Southern Living
2016 Annual Recipes

Oxmoor House®

Soulful Chicken Soup
(page 34)

clockwise from top left:
- Chimichurri Beef Meatball Hoagies (page 35)
- Ginger Shortbread Cookies with Lemon-Cream Cheese Frosting (page 27)
- Coriander-Coconut-Braised Ribs (page 33)
- Honey-Apricot-Glazed Chicken (page 33)

San Antonio Beef
Puffy Tacos (page 38)

The Red Velvet Cake
(page 64)

Chewy Peanut Bars
(page 55)

Freezer Coleslaw
(page 55)

clockwise from top left:

- Cream Cheese Pound Cake (page 56)
- Tee's Corn Pudding (page 56)
- Chocolate-Bourbon Pecan Pie (page 57)
- Gulf Coast Seafood Stew (page 58)

Chocolate Truffle Pie with Amaretto Cream (page 79)

Dad's Famous Chocolate Pie

Lemon Sherbet Cupcakes with Buttercream Frosting (page 81)

Pam's
Citrus Cupcakes

Champagne Punch, Mint-Lime-Champagne Punch, Blueberry-Lavender-Champagne Punch, and Strawberry-Ginger-Champagne Punch (page 78)

Sarah's Signature Punch

Mint-Lime

Blueberry-La

Strawberry-Ginger

Asparagus, Spring Onion, and Feta Quiche (page 81)

Aunt Rose's Quiche

Spinach-and-Romaine Salad with Cucumbers, Radishes, and Creamy Mint Dressing (page 80)

Janie's Spinach Salad

Spring Pea Pasta with Ricotta and Herbs (page 86)

clockwise from top left:
- Golden Potato-and-Smoked Sausage Hash (page 84)
- Hot Chicken-and-Waffle Sandwiches with Chive Cream (page 82)
- Creamy Baked Eggs with Herbs and Bacon (page 84)
- Breakfast Enchiladas (page 83)

Praline Bread Pudding (page 89)

Grilled Chicken Cutlets with Strawberry Salsa (page 126)

Tangy Strawberry Barbecue Sauce (page 127)

16

Our Year at Southern Living®

Dear Friends,

With the 2016 volume of *Southern Living Annual Recipes,* we share all the great recipes we have featured in the magazine during our yearlong 50th anniversary celebration. In planning our February feature "50 Years of Southern Recipes," our staff pored over every issue ever produced, and one thing became apparent: The foods we Southerners have long revered are as hot as ever...everywhere.

By looking back at the way we cooked and ate when the magazine was first unveiled in 1966 until today, the evolution of Southern food became apparent. Each of the magazine's 600 issues is a reflection of the way Southerners cooked at a particular point in our history. Yet the old adage "What was old is new again" also rang true. Trends do indeed come and go, but we could see them returning again and again. Even today, old-fashioned humble foods like potlikker and johnnycakes are being highlighted on five-star restaurant menus across the country, right beside "artisanal" this and "heritage" that. *Southern Living* has been celebrating and elevating our regional ingredients and dishes for 50 years and has been a key player in putting Southern food on the national culinary map.

Southern Living is in the midst of a renaissance too. We are embracing the digital age and complementing our beloved print publication with handy new digital extensions via the launch of the newly designed SouthernLiving.com, online videos, and social media, so you can get the content you love—including the great recipes from the South's most trusted kitchen—wherever you go and however you like it served to you. Our new 40,000-square-foot, state-of-the-art kitchen studios boast 28 individual kitchen bays with all the bells and whistles a cook could dream up. This is where our recipe developers and testers work their magic to create the delicious recipes that you've counted on us to deliver for the past five decades. Now, when a dish is perfected, it can be photographed just steps away in one of the dozen natural light studios our photographers and stylists use as their sets daily.

Through innovation, integration, and creative collaboration, *Southern Living* is excited to share our next 50 years with you.

Cheers!

Katherine Cobbs
Senior Editor

Contents

Top-Rated Recipes

We cook, we taste, we refine, we rate, and at the end of each year our Test Kitchen shares the highest-rated recipes from each issue exclusively with *Southern Living Annual Recipes* readers.

JANUARY

- Three-Bean Cassoulet with Cornmeal Dumplings (page 25) A medley of beans gives this dish contrasting textures and colors.
- Ginger Shortbread Cookies with Lemon-Cream Cheese Frosting (page 27) Fight the winter chill with these sunny, spicy cookies. Make them sparkle by sprinkling the iced cookies with crystallized ginger.
- Soulful Chicken Soup (page 34) This homey chicken soup is perfect for the busy cook. Simply toss in the ingredients, switch on the slow cooker, and walk away.

FEBRUARY

- Hummingbird Cake (page 53) Mrs. L.H. Wiggins of Greensboro, North Carolina, supplied us with this decadent—and frequently requested—recipe. We consider both the lady and her recipe to be Southern treasures.
- Ham-and-Greens Pot Pie with Cornbread Crust (page 57) Behold the great Southern staples of ham, greens, and cornbread combined in one recipe. You'll never want to separate this prized trio again.
- The Lane Cake (page 63) Emma Rylander Lane's signature cake won the blue ribbon more than 100 years ago, thanks in no small part to the rich, boozy filling. We pick up where she left off, giving her classic cake a peachy, spirited makeover.
- Dolester Miles' Lemon Meringue Tart (page 70) With a graham cracker crust and elegant clouds of meringue, this tart blends Southern soul with European technique.

- Ashley Christensen's Buttermilk Spoonbread with Spaghetti Squash (page 70) This spoonbread packs an extra dose of vegetables by combining spaghetti squash puree and buttermilk for a creamy base.
- Sis' Chicken and Dressing (page 74) Rick Bragg pieces together this classic family recipe from his mother's memory, not a cookbook.

MARCH

- Lemon Sherbet Cupcakes with Buttercream Frosting (page 81) These Easter treats benefit from generous squeezes of fresh lemon juice and tangy notes from sour cream.
- Asparagus, Spring Onion, and Feta Quiche (page 81) Think of this quiche as a celebration of spring produce. Sweet spring onions and tender asparagus are complemented by crumbled feta and a dash of nutmeg.
- Breakfast Enchiladas (page 83) Reimagined for easy weeknight cooking, this Tex-Mex breakfast mash-up has buttery eggs and a homemade cheese sauce to top it off.
- Spring Pea Pasta with Ricotta and Herbs (page 86) In this one-pot primavera, fresh herbs, crunchy sugar snap peas, and sweet peas combine with ricotta cheese and salty pasta water for a creamy main.
- Deviled Potatoes (page 87) These two-bite wonders are a combination of Southern classics: deviled eggs and potato salad.

APRIL

- *SL*'s Stovetop Crawfish Boil (page 99) Our old-fashioned crawfish boil doesn't require fancy equipment. All you need is a sink, a stove, and a big pot.

- Crispy Ramen-Crusted Chicken with Asian Salad (page 102) Trade your panko for a college favorite, ramen noodles, in this crunchy chicken main dish.
- Grilled Chicken and Toasted Couscous Salad with Lemon-Buttermilk Dressing (page 104) With nutty, toasted couscous and a splash of citrus, this dish tastes expensive— but costs only $3.35.
- Spinach-and-Vidalia Dip (page 105) The sweet, mellow flavor of Vidalia onions makes this creamy spinach dip an instant crowd-pleaser.
- Salted Chocolate Matzo Toffee (page 109) Part Passover treat, part Southern candy, this matzo toffee gets a boost from flakes of Maldon sea salt.

MAY

- Green Goddess Soup with Jumbo Lump Crabmeat (page 113) You'll be struck by how perfectly the tart, herbaceous soup pairs with the lush crabmeat.
- Kale Salad with Buttermilk Dressing and Pickled Onions (page 119) With a double hit of acid from the pickled onions and buttermilk, this salad is the tangy side for any barbecue.
- Cured Salmon with Dill-Horseradish Cream (page 119) For an easy starter that never fails to impress, cure your own salmon. Top with the zesty dill-horseradish cream and serve with toasted sourdough bread.
- Strawberry Dream Cake (page 126) Our frosting, made with a dreamy blend of mascarpone and whipping cream, tops an elegant, three-tiered white cake along with fresh sliced strawberries.

- Coconut-Banana Pudding (page 136) For your next big shindig, consider making this tropical take on banana pudding. It serves a crowd, but can be halved and served in individual bowls.

JUNE

- Mouthwatering Marinated Tomatoes (page 138) Treat this recipe for juicy, flavorful tomatoes like a vinaigrette to be added to all kinds of salads or to top a plate of pasta.
- Grilled Flat Iron Steak with Charred Tomato Relish (page 140) The secret to our smoky relish? We grill our tomatoes, as well as our steak, until they get a nice char on both sides.
- BLT Salad with Buttermilk-Parmesan Dressing and Buttery Croutons (page 140) For a lighter alternative to a classic sandwich, we remade the BLT as a salad.
- The *SL* BLT (page 142) Our formula for the perfect Southern BLT includes a slather of garlicky mayo and thick slices of beefsteak tomato.
- Fried Green Tomatoes with Buttermilk-Feta Dressing (page 143) To ensure you get perfectly crisp fried green tomatoes, dredge in flour, then an egg wash, and, finally, a mixture of cornmeal and breadcrumbs.
- Southwest Chicken Tortillas, (page 147) For the best flavor, grill your tortillas before filling with the spicy chicken mixture.
- Grilled Peach Cobbler (page 150) Who says you can't make dessert on the grill? The fire gives this Southern stone fruit an extra-smoky, caramelized flavor.

JULY

- Spiced Peach Galette (page 155) This versatile peach dessert can be made with any combination of spices. Consider cardamom, cinnamon, nutmeg, and ginger for different flavor profiles.
- Cherry-Plum Pie with Cornmeal Crust (page 156) Fine yellow cornmeal gives this piecrust a slightly crunchy and flaky texture.
- Blackberry Cobbler with Almond-Ginger Biscuits (page 157) Southern, seasonal, and simple, this cobbler is best served in individual ramekins for the right berry-to-biscuit ratio.
- Street Corn Salad (page 194) Depending on your needs, this can become an easy side or a fun dip with chips.
- Muffin Pan Tomato Tarts (page 197) For a fun twist on a tomato pie, start with puff pastry sheets tucked in muffin tins and add sharp Cheddar cheese and slices of summer's sweet cherry tomatoes.

AUGUST

- Raspberry and Fig Salad with Lemon-Thyme Dressing (pages 213-214) We pair sweet, mellow figs with bold blue cheese, a match made in salad heaven.
- Buttermilk Dressing (page 214) This superfast and delicious alternative to store-bought dressing will be a new staple for your at-home salad bar.
- Cherry Pie Bars (page 217) For a classic cherry dessert baked into crowd-pleasing treats, drizzle these cherry bars with an almond-scented icing and sprinkle the top with pecan crumbles.

SEPTEMBER

- Chocolate-Coconut Layer Cake (page 223) Layers of coconut cream, dark chocolate frosting, and chocolate cake alternate in this striking dessert.
- Praline Layer Cake (page 226) Topped with candied pecans and packed with praline-like filling, this nutty, caramelized layer cake is a certified showstopper.
- Apple-Spice Bundt Cake with Caramel Frosting (page 227) Our updated take on Bundt cake benefits from the warm spices of a favorite Indian tea: chai.
- Savory Sweet Potato Bread Pudding (page 236) Salty Parmesan custard and smoky bacon balance the sweet richness of sweet potatoes in this company-worthy brunch pudding.
- Cheesy Ham, Corn, and Grits Bake (page 237) With its puffy and golden appearance and the pockets of fresh corn and savory ham, you'll think of this casserole as a soufflé without the work.
- Brown Butter Apple Pie (page 243) To achieve the best flavor, we opted for a combination of sweet Honeycrisp and tart Granny Smith apples.
- Deep-Dish Skillet Cookie (page 246) We start with a traditional chocolate chip cookie base, but offer five fun, flavorful variations including pecan praline, Mississippi mud, and Hummingbird.

OCTOBER

- Hugh's Southern Mac and Cheese (page 252) We revive a Southern staple with slab bacon, leeks, and a gourmet mix of Gruyère and Cheddar cheeses.
- Roasted Pumpkin Soup (page 258) With oodles of pumpkin, carrots, and onions, this soup is like a serving of fall deliciousness in a bowl.
- Spicy Sausage-and-Chickpea Soup with Garlic Oil (page 258) We pair hearty chickpeas, tomatoes with spicy Italian pork sausage, and a drizzle of garlic oil to make comfort food with a kick.
- Classic Skillet Cornbread (page 260) The secret to our crunchy, buttery-crusted cornbread is a screaming-hot cast-iron skillet, yellow cornmeal, butter, and a pinch of sugar.

NOVEMBER

- Roasted Herb Turkey and Gravy (page 267) Simple yet perfect, our traditional roast turkey is basted in butter made with sage, thyme, and fennel seeds.

- Brown Butter Sweet Potato Pie (page 277) Often called "liquid gold" by chefs and bakers alike, brown butter is the secret, nutty ingredient in our update on this Southern pie.
- Sweet Potato-Ginger Scones (page 279) These tender, apricot-hued scones are filled with chunks of candied ginger and sprinkled with a cardamom and turbinado sugar spice mixture.
- Green Tomato Mincemeat Pie (page 280) With the tart combination of green tomatoes, Granny Smith apples, and cranberries, this mince-meat pie benefits from a boozy boost of bourbon and bourbon-pecan ice cream.
- Pumpkin-Lemon Cream Cheese Chess Pie (page 282) We took the traditional concept of chess pie—a simple combination of butter, flour, sugar, and eggs—and added pump-kin, spices, lemon, and cream cheese.
- Ambrosia Pudding Pie (page 284) The ambrosia of old was often a dubious mixture of whipped cream and fruit topped with a maraschino cherry garnish. Our sophisticated update incorporates orange marmalade, crushed pineapple, lemon curd, and homemade coconut custard into a decadent layered pie.
- Cinnamon-Pecan Rolls (page 286) Jam-packed with gooey cinnamon-pecan filling, these fragrant rolls are the perfect Sunday morning wake-up call.
- Turkey Tortellini Soup with Greens (page 287) The base of each of our turkey soups begins with a rich stock made from the carcass of the Thanksgiving turkey. In this soup, cheesy tortellini and spinach accompany leftover shredded turkey.
- Gumbo-Style Turkey Soup (page 287) The gumbo element to our soup is the dark, caramelized roux we start with, not to mention the addition of cut okra.

- Green Chile-Turkey Soup with Hominy (page 289) Tomatillos, hominy, green chiles, and fresh cilantro bring Tex-Mex flavor to after-Thanksgiving leftovers.

DECEMBER
- Baked Brie Bites (page 292) This uncomplicated, five-ingredient appetizer packs sophisticated flavor in a simple phyllo pastry package.
- Peppercorn-Crusted Standing Rib Roast with Roasted Vegetables (page 293) This prime rib roast is the showstopping centerpiece of any Christmas feast but is deceptively easy. Slather it with our special herbed butter the night before, and then let the oven do all the work.
- Baby Hasselback Potatoes with Blue Cheese, Bacon, and Rosemary (page 294) The thin slices of our elegant hasselback potatoes offer more surface area to crisp and more nooks and crannies for the cheesy-bacon filling.
- Red Velvet Cheesecake-Vanilla Cake with Cream Cheese Frosting (page 298) We sandwich fluffy vanilla cake between two crimson layers of red velvet cheesecake, top with clouds of cream cheese icing, and garnish with thick white chocolate curls for wow factor.
- Coconut Cake with Rum Filling and Coconut Ermine Frosting (page 299) A tropical holiday cake that'll have you thinking of Christmas Island, our coconut cake gets crowned with sugar cookie Christmas trees and a lacy collar of shredded coconut.
- Grits and Greens with Brown Butter Hot Sauce (page 303) Any greens will do in this recipe but the spicy, nutty notes of our Brown Butter Hot Sauce is irreplaceable.
- Stewed Tomato Shirred Eggs with Ham Chips (page 304) Our crunchy ham chips might become your go-to topper for all breakfast fare.

- Pecan-Chewy Pie (page 304) Filled with a gooey mix of pecans, brown sugar custard, and white chocolate filling, this pecan pie is finished with a scattering of streusel.
- Sausage-Stuffed Honey Buns (page 305) Melding sweet and savory into one breakfast item, we roll ground sausage in with the brown sugar-honey filling for a meaty surprise.
- No-Bake Fudgy Toffee Bars (page 307) No oven is necessary to make these fudgy treats. All these toffee-studded bars need is a chill in the fridge.
- Red Velvet Crackle Sandwich Cookies (page 313) This bite-sized, chewy sandwich cookie pays homage to one of our favorite Southern cakes.
- Lemony Sandwich Cookies (page 314) For these bright, tart cookies, we pack fresh lemon buttercream in the middle of two citrusy crinkle cookies.
- Spiced Stars with Cookie Butter (page 314) Between two ultra-thin, crunchy spice cookies is a generous spread of speculoos, better known as cookie butter.
- Oyster Casserole (page 319) A Christmas staple throughout the coastal South, this recipe uses plump, briny oysters, buttery breadcrumbs, and a velvety sauce to create a rich, decadent dish for the holiday table.

January

Master One Great Dish

ADD THREE DELICIOUS RECIPES TO YOUR REPERTOIRE THAT REQUIRE
ONLY A DUTCH OVEN, SLOW COOKER, OR SKILLET

IT DOESN'T GET ANY MORE GRATIFYING than making a delicious home-cooked dinner in one pot at the end of a busy day—an all-in-one meal that can be prepared in a Dutch oven, a skillet, or a slow cooker. It's no wonder then, in our ever-busier lives, that one-pot meals have earned their own hashtag in the recipe world. But if you think quick and easy means brown and boring, then we have three bright and flavorful recipes to fix that. The best part? You don't need fancy ingredients or culinary-school skills to make these meals at home. It's as simple as opening a can of crushed tomatoes, slicing carrots, or chopping onions and peppers. Plus, we've collected a handful of foolproof tips from a few of our favorite chefs to freshen up your cooking routine for the New Year.

Three-Bean Cassoulet with Cornmeal Dumplings

Skillet Rice with Shrimp and Chicken

Slow-Cooker Parmesan-Herb Pork Loin with Chunky Tomato Sauce

THREE-BEAN CASSOULET WITH CORNMEAL DUMPLINGS

A mixture of beans gives this dish contrasting textures and colors.

CASSOULET

- 1 cup sliced carrots
- 1/2 cup coarsely chopped red onion
- 1 Tbsp. olive oil
- 2 tsp. minced garlic
- 1 (8-oz.) package cooked cubed ham
- 1 (16-oz.) package frozen baby lima beans
- 1 (16-oz.) package frozen butter peas
- 1 cup frozen black-eyed peas
- 1 (32-oz.) container reduced-sodium chicken broth
- 2 tsp. finely chopped fresh rosemary
- 1/2 tsp. table salt
- 1/4 tsp. freshly ground black pepper

CORNMEAL DUMPLINGS

- 1/2 cup all-purpose flour
- 1/2 cup plain yellow cornmeal
- 1 tsp. baking powder
- 1/4 tsp. baking soda
- 1/4 tsp. kosher salt
- 1/4 tsp. freshly ground black pepper
- 2 Tbsp. cold butter, cubed
- 1 tsp. finely chopped fresh rosemary
- 2/3 cup buttermilk

1. Prepare Cassoulet: Sauté carrots and onion in hot oil in a Dutch oven over medium heat 3 to 4 minutes or until tender. Add garlic, and sauté 1 minute. Add ham, and cook, stirring often, 3 minutes. Stir in lima beans and next 6 ingredients; bring mixture to a boil, reduce heat to low, and simmer, stirring occasionally, 15 minutes.

2. Meanwhile, prepare Dumplings: Whisk together flour and next 5 ingredients in a medium bowl. Cut butter into flour mixture with a pastry blender until mixture resembles coarse meal. Stir in rosemary; add buttermilk, and stir just until dough is moistened.

3. Drop dough by tablespoonfuls 1/2 to 1 inch apart into bean mixture. Cover and simmer 15 to 20 minutes or until dumplings are done and dry to the touch. Serve immediately.

Note: We tested with Swanson Natural Goodness 33% Less Sodium Chicken Broth.

MAKES 6 to 8 servings. **HANDS-ON** 30 min. **TOTAL** 55 min.

SLOW-COOKER PARMESAN-HERB PORK LOIN WITH CHUNKY TOMATO SAUCE

Prep the night before, start cooking in the morning, and it will be ready when you get off work. Or prep it and cook on high for a hearty weekend lunch or dinner in 3 to 4 hours.

- 2 1/2 cups chopped yellow onion
- 1 cup chopped carrots
- 1 3/4 cups chopped fresh fennel
- 6 garlic cloves, chopped
- 2 Tbsp. olive oil
- 1 cup red wine
- 1 (28-oz.) can whole tomatoes
- 1 (14.5-oz.) can crushed tomatoes
- 1/4 cup reduced-sodium chicken broth
- 3 1/2 tsp. kosher salt, divided
- 1 1/2 tsp. black pepper, divided
- 1/4 cup freshly grated Parmesan cheese
- 1 Tbsp. chopped fresh rosemary
- 1 Tbsp. chopped fresh oregano
- 1 Tbsp. chopped fresh flat-leaf parsley
- 1 (2-lb.) boneless pork loin roast Hot cooked pasta

1. Sauté onion and next 3 ingredients in hot oil in a large skillet over medium heat 5 minutes or until tender. Increase heat to high, and stir in wine. Bring to a boil, and boil, stirring occasionally, 2 to 3 minutes or until reduced by half.

2. Add whole tomatoes, crushed tomatoes, and chicken broth, and bring to a boil, stirring occasionally and breaking up tomatoes with spoon. Stir in 1 1/2 tsp. kosher salt and 1/2 tsp. pepper, and transfer to a 6-qt. slow cooker.

3. Stir together Parmesan cheese, next 3 ingredients, and remaining salt and pepper. Rub mixture over all sides of pork roast, pressing to adhere.

4. Place pork roast in slow cooker, and cook on LOW 8 hours. Carefully remove pork from slow cooker, and let stand 5 minutes. Slice pork, and serve with sauce over hot cooked pasta.

Note: We tested with Swanson Natural Goodness 33% Less Sodium Chicken Broth.

MAKES 6 to 8 servings. **HANDS-ON** 30 min. **TOTAL** 8 hours, 35 min.

SKILLET RICE WITH SHRIMP AND CHICKEN

Simple substitutions give these hearty dishes flavorful twists: Swap sausage for chicken, crabmeat for shrimp, or make a vegetarian option by subbing vegetable stock and omitting proteins.

- 1 cup uncooked long-grain white rice
- 2 cups reduced-sodium chicken broth
- 3 fresh thyme sprigs
- 1 lb. boneless, skinless chicken thighs, cut into 1-inch pieces
- 2 1/2 tsp. kosher salt, divided
- 1 tsp. freshly ground black pepper, divided
- 2 Tbsp. olive oil
- 1 small yellow onion, chopped (about 3/4 cup)
- 1 green pepper, chopped (about 1 cup)
- 2 garlic cloves, chopped
- 1 cup frozen sliced okra, thawed
- 1/2 lb. medium-size raw shrimp, peeled and deveined
- 1/4 tsp. ground red pepper
- 3 plum tomatoes, chopped
- 2 green onions (green parts only), sliced

1. Cook rice according to package directions, substituting chicken broth for water and adding fresh thyme sprigs to broth. Spread cooked rice in a thin layer on a baking sheet; discard thyme sprigs. Cool completely (about 30 minutes).

2. Meanwhile, toss together chicken pieces, 2 tsp. kosher salt, and 1/2 tsp. black pepper. Cook chicken in hot oil in a large skillet over medium heat, stirring occasionally, 4 to 5 minutes or until lightly browned. Add yellow onion, green pepper, and garlic, and cook, stirring often, 5 minutes or until onion is tender. Increase heat to high.

3. Stir in okra, rice, shrimp, red pepper, and remaining salt and black pepper, and cook, stirring constantly, 4 to 5 minutes or until shrimp are pink and rice is thoroughly heated. Stir in tomatoes, and cook 5 minutes or until tomatoes are thoroughly heated. Remove from heat, and sprinkle with sliced green onions. Serve immediately.

Note: We tested with Swanson Natural Goodness 33% Less Sodium Chicken Broth.

MAKES 6 servings. **HANDS-ON** 40 min. **TOTAL** 1 hour, 20 min.

SECRETS EVERY BUSY COOK SHOULD KNOW

THREE CELEBRATED CHEFS SHARE EASY-TO-STEAL TIPS THAT WILL SIMPLIFY MEALTIME

Chris Hastings

BIRMINGHAM, ALABAMA

Explore the many flavors of olive oil. The range of flavors in extra virgin olive oils can make a huge impact. Keep smaller bottles of different varieties on hand to add herbaceous, floral, or flinty notes to your favorite dishes.

Cook in-season. I've cooked seasonally all of my life; it's just critical to access products at the very best moment of their very best flavor profiles.

Stock your pantry. Fill your shelves with everything from great grains and a variety of dried pastas to oils and vinegars, herbs, salts, spices and rubs, and things from other cultures.

Hugh Acheson

ATHENS, GEORGIA

Think about how you'll use leftovers. Make more than one meal at a time. If one night is steak and wheat berries, roasted carrots, and fennel slaw, then make extra wheat berries, and use them the next night with salmon and an egg.

Make cooking from scratch feel natural. Use a slow cooker, put corned beef on slow, and let it mellow out until you get home.

Let your cooking skills develop. Your cooking skills and techniques are like LEGO pieces, so let them build and develop over the years.

Kevin Nashan

ST. LOUIS, MISSOURI

Keep favorite seasonings handy. Salt is one of my favorite ingredients; I also love Hatch chiles for spice. I like to use bacon fat too—it's like a Band-Aid for food, but in a good way.

Build your technique. The basics are important. Learn to dice, to make a vinaigrette, to truss a chicken. Know how to fry a perfect egg. Keep it simple.

Practice makes perfect. If there's something you really enjoy eating, make it—and make it again and again until you master it. Then move on to the next thing.

Sunny Delights

BEAT THE WINTER BLUES WITH THESE LEMONY SHORTBREAD TREATS

GINGER SHORTBREAD COOKIES WITH LEMON-CREAM CHEESE FROSTING

- 1 cup butter, softened
- 1/2 cup sugar
- 1/4 tsp. vanilla extract
- 2 1/4 cups all-purpose flour
- 2 Tbsp. minced crystallized ginger
- 1/8 tsp. table salt
  Parchment paper
  Lemon-Cream Cheese Frosting

1. Preheat oven to 275°. Beat butter at medium speed with a heavy-duty electric stand mixer until creamy; gradually add sugar, beating well. Stir in vanilla.

2. Stir together flour, ginger, and salt; gradually add to butter mixture, beating at low speed until blended after each addition.

3. Place dough on a lightly floured surface, and roll dough to 1/4 inch thick. Cut with a 2-inch round cutter. Place 2 inches apart on 2 parchment paper-lined baking sheets (about 12 per sheet). Reroll scraps once.

4. Bake, in batches, at 275° for 40 minutes or until lightly browned on bottom. (Refrigerate second batch while baking first batch.) Cool on baking sheet 2 minutes. Transfer to a wire rack, and cool completely (about 30 minutes).

5. Meanwhile, prepare Lemon-Cream Cheese Frosting. Spread about 1 Tbsp. on each cooled cookie, using a small spatula.

MAKES about 2 dozen. **HANDS-ON** 25 min. **TOTAL** 2 hours, 20 min., including frosting

Lemon-Cream Cheese Frosting

- 1/2 (8-oz.) package cream cheese, softened
- 1/4 cup butter, softened
- 2 cups powdered sugar
- 1 tsp. lemon zest
- 1 tsp. fresh lemon juice

Beat cream cheese and butter with an electric mixer until light and fluffy. Gradually add sugar, and beat well. Stir in zest and juice. Use immediately.

MAKES about 1 cup. **HANDS-ON** 5 min. **TOTAL** 5 min.

SHEET

MEET SIX DELICIOUS HANDS-OFF MEALS

PAN

SPECTACULAR

WITH RECORD-BREAKING CLEANUP TIME

SUPPERS

SCRUMPTIOUS

CHICKEN WITH POTATOES AND CARROTS

The trick to extra-savory veggies is cooking the chicken atop the potatoes and carrots.

- 8 bone-in, skin-on chicken thighs (about 4 lb.)
- 2 Tbsp. olive oil, divided
- 2 tsp. kosher salt
- 1 tsp. freshly ground black pepper
- 1 tsp. finely chopped fresh rosemary
- 1 (24-oz.) package fingerling potatoes, halved
- 8 oz. small carrots with tops
- 1 large sweet onion, cut into 8 wedges
  Vegetable cooking spray

1. Preheat oven to 375°. Rub chicken thighs evenly with 1 Tbsp. olive oil. Stir together salt, pepper, and rosemary in a small bowl. Sprinkle chicken thighs evenly with 3 tsp. salt mixture.

2. Stir together potatoes, carrots, and onions in a large bowl. Drizzle with remaining 1 Tbsp. olive oil, and sprinkle with remaining 1 tsp. salt mixture; toss to coat.

3. Spread potato mixture in an even layer in a lightly greased (with cooking spray) heavy-duty aluminum foil-lined sheet pan. Place chicken thighs 2 to 3 inches apart on potato mixture.

4. Bake at 375° for 55 minutes to 1 hour or until a meat thermometer inserted in thickest portion of chicken registers 170°.

MAKES 6 to 8 servings. **HANDS-ON** 15 min. **TOTAL** 1 hour, 10 min.

PORK CHOPS WITH ROASTED APPLES AND BRUSSELS SPROUTS

For the zestiest flavor, rub the chops with the brown sugar mixture the night before, and let them chill overnight.

- 1 tsp. paprika
- 1 tsp. chili powder
- 1 tsp. garlic salt
- 1/8 tsp. ground red pepper
- 1/8 tsp. ground cinnamon
- 3 Tbsp. light brown sugar, divided
- 2 tsp. finely chopped fresh rosemary, divided
- 1 tsp. kosher salt, divided
- 1/2 tsp. freshly ground black pepper, divided
- 4 (1-inch-thick) bone-in, center-cut pork chops
- 3 Tbsp. plus 2 tsp. olive oil, divided
- 3 Tbsp. apple cider vinegar
- 1 Gala apple (8 to 9 oz.), cut into 1/2-inch wedges
- 1 lb. fresh Brussels sprouts, trimmed and cut in half
  Vegetable cooking spray

1. Preheat oven to 425°. Stir together first 5 ingredients, 1 Tbsp. brown sugar, 1 tsp. rosemary, 1/2 tsp. salt, and 1/4 tsp. black pepper in a small bowl. Rub each pork chop with 1/2 tsp. olive oil; rub both sides of each pork chop with brown sugar mixture (about 2 tsp. on each chop).

2. Whisk together apple cider vinegar and remaining 2 Tbsp. brown sugar, 1 tsp. rosemary, 1/2 tsp. salt, and 1/4 tsp. black pepper in a small bowl; slowly whisk in remaining 3 Tbsp. olive oil until blended. Place apples, Brussels sprouts, and 1/4 cup vinegar mixture in a large bowl, and toss to coat.

3. Place pork chops in center of a lightly greased (with cooking spray) heavy-duty aluminum foil-lined sheet pan; place apple mixture around pork chops.

4. Bake at 425° for 12 minutes; turn pork chops over, and bake 10 to 14 more minutes or until a meat thermometer inserted in thickest portion registers 140°. Transfer pork chops to a serving platter, and cover with foil to keep warm. Stir apple mixture in sheet pan, and spread into an even layer.

5. Increase oven temperature to broil, and broil apple mixture 3 to 4 minutes or until browned and slightly charred. Transfer apple mixture to a medium bowl. Toss together apple mixture and remaining vinegar mixture. Season with kosher salt, and serve with pork chops.

MAKES 4 servings. **HANDS-ON** 15 min. **TOTAL** 40 min.

BRATWURST WITH PEPPERS AND ONIONS

If you're lucky enough to have leftovers, wrap hoagies in foil, and reheat in a 350° oven for 15 minutes.

- 2 large red bell peppers, cut into strips
- 1 large yellow bell pepper, cut into strips
- 2 large sweet onions, cut into strips
- 1 Tbsp. olive oil
- 1 tsp. kosher salt
- 1/4 tsp. freshly ground black pepper
  Vegetable cooking spray
- 6 fresh bratwurst sausages (about 1 1/2 lb.)
- 6 hoagie rolls, lightly toasted and split

1. Preheat oven to 375°. Toss together first 6 ingredients in a large bowl; spread mixture in an even layer in a lightly greased (with cooking spray) heavy-duty aluminum foil-lined sheet pan.

2. Pierce each sausage 6 times with a wooden pick. Place sausages 3 to 4 inches apart on pepper mixture.

3. Bake at 375° for 40 minutes; increase oven temperature to broil. Broil 6 to 8 minutes or until browned, turning sausages halfway through.

4. Place 1 sausage in each roll, and top with desired amount of pepper mixture.

MAKES 6 servings. **HANDS-ON** 15 min. **TOTAL** 1 hour

SIMPLE WHOLE CHICKEN WITH ROASTED BROCCOLI-MUSHROOM RICE

Each member of the family can enjoy his or her favorite piece of the bird with this recipe.

- 1 (3 1/2- to 4-lb.) cut-up whole chicken
- 1/3 cup olive oil, divided
- 3 tsp. kosher salt, divided
- 2 tsp. freshly ground black pepper, divided
- 2 (8.5-oz.) pouches ready-to-serve rice
- 1 lb. fresh broccoli
- 2 (8-oz.) packages fresh cremini mushrooms, stems removed

1. Preheat oven to 425°. Rub chicken pieces with 1 Tbsp. olive oil; sprinkle with 2 tsp. salt and 1 tsp. pepper.

2. Spread ready-to-serve rice in an even layer in a heavy-duty aluminum foil-lined sheet pan, breaking up clumps.

3. Cut broccoli into florets. Toss together broccoli florets, 2 Tbsp. oil, 1/2 tsp. salt, and 1/2 tsp. pepper in a medium bowl; spread in an even layer over rice. Toss together mushrooms and remaining olive oil, salt, and pepper, and spread over broccoli and rice.

QUICK TIP
Evenly space chicken pieces so they distribute their flavorful drippings over the rice and broccoli.

QUICK TIP For better, richer flavor, apply layers of glaze several times throughout the cooking process.

4. Place chicken pieces, skin side up, 1 1/2 inches apart on broccoli and mushrooms.

5. Bake at 425° for about 1 hour or until a meat thermometer inserted in thickest portion of chicken registers 170°. Let stand 5 minutes before serving.

MAKES 4 to 6 servings. **HANDS-ON** 10 min. **TOTAL** 1 hour, 20 min.

HONEY-SOY-GLAZED SALMON WITH VEGGIES AND ORANGES

Here's the delicious proof that you can serve a complete, no-mess fish dinner in 25 minutes.

  4   **Tbsp. honey**
  1   **Tbsp. soy sauce**
  1   **Tbsp. Dijon mustard**
  1   **tsp. seasoned rice wine vinegar**
  1/4 **tsp. dried crushed red pepper**
  1   **lb. fresh medium asparagus**
  8   **oz. fresh green beans, trimmed**
  1   **small orange, cut into 1/4- to 1/2-inch slices**
  1   **Tbsp. olive oil**
  1   **tsp. kosher salt**
  1/4 **tsp. freshly ground black pepper**
  4   **(5- to 6-oz.) fresh salmon fillets**
      Garnish: toasted sesame seeds

1. Preheat broiler with oven rack 6 inches from heat. Whisk together honey and next 4 ingredients in a small bowl.

2. Snap off and discard tough ends of asparagus. Place asparagus, green beans, and next 4 ingredients in a large bowl, and toss to coat.

3. Place salmon in center of a heavy-duty aluminum foil-lined sheet pan. Brush salmon with about 2 Tbsp. honey mixture. Spread asparagus mixture around salmon.

4. Broil 4 minutes; remove from oven, and brush salmon with about 2 Tbsp. honey mixture. Return to oven, and broil 4 more minutes. Remove from oven, and brush salmon with remaining honey mixture. Return to oven, and broil 2 more minutes. Serve immediately.

MAKES 4 servings. **HANDS-ON** 25 min. **TOTAL** 25 min.

ANCHO CHILE FLANK STEAK AND SWEET POTATO TACOS

For an extra burst of flavor, stir a few tablespoons of pan drippings into your sour cream.

- 1 (2-lb.) flank steak
- 1/4 cup fresh lime juice
- 1/4 cup chopped fresh cilantro
- 1/2 tsp. garlic powder
- 1 Tbsp. plus 1 tsp. ground cumin, divided
- 1 Tbsp. plus 1 tsp. ancho chile powder, divided
- 4 tsp. kosher salt, divided
- 1/4 cup plus 2 Tbsp. olive oil
- 1/2 lb. fresh tomatillos, husks removed
- 1 1/2 lb. sweet potatoes, peeled and cut into 3/4-inch pieces
- 1 large red onion, cut into 1/2-inch pieces
  Flour tortillas, sour cream, fresh cilantro

1. Place flank steak in a large zip-top plastic freezer bag. Stir together lime juice, next 2 ingredients, 1 Tbsp. cumin, 1 Tbsp. ancho chile powder, and 2 tsp. kosher salt in a small bowl. Whisk in 1/4 cup olive oil, and pour over flank steak. Seal bag, and turn to coat. Chill 1 to 12 hours.

2. Place oven rack about 6 inches from top of oven. Preheat oven to 450°. Rinse tomatillos, and cut into quarters. Stir together sweet potatoes, red onion, tomatillos, and remaining 1 tsp. cumin, 1 tsp. ancho chile powder, 2 tsp. salt, and 2 Tbsp. oil in a large bowl. Spread sweet potato mixture in an even layer in a heavy-duty aluminum foil-lined sheet pan.

3. Bake at 450° for 20 minutes. Remove from oven, and move sweet potato mixture to outer edges of pan. Place flank steak in center of pan. Increase oven temperature to broil.

4. Broil 6 minutes. Turn steak over, and broil 6 more minutes. (Stir vegetables if they begin to char.) Remove from oven, and let stand 5 minutes. Cut steak across the grain, and drizzle with pan drippings. Serve with sweet potato mixture, tortillas, sour cream, and fresh cilantro.

MAKES 6 to 8 servings. **HANDS-ON** 30 min. **TOTAL** 1 hour, 55 min.

QUICK TIP
One secret to a tender flank steak is to slice it against the grain using a serrated knife.

Comfort Zone

SIX DELICIOUS SLOW-COOKER RECIPES, EACH WITH 30 MINUTES (OR LESS!) OF PREP TIME

Honey-Apricot-Glazed
Chicken

HONEY-APRICOT-GLAZED CHICKEN

- 8 skinless, bone-in chicken thighs (about 3 lb.)
- 1 tsp. table salt
- 1/2 tsp. freshly ground black pepper
- 2 Tbsp. canola oil
- 1 large onion, vertically sliced
- 1/4 cup apricot brandy
- 1/4 cup honey
- 2 Tbsp. Dijon mustard
- 1/2 cup chicken broth
- 1 (6-oz.) package dried apricots, halved
- 1 Tbsp. cold butter
  Garnish: fresh oregano

1. Sprinkle chicken with salt and pepper. Heat 1 Tbsp. oil in a large skillet over medium-high heat until shimmering. Add half of chicken, and cook 3 minutes on each side or until browned. Repeat with remaining oil and chicken. Transfer chicken to a 5-qt. slow cooker.

2. Add onion to skillet; cook, stirring occasionally, 10 minutes or until tender and golden brown. Add brandy, and cook 2 minutes or until liquid is almost evaporated, stirring to loosen browned bits from bottom of skillet.

3. Add onion mixture to slow cooker. Whisk together honey, mustard, and chicken broth. Pour over onions. Cover and cook on LOW 4 hours or until chicken is tender, adding dried apricots halfway through.

4. Transfer chicken, onions, and apricots to a serving platter; cover with foil to keep warm. Pour liquid from slow cooker through a fine wire-mesh strainer into a small saucepan; discard solids. Bring to a boil over medium-high heat; reduce heat to medium, and simmer 10 minutes or until reduced to about 3/4 cup. Whisk in butter, and serve with chicken.

Note: We tested with Swanson 100% Natural Chicken Broth.

MAKES 4 servings. **HANDS-ON** 30 min. **TOTAL** 4 hours, 45 min.

Coriander-Coconut-Braised Ribs

CORIANDER-COCONUT-BRAISED RIBS

- 3 1/2 lb. country-style pork ribs
- 1/4 cup packed brown sugar
- 1 1/2 Tbsp. ground cumin
- 1 1/2 Tbsp. ground coriander
- 1 tsp. kosher salt
- 1/2 tsp. ground black pepper
- 1/2 tsp. ground cinnamon
- 2 Tbsp. canola oil, divided
  Vegetable cooking spray
- 1 1/2 cups chopped sweet onion
- 1 Tbsp. minced garlic
- 1 Tbsp. minced ginger
- 1 Tbsp. red curry paste
- 2 small jalapeño peppers, seeded and finely chopped
- 1 tsp. soy sauce
- 1 (13.66-oz.) can coconut milk
- 2 Tbsp. lime juice

1. Trim excess fat from ribs. Stir together brown sugar and next 5 ingredients. Sprinkle mixture over ribs, pressing to adhere. Brown ribs on all sides, in batches, in 1 Tbsp. hot oil in a large skillet over medium-high heat. Place in a lightly greased (with cooking spray) 6-qt. slow cooker.

2. Wipe skillet clean. Cook onion in remaining 1 Tbsp. hot oil 6 minutes or until tender. Add garlic and next 3 ingredients; cook 1 minute. Add soy sauce and coconut milk, stirring to loosen browned bits from bottom of skillet. Pour over ribs in slow cooker. Cover and cook on LOW 5 hours or until pork is tender.

3. Transfer ribs to a serving platter; cover with foil to keep warm. Pour liquid from slow cooker through a fine wire-mesh strainer into a glass measuring cup; let stand 5 minutes. Skim fat from liquid.

4. Transfer liquid to a saucepan, and bring to a boil over medium-high heat. Reduce heat to medium, and cook 6 minutes or until reduced to 1 1/2 cups. Stir in lime juice. Serve with ribs.

MAKES 6 servings. **HANDS-ON** 30 min. **TOTAL** 5 hours, 30 min.

Soulful Chicken Soup

SOULFUL CHICKEN SOUP

No dish is quite as soothing as a hearty bowl of chicken noodle soup. Slow cookers couldn't have made the road to comfort any easier: Simply toss in the ingredients, switch on, and then walk away. We love old-fashioned, wide egg noodles for this recipe.

- 2 lb. bone-in chicken thighs, skinned and trimmed
- 3 medium carrots, cut into 1/2-inch pieces (1 1/4 cups)
- 1 celery root, cut into 1/2-inch pieces (2 cups)
- 1 medium leek, white and light green parts only, cleaned, chopped
- 2 garlic cloves, peeled and smashed
- 2 fresh thyme sprigs
- 2 fresh sage sprigs
- 1 fresh rosemary sprig
- 1 bay leaf
- 1 1/2 tsp. table salt
- 1 tsp. freshly ground black pepper
- 8 cups chicken broth
- 2 cups wide egg noodles
- 3 Tbsp. finely chopped fresh parsley
- 1 Tbsp. fresh lemon juice

1. Place chicken and next 11 ingredients in a 6-qt. slow cooker. Cover and cook on LOW 6 hours or until chicken and vegetables are tender and chicken separates from bone.
2. Remove chicken from slow cooker. Dice meat, discarding bones. Return meat to slow cooker. Stir in noodles and parsley. Cover and cook on HIGH 15 to 20 minutes or until noodles are tender. Stir in lemon juice. Serve immediately, and garnish with any leftover chopped fresh parsley.

Note: We tested with Swanson 100% Natural Chicken Broth.

MAKES 11 cups. **HANDS-ON** 20 min. **TOTAL** 6 hours, 20 min.

BRAISED FENNEL, CANNELLINI BEANS, AND ITALIAN SAUSAGE

Sweet anise-flavored fennel bulb is paired here with cannellini beans, mild Italian sausage, and bitter radicchio for a hearty fall dish.

- 1 (20-oz.) package mild Italian sausage links
- 1 Tbsp. canola oil
- 2 fennel bulbs, chopped
- 1 1/2 cups chopped onion
- 3/4 cup chicken broth
- 3 garlic cloves, minced
- 3/4 tsp. fennel seeds
- 1/2 tsp. table salt
- 1/4 tsp. freshly ground black pepper
  Vegetable cooking spray
- 2 (15.5-oz.) cans cannellini beans, drained and rinsed
- 1 cup shredded radicchio
- 1/4 to 1/3 cup shaved pecorino Romano or Parmigiano-Reggiano cheese
  Extra virgin olive oil

1. Prick sausage casings with a fork or tip of sharp knife. Cook sausage links in hot oil in a large nonstick skillet over medium-high heat 8 minutes, turning often to brown all sides.
2. Place chopped fennel bulbs and next 6 ingredients in a lightly greased (with cooking spray) 5-qt. slow cooker. Top with sausage in a single layer. Cover and cook on LOW 5 hours or until vegetables are tender and sausage is cooked.
3. Transfer sausage to a cutting board; cool slightly. Cut sausage diagonally into 3/4-inch-thick pieces.
4. Stir sausage, beans, and radicchio into fennel mixture in slow cooker. Cover and cook on HIGH 15 minutes or until radicchio is wilted and tender. Top with cheese, and drizzle with extra virgin olive oil.

Note: We tested with Swanson 100% Natural Chicken Broth.

MAKES 6 servings. **HANDS-ON** 20 min. **TOTAL** 5 hours, 35 min.

ANDOUILLE SAUSAGE JAMBALAYA WITH SHRIMP

Traditionally, rice is cooked in the jambalaya liquid, but for this flavorful slow-cooker version, it's best to stir in the cooked rice at the end.

- 1 lb. andouille sausage, sliced
- 1 Tbsp. canola oil
- 2 (8-oz.) packages prechopped onion, celery, and bell pepper mix
- 4 garlic cloves, minced
- 1 Tbsp. Creole seasoning
- 1 tsp. dried thyme
- 2 (14.5-oz.) cans fire-roasted diced tomatoes

2 cups chicken broth
2 (3.5-oz.) packages boil-in-bag rice
1 lb. medium-size raw shrimp, peeled and deveined
   Chopped fresh parsley
   Sliced green onions
   Hot sauce (optional)

1. Cook sausage in hot oil in a large skillet over medium-high heat, stirring often, 5 minutes or until browned. Remove sausage with a slotted spoon, reserving drippings in skillet. Drain sausage on paper towels, and place in a 5-qt. slow cooker.
2. Add onion, celery, and bell pepper mix; garlic; Creole seasoning; and thyme to hot drippings. Sauté 5 minutes or until vegetables begin to soften. Place in slow cooker, and stir in tomatoes and chicken broth. Cover and cook on LOW 4 hours.
3. Cook rice according to package directions. Stir cooked rice and shrimp into sausage mixture in slow cooker; cover and cook on HIGH 15 minutes or until shrimp turn pink. Top with parsley, green onions, and, if desired, hot sauce.

Note: We tested with Swanson 100% Natural Chicken Broth.

MAKES 8 to 10 servings. **HANDS-ON** 15 min. **TOTAL** 4 hours, 40 min.

CHIMICHURRI BEEF MEATBALL HOAGIES

These deliciously flavored meatballs served on hoagie rolls or French baguette rolls will be the new favorite at your weeknight dinner table or your neighborhood football party. The sauce makes plenty for cooking the meatballs, and there's even enough to spoon over the sandwiches for a boost of flavor.

1 1/2 cups fresh cilantro leaves, divided
1 cup fresh parsley leaves, divided
6 garlic cloves, divided
1 1/2 lb. ground sirloin
1 cup soft, fresh breadcrumbs
1/4 tsp. dried crushed red pepper
1 large egg, lightly beaten

Chimichurri Beef Meatball Hoagies

3/4 tsp. kosher salt, divided
1/2 cup canola oil, divided
1/2 cup red wine vinegar
1 shallot, coarsely chopped
1 jalapeño pepper, coarsely chopped
2 Tbsp. fresh oregano leaves
1/4 cup extra virgin olive oil
6 hoagie rolls, split
   Extra virgin olive oil
1 (10-oz.) package finely shredded (angel hair) cabbage
1 cup crumbled Cotija cheese
   Lime wedges

1. Chop 1/2 cup cilantro leaves and 1/4 cup parsley leaves; place in a large bowl. Mince 2 garlic cloves; add to herbs in bowl. Add ground sirloin, next 3 ingredients, and 1/4 tsp. salt; stir gently to combine. Shape mixture into 18 balls.
2. Heat 1 Tbsp. canola oil in a large nonstick skillet over medium-high heat. Add half of meatballs, and cook 6 minutes, turning often to brown all sides. Transfer meatballs to a 6-qt. slow cooker. Repeat with 1 Tbsp. canola oil and remaining meatballs.
3. Process vinegar, next 4 ingredients, and remaining cilantro leaves, parsley leaves, garlic, salt, and canola oil in a food processor until finely chopped and well combined. Stir together 1/2 cup herb mixture and 1/4 cup water;

pour over meatballs in slow cooker. Reserve remaining herb mixture. Cover and cook on LOW 2 hours.
4. Remove meatballs from slow cooker with a slotted spoon; discard mixture in slow cooker. Toss meatballs with 1/4 cup reserved herb mixture.
5. Preheat broiler with oven rack 6 inches from heat. Brush cut sides of rolls with extra virgin olive oil; place on baking sheet. Broil 2 minutes or until golden brown.
6. Toss together shredded cabbage and 1/2 cup reserved herb mixture. Divide cabbage mixture among rolls; top each roll with 3 meatballs and desired amount of cheese. Serve with lime wedges and any remaining herb mixture.

MAKES 6 servings. **HANDS-ON** 30 min. **TOTAL** 2 hours, 30 min.

OUR NEW SPECIAL EDITION

Transform ordinary ingredients into spectacular, slow-cooked comfort your family will love. With 120 fast and easy recipes, our newest slow-cooker collection includes weeknight meals you can count on like 5-Ingredient Pulled Pork and Poppy Seed Chicken, but it also goes beyond the basics. Try new, inspired dishes like Creole Chicken with Field Pea Succotash or Korean Beef Short Ribs. We even include desserts, from cobblers to cakes.

UNITED TASTES OF
TEXAS

FROM THE SMOKED BRISKET OF CENTRAL TEXAS TO THE TEX-MEX OF THE SOUTH,
EACH REGION OF THE LONE STAR STATE HAS ITS DISTINCT AND DELICIOUS CHARACTER.
IN *UNITED TASTES OF TEXAS*, WRITER AND TEXAS NATIVE **JESSICA DUPUY**
TAKES US ON A CULINARY TOUR OF HER BELOVED HOME STATE. HERE, SHE SHARES
A FEW OF HER FAVORITE RECIPES FOR A FABULOUS REGIONAL FEAST

GULF CRAB CAKES

KING RANCH CHICKEN

Hailing from an era when casseroles were king, this Tex-Mex dish still reigns supreme at church suppers and neighborhood potlucks. Though not an invention of the famed King Ranch—it's more likely the creation of a ladies' Junior League.

6	Tbsp. butter
1 1/2	cups chopped yellow onion
1	cup chopped red bell pepper
1	cup chopped poblano peppers (about 2 medium peppers)
1	jalapeño pepper, seeded and chopped
2	garlic cloves, chopped
1	Tbsp. chili powder
1	Tbsp. ground cumin
1	tsp. kosher salt
1/2	tsp. freshly ground black pepper
1/4	cup all-purpose flour
1 3/4	cups reduced-sodium chicken broth
1	(10-oz.) can diced tomatoes with green chiles, drained
1 1/2	cups sour cream
2	lb. coarsely chopped smoked chicken (about 5 cups)
1	cup loosely packed fresh cilantro leaves, chopped
2	cups (8 oz.) shredded Monterey Jack cheese
2	cups (8 oz.) shredded sharp Cheddar cheese
18	(8-inch) soft taco-size corn tortillas
1/4	cup canola oil
	Vegetable cooking spray

1. Preheat oven to 375°. Melt butter in a large skillet over medium-high heat. Add onion and next 3 ingredients; cook, stirring occasionally, 8 to 10 minutes or until softened and lightly browned. Stir in garlic, chili powder, cumin, salt, and black pepper; cook, stirring occasionally, 1 minute.

2. Sprinkle flour over vegetable mixture, and cook, stirring constantly, 1 minute. Whisk in broth, and increase heat to high. Bring to a boil, stirring constantly. Boil, stirring occasionally, 1 to 2 minutes or until thickened. Remove from heat. Stir in tomatoes and sour cream.

3. Stir together chicken and cilantro in a large bowl; stir in vegetable mixture. Combine both cheeses in a small bowl.

4. Heat a large cast-iron skillet over high heat. Lightly brush each tortilla on both sides with oil. Cook tortillas, in batches, in hot skillet 1 to 2 minutes each side or until lightly browned and crisp on both sides.

5. Line bottom of a lightly greased (with cooking spray) 13- x 9-inch baking dish with 6 tortillas, overlapping slightly, to cover bottom of dish. Top with half of chicken mixture and one-third of cheese. Repeat layers once. Top with remaining tortillas and cheese. Lightly coat a sheet of aluminum foil with cooking spray, and cover baking dish.

6. Bake at 375° for 20 minutes. Uncover and bake 10 minutes or until bubbly and lightly browned on top. Let stand 10 minutes before serving.

Note: We tested with Swanson Natural Goodness 33% Less Sodium Chicken Broth.

MAKES 12 servings. **HANDS-ON** 1 hour **TOTAL** 1 hour, 40 min.

GULF CRAB CAKES WITH LEMON BUTTER

For these plump Coastal Texas treats, make sure to handle the delicate mixture carefully; the chilling process helps the cakes hold their shape during cooking.

1/2	cup finely diced red bell pepper
1/2	cup finely diced green bell pepper
1/2	cup finely diced yellow onion
2	Tbsp. minced garlic
8	Tbsp. extra virgin olive oil, divided
2	Tbsp. Creole or Dijon mustard
2	Tbsp. Worcestershire sauce
1	tsp. kosher salt
1/2	tsp. freshly ground black pepper
1/8	tsp. ground red pepper
3/4	cup fine, dry breadcrumbs
2	large eggs, lightly beaten
1 1/2	lb. fresh lump crabmeat, picked and drained
1/2	cup minced green onions
3	Tbsp. butter
	Lemon Butter

1. Sauté bell peppers, yellow onion, and garlic in 2 Tbsp. hot oil over medium-high heat 8 to 10 minutes or until tender. Stir in mustard and next 4 ingredients. Add breadcrumbs, and sauté 1 minute. Transfer mixture to a large bowl. Cool 15 minutes.

2. Fold eggs into breadcrumb mixture until blended. Gently stir in crabmeat and green onions. Shape into 12 (3-inch) crab cakes (about 1/3 cup each). Cover and chill 30 to 40 minutes.

3. Melt 1 Tbsp. butter with 2 Tbsp. oil in a large nonstick skillet over medium heat. Add 4 crab cakes to skillet; cook 3 to 4 minutes on each side or until browned. Remove from skillet, and keep warm in a 200° oven. Repeat procedure with remaining oil, butter, and crab cakes, wiping skillet clean after each batch. Serve with Lemon Butter.

MAKES 12 servings. **HANDS-ON** 50 min. **TOTAL** 1 hour, 55 min., including Lemon Butter

Lemon Butter

1	lemon, peeled and quartered
1	shallot, minced
1/4	cup dry white wine
1	bay leaf
1 1/2	tsp. whole peppercorns
2	cups unsalted butter, cut into tablespoon-size pieces
1/2	tsp. table salt
	Pinch of ground white pepper

1. Bring first 5 ingredients to a simmer in a heavy saucepan over medium heat. Cook 3 to 5 minutes or until liquid almost completely evaporates. Reduce heat to low, and whisk in butter, 1 piece at a time, whisking constantly and allowing butter to melt between each addition.

2. Pour mixture through a fine wire-mesh strainer into a bowl, discarding solids. Stir in salt and white pepper. Cover with foil to keep warm.

MAKES 2 cups. **HANDS-ON** 20 min. **TOTAL** 20 min.

SAN ANTONIO BEEF PUFFY TACOS

Original tacos were a little different than the U-shaped tortillas invented by entrepreneur Glen Bell of Taco Bell. The real deal begins with a ball of masa flattened into a thin round that's fried to a golden crispness. The masa puffs up a bit, which is how the moniker "puffy taco" came into play.

- 2 lb. fresh masa (available at Mexican markets)*
  Wax paper
  Vegetable oil
  Kosher salt
- 1 white onion, chopped
- 1 jalapeño pepper, seeded and minced
- 2 garlic cloves, minced
- 2 Tbsp. vegetable oil
- 1 lb. ground beef
- 2 plum tomatoes, chopped
- 4 tsp. chili powder
- 1 Tbsp. ground cumin
- 2 tsp. kosher salt
- 1/2 cup Mexican beer
  Toppings: shredded cheese, salsa, lettuce, sour cream, guacamole

1. Shape masa into 18 golf ball-size portions (about 2 Tbsp. each). Cut sides off a zip-top plastic freezer bag. Line top and bottom of a tortilla press with freezer bag. Place masa rounds in freezer bag, 1 at a time, and close tortilla press to form tortillas. (If you don't have a tortilla press, use a flat plate, skillet, or flat-bottomed bowl, and press masa balls between sheets of wax paper against countertop into flat rounds. To ensure even thickness, press dough rounds once, rotate 180°, and press again.) Gently stack tortillas between layers of wax paper.
2. Pour oil to a depth of 3 inches into a Dutch oven; heat to 375°.
3. Gently lower 1 uncooked tortilla into hot oil. Once tortilla rises to surface and begins to bubble, cook 10 seconds. Gently flip tortilla, and lightly press center of tortilla, using a metal spatula, to create a U-shape. Cook 30 seconds or until golden brown. Carefully remove from oil, sprinkle with desired amount of salt, and drain upside down on a paper towel-lined wire rack. Repeat procedure with remaining tortillas. Keep warm in a 200° oven.
4. Cook onion and next 2 ingredients in 2 Tbsp. hot oil in a large nonstick skillet over medium-high heat 4 to 5 minutes or until softened. Add beef, and cook, stirring often, 8 minutes or until meat crumbles and is no longer pink; drain. Reduce heat to medium.
5. Return beef mixture to skillet; add tomatoes, chili powder, cumin, and 2 tsp. salt, and cook 4 minutes. Add beer, and reduce heat to medium-low. Cover and simmer 15 minutes.

Uncover and cook 3 minutes or until liquid is absorbed. Serve mixture in tortillas with desired toppings.

*If you can't find fresh masa, you may substitute the following recipe: Whisk together 3 cups masa harina (corn flour), 1 1/2 Tbsp. all-purpose flour, 1 1/2 tsp. baking powder, and 1 1/2 tsp. kosher salt. Whisk in 2 1/4 cups very hot water until dry ingredients are moistened. (Add more hot water if needed, 1 tsp. at a time.) Knead 3 or 4 times to make a smooth dough.

MAKES 8 to 9 servings. **HANDS-ON** 1 hour, 5 min. **TOTAL** 1 hour, 20 min.

TEXAS SHEET CAKE WITH FUDGE ICING

Somehow, Texas claimed the sheet cake as its own in the mid-20th century, perhaps because of the pecans, an ingredient that grows in abundance throughout the Lone Star State. The defining element is its shape—and, of course, the icing, which has to be heated and poured on the warm, just-out-of-the-oven cake. The result is a rich, chocolaty treat that's iconic in Texas.

- 1 ½ cups spicy, fruity cola soft drink (such as Dr Pepper)
- 1 cup vegetable or canola oil
- ½ cup unsweetened cocoa
- 2 cups all-purpose flour
- 1 cup granulated sugar
- 1 cup firmly packed light brown sugar
- 1 ½ tsp. baking soda
- ½ tsp. table salt
- ½ cup buttermilk
- 2 large eggs, lightly beaten
- 2 tsp. vanilla extract
  Vegetable cooking spray
  Fudge Icing
- 1 ¼ cups chopped toasted pecans

1. Preheat oven to 350°. Bring first 3 ingredients to a boil in a medium saucepan over medium-high heat, stirring often. Remove from heat.
2. Whisk together flour and next 4 ingredients in a large bowl. Add soft drink mixture, and whisk until blended. Whisk in buttermilk, eggs, and vanilla. Pour batter into a lightly greased (with cooking spray) 17 ½- x 12 ½-inch sheet pan.
3. Bake at 350° for 18 to 22 minutes or until a wooden pick inserted in center comes out clean.
4. Prepare Fudge Icing, and pour over warm cake. Sprinkle with pecans. Cool completely in pan (about 1 hour).

MAKES 20 servings. **HANDS-ON** 20 min.
TOTAL 1 hour, 50 min., including icing

TEXAS SHEET CAKE

Fudge Icing

- ½ cup butter
- ½ (4-oz.) unsweetened chocolate baking bar, chopped
- 3 Tbsp. milk
- 3 Tbsp. spicy, fruity cola soft drink (such as Dr Pepper)
- 4 cups powdered sugar
- 1 tsp. vanilla extract

1. Cook butter and chocolate in a medium saucepan over medium-low heat, whisking often, until melted and smooth.
2. Remove from heat, and whisk in milk and soft drink until blended. Gradually sift in powdered sugar, whisking constantly. Whisk in vanilla. Use immediately.

MAKES 2 ¼ cups. **HANDS-ON** 10 min.
TOTAL 10 min.

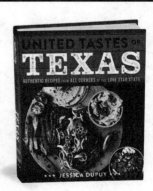

UNITED TASTES OF TEXAS
AUTHENTIC RECIPES FROM ALL CORNERS OF THE LONE STAR STATE

JESSICA DUPUY

THE NEW GUIDE TO TEXAS CUISINE

United Tastes of Texas is more than a cookbook—it's an introduction to the five distinct regions and the many international cuisines that compose the delicious patchwork of Texas. In addition to recipes, you can dig into regional history and tips and meet the chefs and restaurants that feed the Lone Star State.

Light and Cheesy

TASTE WHY READERS LOVE THE *COOKING LIGHT* DIET WITH THIS FRESHENED-UP MAC AND CHEESE

ONLY
343 CAL
SL

NUTRITIONAL INFORMATION *(per serving)*
CALORIES 343; FAT 12.2g (SATURATED FAT 6.5g);
PROTEIN 26g; FIBER 2g; CARBOHYDRATES 31g;
SODIUM 647mg

"THIS RECIPE SHOWS OFF WHAT I LOVE ABOUT THE COOKING LIGHT DIET: I NEVER FEEL LIKE I'M MISSING OUT ON FLAVOR. I LOVE ANYTHING CHEESY AND MELTY, AND WHEN CL FINDS A WAY TO LIGHTEN IT UP, IT'S EVEN BETTER."

COOKING LIGHT DIET SUBSCRIBER OF THE MONTH:
DARCI ROGOJIN
SEATTLE, WA

Cooking Light.
DIET

CHICKEN-BROCCOLI MAC AND CHEESE WITH BACON

To subscribe to the Cooking Light *Diet, visit diet.cookinglight/southernjan.*

- **6** oz. uncooked large or regular elbow macaroni
- **3** cups prechopped broccoli florets
- **3** bacon slices, chopped
- **12** oz. skinless, boneless chicken breasts, cut into 1/2-inch pieces
- **1** tsp. kosher salt, divided
- **1** Tbsp. minced fresh garlic
- **1/8** tsp. ground turmeric
- **1 1/4** cups 1% low-fat milk
- **1** cup unsalted chicken stock (such as Swanson)
- **1/4** cup plus 1 tsp. all-purpose flour
- **5** oz. sharp Cheddar cheese, shredded (about 1 1/4 cups)

1. Preheat broiler to high. Cook pasta according to package directions, omitting salt and fat. Add broccoli to pan during last 2 minutes of cooking. Drain.

2. Cook bacon in a large ovenproof skillet over medium-high heat, stirring occasionally, 4 minutes or until browned. Remove bacon with a slotted spoon; reserve 1 1/2 tsp. drippings in skillet. Sprinkle chicken with 1/4 tsp. salt. Cook chicken in hot drippings 4 minutes. Sprinkle with garlic; cook, stirring occasionally, 2 minutes. Sprinkle with turmeric; cook, stirring often, 30 seconds.

3. Whisk together milk, stock, flour, and remaining salt; add to skillet. Bring to a boil, stirring often. Cook 2 minutes or until thickened. Stir in pasta mixture and 2 oz. cheese. Top with bacon and remaining cheese. Broil 2 minutes.

MAKES 6 servings (serving size: about 1 1/3 cups). **HANDS-ON** 25 min. **TOTAL** 30 min.

Community Cookbook

BUILD A BETTER LIBRARY, ONE GREAT BOOK AT A TIME

Chocolate Pudding Cake, Pumpkin-Hazelnut Layered Cheesecake, Milk Chocolate and Amaretto Crème Brûlée: *Incredibly Decadent Desserts* is filled with 100 delectable confections—**each only 300 calories or less!** Author **Deb Wise,** who has spent eight years honing her craft in the *Cooking Light* Test Kitchen, has assembled her trusted recipes, from Bundt cakes for beginners to Torched Alaska—all indulgent, impressive, and guilt-free.

MEYER LEMON PANNA COTTA

Lemon fans will love this silky custard. In a pinch, substitute regular lemon juice for the Meyer lemon, and stir it in at the end to keep the milk from curdling.

- 1 **Meyer lemon**
- 3/4 **cup 2% reduced-fat milk, divided**
- 1/2 **cup half-and-half**

- 1/3 **cup sugar**
- 1/8 **tsp. table salt**
- 1 3/4 **tsp. unflavored gelatin**
- 1 1/2 **cups reduced-fat buttermilk**
  Vegetable cooking spray
- 1/2 **cup frozen reduced-calorie whipped topping (such as Cool Whip), thawed**
  Mint sprigs (optional)
  Lemon rind strips (optional)

1. Remove rind from lemon using a vegetable peeler, avoiding the white pith. Squeeze 3 Tbsp. juice from lemon. Combine rind, 1/2 cup milk, half-and-half, sugar, and salt in a small saucepan; bring to a simmer. (Do not boil.) Remove pan from heat; cover and let stand 20 minutes. Discard lemon rind.
2. Sprinkle gelatin over remaining 1/4 cup milk in a small bowl; let stand 5 minutes. Return milk mixture in pan to medium heat; cook 1 minute or until mixture reaches a simmer. Whisk in gelatin mixture, stirring until gelatin completely dissolves. Stir in buttermilk and 3 Tbsp. lemon juice. Divide mixture among 4 (6-oz.) ramekins or custard cups coated with cooking spray. Cover and chill 4 hours or overnight.
3. To serve, run a knife around outside edges of panna cottas. Place a plate upside down on top of each cup; invert onto plate. Top servings with

whipped topping, and garnish with mint and lemon rind, if desired.

MAKES 4 servings. **HANDS-ON** 35 min. **TOTAL** 4 hours, 55 min.

CHOCOLATE PUDDING CAKE

This dessert is warm, gooey, and rich with chocolaty goodness.

- 4.5 **oz. all-purpose flour (about 1 cup)**
- 3/4 **cup granulated sugar, divided**
- 1/4 **cup unsweetened cocoa, divided**
- 2 **tsp. baking powder**
- 1/4 **tsp. table salt**
- 1/2 **cup 2% reduced-fat milk**
- 2 **Tbsp. unsalted butter, melted**
- 1 **tsp. vanilla extract**
  Baking spray with flour
- 1/4 **cup firmly packed brown sugar**
- 1 1/4 **cups strong hot coffee**
- 9 **Tbsp. frozen reduced-calorie whipped topping (such as Cool Whip), thawed**

1. Preheat oven to 350°.
2. Weigh or lightly spoon flour into a dry measuring cup; level with a knife. Combine flour, 1/2 cup granulated sugar, 2 Tbsp. cocoa, baking powder, and salt in a bowl, stirring with a whisk. Add milk, butter, and vanilla; stir until just combined. Scrape batter into a 9- x 9-inch metal baking pan coated with baking spray. Combine remaining 1/4 cup granulated sugar, 2 Tbsp. cocoa, and brown sugar; sprinkle mixture over top of batter. Carefully pour coffee over top. (Do not stir in.)
3. Bake at 350° for 28 to 30 minutes or until just set. (Do not overbake.) Let stand 10 minutes; top with whipped topping.

MAKES 9 servings. **HANDS-ON** 15 min. **TOTAL** 1 hour

➤➤ To purchase *Incredibly Decadent Desserts,* visit your local bookstore or *amazon.com.*

February

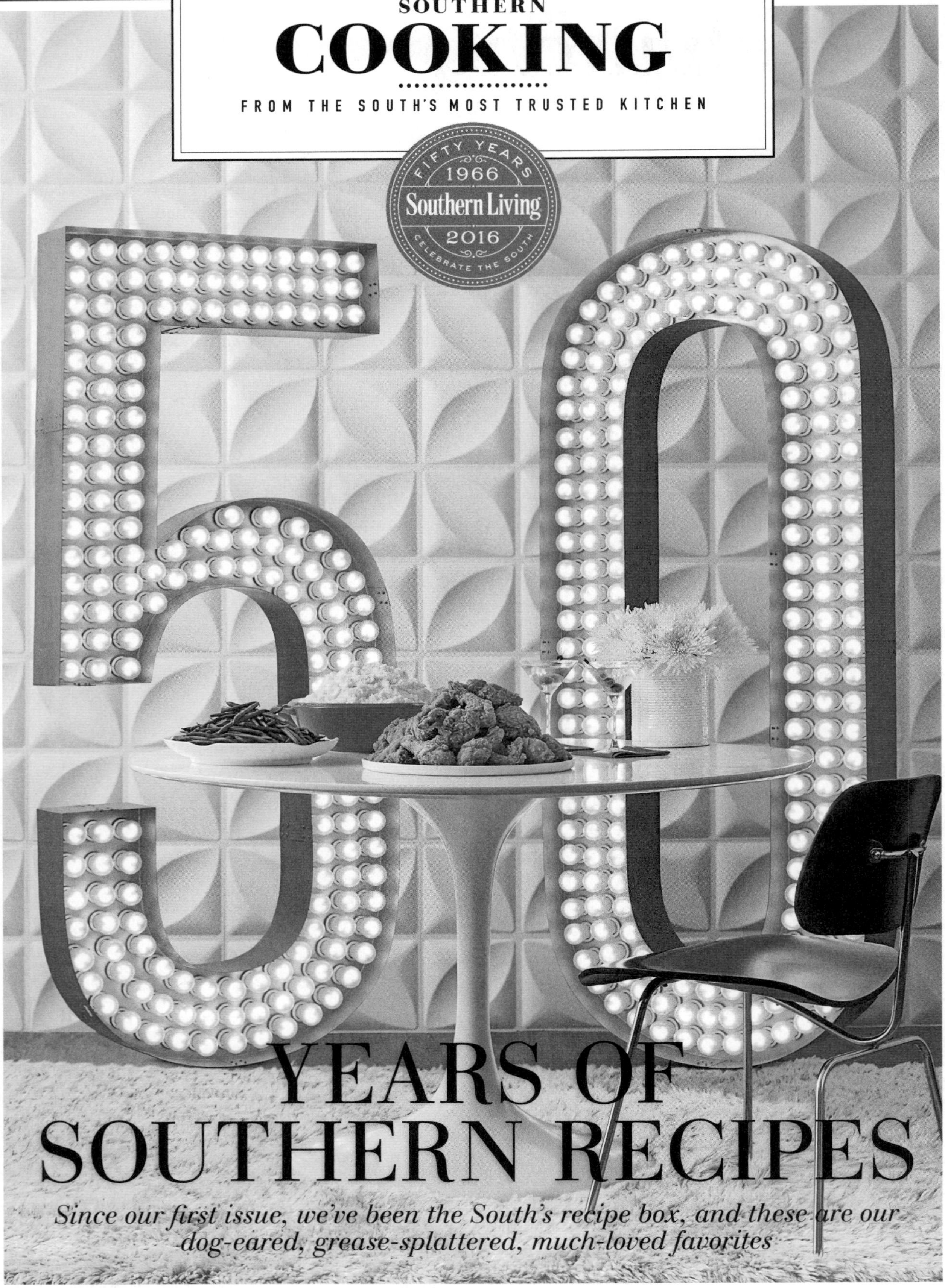

FIFTY YEARS
1966
Southern Living
2016
CELEBRATE THE SOUTH

YEARS OF
SOUTHERN RECIPES

Since our first issue, we've been the South's recipe box, and these are our
dog-eared, grease-splattered, much-loved favorites

Molded Cranberry
Salad

WITH TWO LINES, IT BEGAN.

"We are looking for recipes using peaches and will pay $3 for each one we use in *Southern Living*. In submitting your recipes, tell us something of its origin and other foods you would serve with it for a complete meal." Since the publication of our second issue in March 1966, millions of recipes have arrived in our mailboxes and, now, inboxes. Nearly every issue of *Southern Living* since has included at least one reader-submitted recipe. It's the hallmark of our pages. When *Southern Living* first began, the times, they were a-changin' both culturally and in our kitchens. Our readers still liked formal dinner parties where they served fancy dishes with flair. Julia Child and the Kennedy White

House made French cuisine wildly popular. And at cocktail parties, gracious hostesses would pass delicate hors d'oeuvres on monogrammed silver trays and inherited chafing dishes. But our readers also began their exploration of fun, casual, and convenient family meals. Perhaps the biggest change was the Space Race and with it, the fascination with foods like freeze-dried ice cream and Tang, but none more revelatory than gelatin. The recipes during its wiggly, jiggly reign suggested that with a little determination and imagination, there was no type of food—sweet or savory—that could not be molded and congealed.

1966

The first issue of *Southern Living* is published, while Cool Whip and Snack Mate spray cheese hit the market.

1967

Bundt pan **sales skyrocket** after a Tunnel of Fudge Bundt cake placed second in the 17th annual Pillsbury Bake-Off. Today, more than 70 million households have a Bundt pan.

Hamburger Helper first offers to lend a hand in quick-meal preparation.

1971

1972

Mr. Coffee introduces us to automatic drip coffee makers.

1973

Cuisinart food processors **make their debut at the National Housewares Expo in Chicago.**

1974

A pack of Wrigley's Juicy Fruit **gum—in an Ohio store—becomes the first grocery item to be scanned with a UPC code.**

McDonald's introduces the Happy Meal.

1979

1980

In this year, *Southern Living* **tests** over 1,800 recipes, using ¼ ton of sugar, ⅕ ton of flour, and over ½ mile of aluminum foil.

Gallo Wine introduces Bartles and Jaymes wine coolers.

1981

1982

Diet Coke, **Bud Light, and Equal artificial sweetener hit the market.** Jell-O releases pudding pops, advertising them as a wholesome snack.

1986

Louisiana chef Paul Prudhomme releases a cookbook on video.

1987

The first edition of *The Southern Living Cookbook* **introduces the nation to the food of the New South.**

1988

Oat bran **is the most popular cure-all food craze.**

1992

The USDA creates the Food Pyramid.

1993

The Food Network **premieres.**

1994

The U.S. Food and Drug Administration **(FDA) declares the** first genetically engineered tomato, **the Flavr Savr, safe for human consumption.**

John Egerton convenes 50 people at the Birmingham *Southern Living* **headquarters to found the** Southern Foodways Alliance.

1999

2000

Southern writer and *New York Times* **food critic** Craig Claiborne passes away.

The cupcake **craze begins.**

2001

2002

Small, neighborhood restaurants **steal the spotlight from fine dining.**

2006

Wal-Mart becomes the largest seller of organic milk in the United States.

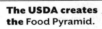

The 7 billionth can of Spam **is sold.**

2007

2008

The McIlhenny Company, makers of Tabasco hot sauce, turns 140.

The soaring popularity of all things bacon **causes prices to increase 240% since 2005.**

2013

A surprising surge in **demand for** bourbon creates a barrel shortage.

2014

2015

Food trend prognosticators **predict that restaurants will start using** biscuits **to make sandwiches in the coming year.** Southerners shake their heads and mutter "Bless their hearts."

1968

Electric toasters **are the most-owned small appliance in the United States.**

1969

The moon landing fuels fascination with "space food" **consumed by astronauts, such as freeze-dried trail mix in a Mylar bag and Tang, an orange-flavored breakfast drink.**

1970

Hawaiian-themed cocktail parties, tiki drinks, **and anything with pineapple are all the rage.**

1975

Push-tab cans are touted as a safer alternative to pull tabs.

1976

Chef Edna Lewis publishes her masterpiece, A Taste of Country Cooking, **which champions authentic Southern cooking and the use of local ingredients.**

Chili is proclaimed the official state food of Texas.

1977

1978

Garfield debuts, and lasagna's **popularity soars.**

1983

Southern Living **introduces "From Our Kitchen to Yours," a column designed to answer common how-to questions from busy home cooks.**

1984

Hidden Valley Ranch dressing quickly overtakes Italian dressing as the national favorite.

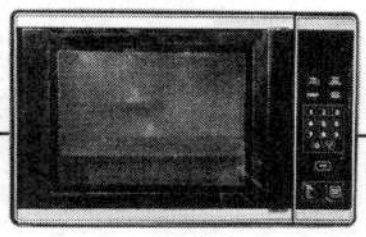

1985

67% of subscribers now own a microwave versus 10% just a decade before.

Ready-to-eat salad in a bag **lands in the produce aisle.**

1989

1990

The Vidalia onion **is named Georgia's official state vegetable.**

1991

Mexican sauces, such as salsa, **overtake ketchup as the best-selling condiment in the United States in total dollar sales.**

1995

Southern Living **features a coconut-lemon layer cake on the December cover, beginning our annual big white cake tradition.**

A voluntary ban of hard liquor ads **on television and radio in effect since 1936 is lifted.**

1996

1997

Red Bull energy drink comes to the United States.

Memphis BBQ destination Charlie Vergos' Rendezvous **celebrates its 50th anniversary.**

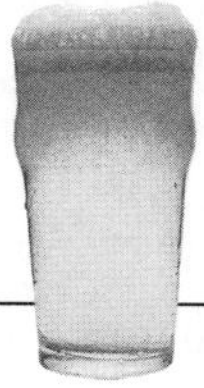

1998

Demand for craft beer is at an all-time high, and breweries pop up all over the South.

2003

2004

Willie Nelson opens his own restaurant, Willie's Roadhouse Grill, **in Austin, Texas.**

Arnaud's and Antoine's **in New Orleans resiliently reopen just a few months after Hurricane Katrina.**

2005

The film Julie and Julia **renews interest in** Julia Child.

2010

2009

Sean Brock opens his lauded Husk **in Charleston, SC.**

Food trucks take off, giving a whole new meaning to the term "meals on wheels."

2011

2012

The final 6.5 ounce iconic returnable glass Coca-Cola **bottle was filled and capped.**

Hummingbird Cake

THE 1970s

WE MAKE MAGIC OUT OF CANNED PINEAPPLE

Things took an international turn on our pages during the seventies. Our fascination for all things French continued; we ate lots of quiche and rolled lots of crêpes. Asian food from China to Polynesia had us experimenting with woks and cranking open a few thousand cans of pineapple. Italian food increased in popularity as well, especially pasta dishes. In the early 1970s, three different restaurants claimed to have invented Pasta Primavera. Our recipes have always reflected trends, and just like our readers, our Test Kitchen pros in the 1970s were using fondue pots, Ginsu knives, and slow cookers. An advertisement for Rival Crock-Pots proclaimed that their product "cooks all day while the cook's away" to appeal to working mothers, and recipes for slow cooking soon followed on our pages. After hearing that readers loved to clip out our recipes but hated to cut up their issues, we published the first *Southern Living Annual Recipes* cookbook in 1979, which aggregated the hundreds of recipes featured in our magazine that year. We still hear from readers who display the entire collection on their shelves with family photos. Although a recipe is published only after due deliberation, we can't predict which ones will become classics. The best example of that phenomenon is the 1978 publication of Hummingbird Cake, which became one of our most requested recipes in the magazine's history.

Chicken-Spaghetti Casserole

THE 1980s

WE GIVE RISE TO THE GOLDEN AGE OF CASSEROLES

Women entered the workforce outside the home in record numbers in the eighties. Time for cooking shrank, but expectations for scratch-made dinners and impressive entertaining did not. *Southern Living* responded by providing time-strapped cooks with quick and easy recipes, one-pan wonders, and make-ahead meals. The need for speed influenced our appliance purchases as well. By 1989, most kitchens included a microwave oven. The eighties were challenging for many family cooks due to soaring grocery prices and beef shortages. Our staff responded by helping cooks on tight budgets make the most of their groceries. The secret to stretching ingredients, it turned out, was casseroles. But affordable didn't equate unappealing. In the eighties, readers liked their food, at least in photos, all gussied up with garnishes like radish roses, chocolate curls, and paper frills on crown roasts. In turn, food styling and photography took on new importance. Cooking light went from a buzzword to a legacy in the 1980s, the decade that ushered in calorie-conscious Southern recipes on our pages. A Cooking Light column written by staff dieticians debuted in 1982. Readers couldn't get enough of our oven-fried chicken and lightened-up layer cakes, and five years later the column became *Cooking Light* magazine, lauded in the publishing world as the best new magazine launch in the past 20 years.

Tex-Mex Deviled Eggs

THE 1990s

WE DISCOVER TEX-MEX

The idea of a celebrity chef emerged in the nineties, and *Southern Living* offered more recipes from revered regional chefs than ever before. Talents featured on our pages included Frank Stitt, Emeril Lagasse, and Bill Smith—often featuring the foods they prepared at home for their families. Some chefs became household names with huge fan bases, especially after the premiere of the Food Network in 1993, which enabled viewers to have ringside seats at the world of professional cooking. Inspired by the availability of foreign foods and gourmet groceries, many chefs began combining cuisines in a trend known as fusion cooking, and so did we. Spurred by the runaway hit show *Dallas*, readers clamored for Tex-Mex and Southwestern fare. Seven-layer dip, nachos, and queso dip made from Velveeta cheese and Ro-Tel tomatoes and chiles became wildly popular party foods to enjoy while we wondered who shot J.R. when the final episode aired in 1991. The Mediterranean Diet and the rise of restaurants like Olive Garden and Pizza Hut led to a renewed fascination with Italian food, and we quickly discovered that a cast-iron skillet made a great pan for homemade pizzas. Although we continued developing healthier recipes during the advent of artificial sweeteners and low-fat cookies, we still ran the classics, never losing sight of our belief that Southern home cooking is healing for the heart and soul.

Sweet Tea-Brined Chicken

THE 2000s AND BEYOND...

It's a new century and we're all online. Now readers need only type in southernliving.com to access our enormous archive of recipes. We tweet, blog, pin, snap, and post, and our video channel shares tutorials on everything from potato salad to piecrusts. Our first viral video featuring red velvet pancakes lets us know that Southerners might be pioneers of the farm-to-table craze but they still won't be putting away their red food coloring any time soon. Nationally, Southern cooking has finally earned the respect it deserves, and native dishes and drinks like BBQ and bourbon become red-hot trends globally. While our best Southern restaurants list trended on Twitter, the newest thing in restaurants is no restaurant at all; we're walking up to food trucks and buying tickets for neighborhood pop-ups. Small plates are popular, letting us build a meal from an array of this and that— just like old-fashioned Southern covered-dish dinners. Although we still love finding new hot spots, we also can't get enough of lost domestic arts like canning and pickling. Our readers crave the classics but love updated flavors that make the familiar feel inventive— like Boiled Peanut Hummus and tomato salads made with heirloom varieties. With new, state-of-the-art Food Studios and a website redesign ahead this year, the possibilities for the future feel limitless.

the '60s

MOLDED CRANBERRY SALAD

We'll admit it: We wouldn't want to revisit many of the congealed salads we published in the sixties, but rediscovering this jewel of a recipe was like finding a timeless dress at a vintage store.

- 1 **(8-oz.) can crushed pineapple in syrup**
  Boiling water
- 1 **(3-oz.) package raspberry-flavored gelatin**
- 1 **(14-oz.) can whole-berry cranberry sauce**
- 1 **cup drained mandarin oranges**
- 1 **tsp. orange zest**

Drain syrup from pineapple into a 2-cup measuring cup. Add boiling water to equal 1 1/4 cups. Transfer to a large bowl. Dissolve gelatin in hot syrup mixture; chill 1 hour and 30 minutes or until partially set. Fold in cranberry sauce, oranges, zest, and crushed pineapple. Pour into 1 (4-cup) mold, and chill 2 hours or until set.

MAKES 6 to 8 servings. **HANDS-ON** 15 min. **TOTAL** 3 hours, 45 min.

BRENNAN'S BANANAS FOSTER

Flambéed desserts were a must-have tableside sensation both at restaurants and at home. This recipe we ran from Brennan's in New Orleans is just as delicious as it was when they invented it more than 60 years ago.

- 4 **medium-size ripe bananas**
- 1/2 **cup butter**
- 1 **cup packed light brown sugar**
  Dash of ground cinnamon
- 1/4 **cup banana liqueur**
- 1/2 **cup rum**
  Vanilla ice cream

1. Cut bananas in half crosswise, then lengthwise. Melt butter in a large skillet over medium heat; add brown sugar, and cook, stirring constantly, 2 minutes.

2. Add bananas to skillet, and sprinkle with cinnamon. Remove skillet from heat. Stir in liqueur and rum, and carefully ignite the fumes just above mixture with a long match. Let flames die down.

3. Return to heat, and cook 3 to 4 minutes or until soft. Serve over ice cream.

MAKES 4 to 6 servings. **HANDS-ON** 10 min. **TOTAL** 10 min.

BEEF BURGUNDY STEW

The vice president for the Southern division of Sears, Roebuck and Co. sent us this recipe after a trip to France.

- 3 **lb. beef stew meat**
- 2 **cups red wine**
- 2 **Tbsp. butter**
- 2 **Tbsp. olive oil**
- 1 **yellow onion, coarsely chopped**
- 2 **large carrots, sliced**
- 3 **garlic cloves, chopped**
- 2 **tsp. chopped fresh thyme**
- 1 **Tbsp. all-purpose flour**
- 2 **tsp. table salt**
- 1 **tsp. freshly ground black pepper**
- 1/4 to 1/2 **cup beef broth**

1. Place meat and wine in a medium bowl; chill 1 hour. Remove meat using a slotted spoon; reserve wine in a small saucepan. Pat meat dry with paper towels.

2. Cook reserved wine over medium-high heat, stirring occasionally, 15 minutes or until reduced to 1 cup.

3. Melt butter with oil in a Dutch oven over medium-high heat; add meat, and cook 5 minutes, stirring to brown all sides. Add onion and next 3 ingredients, and cook, stirring often, 15 minutes or until vegetables and meat are cooked. Sprinkle flour over meat mixture, and cook, stirring constantly, 1 minute. Stir in reduced wine, salt, pepper, and 1/4 cup beef broth. Cover and reduce heat to low; simmer, stirring occasionally, 2 hours, adding up to 1/2 cup beef broth if needed.

Note: We tested with Swanson 100% Natural 50% Less Sodium Beef Broth.

MAKES 4 to 6 servings. **HANDS-ON** 45 min. **TOTAL** 3 hours, 45 min.

CHEESE SNAPPY WAFERS

Southern hostesses have long relied on cheese wafers to keep their party guests satiated.

- 1 **cup butter, cubed**
- 2 **cups all-purpose flour**
- 8 **oz. sharp Cheddar cheese, grated**
- 1/2 **tsp. ground red pepper**
- 1/2 **tsp. table salt**
- 2 **cups crisp rice cereal (such as Rice Krispies)**

Preheat oven to 350°. Cut butter into flour until mixture resembles coarse meal. Stir in cheese, red pepper, and salt. Fold in cereal. Shape into 1-inch balls, and place 2 inches apart on ungreased baking sheets. Flatten each dough ball. Bake, in batches, 15 minutes. (Refrigerate remaining baking sheet while first batch is baking.)

MAKES 32 wafers. **HANDS-ON** 20 min. **TOTAL** 35 min.

Cheese Snappy Wafers

the '70s

HUMMINGBIRD CAKE

Thanks to Mrs. L.H. Wiggins of Greensboro, North Carolina, this pineapple-banana spice cake with cream cheese frosting became one of our most requested recipes. We still stand by Mrs. Wiggins' original, indulgent creation.

- 3   **cups all-purpose flour**
- 2   **cups sugar**
- 1   **tsp. table salt**
- 1   **tsp. baking soda**
- 1   **tsp. ground cinnamon**
- 3   **large eggs, lightly beaten**
- 1 1/2   **cups vegetable oil**
- 1 1/2   **tsp. vanilla extract**
- 1   **(8-oz.) can crushed pineapple in juice, undrained**
- 2   **cups chopped bananas (about 4 medium bananas)**
- 1   **cup chopped toasted pecans**
     Shortening
     Cream Cheese Frosting
- 1   **cup toasted pecan halves**

1. Preheat oven to 350°. Whisk together flour and next 4 ingredients in a large bowl; add eggs and oil, stirring just until dry ingredients are moistened. Stir in vanilla, pineapple, bananas, and 1 cup chopped toasted pecans. Spoon batter into 3 well-greased (with shortening) and floured 9-inch round cake pans.
2. Bake at 350° for 25 to 30 minutes or until a wooden pick inserted in center comes out clean. Cool cake layers in pans on wire racks 10 minutes; remove from pans to wire racks, and cool completely (about 1 hour).
3. Place 1 cake layer on a serving platter. Spread 1 cup Cream Cheese Frosting over cake layer. Top with second layer, and spread 1 cup frosting over cake layer. Top with third cake layer, and spread top and sides of cake with remaining frosting. Arrange toasted pecan halves in a circular pattern over top of cake.

MAKES 12 servings. **HANDS-ON** 30 min.
TOTAL 2 hours, 15 min., including frosting

Cream Cheese Frosting

- 2   **(8-oz.) packages cream cheese, softened**
- 1   **cup butter, softened**
- 2   **(16-oz.) packages powdered sugar**
- 2   **tsp. vanilla extract**

Beat cream cheese and butter at medium-low speed with an electric mixer until smooth. Gradually add sugar, beating at low speed until blended. Stir in vanilla. Increase speed to medium-high, and beat 1 to 2 minutes or until fluffy.

MAKES about 5 1/2 cups. **HANDS-ON** 10 min.
TOTAL 10 min.

COCKTAIL MEATBALLS

Cocktail meatballs hold a special place in the canon of Southern party appetizers. While we love the ones our mamas made with chili sauce and grape jelly, this recipe is the one we still pull out for company.

- 1 1/2   **lb. ground chuck**
- 1/4   **cup seasoned breadcrumbs**
- 2   **tsp. prepared horseradish**
- 2   **garlic cloves, crushed**
- 3/4   **cup tomato juice**
- 2   **tsp. kosher salt**
- 1/4   **tsp. freshly ground black pepper**
- 2   **medium-size yellow onions, chopped (about 1 1/2 cups), divided**
     Vegetable cooking spray
- 2   **Tbsp. butter**
- 2   **Tbsp. all-purpose flour**
- 1 1/2   **cups beef broth**
- 1/2   **cup dry red wine**
- 2   **Tbsp. light brown sugar**
- 2   **Tbsp. ketchup**
- 1   **Tbsp. fresh lemon juice**
- 3   **gingersnaps, crumbled (about 3 Tbsp.)**

Cocktail Meatballs

1. Preheat oven to 450°. Gently stir together ground chuck, next 6 ingredients, and 3/4 cup chopped onions. Shape into 1-inch balls; place in a lightly greased (with cooking spray) 13- x 9-inch baking dish. Bake at 450° for 20 minutes. Remove from oven, and drain off excess fat.
2. Heat butter in a large skillet over medium heat; add remaining onions, and sauté 4 to 6 minutes or until tender. Whisk in flour; cook, whisking constantly, 1 minute. Gradually whisk in beef broth, and cook, whisking constantly, until smooth. Stir in wine and next 4 ingredients. Reduce heat to low, and cook, stirring often, 15 minutes. Add meatballs, and simmer, stirring occasionally, 5 minutes.

Note: We tested with Swanson 100% Natural 50% Less Sodium Beef Broth.

MAKES 4 dozen. **HANDS-ON** 40 min.
TOTAL 1 hour

QUICHE LORRAINE

A quiche was featured in nearly every issue of the seventies, but none was more popular than Quiche Lorraine. Our favorite version, of course, uses bacon.

- 1/2 (14.1-oz.) package refrigerated piecrusts
- 1 lb. bacon, cut into 1/2-inch pieces
- 1/4 cup chopped green onions
- 8 oz. Swiss cheese, grated and divided
- 6 large eggs, beaten
- 1 cup heavy cream
- 1/2 tsp. table salt
  Dash of ground red pepper
  Dash of white pepper
- 1/8 tsp. ground nutmeg

1. Preheat oven to 425°. Fit piecrust into a 9-inch pie plate; fold edges under, and crimp. Prick bottom and sides of crust with a fork; bake 6 to 8 minutes or until lightly browned. Reduce oven temperature to 350°. Cool piecrust on a wire rack while preparing filling.
2. Cook bacon in a large skillet over medium heat, stirring often, 7 to 8 minutes or until crispy; drain on paper towels. Sprinkle bacon over bottom of pie shell. Sprinkle green onions over bacon; sprinkle half of Swiss cheese over onions.
3. Whisk together beaten eggs and next 5 ingredients. Carefully pour egg mixture over cheese. Sprinkle remaining Swiss cheese over egg mixture.
4. Bake at 350° for 35 to 40 minutes or until lightly browned and set in middle. Cool 15 minutes before serving.

MAKES 6 servings. **HANDS-ON** 35 min. **TOTAL** 1 hour, 25 min.

CHICKEN WITH CASHEWS

Our Test Kitchen staffers declared that this Chinese-inspired recipe from 1979 beats any takeout meal.

- 2 large boneless, skinless chicken breasts (about 14 oz.)
- 1/4 cup dry sherry
- 1/4 cup soy sauce
- 1 Tbsp. plus 1 tsp. cornstarch
- 2 Tbsp. dark corn syrup
- 1 Tbsp. distilled white vinegar
- 1/4 cup peanut oil
- 1/2 cup coarsely chopped green pepper
- 1/2 cup cashews
- 2 Tbsp. sliced green onions (white and green parts only)
- 2 garlic cloves, minced
- 1/4 tsp. ground ginger
  Hot cooked long-grain rice

1. Cut chicken into 1-inch pieces. Stir together sherry, next 4 ingredients, and 1/4 cup water in a small bowl.
2. Heat a large skillet over high heat for 2 minutes. Add peanut oil, and tilt skillet to coat sides; heat 2 minutes.
3. Add chicken, and stir-fry 2 to 3 minutes or until chicken turns white. Move chicken to perimeter of skillet. Add green pepper and cashews; stir-fry 30 seconds, and move to perimeter of skillet. Add onions, garlic, and ginger; stir-fry 1 minute, and move to perimeter of skillet.
4. Add sherry mixture, and bring to a boil, stirring constantly. Cook 1 minute, stirring all ingredients into sauce. Serve over rice.

MAKES 4 servings. **HANDS-ON** 30 min. **TOTAL** 30 min.

the '80s

CHICKEN-SPAGHETTI CASSEROLE

Casseroles are where you can see Southern ingenuity at its best, and the eighties had no shortage of inventive ideas. This particular Southern standard gave us all the warm and fuzzy memories we were craving.

- 1 (4-lb.) whole chicken
- 4 Tbsp. kosher salt
- 1 bay leaf
- 8 oz. uncooked spaghetti
- 3 Tbsp. butter
- 1 large yellow onion, chopped
- 1/2 medium-size green pepper, coarsely chopped
- 2 celery ribs, chopped
- 2 garlic cloves, minced
- 1 (10 3/4-oz.) can cream of mushroom soup
- 1 (28-oz.) can diced tomatoes, drained and chopped
- 1 tsp. Worcestershire sauce
- 4 drops of hot sauce
- 1/8 tsp. freshly ground black pepper
  Vegetable cooking spray
- 1 cup (4 oz.) shredded medium Cheddar cheese

1. Place first 3 ingredients and water to cover in a large Dutch oven. Bring to a boil over high heat. Cover and reduce heat to medium-low. Simmer 1 hour or until tender. Remove chicken, reserving broth in Dutch oven. Cool chicken completely (about 20 minutes). Discard bay leaf. Skin and bone chicken, and cut meat into pieces.
2. Preheat oven to 350°. Remove and reserve 1/4 cup chicken broth. Bring remaining broth in Dutch oven to a boil over high heat. Break spaghetti into thirds, and cook in broth 12 to 15 minutes or until tender; drain well,

Chicken with Cashews

discarding broth. Return spaghetti to Dutch oven.

3. Melt butter in a large skillet over medium-high heat. Add onion and next 3 ingredients, and sauté 5 minutes or until tender; add to spaghetti. Stir together soup and 1/4 cup reserved broth; stir into spaghetti mixture. Stir in chicken, tomatoes, and next 3 ingredients. Add salt to taste. Spoon mixture into a lightly greased (with cooking spray) 13- x 9-inch baking dish. Top with cheese.

4. Bake at 350° for 15 to 20 minutes or until cheese melts.

MAKES 8 servings. **HANDS-ON** 1 hour **TOTAL** 2 hours, 35 min.

LEAN LASAGNA

Our favorite recipe from the Cooking Light column, this lightened-up lasagna tastes every bit as flavorful as the traditional version.

- 1/2 **lb. ground turkey**
- 1 **(14.5-oz.) can tomato puree**
- 3 **(8-oz.) cans no-salt-added tomato sauce**
- 1/3 **cup chopped green pepper**
- 1/3 **cup chopped yellow onion**
- 1 **garlic clove, crushed**
- 1 **bay leaf**
- 1 1/4 **tsp. dried Italian seasoning**
- 1/2 **tsp. dried oregano**
- 1/4 **tsp. fennel seeds**
- 1/8 **tsp. ground red pepper**
  Dash of ground nutmeg
- 1 **(12-oz.) container 2% reduced-fat cottage cheese**
- 1 **(10-oz.) package frozen chopped spinach, thawed and pressed dry**
- 2 **Tbsp. grated Parmesan cheese**
  Vegetable cooking spray
- 18 **wonton wrappers**
- 1 **cup (4 oz.) shredded part-skim mozzarella cheese**

1. Cook ground turkey in skillet over medium heat, stirring often, 8 minutes or until brown; drain well on paper towels. Stir together turkey, tomato puree, and next 10 ingredients in a large saucepan; cover and cook over low heat, stirring occasionally,

30 minutes. Discard bay leaf.

2. Preheat oven to 350°. Stir together cottage cheese, spinach, and Parmesan.

3. Coat a 13- x 9-inch baking dish with cooking spray. Spread 1 cup turkey mixture into baking dish. Top with 6 wonton wrappers in a single layer (slightly overlapping), 1 cup spinach mixture, and 1 1/2 cups turkey mixture. Repeat layers twice, beginning with wontons and ending with turkey mixture.

4. Bake at 350° for 40 minutes or until thoroughly heated. Remove from oven. Top with mozzarella cheese, and bake 5 more minutes.

MAKES 8 servings. **HANDS-ON** 1 hour **TOTAL** 1 hour, 45 min.

FREEZER COLESLAW

Freezer coleslaws repeated throughout our eighties issues, and we can see why. This sweet and tangy slaw is perfect for pulled pork and hot dogs. Plus, it stays cold and crunchy longer.

- 1 **cup sugar**
- 1 **cup vinegar**
- 1/2 **tsp. celery seeds**
- 1 **medium cabbage, shredded (about 8 cups)**
- 1 **large carrot, shredded**
- 1/2 **cup chopped green pepper**
- 1/2 **cup chopped sweet red pepper**
- 1 **medium-size sweet onion, finely chopped**
- 1 **tsp. table salt**

1. Stir together first 3 ingredients and 1 cup water in a saucepan; bring to a boil over high heat, stirring occasionally. Boil 1 minute. Cool completely (about 30 minutes).

2. Stir together shredded cabbage and next 5 ingredients in a large bowl. Pour dressing over cabbage mixture; toss gently. Divide coleslaw evenly among 4 (1-qt.) zip-top plastic freezer bags. Seal and freeze 3 days. Store in freezer up to 1 month. Thaw coleslaw at room temperature 3 hours before serving.

MAKES 4 pt. **HANDS-ON** 25 min. **TOTAL** 55 min., plus 3 days for freezing

CHEWY PEANUT BARS

We weren't exactly excited to test our old microwave column recipes again, but these chocolate-peanut blondies truly surprised us.

- 6 **Tbsp. butter**
- 1 **cup firmly packed light brown sugar**
- 1/4 **cup creamy peanut butter**
- 2 **large eggs, lightly beaten**
- 1 **cup all-purpose flour**
- 1/2 **tsp. baking powder**
- 1/2 **tsp. table salt**
- 1 **tsp. vanilla extract**
- 3/4 **cup chopped salted peanuts, divided**
  Vegetable cooking spray
- 1 **(4-oz.) semisweet chocolate baking bar, chopped**

Microwave butter in a large microwave-safe bowl at MEDIUM-HIGH (70%) for 45 to 60 seconds or until melted. Stir together brown sugar and peanut butter. Add eggs, next 4 ingredients, and 1/2 cup peanuts. Spoon batter into a lightly greased (with cooking spray) 8-inch square microwave-safe baking dish. Microwave at MEDIUM-HIGH (70%) for 4 minutes. Microwave at HIGH (100%) for 3 to 6 minutes or until top is almost dry. Remove from microwave, and immediately top with chopped chocolate. Let stand 5 minutes; spread melted chocolate evenly over top, and sprinkle with remaining peanuts. Cool 15 minutes. Cut into squares.

MAKES 16 squares. **HANDS-ON** 15 min. **TOTAL** 50 min.

the '90s

TEX-MEX DEVILED EGGS

The South's iconic appetizer fuses with the nineties' obsession with Tex-Mex.

- 6 hard-cooked eggs, peeled
- 1 Tbsp. diced green onions
- 1 Tbsp. chopped fresh cilantro
- 1 small serrano or jalapeño pepper, seeded and finely chopped
- 1/4 cup mayonnaise
- 1 tsp. yellow mustard
- 1/2 tsp. table salt
- 1/4 cup (1 oz.) shredded Cheddar cheese
  Chili powder

1. Cut eggs in half crosswise; carefully remove yolks, and place in a small bowl.
2. Mash egg yolks; stir in green onions and next 5 ingredients.
3. Spoon yolk mixture into egg white halves; sprinkle with Cheddar cheese and desired amount of chili powder. Serve immediately, or cover and chill until ready to serve.

MAKES 1 dozen. **HANDS-ON** 15 min. **TOTAL** 45 min.

CREAM CHEESE POUND CAKE

This ultra-moist pound cake received our Test Kitchen's highest rating. It can be dressed up for any occasion: Fresh berries and a dollop or two of whipped cream do the trick.

- 1 1/2 cups butter, softened
- 1 (8-oz.) package cream cheese, softened
- 3 cups sugar
- 6 large eggs
- 1 1/2 tsp. vanilla extract
- 3 cups all-purpose flour

- 1/8 tsp. table salt
  Shortening

1. Preheat oven to 300°. Beat softened butter and cream cheese at medium speed with a heavy-duty electric stand mixer 2 minutes or until creamy.
2. Gradually add sugar, beating at medium speed until mixture is light and fluffy. Add eggs, 1 at a time, beating just until yellow disappears after each addition. Add vanilla, and beat just until blended.
3. Stir together flour and salt in a small bowl; gradually add to butter mixture, beating at low speed just until blended after each addition. Pour batter into a greased (with shortening) and floured 10-inch tube pan.
4. Bake at 300° for 1 hour and 25 to 30 minutes or until a wooden pick inserted in center of cake comes out clean. Cool cake in pan on a wire rack 10 to 15 minutes; remove from pan, and cool completely on wire rack (about 1 hour).

MAKES 12 servings. **HANDS-ON** 15 min. **TOTAL** 2 hours, 50 min.

LATE-NIGHT PASTA CHEZ FRANK

Our Test Kitchen Director, Robby Melvin, still loves to prepare this fresh and easy pasta dish from his mentor, Birmingham chef Frank Stitt.

- 4 jalapeño peppers or other chile peppers, seeds removed
- 6 garlic cloves, pressed
- 2 Tbsp. olive oil
- 8 plum tomatoes, chopped
- 1/2 tsp. kosher salt
- 1/3 to 1/2 cup chopped fresh basil
- 1 (8-oz.) package spaghettini or vermicelli, cooked
  Freshly grated Parmesan cheese

1. Finely chop jalapeño or other peppers; set aside.
2. Cook garlic in hot oil in a large nonstick skillet over medium heat, stirring constantly, 1 to 2 minutes or until golden.
3. Add peppers to garlic, and cook, stirring constantly, 1 minute.

Late-Night Pasta /Chez Frank

4. Add chopped plum tomatoes and kosher salt; cook 3 minutes or until thoroughly heated. Stir in desired amount of chopped fresh basil. Serve immediately over hot pasta, and sprinkle with Parmesan cheese.

MAKES 2 to 3 servings. **HANDS-ON** 25 min. **TOTAL** 25 min.

TEE'S CORN PUDDING

The ultimate creamed corn, this in-demand recipe has run in our magazine more than 10 times after its debut in 1995. We like to add chopped fresh chives on top.

- 1/4 cup sugar
- 3 Tbsp. all-purpose flour
- 2 tsp. baking powder
- 2 tsp. table salt
- 6 large eggs
- 2 cups heavy cream
- 1/2 cup butter, melted
- 6 cups fresh corn kernels*
  Vegetable cooking spray

1. Preheat oven to 350°. Stir together sugar, flour, baking powder, and salt in a small bowl.
2. Whisk eggs together in a large bowl; whisk in cream and melted butter.
3. Gradually add sugar mixture, whisking until smooth; stir in corn. Pour mixture into a lightly greased (with cooking spray) 13- x 9-inch baking dish.
4. Bake at 350° for 40 to 45 minutes or until mixture is deep golden and set. Let stand 5 minutes.

*Frozen whole kernel corn may be substituted.

MAKES 8 to 10 servings. **HANDS-ON** 15 min. **TOTAL** 1 hour

the
'00s
and beyond

SWEET TEA-BRINED CHICKEN

Sweet tea has become an iconic Southern flavor for pound cakes, ice cream, and even fried chicken. In this recipe, we brined pieces of chicken in the elixir before grilling to impart subtle sweetness and moisture.

- 2 family-size tea bags
- 1/2 cup firmly packed light brown sugar
- 1/4 cup kosher salt
- 1 small sweet onion, thinly sliced
- 1 lemon, thinly sliced
- 3 garlic cloves, halved
- 2 (6-inch) fresh rosemary sprigs
- 1 Tbsp. freshly cracked pepper
- 2 cups ice cubes
- 1 (3 1/2- to 4-lb.) cut-up whole chicken

1. Bring 4 cups water to a boil in a 3-qt. heavy saucepan; add tea bags. Remove from heat; cover and steep 10 minutes.
2. Discard tea bags. Stir in sugar and next 6 ingredients, stirring until sugar dissolves. Cool completely (about 45 minutes); stir in ice cubes. (Mixture should be cold before adding chicken.)
3. Place tea mixture and chicken in a large zip-top plastic freezer bag; seal. Place bag in a shallow baking dish, and chill 24 hours. Remove chicken from marinade, discarding marinade; pat chicken dry with paper towels.
4. Light 1 side of grill, heating to 300° to 350° (medium) heat; leave other side unlit. Place chicken, skin side down, over unlit side, and grill, covered with grill lid, 20 minutes. Turn chicken, and grill, covered with grill lid, 40 to 50 minutes or until done. Transfer chicken, skin side down, to lit side of grill, and grill 2 to 3 minutes or until skin is crispy. Let stand 5 minutes before serving.

MAKES 6 to 8 servings. **HANDS-ON** 30 min. **TOTAL** 2 hours, 35 min., plus 1 day for marinating

HAM-AND-GREENS POT PIE WITH CORNBREAD CRUST

From bacon to carnitas to BBQ, pork has hit prime time nationally. This recipe featuring ham and the Southern staples greens and cornbread continues to be a go-to dinner for our food editors.

FILLING:
- 4 cups chopped cooked ham
- 2 Tbsp. vegetable oil
- 3 Tbsp. all-purpose flour
- 3 cups chicken broth
- 1 (14-oz.) package frozen diced onion, bell pepper, and celery mix
- 1 (16-oz.) package frozen chopped collard greens
- 1 (15.8-oz.) can black-eyed peas, drained and rinsed
- 1/2 tsp. dried crushed red pepper
  Vegetable cooking spray

CRUST:
- 1 1/2 cups self-rising white cornmeal mix
- 1/2 cup all-purpose flour
- 1 tsp. sugar
- 2 large eggs, lightly beaten
- 1 1/2 cups buttermilk

1. Prepare Filling: Preheat oven to 425°. Sauté chopped ham in hot oil in a Dutch oven over medium-high heat 5 minutes or until lightly browned. Add 3 Tbsp. flour to Dutch oven, and cook, stirring constantly, 1 minute. Gradually add chicken broth, and cook, stirring constantly, 3 minutes or until broth begins to thicken.
2. Bring mixture to a boil, and add onion, bell pepper, and celery mix and collard greens; return to a boil, and cook, stirring often, 15 minutes.
3. Stir in black-eyed peas and dried crushed red pepper; spoon hot mixture into a lightly greased (with cooking spray) 13- x 9-inch baking dish.
4. Prepare Crust: Stir together cornmeal mix and next 2 ingredients in a large bowl, and make a well in the center of mixture. Add eggs and buttermilk, stirring just until dry ingredients are moistened. Pour batter evenly over hot filling mixture.
5. Bake at 425° for 20 to 25 minutes or until crust is golden brown and set.

Note: We tested with Swanson 100% Natural Chicken Broth.

MAKES 8 to 10 servings. **HANDS-ON** 35 min. **TOTAL** 1 hour

CHOCOLATE-BOURBON PECAN PIE

The new appreciation for whiskey goes beyond drinking and finds its way into sauces, braises, and especially desserts. Now bourbon and pecan pie fit together like peanut butter and jelly or Tom Petty and the Heartbreakers.

- 1/2 (14.1-oz.) package refrigerated piecrusts
- 1 1/2 cups chopped toasted pecans
- 1 cup (6 oz.) semisweet chocolate morsels
- 1 cup dark corn syrup
- 1/2 cup granulated sugar
- 1/2 cup firmly packed light brown sugar
- 1/4 cup bourbon or water
- 4 large eggs
- 1/4 cup butter, melted
- 2 tsp. plain white cornmeal
- 2 tsp. vanilla extract
- 1/2 tsp. table salt

1. Preheat oven to 325°. Fit piecrust into a 9-inch deep-dish pie plate according to package directions; fold edges under, and crimp. Sprinkle pecans and chocolate morsels onto bottom of piecrust.
2. Stir together corn syrup and next 3 ingredients in a large saucepan, and bring to a boil over medium heat. Cook, stirring constantly, 3 minutes. Remove from heat.
3. Whisk together eggs and next 4

ingredients. Gradually whisk one-fourth of hot corn syrup mixture into egg mixture; add to remaining hot corn syrup mixture, whisking constantly. Pour filling into prepared piecrust.

4. Bake at 325° for 55 minutes or until set; cool pie completely on a wire rack (about 1 hour).

MAKES 6 to 8 servings. **HANDS-ON** 15 min. **TOTAL** 2 hours, 10 min.

GULF COAST SEAFOOD STEW

Hurricane Katrina and a subsequent oil spill off the coast of Louisiana renewed appreciation for our region's seafood. This stew shows off its incomparable flavors, colors, and beauty.

- 1 1/2 **lb. unpeeled, medium-size raw shrimp**
- 2 **celery ribs**
- 1 **large sweet onion**
- 2 **qt. reduced-sodium fat-free chicken broth**
- 12 **oz. andouille sausage, cut into 1/2-inch pieces**
- 1 **poblano pepper, seeded and chopped**
- 1 **green bell pepper, chopped**
- 1 **Tbsp. canola oil**
- 3 **garlic cloves, chopped**
- 1 **lb. small red potatoes, halved**
- 1 **(12-oz.) bottle beer**
- 1 **Tbsp. fresh thyme leaves**
- 2 **fresh bay leaves**
- 2 **tsp. Creole seasoning**
- 1 1/2 **lb. fresh white fish fillets (such as snapper, grouper, or catfish), cubed**
- 1 **lb. cooked crawfish tails (optional)**
  Kosher salt and freshly ground black pepper

1. Peel shrimp; place shells in a saucepan. (Refrigerate shrimp until ready to use.) Add celery ends and onion peel to pan; chop remaining celery and onion, and reserve. (Using the leftover bits of onion and celery will result in a flavorful broth.) Add broth; bring to a boil over medium-high heat. Reduce heat to low; simmer 30 minutes.

2. Meanwhile, cook sausage in a large

Gulf Coast Seafood Stew

Dutch oven over medium-high heat, stirring often, 7 to 8 minutes or until browned. Remove sausage; pat dry. Wipe Dutch oven clean. Sauté celery, onion, and peppers in hot oil in Dutch oven over medium-high heat 5 to 7 minutes or until onion is tender. Add garlic, and sauté 45 seconds to 1 minute or until fragrant. Stir in potatoes, next 4 ingredients, and sausage.

3. Pour broth mixture through a fine wire-mesh strainer into Dutch oven, discarding solids. Increase heat to high; bring to a boil. Reduce heat to low, and cook, stirring occasionally, 20 minutes or until potatoes are tender.

4. Add fish, and cook 2 to 3 minutes or until just opaque. Add shrimp, and cook 2 to 3 minutes or just until shrimp turn pink. If desired, stir in crawfish, and cook 2 to 3 minutes or until hot. Add salt and pepper to taste.

5. Spoon seafood into warmed soup bowls. Top with broth mixture.

Note: We tested with Swanson Natural Goodness 33% Less Sodium Chicken Broth.

MAKES 6 to 8 servings. **HANDS-ON** 55 min. **TOTAL** 1 hour, 35 min.

The South's Most Storied Cakes

FROM BAPTISMS TO FUNERALS, NO OCCASION IS COMPLETE
WITHOUT A CAKE. HERE, WE SHARE FIVE TWISTS ON ICONIC RECIPES
AND HOW THEY BECAME OUR SWEETEST TRADITIONS

Coconut Chiffon Cake

Red Velvet Cake

Lane Cake

Jam Cake

Lemon Cheese Layer Cake

Southerners have had a long-standing love affair with layer cakes.

We bake them for birthdays and christenings, mount them on heirloom cake stands in honor of anniversaries and holiday home-comings, and immortalize them in great works of fiction. Few desserts are more impressive on a buffet. Vying with a dazzling parade of pies and meringue-topped banana puddings, a decadent layer cake will always be the star of the show at a church dinner. Tattered and scribbled with marginalia, the best-loved recipes are passed down from one generation to the next. Stories of their origin, both real and apocry-phal, are as multilayered as the cakes themselves. Over the years, hundreds of readers, and *SL* staffers, have shared their favorite cake recipes in the pages of *Southern Living*. In celebration of our 50th Anniversary, we offer a deliciously fresh take on a few of the classics.

THE LANE CAKE

MORE THAN 100 YEARS AGO, Emma Rylander Lane of Clayton, Alabama, entered the annual baking competition at the county fair in Columbus, Georgia. She took first prize. No doubt the judges were swayed by her cake's filling: a richly yolked custard heavily spiked with bourbon. The recipe, entitled Prize Cake, can be found in *Some Good Things To Eat,* a collection of personal favorites she published in 1898. Though later versions add shredded coconut and pecans to the filling, the original recipe calls for raisins only. Like Lady Baltimore Cake, it's one of many spirited fruit-filled cakes of the era that became a holiday tradition. In July 1960, Lane Cake gained literary fame in *To Kill A Mockingbird.* And in March 1966, *Southern Living* featured a recipe for Lane Cake in its second issue. Our latest twist? Dried peaches (finely diced and ridiculously delicious) stand in for raisins, and the traditional meringue frosting gets a spirited makeover with a triple shot of peach schnapps. ***Recipe, page 63***

THE LEMON CHEESE LAYER CAKE

EXPECTING A TWIST ON CHEESECAKE? You're in for an even sweeter surprise. These layers are filled with a buttery rich lemon curd instead. Recipes dating back to the early 1800s called for acidulating cream with lemon juice, then separating the curds and whey. Over the years, the original recipe for lemon cheese evolved into one using butter and eggs. By the 1940s, almost every good cook south of the Mason-Dixon Line had a recipe for lemon cheese layer cake in her repertoire. And if you've ever lived anywhere near Hartford in southeast Alabama, you know of the local ladies still famous for their 14-layer lemon cheese cakes. Numerous versions of this nostalgic classic pay homage to Robert E. Lee, who allegedly fancied sponge cakes filled with a sugary mix of finely grated lemons and oranges. Until now, a lemon cheese riff on Robert E. Lee Cake from the *Southern Living* 1990 Five-Star Recipe Collection used to be our favorite. But this one trumps them all. ***Recipe, page 63***

THE RED VELVET CAKE

VELVET CAKES (MINUS THE JOLT OF RED) were popular in Victorian times when savvy cooks blended flour and cornstarch to create fine-crumbed cake layers with a velvety texture. The subtle hue of Mahogany Velvet Cake, and later Red Devil's Food Cake, was the result of baking soda interacting with natural cocoa and other acids in the batter. Legend has it that chefs at the Waldorf Astoria dreamed up a hybrid "Red Velvet" cake during the 1930s and served a slice to the owner of the Texas-based Adams Extract Company while he was a hotel guest. By the 1940s, Mr. John Adams was marketing red food coloring to the masses with recipe cards for a Red Velvet Cake his wife, Betty, developed. In 1989, an armadillo-shaped groom's cake in *Steel Magnolias* kicked off a cult following for red velvet. The craze has continued, fueled in part by the red velvet cakes that have graced the *Southern Living* Christmas cover three times. ***Recipe, page 64***

THE JAM CAKE

THE ORIGINS OF JAM CAKE lie deep in Appalachia where store-bought sugar was once scarce. Cakes were often sweetened with homemade jams, filled with wild berries and mountain fruits. The payoff for the genius swap? Rich, dense cake layers with a depth of flavor sugar alone can't deliver. Vintage cookbooks offer century-old favorites, from Alice May Cresswell's Blackberry Jam Cake to Zella McDowell's extravaganza made with strawberry jam and fig preserves. Most recipes start with a tangy buttermilk batter ramped up with one or more flavors of jam and a flurry of ground spices. Foraged hickories and black walnuts, or wind-fallen pecans were added along with raisins and dates. Optional flourishes ranged from cocoa and freshly grated apple to pickled watermelon rind. This latest addition to our archives is finished with a quick caramel cream cheese frosting instead of the traditional burnt sugar icing. And yes, it's every bit as luscious as it looks. ***Recipe, page 64***

THE COCONUT CHIFFON CAKE

WHITE AS A SUNDAY GLOVE, coconut is the doyenne of Southern layer cakes, a masterpiece of home cookery that has crowned dining room sideboards for more than a hundred years. Purists sing the praises of simple but divine, opting for coconut water-doused cake layers and dreamy swirls of meringue. No argument there. In fact, it's one of our favorites too. But flip through back issues of *Southern Living* and you'll find more than 40 top-rated twists too good to pass up. Often requested: Nanny's Famous Coconut-Pineapple Cake leavened with 7-Up, sent in by a reader in 1997. Fifty-one years earlier, Eudora Welty chose a coconut cake as the culinary centerpiece of *Delta Wedding*. Faulkner even gives it a shout-out in *The Unvanquished*. One of the earliest published recipes appears in *Mrs. Hill's New Cook Book*. Writing from her rural Georgia kitchen in 1867, Mrs. Hill advises to make the filling "as thick and rich as desired," which is exactly what we did with our latest creation. ***Recipe, page 65***

THE LANE CAKE

CAKE LAYERS:

2 1/4 cups sugar

1 1/4 cups butter, softened

8 large egg whites, at room temperature

3 cups all-purpose soft-wheat flour (such as White Lily)

4 tsp. baking powder

1 Tbsp. vanilla extract

Shortening

PEACH FILLING:

Boiling water

8 oz. dried peach halves

1/2 cup butter, melted

1 cup sugar

8 large egg yolks

3/4 cup sweetened flaked coconut

3/4 cup chopped toasted pecans

1/2 cup bourbon

2 tsp. vanilla extract

PEACH SCHNAPPS FROSTING:

2 large egg whites

1 1/2 cups sugar

1/2 cup peach schnapps

2 tsp. light corn syrup

1/8 tsp. table salt

1. Prepare Cake Layers: Preheat oven to 350°. Beat first 2 ingredients at medium speed with an electric mixer until fluffy. Gradually add 8 egg whites, 2 at a time, beating well after each addition.

2. Sift together flour and baking powder; gradually add to butter mixture alternately with 1 cup water, beginning and ending with flour mixture. Stir in 1 Tbsp. vanilla. Spoon batter into 4 greased (with shortening) and floured 9-inch round shiny cake pans (about 1 3/4 cups batter in each pan).

3. Bake at 350° for 14 to 16 minutes or until a wooden pick inserted in center comes out clean. Cool in pans on wire racks 10 minutes; remove from pans to wire racks, and cool completely (about 30 minutes).

4. Prepare Filling: Pour boiling water to cover over dried peach halves in a medium bowl; let stand 30 minutes. Drain well, and cut into 1/4-inch pieces. (After plumping and dicing, you should have about 2 cups peaches.)

5. Whisk together melted butter and next 2 ingredients in a heavy saucepan. Cook over medium-low heat, whisking constantly, 10 to 12 minutes or until thickened. Remove from heat, and stir in diced peaches, coconut, and next 3 ingredients. Cool completely (about 30 minutes).

6. Spread filling between cake layers (a little over 1 cup per layer). Cover cake with plastic wrap, and chill 12 hours.

7. Prepare Frosting: Pour water to a depth of 1 1/2 inches into a small saucepan; bring to a boil over medium heat. Whisk together 2 egg whites, 1 1/2 cups sugar, and next 3 ingredients in a heatproof bowl; place bowl over boiling water. Beat egg white mixture at medium-high speed with a handheld electric mixer 12 to 15 minutes or until stiff glossy peaks form and frosting is spreading consistency. Remove from heat, and spread immediately over top and sides of cake.

Note: Find dried peaches at Sprouts Farmers Market and Whole Foods Market.

MAKES 12 to 16 servings. **HANDS-ON** 1 hour, 30 min. **TOTAL** 15 hours, 35 min.

THE LEMON CHEESE LAYER CAKE

LEMON CURD:

1 3/4 cups granulated sugar

3/4 cup butter, softened

4 large eggs

3 large egg yolks

1 Tbsp. lemon zest

3/4 cup fresh lemon juice

CAKE LAYERS:

1 3/4 cups granulated sugar

1 cup butter, softened

4 large eggs, separated, at room temperature

1 Tbsp. orange zest

3 cups cake flour

2 1/2 tsp. baking powder

1/4 tsp. table salt

1 cup fresh orange juice

Shortening

3 (4-inch) wooden skewers

LEMON-ORANGE BUTTER-CREAM FROSTING:

3 cups powdered sugar, sifted and divided

1/2 cup butter, softened

1 Tbsp. orange zest

1. Prepare Lemon Curd: Beat first 2 ingredients at medium speed with an electric mixer until blended. Add 4 eggs and 3 egg yolks, 1 at a time, to butter mixture, beating just until blended after each addition. Stir in lemon zest. Gradually add lemon juice to butter mixture, beating at low speed just until blended after each addition. (Mixture will look curdled.) Transfer to a large heavy saucepan.

2. Cook mixture over medium-low heat, whisking constantly, 14 to 16 minutes or until mixture thickens, coats the back of a spoon, and starts to mound slightly when stirred. Transfer mixture to a bowl.

3. Place heavy-duty plastic wrap directly on surface of warm curd (to prevent a film from forming), and cool 1 hour. Chill 8 hours.

4. Prepare Cake Layers: Preheat oven to 350°. Beat 1 3/4 cups granulated sugar and 1 cup softened butter at medium speed with an electric mixer until fluffy. Add 4 egg yolks, 1 at a time, beating just until blended after each addition. Stir in orange zest.

5. Sift together cake flour and next 2 ingredients; gradually add to butter mixture alternately with 1 cup orange juice, beginning and ending with flour mixture, beating just until blended after each addition.

6. Beat 4 egg whites at medium-high speed with mixer until stiff peaks form. Fold one-third of egg whites into batter; fold remaining egg whites into batter. Pour batter into 4 greased (with shortening) and floured 8-inch round shiny cake pans (about 1 3/4 cups batter in each pan).

7. Bake at 350° for 17 to 20 minutes or until a wooden pick inserted in center comes out clean. Cool in pans on wire racks 10 minutes; remove from pans to wire racks, and cool completely (about 30 minutes).

8. Reserve and refrigerate 1 cup Lemon Curd. Spread remaining Lemon Curd between cake layers and on top of cake (about 1/2 cup per layer). Insert skewers 2 to 3 inches apart into cake to prevent layers from sliding. Immediately wrap cake tightly in plastic wrap, and chill 12 to 24 hours. (The layers of cake and Lemon Curd will set and firm up overnight, ripening the flavor and making the cake more secure and easier to frost.)

9. Prepare Frosting: Beat 1 cup powdered sugar, 1/2 cup softened butter, and 1 Tbsp. orange zest at low speed with electric mixer until blended. Add 1/2 cup reserved Lemon Curd alternately with remaining 2 cups powdered sugar, beating until blended after each addition. Increase speed to high, and beat 1 to 2 minutes or until fluffy.

10. Remove skewers from cake; discard skewers. Spread frosting on sides of cake. Spread remaining 1/2 cup reserved Lemon Curd over top of cake. (Adding a bit of extra Lemon Curd to the top of the cake creates a luxe decorative finish.)

Note: Lemon Curd may be stored in an airtight container in refrigerator up to 2 weeks.

MAKES 12 to 16 servings. **HANDS-ON** 1 hour, 30 min. **TOTAL** 22 hours, 45 min.

THE RED VELVET CAKE

CAKE LAYERS:

- 1 1/2 cups granulated sugar
- 1 cup butter, softened
- 1/2 cup firmly packed light brown sugar
- 4 large eggs, at room temperature
- 2 Tbsp. red liquid food coloring
- 1 Tbsp. vanilla extract
- 1 (8-oz.) container sour cream
- 2 1/2 cups all-purpose soft-wheat flour (such as White Lily)
- 1/2 cup unsweetened cocoa
- 1 tsp. baking soda
- 1/2 tsp. table salt
  Shortening

STRAWBERRY GLAZE:

- 3/4 cup strawberry preserves
- 1/4 cup almond liqueur

STRAWBERRY FROSTING:

- 3/4 cup butter, softened
- 5 cups powdered sugar, sifted
- 1 3/4 cups diced fresh strawberries, divided

1. Prepare Cake Layers: Preheat oven to 350°. Beat first 3 ingredients at medium speed with an electric mixer until fluffy. Add eggs, 1 at a time, beating just until blended after each addition. Add red food coloring and vanilla, beating at low speed just until blended.

2. Stir together sour cream and 1/2 cup water until blended. Sift together flour and next 3 ingredients; gradually add to butter mixture alternately with sour cream mixture, beginning and ending with flour mixture. Spoon batter into 3 greased (with shortening) and floured 9-inch round shiny cake pans (about 2 1/2 cups batter in each pan).

3. Bake at 350° for 20 to 24 minutes or until a wooden pick inserted in center comes out clean. Cool in pans 10 minutes; remove from pans to wire racks, and cool completely (about 30 minutes).

4. Prepare Glaze: Pulse strawberry preserves in a food processor until smooth; transfer to a microwave-safe bowl. Microwave strawberry preserves at HIGH 30 to 45 seconds or until melted; stir in almond liqueur. Brush 1/4 cup warm glaze over top of each cooled cake layer. Reserve remaining 1/4 cup glaze.

5. Prepare Frosting: Beat 3/4 cup softened butter at medium speed 20 seconds or until fluffy. Gradually add 5 cups powdered sugar and 1/2 cup diced strawberries, beating at low speed until creamy. Add 1/4 cup diced strawberries, 1 Tbsp. at a time, beating until frosting reaches desired consistency. Reserve remaining 1 cup diced strawberries.

6. Place 1 cake layer, glazed side up, on serving platter. Spread one-third of frosting over cake layer; sprinkle with 1/2 cup reserved diced strawberries. Repeat procedure with second cake layer. Top with remaining cake layer; spread with remaining frosting. Drizzle remaining 1/4 cup strawberry glaze over cake.

Note: If your berries are juicy, you may not need the entire amount in the frosting.

MAKES 12 to 16 servings. **HANDS-ON** 1 hour, 10 min. **TOTAL** 2 hours, 10 min.

THE JAM CAKE

Make sure spices and baking soda are fresh.

CAKE LAYERS:

- 1 1/2 cups sugar
- 1 cup butter, softened
- 4 large eggs, at room temperature
- 3 cups all-purpose flour
- 2 Tbsp. unsweetened cocoa
- 2 tsp. pumpkin pie spice
- 1 cup buttermilk
- 1 tsp. baking soda
- 1 1/2 cups seedless blackberry jam
- 1 Tbsp. vanilla extract
- 1 1/2 cups finely chopped toasted pecans
- 1 cup peeled and grated Granny Smith apple (about 1 large)
  Shortening

CARAMEL-CREAM CHEESE FROSTING:

- 2 (8-oz.) packages cream cheese, softened

¼ cup butter, softened
2 (13.4-oz.) cans dulce de leche
2 to 4 Tbsp. whipping cream

1. Prepare Cake Layers: Preheat oven to 350°. Beat first 2 ingredients at medium speed with an electric mixer until light and fluffy. Add eggs, 1 at a time, beating just until blended after each addition.

2. Stir together flour and next 2 ingredients. Stir together buttermilk and baking soda in a 2-cup glass measuring cup. Add flour mixture to butter mixture alternately with buttermilk mixture, beginning and ending with flour mixture. Beat at low speed just until blended after each addition.

3. Stir jam until smooth. Add jam and vanilla to butter mixture, and beat at low speed just until blended. Stir in toasted pecans and grated apple. Spoon batter into 4 greased (with shortening) and floured 9-inch round shiny cake pans (about 2 ½ cups batter in each pan).

4. Bake at 350° for 20 to 22 minutes or until a wooden pick inserted in center comes out clean. Cool in pans 10 minutes; remove from pans to wire racks, and cool completely (about 30 minutes).

5. Prepare Frosting: Beat cream cheese and ¼ cup softened butter at medium speed with an electric mixer until creamy. Add dulce de leche, 1 can at a time, beating until blended after each addition. Gradually add 2 Tbsp. whipping cream, 1 Tbsp. at a time, and beat at medium speed. Add up to 2 Tbsp. additional cream, 1 Tbsp. at a time, and beat until frosting is desired spreading consistency. Spread frosting between each layer and on top and sides of cake.

Note: We tested with Nestlé La Lechera Dulce de Leche.

MAKES 12 to 16 servings. **HANDS-ON** 1 hour **TOTAL** 1 hour, 30 min.

THE COCONUT CHIFFON CAKE

CAKE LAYERS:
2 ½ cups sifted cake flour
1 ⅓ cups granulated sugar
1 Tbsp. baking powder
½ tsp. table salt
½ cup canola oil
5 large eggs, separated, at room temperature
1 Tbsp. vanilla extract
½ tsp. cream of tartar
Shortening

COCONUT-MASCARPONE FILLING:
1 (8-oz.) container mascarpone cheese
½ cup powdered sugar
1 Tbsp. vanilla extract
¾ cup whipping cream
1 (6-oz.) package frozen grated coconut, thawed

WHITE CHOCOLATE BUTTER-CREAM FROSTING:
1 ½ (4-oz.) white chocolate baking bars, chopped
2 Tbsp. whipping cream
1 cup butter, softened
3 cups sifted powdered sugar, divided
2 tsp. vanilla extract
3 cups sweetened flaked coconut

1. Prepare Cake Layers: Preheat oven to 350°. Stir together sifted cake flour and next 3 ingredients in bowl of an electric stand mixer. Make a well in center of flour mixture; add oil, egg yolks, vanilla, and ¾ cup water. Beat at medium speed 1 to 2 minutes or until smooth.

2. Beat egg whites and cream of tartar at medium-high speed until stiff peaks form. Fold one-third of egg whites into batter; fold remaining whites into batter. Spoon batter into 4 greased (with shortening) and floured 8-inch round shiny cake pans (about 2 cups batter in each pan).

3. Bake at 350° for 12 to 14 minutes or until a wooden pick inserted in center comes out clean. (Do not overbake—cakes will be a very pale golden color.) Cool in pans on wire racks 10 minutes; remove from pans to wire racks, and

cool completely (about 30 minutes).

4. Prepare Filling: Stir together mascarpone cheese, ½ cup powdered sugar, and 1 Tbsp. vanilla in a large bowl just until blended.

5. Beat ¾ cup cream at low speed with an electric mixer until foamy; increase speed to medium-high, and beat until soft peaks form. Fold whipped cream into mascarpone mixture until well blended. Add thawed grated coconut, and stir just until blended. Spread mixture between cake layers (about 1 ⅓ cups per layer). Cover with plastic wrap, and chill 12 hours.

6. Prepare White Chocolate Butter-cream Frosting: Microwave chopped white chocolate and 2 Tbsp. whipping cream in a microwave-safe bowl at MEDIUM (50% power) 1 to 1 ½ minutes or until melted and smooth, stirring at 30-second intervals. Cool completely (about 20 minutes).

7. Beat 1 cup softened butter and 2 cups powdered sugar at low speed with an electric mixer until blended. Add white chocolate mixture, 2 tsp. vanilla, and remaining 1 cup powdered sugar, and beat at high speed 2 to 3 minutes or until fluffy. Spread frosting on top and sides of cake. Cover top and sides of cake with 3 cups flaked coconut, gently pressing coconut into frosting.

Test Kitchen Tip: Be sure to measure flour after sifting. (If you measure before sifting, you'll end up with too much flour and a dry cake.) Check for doneness at the minimum bake time—even 1 or 2 minutes of extra baking can also create a dry cake.

Note: We tested with Birds Eye Tropic Isle Fresh Frozen Flake Grated Coconut and Mounds Sweetened Coconut Flakes.

MAKES 10 to 12 servings. **HANDS-ON** 1 hour, 15 min. **TOTAL** 14 hours, 25 min.

FIVE SOUTHERN KITCHEN MAGICIANS

SOME OF OUR FAVORITE CHEFS SHARE THEIR STORIES, THEIR INSPIRATION, AND THEIR PRIZED RECIPES

IN OUR VERY FIRST ISSUE, a column called Prized Recipes featured five women and their dishes, from Mrs. George L. Chapman of Timmonsville, South Carolina's Party Cherry Pie to Mrs. J.C. Biddy of Blair, Oklahoma's Peanut Butter Soup. These women were home cooks, and their recipes set the tone for how this magazine would cover food over the next 50 years. Showing hospitality and feeding our families well would become a core mission of *Southern Living.* Today we're proud to feature five professional chefs, all Southern, all female, who are making their mark across the nation. Each has demonstrated not only a reverence for home cooking but also the tenacity, fearlessness, and talent it takes to become leaders in an industry that hasn't always been receptive to women.

DOLESTER MILES'
LEMON MERINGUE TART

Birmingham's pioneering pastry chef has been combining European technique with Southern soul for 34 years.

DOL, AS SHE'S affectionately known, has been Frank Stitt's pastry ninja since shortly after he first opened Highlands Bar & Grill in Birmingham, nearly 34 years ago. She now oversees the desserts in all four of his restaurants. "My mother showed me how to make meringues, how to make a good graham cracker crust," Miles says. "I started baking brown sugar pound cakes when I was 15 years old with her recipe." Over the decades, Stitt has offered guidance in French and Italian technique, and now Miles leads a team of cooks—she is quick to point out it's not a solo effort—in preparing enough desserts to feed 400 people each day.

Miles' Lemon Meringue Tart, page 70

ASHLEY CHRISTENSEN'S
BUTTERMILK SPOONBREAD

The James Beard Award-winner and
North Carolina restaurant mogul is also
a self-described "hospitalitarian."

ASHLEY CHRISTENSEN grew up surrounded by food:
Her father, a truck driver, would drape freshly made
strands of pasta over chair backs and broom handles, and
her parents cooked dinner nearly every night. In college,
she often threw dinner parties, and fell in love with hosting people. That background drives this beloved chef to
nurture her business—and her diners—with a deep sense of
hospitality. Not yet 40, Christensen oversees 250 employ-
ees, from Poole's Diner, where people pack into banquettes
for the richest, gooiest mac and cheese in the land, to
Death & Taxes—her first real foray into fine dining—with its
flame-licked oysters, whole roasted fish, and 93-day aged
beef. And we get the sense she's just hitting her stride.

Christensen's Buttermilk Spoonbread with Spaghetti Squash, page 70

ASHA GOMEZ'S
COUNTRY CAPTAIN

This Indian-born Atlanta chef
gives Southern comfort food a
delightfully global twist

ASHA GOMEZ personifies the modern South. Born in
the southern Indian state of Kerala, she claims Atlanta as
home. Though the Georgia capital, a modern port city by
way of its heavily trafficked airport, has its share of global
influence, Gomez stands apart. She reinterprets flavors
using things native to both lands—catfish, okra, rice. Just
don't call it fusion. "For me, that's the other 'f word.' I'm
not trying to put two things together that don't belong,"
she says. When she opened Cardamom Hill, in 2013,
people went crazy for her fried chicken, cooked in coconut
oil and crowned with curry leaves. It's since closed, but
Gomez has the gumption to reinvent herself. (In fact,
before becoming a chef, she owned an Ayurvedic spa.) She
now runs Spice to Table, a patisserie near the new Krog
Street Market, where she accents traditional recipes with
next-generation flair (carrot cake with cardamom), and
leads cooking classes to initiate people to her two Souths.

Gomez's Country Captain, page 71

KELLY FIELDS'

BLACKBERRY-AND-BOURBON COBBLER

John Besh's pastry ace has branched out with her own New Orleans café.

SARAH GAVIGAN'S

SAVORY REFRIGERATOR SOUP

In three short years, this up-and-comer has gone from cooking at pop-up restaurants to being the Noodle Queen of Nashville.

WHEN YOU ASK KELLY FIELDS ABOUT the rise of female chefs, her response raises a good point: "Why should it be such a big deal?" Quality is quality. In fact, all of her sous chefs are women. "I've never known women not to be in a kitchen," she says. Though she has made her name with fantastical sugar creations as the Executive Pastry Chef for John Besh's Restaurant Group, that's not her only job. At her newly opened bakery and café, Willa Jean, she cooks the way she learned from her mother and her two grandmothers, Audrey and Willa Jean: simple, straightforward, honest. "You can't hide behind technique. It's either good or it's not." Fields has worked the line in every Besh restaurant she's set foot in. Fields is responsible for empowering a whole new generation of chefs. "I have the best team in the world surrounding me. Most of my cooks are mothers, and they are all 100% heart."

SARAH GAVIGAN DIDN'T START COOKING professionally until she was nearly 40. After a career in film production in California, she moved back to the South and began tinkering with ramen (albeit with a healthy dose of collards and field peas). "My 'kitchen' experience is based on being a home cook" and taking pride in doing a lot with a little, she explains. When she was a child, her grandmother would visit for a week at a time and turn the scraps—a rind of Parmesan, a cauliflower stump—into a stew she called "refrigerator soup" at the end of the week. To this day, Sarah revels in what she terms "kitchen sink challenges," where she raids her pantry to create a feast for 10. That ingenuity has fueled the success of her ramen venture Otaku South—and earned her serious respect.

Gavigan's Refrigerator Soup, page 71

Fields' Blackberry-and-Bourbon Cobbler, page 71

DOLESTER MILES' LEMON MERINGUE TART

TART SHELL:

- 2 1/2 cups all-purpose flour
- 1/8 tsp. table salt
- 1 cup cold unsalted butter, cubed
- 1 cup powdered sugar
- 3 large egg yolks
  Parchment paper

FILLING:

- 7 Tbsp. lemon zest (about 7 lemons)
- 1 1/4 cups fresh lemon juice
- 1 3/4 cups granulated sugar
- 6 large eggs
- 9 large egg yolks
- 1 1/4 cups unsalted butter, softened

MERINGUE:

- 1 cup egg whites (from 6 to 7 large eggs)
- 2 cups granulated sugar

1. Prepare Tart Shell: Pulse flour and salt in a food processor until combined. Add cubed butter, and pulse 10 to 12 times or until mixture resembles coarse breadcrumbs. Add powdered sugar and 3 egg yolks, and pulse just until mixture comes together and pulls away from sides of bowl. Divide dough in half, and flatten each half into a disk. Wrap in plastic wrap, and chill 1 to 12 hours.

2. Preheat oven to 350°. Place dough disks on a lightly floured surface, and roll each into a 12-inch circle. Fit dough circles into 2 (9-inch) fluted tart pans with removable bottoms; trim edges. Line tart shells with parchment paper, and fill with pie weights or dried beans. Bake at 350° for 20 minutes or until edges are light brown. Remove weights and parchment paper, and bake 5 to 10 minutes more or until light golden. Cool on a wire rack while preparing Filling.

3. Prepare Filling: Stir together lemon zest and next 4 ingredients in a large saucepan. Cook over low heat, whisking constantly, 3 minutes or until eggs have broken up and sugar has dissolved.

4. Whisk in 3/4 cup softened butter. (Eggs will start to cook, and mixture will coat the back of a spoon.) Whisk in remaining butter, and cook, whisking constantly, about 22 minutes or until mixture becomes very thick. (Continue whisking throughout the cooking process to prevent mixture from curdling.) Remove from heat, and pour through a fine wire-mesh strainer into a bowl, discarding solids. Whisk 10 minutes or until mixture has cooled slightly.

5. Increase oven temperature to 450°. Spoon lemon filling into tart shells, and bake 5 to 8 minutes or until top is set.

6. Prepare Meringue: Pour water to a depth of 1 1/2 inches in a small saucepan; bring to a boil over medium-high heat. Reduce heat to medium-low, and maintain at a simmer. Stir together egg whites and 2 cups granulated sugar in bowl of a heavy-duty electric stand mixer. Place bowl over simmering water, and cook, whisking constantly, 3 minutes or until sugar has dissolved and mixture is hot.

7. Beat hot mixture at medium-high speed with stand mixer, using whisk attachment, about 2 minutes. Increase speed to high, and beat 4 to 6 minutes or until stiff, glossy peaks form. Spoon meringue over tarts. Brown meringue using a kitchen torch, holding torch 2 inches from meringue and moving torch back and forth. (If you do not have a torch, preheat broiler with oven rack 8 inches from heat; broil 30 to 45 seconds or until golden.)

MAKES 8 to 10 servings. **HANDS-ON** 1 hour, 10 min. **TOTAL** 2 hours, 40 min.

ASHLEY CHRISTENSEN'S BUTTERMILK SPOONBREAD WITH SPAGHETTI SQUASH

- 1 small spaghetti squash (2 1/2 to 2 3/4 lb.)
  Vegetable cooking spray
- 1 1/2 cups buttermilk
- 1 1/2 cups heavy cream
- 6 large eggs
- 3/4 cup grated Parmesan cheese
- 3/4 tsp. sea salt
- 5 cups crumbled cornbread
- 1 Tbsp. butter

1. Preheat oven to 375°. Cut spaghetti squash in half lengthwise; discard seeds. Bake squash, cut sides down, on a lightly greased (with cooking spray) baking sheet at 375° for 40 to 45 minutes or until tender. Cool 10 minutes. Scrape inside of squash to remove spaghetti-like strands.

2. Whisk together buttermilk, cream, eggs, Parmesan cheese, and salt in a large bowl. Process half of squash strands in a food processor until smooth; stir into cream mixture. Process squash-cream mixture in batches until smooth.

3. Return mixture to bowl, and stir in cornbread and remaining squash. Let stand at room temperature 1 hour.

4. During last 20 minutes of stand time, place a 12-inch cast-iron skillet in oven, and preheat oven to 375°. Add butter to skillet, and tilt to coat sides and bottom. Transfer squash mixture to skillet.

5. Bake at 375° for 35 to 40 minutes or until a wooden pick inserted in center of spoonbread comes out clean. Cool 5 minutes before serving.

MAKES 8 to 10 servings. **HANDS-ON** 20 min. **TOTAL** 2 hours, 50 min.

ASHA GOMEZ'S COUNTRY CAPTAIN

- 1 (3- to 4-lb.) whole chicken, cut into 8 pieces
- 3 1/2 tsp. kosher salt, divided
- 1 1/2 tsp. freshly ground black pepper, divided
- 1/4 cup vegetable oil
- 1 large yellow onion, chopped
- 4 celery ribs, chopped
- 1 red bell pepper, chopped
- 1 green bell pepper, chopped
- 6 garlic cloves, finely chopped
- 1 (1-inch) piece fresh ginger, finely chopped
- 2/3 cup dried currants, divided
- 2 Tbsp. garam masala
- 1 Tbsp. ground coriander
- 1 Tbsp. paprika
- 1 tsp. ground turmeric
- 1 (14.5-oz.) can whole, peeled tomatoes, chopped
- 1 Tbsp. tomato paste
- 2 Tbsp. cane syrup
- 1/3 cup slivered almonds
  Cooked white long-grain rice

1. Sprinkle chicken with 1 1/2 tsp. salt and 1 tsp. black pepper. Cook chicken, skin side down, in hot oil in a 5-qt. Dutch oven over medium heat, turning once or twice, about 10 minutes or until golden brown. Transfer chicken pieces to a platter, reserving 2 Tbsp. drippings in Dutch oven.
2. Cook chopped yellow onion, next 5 ingredients, and 1/3 cup dried currants in hot drippings over medium heat, stirring occasionally, 8 to 10 minutes or until onions are tender.
3. Stir garam masala, next 3 ingredients, and remaining 2 tsp. salt and 1/2 tsp. black pepper into onion mixture, and cook, stirring often, 3 to 4 minutes or until spices are toasted. Stir in tomatoes, tomato paste, and cane syrup. Cover and reduce heat to low.
4. Preheat oven to 350°. Simmer mixture in Dutch oven over low heat, stirring occasionally, 25 minutes or until mixture thickens into a chunky sauce. Add chicken pieces, pressing gently to submerge in sauce; cover.
5. Bake at 350° for about 1 hour or until chicken is tender. Sprinkle with almonds and remaining 1/3 cup currants. Serve chicken and sauce over hot cooked rice.

MAKES 4 servings. **HANDS-ON** 50 min. **TOTAL** 2 hours, 15 min.

KELLY FIELDS' BLACKBERRY-AND-BOURBON COBBLER

- 12 cups fresh blackberries
- 3/4 cup turbinado sugar
- 1/4 cup bourbon
  Vegetable cooking spray
- 1/2 vanilla bean
- 1 cup granulated sugar
- 2 cups all-purpose flour
- 1 Tbsp. plus 2 tsp. baking powder
- 1/2 tsp. table salt
- 1 tsp. lemon zest
- 1 1/2 cups milk
- 1 large egg
- 3/4 tsp. vanilla extract
- 6 Tbsp. butter, melted

1. Preheat oven to 350°. Toss together first 3 ingredients in a large bowl. Transfer mixture to a lightly greased (with cooking spray) 13- x 9-inch baking dish.
2. Split vanilla bean, and scrape seeds into granulated sugar. (Rub the sugar between your fingers to distribute the vanilla bean seeds evenly.)
3. Sift together flour, next 2 ingredients, and granulated sugar mixture into a large bowl. Stir in lemon zest. Whisk together milk, egg, and vanilla; stir into dry ingredients. Stir in melted butter.
4. Pour batter evenly over fruit; place dish on a baking sheet.
5. Bake at 350° for 1 hour and 5 minutes to 1 hour and 15 minutes or until crust is dark golden brown and done in center.

MAKES 8 to 10 servings. **HANDS-ON** 20 min. **TOTAL** 1 hour, 25 min.

SARAH GAVIGAN'S REFRIGERATOR SOUP

- 1/2 cup chopped red onion
- 1/2 cup chopped celery
- 1/2 cup chopped carrot
- 1/2 cup extra virgin olive oil
- 3 cups chopped red cabbage
- 3 cups chopped green cabbage
- 3 cups coarsely torn collard greens
- 3 cups coarsely torn turnip greens
- 3 cups medium cauliflower florets
- 2 tsp. kosher salt
- 1 medium zucchini, cut into half moons
- 3/4 lb. small potatoes, halved
- 2 cups canned crushed tomatoes
- 1 (12-oz.) package frozen lima beans
- 1 Parmesan cheese rind
- 3 cups day-old whole wheat bread pieces
  Shaved Parmesan cheese

1. Cook first 3 ingredients in hot oil in a large Dutch oven over medium heat, stirring occasionally, 5 minutes or until tender. (Do not brown.)
2. Stir in red cabbage and next 5 ingredients, and cook over medium heat 3 minutes. Add 1/2 cup water, and reduce heat to medium-low. Cook, stirring occasionally, 20 minutes. Stir in zucchini, next 4 ingredients, and remaining 4 cups water.
3. Increase heat to medium-high, and bring to a boil. Reduce heat to medium-low, and simmer, stirring occasionally, 20 to 25 minutes or until the potatoes are tender. Discard cheese rind. Stir in bread pieces 15 minutes before serving. Spoon into bowls, and drizzle with extra virgin olive oil; sprinkle with shaved Parmesan cheese.

Note: This soup can be cooked a day in advance. It's always better the second day, so make a big batch.

MAKES 12 cups. **HANDS-ON** 1 hour, 20 min. **TOTAL** 1 hour, 30 min.

My Mama's Cookbook

LESSONS ON LIFE AND COOKING FROM A WOMAN WHO'S NEVER CONSULTED A RECIPE

"**A** person can't cook from a book," she told me, once. "A person," she said, "can't cook from numbers."

What she meant was, a cook can't just read off ingredients, temperatures, and times, and do the magic she can do with a scorched, ancient, ragged pot holder in her hands. I have tasted her work across half a century, enough to wonder if the old men and women she learned from really were dabbling in some kind of alchemy. The very life itself was the seasoning. You ate your chicken and dumplings with an illegal smile, because sometimes you had to range all the way to a neighbor's coop in the dead of night to procure the principal ingredient. "Chicken tastes better if it's stole," my uncles liked to say, and I used to think they were kidding. Now, I don't know. How, I wonder, would that recipe begin?

> *One pan cornbread, crumbled*
> *One onion, diced*
> *One chicken, stole*

But never, in her long life, has my mother cooked from a recipe. She cooked by instinct, memory, and feel, from scenes and stories, from riverbanks, hog killings, and squirrel hunts. She learned to bake the perfect biscuit as her sister's first child was born, taught by her brother-in-law, a Navy man. She learned Brunswick stew beside a bonfire on the Coosa, just before a gathering of drunken men settled a feud with a hawk-billed knife. Such people will not eat dull food any more than they will tolerate a dull story.

No, Mama never needed any recipes. The craft and ingredients were locked inside her. If I wanted to capture those recipes for the generations to come, I would have to tell the story of a cooking education, to walk through it beside her one skillet, pan, and pinch at a time. But you can't, if you know my mama, compel her to remember. You just have to listen closely, and bide your time.

THE SONG WAS THE LAST ONE I expected her to know. We were driving to the doctor's office that morning; it seems like going to the doctor is what we do. We go to the heart doctor, kidney doctor, toe doctor, eye doctor, and a dermatologist she calls "Dr. Butcher." She tells me stories when we are in the car, and she does not have to hurry because she lives 45 minutes and at least one drive-through sausage biscuit away from the closest physician. She likes to get one on the way to the cardiologist. I do not play the radio when we are in the car, because you never know when she will crack the seal on some memory, and I don't want her to have to shout over Merle Haggard to tell about picking highland watercress in 1945. "Cook it

Rick Bragg and his mother, Margaret Bragg, at her Jacksonville, Alabama, home in September 2015

in bacon grease," she said, "with slivered wild onion."

We do, sometimes, sing, and I had an old song in my head that day as we rolled through the foothills where my grandfather used to cook his liquor. He was bad to taste-test his recipe, and so was inclined to go to jail. That made me think of chain gangs, and I started to sing, under my breath...

Well, you wake up in the morning
Hear the ding-dong rang
You go a-marching to the table
See the same damn thang
Ain't no food upon the table
Ain't no pork up in the pan
But you better not complain, boys,
You'll get in trouble with the man

Then, right on cue, the old woman next to me began to sing...

So let the Midnight Special
Shine her light on me

It was as if I had been sitting with her in the living room, watching *Gunsmoke*, and she leapt to her feet and did the Charleston. Her musical history runs more to "The Church in the Wildwood," not a prison anthem. Still, I knew better than to ask; she would tell it to me, eventually, in a story. "My mind ain't too good, but that shouldn't surprise nobody," she said. "But I remember how Daddy and Mama used to cook together on a Sunday morning, and sometimes when they'd cook, they'd sing..."

You live 78 years, there's a story in everything.

THEY LIVED IN ALABAMA then, but it might have been Georgia. Across seven decades, her geography is uncertain, as if geography matters. The world did not change much at Cedartown, coming or going. But she is sure it was Sunday. Some of the little stores in the highlands opened

Margaret's secret to good beans is "not to let a bad one slip in."

"DADDY ALWAYS COOKED THE MEAT AND MADE THE GRAVY...AND MAMA ALWAYS MADE THE **BIReadsCUITS AND THE COFFEE.** THEY COOKED TOGETHER."

on Sunday then, and in the dawn her daddy would load his girls in his Model A cutdown—that's a Ford that has been converted to a truck with a blowtorch and a homemade bed of two-by-fours—and go see the butcher.

Funny how you can see a man, so long after he is dust. And she made me see him, there at the counter, towering over the little man in the white apron. My grandpa, Charlie Bundrum, was thin but indestructible, cured and hardened in his flesh and bones like a hickory handle on a good hammer. His Sunday overalls sagged over his bones, and his work boots were filmed in red dust.

He would ask the man if he had any T-bones—they cost a dear 39 cents apiece—and would nod his head as the butcher talked, as if it had been a possibility. Then he would say his mouth wasn't set right for steak,

but maybe ham, or streak o' lean. The Depression lingered a long, long time in the foothills of the Appalachians, so usually it was side meat the butcher sold him.

If it was too soon for tomatoes from the garden, he would look at the ones that had traveled up from Florida on the freights, from the tip of the Sunshine State where winter didn't go. If they looked passable, he would take two of the ripest; they had to be dead ripe, for what he had in mind.

He would leave the store trailed by his girls like baby ducks, with a package wrapped in white paper under his arm. At home, he would stoke up the fire on the woodstove and reach for an iron skillet that had never seen soap and water, a skillet that had the lives of generations burned into the black.

"Daddy always cooked the meat and made the gravy," my mother remembered, "and Mama always made the biscuits and the coffee. They cooked together." Her daddy would leave the rind on and fry the fatback until it was so crisp it crumbled.

And her mama, Ava, who had gone with a baby on her hip to get the big rascal out of jail more than once, would pat out her biscuits and battle him word for word, and sing of the power and the glory in what must have seemed like a losing battle...

What a friend we have in Jesus
All our sins and grief to bear

She can still see her mother's hands in the flour. Ava made her biscuits in the battered old flour barrel itself, then sifted the leftover flour back into the barrel so as not to waste. Their recipes vary a little, hers and her mother's, but the principle, the doctrine, is the same. The biscuits began with a small bowl fashioned from the flour itself, to hold the wet ingredients. "You start with White Lily. Use a handful of Crisco, and half-and-half buttermilk and water. Mama liked to use sweet milk, mostly. And you make them like the old people do. Careful. The dough has to be just right, just thick enough so the biscuit will form a dome. Feel the flour as you do it. If the flour's old, I can feel it, feel it grainy, and if the flour's old the biscuits won't rise, and…when you've got it just right I pat 'em out with my hands, I don't cut 'em. It's pretty much like surgery." It probably does not hurt to sing about Jesus as you do it; she still sings as she does, as if Ava was in the kitchen with her, still.

What a privilege to carry
Everything to God in prayer

"Daddy would start the gravy as soon as the meat was done. He'd put flour in that skillet and brown it and brown it till it was nearly burned, then he'd thicken it with water. He might have made milk gravy ever' now and then but I don't remember it. It was water gravy, seasoned with black pepper, and good meat.

"But sometimes, we'd have what some people call red-eye gravy, and I still think it's the best thing, about, I've ever eaten. He'd take the clear, hot grease from the meat, and spoon in fresh-brewed, black coffee till it was about half and half. Then, he'd take a ripe tomato or two and dice 'em up, and use a little salt on 'em and a lot of black pepper. He'd take two of Mama's biscuits and open them up, and pile that diced tomato on top. Then he'd spoon that mixture, that red-eye gravy—nothin' but coffee and grease and the leavings of the fried meat from the bottom of the skillet—onto that tomato. And that hot grease, it causes that tomato to kind of wilt. I don't know if that's the right word for it, but it does, and…well, the trick to it is, you have to eat it right then or it's not fit to eat. But if you eat it right then…Lord, I have done made myself hungry."

Ava was prone to spells then, a kind of falling darkness that would suck the joy from the very air, but she was still young then and all right most of the time, and as she drizzled the red-eye gravy onto her children's plates she sang her displeasure at her big lout, but there was no darkness in it.

Single life is a happy life
Single life is a pleasure
For I am single and no man's wife
And no man can control me

"She only sung it when she was mad at Daddy," said my mother, remembering, and she smiled the way I wished she could always smile. She just remembered for a while then, how the great rascal, the great hammer swinger and liquor maker, would wink at her, and his girls.

It was the happiest she ever saw them. "I still remember all of that, with Mama and Daddy. I think it's what made me want to cook. And I can cook."

We rode awhile in silence.

"Could you teach me," I said, "how to make a biscuit?"

"Oh Lord" was all she said.

Sis' Chicken and Dressing

	6 or 7 chicken thighs, skin on
1	large iron skillet of corn-bread (or enough to fill a 9- x 13-inch pan)
2	cups (or so) of chicken broth
1	egg, beaten
1	large onion, chopped
½	cup celery, diced
¼	tsp. black pepper
¼	tsp. sage *("Do not ruin it with sage. Too much and it's all you taste.")*
1	tsp. poultry seasoning (also contains sage)

1. Boil chicken in salted water until done, *"till it's so tender it falls off the bone."* (Boil for at least 1 hour.) Chicken legs can be substituted.

Chicken breasts can also be substituted, *"but it ain't as good,"* Mama says. Break the chicken into small pieces, but do NOT shred. Be careful to discard small pieces of bone and gristle, but do NOT discard the skin. *"That's where your flavor is."*

2. In a large bowl, break up cooked cornbread into small pieces; gradually stir in the chicken broth, mixing until you have a moist, pudding–like consistency. Stir in chicken, beaten egg, onion, celery, and seasonings. Pour into iron skillet. A pan is fine, if you are a Philistine.

3. Bake in preheated oven at 375° until the top of the dressing is crisp and golden brown and the inside is creamy. (This could be anywhere from a half hour to 45 minutes, depending on the oven.) A spoon should make a faint cracking noise as it breaks the surface of the dressing.

4. Serve with green beans, mashed potatoes, and cabbage-and-carrot slaw.

Margaret Bragg with Sam, Rick's older brother, circa 1957

March

The Elegant Easter Potluck

WANT TO PLAN AN EVERYONE-PITCHES-IN-MEAL THAT STILL LOOKS STUNNING? HERE'S HOW

IT'S A SCENE THAT HAS BEEN PLAYED OUT ACROSS THE SOUTH FOR GENERATIONS: a crowd of close friends and family gather together for a celebration that is centered around cooking and sharing signature dishes, from classic deviled eggs and cheesy casseroles to jiggly congealed salads and mile-high layer cakes. Known as a potluck, this type of impromptu, "no-rhyme-or-reason" get-together was historically a casual event—not a well-planned menu.

Today's hostess organizes a potluck with more attention to detail and less of that "just surprise us with something special" attitude. But despite the differences, the purpose behind these parties still rings true: gathering around the holiday table to enjoy delicious fare with people we love. On the following pages, find our secrets for stress-free hosting, tips for being a good guest, and our favorite recipes for this Easter's feast.

Asparagus, Spring Onion, and Feta Quiche

reese

Aunt Ros Quiche

Green Bean Potato Salad

With most of the food-making duties off your shoulders, focus on the details that will bring this insta-feast together.

CHOOSE A THEME.
Let guests know if you're planning a traditional holiday buffet or a casual Tex-Mex fiesta. No one wants to set their disposable aluminum pan of baked beans next to a trifle served in Grandmother's finest china.

KNOW YOUR NUMBERS.
Decide how many appetizers, sides, and desserts you will need based on the number of people attending. Obviously, if you have 20 guests and two are making desserts, they should each prepare something that serves at least 10 people. However, before dessert, most guests usually won't eat a full portion of a dish when other options are on the table.

ASK GUESTS TO SIGN UP.
To avoid ending up with too much of one thing, make a list—two green vegetables, three starches, one chocolate dessert—and ask guests to take one. Communicate this however you feel comfortable: Make phone calls, e-mail a sign-up sheet, or use an online service. (We recommend *signupgenius.com/potluck*.)

MAKE SPECIAL REQUESTS.
If your crowd will be looking forward to Aunt Susan's famous squash casserole, then ask her to bring it to the party.

LABEL DISHES.
Personalize your table by letting guests know what they're digging into and who made it.

PREP YOUR SERVEWARE.
There's a good chance someone will forget to bring a serving utensil for their dish, so be prepared with the essentials like salad tongs, pie servers, and slotted spoons.

PLAN FOR LEFTOVERS.
Should guests divide up any food that remains? Are to-go plates approved? Leave it up to the person who made the dish. Stock up on extra paper plates, aluminum foil, and plastic wrap so you're also prepared for the meal's end.

PUNCH BAR

While this simple Champagne punch is tasty on its own, the fruity stir-ins add an extra flavorful touch. For a nonalcoholic option, have lemon-lime soda or seltzer water on hand.

CHAMPAGNE PUNCH

- 1 (750-milliliter) bottle Champagne or prosecco
- 1 cup dry gin
- 1/3 cup simple syrup
- 1/4 cup fresh lemon juice

Stir ingredients together in a punch bowl or pitcher. Garnish with frozen fruit.

MAKES about 2 qt. (serving size: 5 oz.) **ACTIVE** 5 min. **TOTAL** 5 min.

MINT-LIME-CHAMPAGNE PUNCH

Bring 1 1/2 cups **water** to a simmer in a saucepan over medium. Stir in 2 cups firmly packed torn **mint** leaves and 1/4 cup **sugar.** Cover, remove from heat, and steep 10 to 12 minutes. Cool completely, about 35 minutes, and remove mint leaves. Stir in 4 tablespoons fresh **lime juice.** Stir desired amount into 1 serving of **Champagne Punch.** Garnish with **mint** or **lime slices.**

MAKES 1 1/2 cups. **ACTIVE** 15 min. **TOTAL** 1 hour

BLUEBERRY-LAVENDER-CHAMPAGNE PUNCH

Stir together 1 cup mashed fresh **blueberries,** 2/3 cup **sugar,** 1 cup **water,** and 1/2 teaspoon **dried lavender** in a saucepan, and bring to a simmer over medium. Simmer, stirring occasionally, 20 minutes. Pour through a fine wire-mesh strainer, discarding solids. Cool completely, about 45 minutes. Stir desired amount into 1 serving of **Champagne Punch.** Garnish with **blueberries** or **lavender sprigs.**

MAKES 1 cup. **ACTIVE** 25 min. **TOTAL** 1 hour, 10 min.

STRAWBERRY-GINGER-CHAMPAGNE PUNCH

Stir together 1 (12-ounce) jar **strawberry jelly,** 1/2 cup **water,** and 1 tablespoon finely grated fresh **ginger** in a saucepan. Bring to a simmer over low, and simmer until mixture is smooth, about 5 minutes. Cool completely, about 30 minutes. Stir desired amount into 1 serving of **Champagne Punch.** Garnish with **strawberries** or slices of fresh **ginger.**

MAKES 1 1/3 cups. **ACTIVE** 10 min. **TOTAL** 40 min.

Sarah's Signature Punch

Mint-lime

Blueberry-La

Strawberry-Ginger

Dad's Famous Chocolate Pie

CHOCOLATE TRUFFLE PIE WITH AMARETTO CREAM

(Dad's Famous Chocolate Pie)

- ½ (14.1-oz.) pkg. refrigerated piecrusts
- 1 cup (6 oz.) semisweet chocolate chips
- 1 cup (6 oz.) bittersweet chocolate chips
- ½ cup (4 oz.) salted butter, softened
- ¾ cup packed light brown sugar
- 3 large eggs
- 1 tsp. vanilla extract
- ¼ tsp. almond extract
- 2 oz. (½ cup) all-purpose flour
- 1 cup toasted slivered almonds Amaretto Cream

1. Preheat oven to 350°F. Fit piecrust into a 9-inch pie pan; fold edges under, and crimp. Line piecrust with aluminum foil or parchment paper, and fill to rim with pie weights or dried beans. Place pan on a baking sheet. Bake in preheated oven 10 minutes. Remove weights and foil, and bake until bottom is lightly browned, 10 to 12 more minutes. Cool on baking sheet on a wire rack while preparing filling.
2. Microwave semisweet and bittersweet chocolate chips in a small microwave-safe bowl at MEDIUM (50% power) until melted and smooth, 3 to 4 minutes, stirring at 30-second intervals. Cool 15 minutes.
3. Beat butter and brown sugar at medium speed with an electric mixer until light and fluffy. Add eggs, 1 at a time, beating after each addition. Stir in melted chocolate, vanilla, and almond extract; stir in flour and toasted almonds. Spread mixture evenly in pastry shell.
4. Bake in preheated oven until set, 30 to 35 minutes, covering edges during last 10 minutes to prevent overbrowning, if needed. Cool completely on a wire rack (about 1 hour). Chill 1 hour. Serve with Amaretto Cream. Store leftover pie, covered, in refrigerator.

SERVES 8 (serving size: 1 slice). **ACTIVE** 25 min.
TOTAL 3 hours, including Amaretto Cream

Amaretto Cream

Beat 1 cup **heavy cream** and 2 teaspoons **almond-flavored liqueur** at medium-high speed with an electric mixer until foamy. Gradually add ¼ cup **powdered sugar,** beating until soft peaks form. Chill until ready to serve.

Note: ¼ teaspoon almond extract may be substituted for liqueur.

MAKES 2 cups (serving size: ¼ cup).
ACTIVE 5 min. **TOTAL** 5 min.

GREEN BEAN POTATO SALAD WITH LEMON-SOY VINAIGRETTE

(Wade's Potato Salad)

~~~~~~~~~~

2 (12-oz.) pkg. fresh green beans
3/4 tsp. table salt, divided
1 lb. petite red potatoes
1 large yellow bell pepper, cut into thin strips
1/3 cup thinly sliced red onion
Lemon-Soy Vinaigrette
3 Tbsp. chopped fresh mint
2 Tbsp. toasted sliced almonds
1 Tbsp. toasted sesame seeds

1. Cook green beans and 1/2 teaspoon salt in boiling water to cover in a large saucepan until crisp-tender, 3 to 4 minutes; drain. Plunge into ice water to stop cooking process; drain and pat dry with paper towels.

2. Bring potatoes and cold water to cover to a boil in large saucepan over medium-high; reduce heat to medium-low, and simmer until just tender, about 20 minutes total. Drain and let cool 30 minutes. Slice potatoes into 1/4- to 1/2-inch rounds.

3. Gently toss together green beans, potatoes, bell pepper, red onions, and remaining 1/4 teaspoon salt in a large bowl. Add Lemon-Soy Vinaigrette, and gently toss to combine. Transfer mixture to a serving platter, and top with mint, almonds, and sesame seeds. Serve at room temperature or chilled.

SERVES 8 (serving size: about 3/4 cup)
ACTIVE 20 min. **TOTAL** 1 hour, 15 min.

Lemon-Soy Vinaigrette

Whisk together 1/4 cup packed **light brown sugar,** 1/4 cup fresh **lemon juice,** 2 tablespoons **soy sauce,** 2 teaspoons **sesame oil,** and 1/2 teaspoon **red pepper flakes** in a small bowl until combined.

MAKES about 1/2 cup (serving size: about 1 Tbsp.).

CREAMY SPRING PASTA BAKE

(Julia's Pasta Bake)

~~~~~~~~~~

PASTA

1/2 cup (4 oz.) salted butter
1/2 cup (2 oz.) all-purpose flour
2 tsp. dry mustard
1 tsp. table salt
1/2 tsp. black pepper
1/4 tsp. cayenne pepper
2 cups half-and-half
2 cups whole milk
1 (16-oz.) block Swiss cheese, shredded
2 oz. Parmesan cheese, shredded (about 2/3 cup)
1 (16-oz.) pkg. farfalle (bow-tie pasta), prepared according to pkg. directions
1 (12-oz.) pkg. cubed boneless ham (about 2 cups)
1 1/2 cups frozen baby sweet peas, thawed

TOPPING

1 cup sea salt-and-pepper croutons
2 oz. Parmesan cheese, shredded (about 2/3 cup)
1 Tbsp. butter, melted

1. Preheat oven to 350°F. Melt butter in a Dutch oven over medium. Gradually whisk in flour until smooth; cook, whisking constantly, 2 minutes. Whisk in dry mustard, salt, black pepper, and cayenne pepper. Gradually whisk in half-and-half and milk; cook, whisking constantly, until thickened, 8 to 10 minutes.

2. Whisk in Swiss cheese and 2 oz. Parmesan cheese. Remove from heat. Stir in pasta, ham, and peas. Pour mixture into a lightly greased 13- x 9-inch baking dish.

3. Prepare Topping: Process croutons and 2 oz. Parmesan cheese in a food processor until finely ground. Add 1 tablespoon melted butter, and process until combined. Sprinkle over pasta mixture.

4. Bake in preheated oven until golden, about 30 minutes. Let stand 10 minutes.

Note: We tested with Hormel Cure 81 Premium Cubed Boneless Ham and

New York Texas Toast Sea Salt and Pepper Croutons.

SERVES 8 (serving size: about 1 1/2 cups).
ACTIVE 25 min. **TOTAL** 1 hour, 5 min.

SPINACH-AND-ROMAINE SALAD WITH CUCUMBERS, RADISHES, AND CREAMY MINT DRESSING

(Janie's Spinach Salad)

~~~~~~~~~~

1 (5-oz.) pkg. baby spinach
2 romaine lettuce hearts, chopped
2 cucumbers, cut into 1-inch pieces
1 cup thinly sliced radishes
1 small shallot, minced
2 Tbsp. white wine vinegar
2 Tbsp. fresh lemon juice
1/4 cup sour cream
1 cup half-and-half
1/2 cup chopped fresh mint, plus leaves for garnish
1/4 tsp. kosher salt
1/8 tsp. black pepper
1/2 cup crumbled feta cheese

1. Toss together spinach, romaine, cucumbers, and radishes in a large bowl.

2. Stir together shallot, vinegar, and lemon juice in a medium bowl; let stand 5 minutes. Stir in sour cream, and gradually whisk in half-and-half. Stir in chopped mint, salt, and black pepper.

3. Top spinach mixture with feta cheese; serve with dressing.

SERVES 6 (serving size: about 1/4 cup)
ACTIVE 20 min. **TOTAL** 25 min.

LEMON SHERBET CUPCAKES WITH BUTTERCREAM FROSTING

(Pam's Citrus Cupcakes)

CUPCAKES

- 1 cup (8 oz.) salted butter, softened
- 2 1/2 cups granulated sugar
- 6 large eggs
- 3 cups (12 oz.) all-purpose flour
- 1 tsp. baking powder
- 1/2 tsp. baking soda
- 1/4 tsp. table salt
- 1 (8-oz.) container sour cream
- 1 Tbsp. lemon zest
- 1 Tbsp. fresh lemon juice
- 1 tsp. vanilla extract
- 30 paper baking cups

FROSTING

- 1 cup (8 oz.) salted butter, softened
- 3 Tbsp. lemon zest
- 1 (32-oz.) pkg. powdered sugar
- 8 to 9 Tbsp. fresh lemon juice
- 1 to 2 drops yellow liquid food coloring

1. Prepare Cupcakes: Preheat oven to 350°F. Beat 1 cup softened butter at medium speed with a heavy-duty stand mixer until creamy; gradually add granulated sugar, beating until light and fluffy. Add eggs, 1 at a time, beating just until blended after each addition.

2. Stir together flour, baking powder, baking soda, and salt. Add flour mixture to butter mixture alternately with sour cream, beginning and ending with flour mixture. Beat at low speed just until blended after each addition. Stir in 1 tablespoon zest, 1 tablespoon juice, and 1 teaspoon vanilla. Place 30 paper baking cups in three 12-cup standard-size muffin pans; spoon 1/4 cup batter into each baking cup.

3. Bake in preheated oven until a wooden pick inserted in centers comes out clean, 20 to 23 minutes. Remove from pans to wire racks, and cool completely (about 20 minutes).

4. Prepare Frosting: Beat 8 ounces softened butter and 3 tablespoons lemon zest at medium speed until creamy, 1 to 2 minutes. Gradually add powdered sugar alternately with 8 tablespoons lemon juice, beating at low speed until blended after each addition. Add up to 1 tablespoon lemon juice, 1 teaspoon at a time, beating until desired consistency is reached. Add food coloring, and beat at high speed until well blended and frosting is light and fluffy, 1 to 2 minutes.

5. Spoon frosting into a ziplock plastic freezer bag. Snip 1 corner of bag to make a small hole. Pipe about 1 1/2 tablespoons frosting onto each cupcake.

MAKES about 30 cupcakes (serving size: 1 cupcake). **ACTIVE** 30 min. **TOTAL** 1 hour, 10 min.

Lime Sherbet Cupcakes

Substitute **lime zest** for lemon zest and fresh **lime juice** for lemon juice. For frosting, substitute fresh **lime juice** for lemon juice, and 1 to 2 drops **green liquid food coloring** for yellow.

Orange Sherbet Cupcakes

Substitute **orange zest** for lemon zest and fresh **orange juice** for lemon juice. For frosting, substitute **orange zest** for lemon zest and 1 tablespoon **lemon juice** and 7 to 8 tablespoons **fresh orange juice** in place of 8 to 9 tablespoons lemon juice. Substitute 1 drop **red liquid food coloring** for yellow.

ASPARAGUS, SPRING ONION, AND FETA QUICHE

(Aunt Rose's Quiche)

- 1 (14.1-oz.) pkg. refrigerated piecrusts
- 2 Tbsp. (1 oz.) salted butter
- 2 cups thinly sliced spring onions
- 1 bunch fresh asparagus, trimmed and cut into 1-inch pieces)
- 2 tsp. kosher salt, divided
- 3/4 tsp. black pepper, divided
- 1 cup heavy cream
- 8 large eggs
- 2 Tbsp. thinly sliced chives
- 2 Tbsp. chopped flat-leaf parsley
- 1/8 tsp. ground nutmeg
- 3/4 cup crumbled feta cheese, divided

1. Preheat oven to 425°F. Unroll piecrusts; stack on a lightly floured surface. Roll stacked piecrusts into a 12-inch circle. Fit piecrust into a 10-inch deep-dish, lightly greased tart pan with removable bottom; press into fluted edges. Trim off excess piecrust along edges. Line piecrust with aluminum foil or parchment paper, and fill to rim with pie weights or dried beans. Place pan on a baking sheet. Bake in preheated oven 14 minutes. Remove weights and foil, and bake until golden brown, 10 to 12 more minutes. Reduce oven temperature to 350°F. Cool piecrust completely on baking sheet on a wire rack, about 15 minutes.

2. Meanwhile, melt butter in a medium skillet over medium-high. Add onions, and cook, stirring occasionally, until tender and lightly browned, about 10 minutes. Stir in asparagus; sprinkle with 1/2 teaspoon salt and 1/4 teaspoon pepper. Remove from heat, and cool 5 minutes.

3. Whisk together cream, eggs, chives, parsley, nutmeg, and remaining 1 1/2 teaspoons salt and 1/2 teaspoon pepper.

4. Place half of onion mixture (about 1 cup) in tart shell; sprinkle with 1/4 cup feta. Spoon half of cream mixture (about 1 1/2 cups) over feta. Repeat layers once, and sprinkle top with remaining 1/4 cup feta.

5. Bake in preheated oven until set, about 1 hour. Cool on baking sheet on a wire rack 20 minutes before serving.

SERVES 6 (serving size: 1 slice). **ACTIVE** 30 min. **TOTAL** 2 hours, 30 min.

Breakfast for Dinner

OUR BEST MORNING RECIPES, REIMAGINED FOR EASY WEEKNIGHT COOKING

RECIPE SHORTCUT
No time to whip up homemade waffles? Head to your grocer's freezer section. We like Van's Belgian Homestyle Waffles.

HOT CHICKEN-AND-WAFFLE SANDWICHES WITH CHIVE CREAM

We did a taste test and loved the just-fried tenders from the Publix grocery store deli.

HOT CHICKEN
- 9 fried chicken breast tenders
- 1 Tbsp. cayenne pepper
- 1 tsp. paprika
- 1/2 tsp. garlic powder
- 2 Tbsp. sugar, divided
- 1/2 cup peanut oil

WAFFLES
- 2 cups (about 9 oz.) all-purpose flour
- 1 1/2 tsp. baking powder
- 3/4 tsp. baking soda
- 3/4 tsp. table salt
- 1 1/2 cups buttermilk
- 1/4 cup (2 oz.) salted butter, melted
- 2 large eggs

CHIVE CREAM
- 1/2 cup sour cream
- 2 Tbsp. thinly sliced chives
- 1 tsp. water

1. Prepare Hot Chicken: Preheat oven to 200°F. Place chicken tenders in a single layer on a baking sheet, and keep warm in oven until ready to use.
2. Stir together cayenne pepper, paprika, garlic powder, and 1 tablespoon of the sugar in a small saucepan. Whisk in peanut oil, and cook over low, whisking constantly, until well combined, about 5 minutes. Set aside.
3. Prepare Waffles: Whisk together flour, next 3 ingredients, and remaining 1 tablespoon sugar in a medium bowl. Whisk buttermilk, butter, and eggs in a small bowl. Stir buttermilk mixture into flour mixture until combined.

Cook batter, in batches, in a preheated, lightly greased waffle iron until golden brown, 4 to 5 minutes.

4. Prepare Chive Cream: Stir together sour cream, chives, and 1 teaspoon water in a small bowl.

5. Assemble Sandwiches: Toss tenders and cayenne mixture in a large bowl. Place 1 1/2 tenders on each of 6 waffles; top each with 2 tablespoons chive cream and 1 waffle. Serve immediately.

SERVES 6 (serving size: 1 sandwich). **ACTIVE** 40 min. **TOTAL** 40 min.

BREAKFAST ENCHILADAS

Remove eggs from stove-top while they're still a bit wet; they'll finish cooking in the oven. To make this a day ahead, go through Step 2; cover and chill the casserole. Let stand at room temperature about 20 minutes before baking.

- 2 Tbsp. (1 oz.) **unsalted butter**
- 3/4 cup **chopped red bell pepper**
- 1/2 cup **chopped sweet onion**
- 12 **large eggs**
- 1/2 tsp. **table salt**
- 1/4 tsp. **black pepper**
- 2 Tbsp. **water**
- 1 (16-oz.) **jar salsa verde**
- 12 (6-in.) **flour tortillas**
- 2 1/2 cups (10 oz.) **shredded Colby Jack cheese**
- 2 Tbsp. **chopped fresh cilantro**
  Cheese Sauce
  Toppings: halved grape tomatoes, chopped fresh cilantro, chopped avocado

1. Preheat oven to 350°F. Melt butter in large nonstick skillet over medium. Add bell peppers and onions; sauté until tender, 4 to 5 minutes. Stir together eggs and next 3 ingredients in a medium bowl. Add egg mixture to bell pepper mixture, and cook, without stirring, until eggs begin to set on bottom, about 1 to 2 minutes. Draw a spatula across pan to form large curds. Cook, stirring occasionally, until eggs are thickened, about 6 to 7 minutes. (Do not overstir.)

2. Spread 2 tablespoons salsa verde in center of each tortilla. Spoon about

1/4 cup egg mixture over salsa; sprinkle with 2 tablespoons cheese and 1/2 teaspoon cilantro. Roll up, and place, seam side down, in lightly greased 13- x 9-inch baking dish. Add Cheese Sauce and remaining cheese.

3. Bake in preheated oven until sauce is bubbly, 30 minutes. Serve with desired toppings.

SERVES 6 (serving size: 2 tortillas). **ACTIVE** 20 min. **TOTAL** 1 hour, including sauce

MAKE AHEAD Assemble up to 24 hours prior to serving, and store in the fridge. Before baking, bring the casserole to room temperature.

Cheese Sauce

Melt 1/4 cup (2 oz.) **salted butter** in heavy saucepan over medium-low; whisk in 1/4 cup (about 1 oz.) all-purpose **flour** until smooth. Cook, whisking constantly, 1 minute. Increase heat to medium. Gradually whisk in 2 cups **milk**; cook, whisking constantly, until thickened, 5 minutes. Remove from heat, and whisk in 1 1/2 cups (6 oz.) shredded **Colby Jack cheese,** 1 (4.5-oz.) can chopped **green chiles,** and 1/2 teaspoon table **salt.** Use immediately.

GOLDEN POTATO-AND-SMOKED SAUSAGE HASH

Make this hash even heartier by adding a fried egg on top. (See page 88 to learn our foolproof frying technique.)

- 1 **lb. baby golden potatoes, each cut into 8 pieces**
- 1/4 **cup kosher salt**
- 1 **lb. smoked sausage, sliced**
- 1 **medium-size sweet onion, thinly sliced**
- 2 **Tbsp. red wine vinegar**
- 3 **cups arugula**
- 1/4 **cup shaved Parmesan cheese**

1. Place potatoes, salt, and water to cover in a medium saucepan. Bring to a boil over high; reduce heat to medium-low, and simmer until tender when pierced, 10 minutes. Drain and place in a single layer on a baking sheet. Cool completely, 15 minutes.
2. Meanwhile, cook the sausage in a large skillet over medium-high, stirring often, until browned, 10 minutes. Remove with a slotted spoon, and drain on paper towels, reserving drippings in skillet.
3. Cook potatoes in hot drippings over medium, stirring occasionally, until potatoes are brown and crisp, 10 minutes. Add onions, and cook, stirring occasionally, until tender, 10 minutes. Add vinegar, and cook 30 seconds.
4. Stir in sausage and arugula, and cook, stirring until arugula is wilted, about 5 minutes. Transfer to a serving platter. Top with Parmesan.

SERVES 6 (serving size: about 3/4 cup). **ACTIVE** 55 min. **TOTAL** 1 hour, 5 min.

RECIPE SHORTCUT
Speed up cooking time by using parboiled potatoes from your grocer's freezer section.

Golden Potato-and-Smoked Sausage Hash

CREAMY BAKED EGGS WITH HERBS AND BACON

Serve with toasted bread and a leafy green side salad.

- 1/2 **cup heavy whipping cream**
- 2 **Tbsp. thinly sliced chives**
- 2 **Tbsp. chopped fresh flat-leaf parsley**
- 2 **tsp. chopped fresh dill**
- 1/2 **tsp. kosher salt**
- 1/4 **tsp. black pepper**
- 8 **large eggs**
- 4 **cooked bacon slices, crumbled (about 1/2 cup)**

1. Preheat oven to 425°F. Stir together first 6 ingredients in a large ovenproof skillet. Bring to a simmer over medium-low. Break eggs into cream mixture; do not stir.
2. Bake in preheated oven until whites are set and yolks are at desired degree of doneness, 6 to 8 minutes. Sprinkle with bacon, and serve immediately.

SERVES 4 (serving size: 2 eggs, about 1/4 cup sauce). **ACTIVE** 15 min. **TOTAL** 20 min.

Creamy Baked Eggs with Herbs and Bacon

MAKE AHEAD
Up to 24 hours before, stir together cream, herbs, salt, and pepper. Keep chilled in an airtight container until ready to use.

Pasta That Tastes Like Spring

TWO TYPES OF SPRING PEAS ENLIVEN THIS QUICK AND SATISFYING ONE-POT PASTA DISH

SPRING PEA PASTA WITH RICOTTA AND HERBS

Our one-pot primavera brings together seasonal favorites: fresh herbs, crunchy sugar snap peas, and sweet peas. Combining ricotta cheese with the salty water left over from boiling the pasta makes a super-easy, creamy sauce.

- **4** qt. water
- **1/4** cup kosher salt
- **8** oz. gemelli, penne, or other short pasta
- **2** (8-oz.) pkg. sugar snap peas, trimmed and strings removed
- **1** (13-oz.) pkg. frozen sweet peas, thawed
- **1** cup ricotta cheese
- **1/2** cup firmly packed fresh flat-leaf parsley leaves
- **2** Tbsp. (1 oz.) salted butter
- **2** Tbsp. thinly sliced fresh chives
- **2** Tbsp. chopped fresh tarragon

1. Bring 4 quarts water to a boil in a stockpot over high. Add 1/4 cup salt; return to a boil. Add pasta; boil, stirring occasionally, until al dente, about 8 minutes. Stir in sugar snap peas, and cook 2 minutes. Stir in sweet peas, and cook 1 minute. Drain pasta mixture, reserving 1/2 cup cooking water.

2. Return pasta mixture to pot. Add ricotta, parsley, butter, chives, tarragon, and reserved cooking water; stir to coat. Serve immediately.

SERVES 4 (serving size: about 1 cup).
ACTIVE 20 min. **TOTAL** 30 min.

MEET YOUR NEW FAVORITE APPETIZER...

Deviled Potatoes

Two Southern classics, deviled eggs and potato salad, join forces to create these two-bite wonders. Make them a day before your get-together, and chill until you head out. When you arrive, they'll be the right serving temperature.

1 **lb. petite red potatoes (about 15)**
1 **Tbsp. olive oil**
1 1/2 **tsp. kosher salt, divided**
1/2 **cup sour cream**
2 **Tbsp. brined capers, drained and rinsed**
2 **tsp. chopped fresh flat-leaf parsley**
2 **tsp. chopped fresh dill**
2 **tsp. whole grain mustard**
1 **tsp. lemon zest**
Garnishes: chopped fresh flat-leaf parsley, lemon zest, chopped fresh dill

1. Preheat oven to 350°F. Place potatoes in a small bowl, and drizzle with oil. Sprinkle with 1 teaspoon of the salt; toss to coat. Spread potatoes in a single layer on a baking sheet, and bake until tender when pierced, about 40 minutes. Remove from oven, and cool 15 minutes.

2. Cut each potato in half crosswise. Carefully scoop out potato pulp into a medium bowl, leaving shells intact. Place shells, cut side up, on baking sheet, and bake in preheated oven until dry, about 10 more minutes. Cool completely, about 30 minutes.

3. Stir together potato pulp, sour cream, capers, parsley, dill, mustard, zest, and remaining 1/2 teaspoon salt. Spoon mixture generously into each potato shell.

SERVES 10 (serving size: 3 pieces).
ACTIVE 25 min. **TOTAL** 2 hours

BEST WAY TO FRY AN EGG

WANT CRISP BROWN EDGES AND A RUNNY, SOAK-UP-WITH-TOAST YOLK? HERE'S HOW

USE OLIVE OIL It has a higher smoke point than butter, which keeps the edges from burning. Heat 2 tablespoons of extra-virgin olive oil in a nonstick skillet over medium for about 1 to 2 minutes.

WATCH FOR BUBBLES Once the oil is hot, gently crack the egg into the skillet. The oil should bubble around the whites from the start.

STICK THE LANDING Cook the egg for 2 minutes, rotating the skillet a few times so it cooks evenly. Use a thin, flat-edged spatula to slide under the egg, and carefully lift it from the pan.

FIVE FRESH WAYS WITH SCALLIONS

SERVE AS A SIDE
Coat bunches of scallions with olive oil, salt, and pepper; then grill until wilted and slightly charred for a quick and simple side dish.

PICK UP YOUR PESTO GAME
Use scallions in place of basil for a springy pesto sauce that's delicious on pizza, pasta, or crostini.

SPREAD ON SANDWICHES
Stir chopped scallions and lemon juice into your favorite mayonnaise for an elevated sandwich spread.

WHIP UP SAVORY PANCAKES
For a flaky, fragrant stack, add thinly sliced scallions to your favorite batter—minus the sugar—and enjoy a delicious snack.

TOP SALADS AND SOUPS
Infuse canola oil with scallions by heating the oil, adding scallions for about 10 seconds, and then giving a quick stir. Remove from heat, chill, and store in the fridge. Serve over rice, soup, salad, or anything you think needs a hint of delicate onion flavor.

Drizzle and Delight

WE GAVE OUR FAVORITE BREAD PUDDING A LOUISIANA-STYLE REVIVAL

PRALINE BREAD PUDDING

- 6 large eggs
- 3 cups heavy whipping cream
- 3 cups milk
- 2 cups packed dark brown sugar
- 2 Tbsp. vanilla extract
- 1/4 tsp. table salt
- 1/4 tsp. ground nutmeg
- 1 (16-oz.) day-old French bread loaf, cut into 1-inch cubes (about 14 cups)
- 2 cups coarsely chopped toasted pecans
  Praline Sauce

1. Whisk together first 7 ingredients in a large bowl. Add bread cubes, stirring to coat thoroughly. Let stand 1 hour, stirring occasionally to ensure an even coating. Stir in pecans.
2. Preheat oven to 350°F. Lightly grease a 13- x 9-inch baking dish; pour bread mixture into dish. Bake in preheated oven until bubbly around edges and firm in center, about 1 hour, shielding with aluminum foil after 45 to 50 minutes to prevent excessive browning. Let stand 5 minutes. Serve with Praline Sauce.

SERVES 12 (serving size: about 1 cup pudding, 2 Tbsp. sauce). **ACTIVE** 30 min. **TOTAL** 3 hours, including sauce

Praline Sauce

- 3 Tbsp. (1 1/2 oz.) salted butter
- 1 Tbsp. all-purpose flour
- 1 cup heavy whipping cream
- 1/2 cup packed dark brown sugar
- 2 Tbsp. vanilla extract
- 1/4 tsp. ground nutmeg
- 1/8 tsp. table salt

Melt butter in a small saucepan over medium-low; whisk in flour, and cook, whisking constantly, until foamy and golden brown, 3 to 4 minutes. Whisk in cream and brown sugar; cook, whisking constantly, until thickened, about 3 minutes. Whisk in vanilla, nutmeg, and salt; cook, whisking constantly, until bubbly, 2 to 3 minutes.

MAKES about 1 1/2 cups. **ACTIVE** 20 min. **TOTAL** 20 min.

Community Cookbook

BUILD A BETTER LIBRARY, ONE GREAT BOOK AT A TIME

Delicious Reads

Five cookbooks packed with authentic Southern recipes, personal stories, and regional travel inspiration

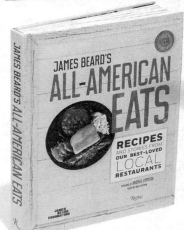

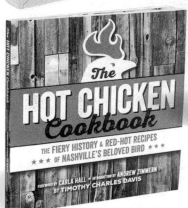

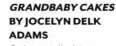

BESH BIG EASY BY JOHN BESH

In his latest cookbook, New Orleans chef John Besh shares personal anecdotes along with the history behind the food he grew up loving and eating in his hometown. He also reveals why it's all right to keep a can of breadcrumbs handy in your pantry.

JAMES BEARD'S ALL-AMERICAN EATS BY THE JAMES BEARD FOUNDATION (WITH INTRODUCTION BY JOHN T. EDGE)

Since 1991, the James Beard Foundation has been honoring regional restaurants. While this book includes the entire country, many Southern spots reap high praise. Get it for the recipes, but read it for the history.

THE HOT CHICKEN COOKBOOK BY TIMOTHY CHARLES DAVIS

Arguably Music City's most iconic food, hot chicken is having its moment. Part history book, part travelogue, and part love letter, this includes interviews with the likes of chef Edward Lee and former mayor of Nashville Karl Dean.

CRABS & OYSTERS (A SAVOR THE SOUTH COOKBOOK) BY BILL SMITH

Chef Bill Smith shares his passion for the South's favorite shellfish. You'll also find terrific recipes from the classic regional cookbooks of coastal communities, as well as Smith's own charmingly reported research and memorable headnotes.

GRANDBABY CAKES BY JOCELYN DELK ADAMS

Only grandbabies are sweeter than a book devoted to desserts. And—as if the decadent cakes, glazes, and frostings weren't already enticing enough—Adams' debut cookbook is sprinkled with the heartfelt stories behind her delicious recipes and also features beautiful vintage family photos.

April

A Colorful Spring Luncheon

JULIA REED KEEPS HER PALETTE AND PALATE IN SYNC FOR THIS OUTDOOR AFFAIR

SPRING TO ME ALWAYS means acres of yellow and white blooms because as soon as the winter weather abates, my mother's expansive front lawn in Greenville, Mississippi, is covered in thousands of daffodils. When I'm back home in The Delta, I love to stage "welcome spring" lunches outside in the midst of all the beauty, where even the food is inspired by the color palette. In New Orleans, where the soggy soil keeps bulbs from thriving, I still head outdoors, but my golden table flowers are usually from the flower shop: tulips, roses, ranunculus, and (when I'm especially lucky) glorious pale yellow peonies.

These lunches are almost always set on a background of blue and white, not least because I have a dozen tablecloths in an indigo toile left over from my step-daughter's wedding reception. As it happens, the tablecloths are not only the perfect foil for flowers of almost every color but also for food. "One reason blue and white is so special for a table setting is because there are few blue foods," says über-decorator Bunny Williams. "So anything you serve looks fabulous on it." Williams and her husband, John Rosselli, are avid collectors of blue-and-white porcelain, including lots of 18th- and 19th-century Canton ware (George Washington was a

Varying shades of yellow are always a pretty complement to blue and white.

Raspberry china and deep-pink flowers also pop against the blue toile.

Add a pinch more saffron to your stew (recipe, page 95) for a deeper color and slightly more exotic flavor.

fan), but Williams has never been a snob. She mixes in new inexpensive pieces from *pearlriver.com*. I add similar plates and bowls from shops in various Chinatowns around the country to my own collection of Blue Willow. The latter is a late-18th-century English pattern designed by Thomas Minton, who was inspired by the masses of Canton ware heading west from China.

While it's fun to add the cheap stuff to far finer blue and white (which might also include antique Wedgwood or Delftware, Royal Crown Derby's lush Blue Aves, or Royal Copenhagen's graceful Half Lace), I also inject color by mixing in other china patterns. With yellow flowers, I pull out my set of antique yellow-and-white tableware. But with deep-pink roses and peonies, I pull out my Herend Chinese Bouquet in Raspberry. The same pattern in Rust would look swell with a center-piece of orange tulips.

Williams is right that pretty much anything you serve will look terrific against the blue design, but I couldn't resist throwing in a touch of saffron and Parmesan cheese to a typically white *blanquette de veau*, the classic veal stew featured here. Not only do the additions give this all-too-often bland dish some zing, but also the end result goes nicely with our color scheme. With it I serve rice, noodles, or even a potato puree, along with a simple butter lettuce salad and some fresh spring peas or tender asparagus. For an aperitif, I offer a refreshing Champagne cocktail (at right), and for dessert, a cold lemon mousse. Not only does it match the yellow scheme, but also its light texture and fresh, zesty flavor speak to me of spring.

Finding the Tablecloth

There are plenty of affordable blue toiles out there, including Waverly's Sunny Field Toile Delft or Charmed Life Toile Cornflower. (Both of these patterns are similar to mine and are available for purchase on fabric.com.) You could also use a simple blue-and-white ticking or even a small check. For a splurge, be sure to check out Bennison Fabric's stunning Waikiki in Faded Blue on Oyster (bennisonfabrics.com).

JULIA'S SPRING STEW

THE RECIPE

SAFFRON VEAL STEW

Serve over noodles, rice, or potato puree.

- **4 lb. veal stew meat, cut into 2-inch pieces**
- **3 1/2 tsp. kosher salt, divided**
- **1 1/2 tsp. black pepper, divided**
- **3 Tbsp. all-purpose flour**
- **1/4 cup olive oil, divided**
- **1 cup dry white wine**
- **2 leeks**
- **1 large onion, halved and studded with 2 whole cloves**
- **2 carrots, quartered**
- **2 celery ribs, roughly chopped**
- **4 garlic cloves, sliced**
- **1 lemon, peel removed in strips with a vegetable peeler**
- **2 bay leaves**
- **2 fresh thyme sprigs**
- **4 cups chicken broth, divided**
- **1 tsp. saffron threads**
- **1 cup peeled pearl onions**
- **3 Tbsp. (1 1/2 oz.) salted butter, divided**
- **2 (8-oz.) pkg. button mushrooms**
- **1 cup crème fraîche**
- **3 Tbsp. grated Parmesan cheese**
- **3 Tbsp. minced fresh chives**
- **1 Tbsp. chopped fresh tarragon leaves**

1. Sprinkle veal with 2 teaspoons salt and 1 teaspoon pepper; sprinkle with flour, and toss to coat.

2. Heat 2 tablespoons oil in a large Dutch oven over high. Add veal, and cook, in batches if necessary, until browned on all sides, 5 to 6 minutes. Transfer veal to a paper towel–lined sheet pan. Add wine to Dutch oven, and stir, scraping up any browned bits from bottom of pot. Reduce heat to medium, and simmer until wine is reduced by half.

3. Cut and discard root ends and dark green tops from leeks, reserving white and pale-green parts only. Cut into 1-inch pieces, and rinse thoroughly.

4. Return veal to Dutch oven. Add leeks and next 7 ingredients, and cook, stirring often, until vegetables begin to soften, 8 to 10 minutes. Stir in 3 cups broth, and bring to a boil over high. Reduce heat to low, add saffron, and cover. Simmer until meat is tender, about 1 hour.

5. Meanwhile, bring remaining 1 cup broth to a boil in a saucepan. Add pearl onions, 1 tablespoon butter, and 1/2 teaspoon salt. Reduce heat to low; cover and simmer until onions are tender, about 10 minutes. Drain over a small bowl, reserving onion liquid. Set cooked pearl onions aside.

6. Melt remaining 2 tablespoons butter with remaining 2 tablespoons oil in a large skillet over high. Add mushrooms; sprinkle with remaining 1 teaspoon salt and 1/2 teaspoon pepper. Sauté until mushrooms are browned, about 5 minutes. Remove from heat.

7. Pour veal mixture in Dutch oven through a colander into a large bowl. Remove veal pieces, and reserve; discard vegetables. Transfer veal sauce in bowl to Dutch oven, and bring to a boil over high. Reduce heat to medium, and cook 5 minutes, stirring occasionally. Whisk in crème fraîche and Parmesan until blended and smooth, adding desired amount of reserved onion liquid if sauce is too thick. Stir in cooked veal, pearl onions, and mushrooms. Stir in chives and tarragon.

SERVES 8 (serving size: about 1 cup)
ACTIVE 50 min. **TOTAL** 1 hour, 40 min.

LAVENDER-AND-MINT CHAMPAGNE COCKTAIL

Bring 1 cup of **lavender sugar** (available online) and 1 cup water to a boil; cook until the sugar is dissolved. Remove from heat, add a bunch of **mint,** and let it steep for 30 minutes. Strain syrup, and chill. Add a teaspoon or two (depending on size of your glass) to a Champagne flute, and top with cold **Champagne.**

BEYOND THE BOIL

FROM BISQUE TO ÉTOUFFÉE, CELEBRATE THE MANY
WAYS TO COOK CRAWFISH

IN NEW ORLEANS, YOU CAN TELL IT'S CRAWFISH SEASON BEFORE YOU ACTUALLY GET YOUR HANDS ON ANY.

Boiling crawfish is an outdoor activity that thickens the city's air with a tingly, cayenne-spiked aroma. This time of year, the scent is an inescapable reminder that sucking the meat from a whole boiled crawfish's tail is one of the South's spiciest culinary pleasures. It's also a messy endeavor, one that you know is captivating South Louisiana when you start finding discarded crawfish shells covering the grounds of music festivals or on the street following second line parades, like spent peanut shells on the floor of a beer bar.

While freshly harvested Louisiana crawfish start making appearances on menus around the holidays, the height of the season runs roughly from February to late spring, weather depending. The freshwater crustacean is South Louisiana's unofficial culinary mascot, so crawfish iconography—on neon signs, flags, even golf shirts—is inescapable all year long.

Louisiana's love affair with crawfish is tightly connected with the ritual of the crawfish boil. The primal exercise of boiled crawfish eating—"pinching" and "sucking" are socially acceptable in this context—reinforces Louisiana cuisine's lusty reputation, just as eating something that vaguely resembles an insect reinforces the notion that locals will eat anything, provided it's properly spiced. Cayenne is a fairly constant presence in seafood spice blends, but the heat it imparts is not the defining characteristic of all boils. Clove, lemon, garlic, and even lemongrass permeate the air, in varying degrees and combinations, wherever crawfish is boiled.

At least once a year, ideally in March or April, when crawfish are at their sweet and meaty peak, I head west to Cajun Claw's, in Abbeville, or to Hawk's, tucked in the woods behind the rice fields in Rayne. Those two Cajun country seafood joints consistently serve the biggest crawfish, with the pearliest meat and the most finely calibrated seasoning, of any of the countless boiling houses I've frequented over the last 15 years.

But as these recipes demonstrate, Louisiana crawfish cookery extends well beyond the boiling pot. You'll find the meat featured everywhere in New Orleans, from corner saloons to grand temples of French-Creole cuisine. Crawfish bisque is a particularly elegant form, especially when adorned by heads stuffed with herbaceous dressing, as at places like Li'l Dizzy's Café, on Esplanade Avenue. Crawfish étouffée, the classic dish of stewed crawfish served over rice, is a staple from New Orleans clear to the Texas border. It's served at such established Creole restaurants as Dooky Chase and Galatoire's, and at Cajun lunch counters like T-Coon's in Lafayette.

Master cooking crawfish at home and you'll start living like Louisianans do: sautéing tails for your morning omelet, your lunchtime taco, your evening pasta. Once you get a taste for this Southern delicacy, you'll never see the critters the same way again.

— **Brett Anderson**

WHAT YOU NEED TO KNOW ABOUT CRAWFISH

Don't be intimidated by their insect-like looks. Here's a crash course on all things crawfish—or mudbugs, if you want to talk like a local.

BUYING
Many seafood stores in the South carry crawfish in season. Or, you can order them from *lacrawfish.com, deanies.com,* or *cajungrocer.com.* The standard in South Louisiana is about 3 pounds per person. (Unlike shrimp, only a small part of a whole crawfish is actually meat.)

CLEANING
Ask your supplier if the crawfish have been cleaned before purchasing. If not, it's easiest to clean them before bringing them inside. Place them in a cooler with a drink spout at the base. Fill with cool water, and let stand for 10 minutes. Drain the dirty water through the spout until the water runs clear.

SERVING
Enjoying crawfish outdoors is ideal, preferably piled high on a table lined with newspaper. Guests can gather around and dig in with their hands. If weather forces you indoors, serve crawfish the same way, perhaps in a garage or basement, and consider covering tables with plastic beneath the newspaper.

EATING
Pick up the boiled crawfish, and crack or twist off the head from the tail. (Be sure to suck out the juices from the head.) Remove the shell from the widest part of the tail, like you do when peeling a shrimp. Then, hold the end of the tail with one hand and gently pull out the meat from the shell.

CRAWFISH BISQUE

- 6 Tbsp. (3 oz.) salted butter
- 6 Tbsp. all-purpose flour
- 1 medium-size yellow onion, diced
- 1 red bell pepper, diced
- 2 celery ribs, diced
- 2 garlic cloves
- 1 medium tomato, diced
- 1 1/2 tsp. kosher salt
- 1/2 tsp. black pepper
- 1/4 tsp. cayenne pepper
- 3 cups seafood stock
- 4 fresh thyme sprigs
- 2 bay leaves
- 1/2 cup dry sherry cooking wine, divided
- 1 lb. frozen peeled crawfish tails, thawed and divided
- 1/2 cup heavy whipping cream
- 1 Tbsp. fresh lemon juice
- 1 tsp. hot sauce
- 2 Tbsp. chopped chives
  Oyster crackers

1. Melt butter in a saucepan over medium. Whisk in flour until combined. Reduce heat to medium-low, and cook, stirring constantly, until roux is pale brown, about 10 minutes. Add onion, bell pepper, celery, garlic, tomato, salt, black pepper, and cayenne pepper, and cook, stirring occasionally, 5 minutes. Increase heat to medium-high. Whisk in stock, thyme, bay leaves, and 1/4 cup cooking wine, and cook 10 minutes. Add half of crawfish, and cook 2 minutes.

2. Transfer mixture to a blender, and process until smooth, 30 seconds. Return to pan, and place over medium-low. Stir in cream, lemon juice, hot sauce, and remaining crawfish and 1/4 cup cooking wine. Bring to a low simmer, and cook until heated, about 5 minutes. Spoon into six bowls, and top with chives.

SERVES 6 (serving size: 1 1/4 cups)
ACTIVE 30 min. **TOTAL** 40 min.

Crawfish Bisque

"CRAWDOGS"

If you serve our étouffée (recipe on page 100) and have leftovers, slather it on top of grilled 'dogs.

1. Coat cold cooking grate of grill with cooking spray, and place on grill. Preheat grill to medium (350°F to 450°F). Brush 8 **hot dogs** with 1/4 cup **Creole mustard.** Split 8 hot dog **buns** (if necessary), and brush inside with 2 tablespoons melted salted **butter.** Place hot dogs on cooking grate, and grill, turning occasionally, until slightly charred, 3 to 4 minutes. Transfer hot dogs to side of grate, away from heat, and place buns, buttered side down, over heat. Grill buns until golden brown, about 30 seconds.

2. Heat 2 cups **Crawfish Étouffée** in a saucepan over medium-low just until warm. Place hot dogs in buns, and spoon 1/4 cup étouffée over each hot dog. If desired, top with fresh **jalapeño** slices, diced red **onion,** and diced plum **tomato.**

SERVES 8 (serving size: 1 hot dog, 1 bun, 1/4 cup étouffée) **ACTIVE** 15 min. **TOTAL** 15 min.

Crawfish Dip

CRAWFISH DIP

Cook and serve this dip in a slow cooker to keep it warm.

- 2 Tbsp. salted butter
- 1/2 cup diced green bell pepper
- 1 small yellow onion, diced (about 1 cup)
- 1/2 cup diced celery
- 3 garlic cloves, chopped
- 1 jalapeño chile, diced
- 1 tsp. kosher salt
- 1/2 tsp. black pepper
- 2 tsp. paprika
- 1/2 tsp. cayenne pepper
- 1 lb. frozen peeled crawfish tails, thawed according to package directions
- 8 oz. cream cheese, softened
- 2 cups grated extra-sharp Cheddar cheese (about 8 oz.)
- 1/4 cup heavy whipping cream
- 2 Tbsp. Creole mustard
- 1 Tbsp. Worcestershire sauce
- 2 tsp. hot sauce
- 2 Tbsp. fresh lemon juice
- 2 Tbsp. chopped fresh flat-leaf parsley
  Crackers, toasted baguette slices

1. Melt butter in a large sauté pan or skillet over medium. Add bell pepper, onion, celery, garlic, jalapeño, salt, and black pepper, and cook 6 minutes. Add paprika and cayenne pepper, and cook 1 more minute.
2. Place crawfish, cream cheese, Cheddar cheese, and cream in a 6-quart slow cooker. Stir in bell pepper mixture, Creole mustard, Worcestershire sauce, and hot sauce. Cover and cook on HIGH 45 minutes. Reduce heat to WARM. Stir in lemon juice and parsley; serve with crackers or toasted baguette slices.

SERVES 10 as an appetizer (serving size: 3/4 cup) **ACTIVE** 15 min. **TOTAL** 1 hour

SL'S STOVETOP CRAWFISH BOIL

Here's a crawfish boil that you can do at home, without any fancy equipment—all you need is a sink, stove, and big pot.

- 4 1/2 gal. water
- 2 (4-oz.) pkg. seafood boil, such as Zatarain's Crawfish, Shrimp, and Crab Boil
- 2 cups kosher salt
- 1/4 cup Creole seasoning
- 4 bay leaves
- 5 lemons, halved
- 2 garlic heads, halved crosswise
- 4 small yellow onions, halved
- 2 lb. small red potatoes, halved
- 2 large fresh artichokes
- 10 lb. live fresh crawfish, purged (ask your vendor)
- 4 ears corn, husks removed
  Creole Mayo

1. Bring 4 1/2 gallons water to a rolling boil in a 7- to 8-gallon stockpot over high. (Start early! This could take 30 to 40 minutes.) Add seafood boil, salt, Creole seasoning, bay leaves, lemons, garlic, and onions. Stir until spices are dissolved. Add potatoes and artichokes; return to a boil. Boil 20 minutes. Add crawfish, and simmer 5 minutes.
2. Cut each ear of corn into 4 pieces, and add to pot. Simmer 5 minutes. (If you lose your boil at any point, cover with a lid to return it to a simmer.)
3. Line a large sheet pan with newspaper or parchment paper. Pour mixture through a large colander, or remove crawfish and vegetables from water, using a slotted spoon. Place crawfish and vegetables on pan. Serve with Creole Mayo for dipping.

Tip: You'll know the water is seasoned perfectly when it makes your eyes water.

SERVES 6 **ACTIVE** 20 min.
TOTAL 1 hour, 20 min.

Creole Mayo

This tangy dip is a great accompaniment with the veggies in the crawfish boil.

- 1 1/2 cups mayonnaise
- 1/4 cup Creole mustard
- 2 Tbsp. fresh lemon juice
- 2 Tbsp. finely chopped chives
- 2 tsp. Creole seasoning
- 2 tsp. chopped fresh tarragon
- 2 tsp. hot sauce
- 1 tsp. kosher salt
- 1/2 tsp. black pepper
- 2 garlic cloves, finely chopped

Whisk together all ingredients. Chill 30 minutes before serving.

MAKES 2 cups (serving size: 1/4 cup)
ACTIVE 10 min. **TOTAL** 40 min.

CRAWFISH ÉTOUFFÉE

Étouffée is French for "smothered," so don't scrimp when pouring this thick Cajun stew over rice.

- 1 Tbsp. paprika
- 2 tsp. kosher salt
- 1 tsp. black pepper
- 1 tsp. dried thyme
- ½ tsp. cayenne pepper
- ½ cup vegetable oil
- 1 cup (4 oz.) all-purpose flour
- 1 poblano chile, seeds removed, diced
- 3 celery ribs, diced
- 1 medium-size yellow onion, diced
- 3 garlic cloves, chopped
- 1 jalapeño chile, seeds removed (if desired), diced
- 2 cups seafood stock
- 2 lb. frozen peeled crawfish tails, thawed and rinsed
- ¼ cup chopped fresh parsley
- 2 Tbsp. fresh lemon juice
- 1 Tbsp. Worcestershire sauce
- 2 tsp. hot sauce, plus more for serving
- 8 cups cooked white long-grain rice
- ½ cup sliced scallions, white and light green parts only

1. Stir together the first 5 ingredients in a small bowl.

2. Heat oil in a large stockpot over medium-high. Add flour, and stir well to combine. Reduce heat to medium-low, and cook, stirring, until roux is the color of caramel sauce, about 20 minutes. Add poblano, celery, and onion. Cook, stirring, until vegetables are tender, about 10 minutes. Add garlic, jalapeño, and paprika mixture. Cook 2 minutes. Gradually whisk in stock. Return to a simmer over medium-high. Stir in crawfish, parsley, lemon juice, Worcestershire sauce, and 2 teaspoons hot sauce. Cook until warm, 2 to 3 minutes. Serve with hot rice, scallions, and hot sauce.

SERVES 8 (serving size: 1 cup étouffée and 1 cup rice) **ACTIVE** 40 min. **TOTAL** 55 min.

Crawfish Étouffée

SIMPLE CRAWFISH STOCK

Don't toss those heads after the boil. They still pack deep flavor and create a rich seafood stock when simmered with vegetables and herbs.

Bring 2 pounds cooked **crawfish heads,** 6 cups water, 1 quart **chicken broth,** ½ cup dry **white wine,** 6 fresh **thyme** sprigs, 2 **celery** ribs diced, 2 **bay leaves,** and ½ yellow **onion** cut into 1-inch pieces to a boil in a stockpot over high. Reduce heat to low, and simmer 30 minutes. Strain through a colander lined with a coffee filter. Use immediately, or chill and then freeze up to 1 month.

MAKES about 9 cups **ACTIVE** 5 min. **TOTAL** 45 min.

$15 Chicken Dinners

FAST, FRESH, AND BUDGET-FRIENDLY

Southwest
Chicken Cutlet
Rice Bowl

PER
$3.65
SERVING

CAST-IRON CHICKEN PICCATA

- 4 (5- to 6-oz.) chicken cutlets
- ½ cup (2 oz.) all-purpose flour
- 1½ tsp. kosher salt
- ¼ tsp. black pepper
- 1 large egg white, lightly beaten
- 6 Tbsp. (3 oz.) salted butter, divided
- 2 Tbsp. olive oil, divided
- 1 cup reduced-sodium chicken broth
- ¼ cup fresh lemon juice
- 2 Tbsp. brined capers, drained and rinsed
- ⅓ cup chopped fresh flat-leaf parsley
  Hot cooked pasta

1. Place each chicken cutlet between two sheets of heavy-duty plastic wrap, and flatten to ¼-inch thickness, using a rolling pin or flat side of a meat mallet. Stir together flour, salt, and pepper. Dip each cutlet in egg white, and dredge in flour mixture, shaking off excess.

2. Melt 2 tablespoons butter with 1 tablespoon olive oil in a large cast-iron skillet over medium-high. Add 2 cutlets, and cook until golden brown, 2 to 3 minutes on each side. Transfer to a plate. Wipe skillet clean, and repeat process with 2 table-spoons butter and remaining 1 tablespoon olive oil and remaining 2 cutlets. Discard drippings; do not wipe skillet clean.

3. Add broth, lemon juice, and capers to skillet. Bring to a boil over high, stirring and scraping bottom of skillet to loosen browned bits. Reduce heat to medium, and simmer, whisking occasionally, 5 minutes. Whisk in remaining 2 tablespoons butter. Whisk in parsley. Spoon sauce over chicken, and serve immediately with pasta.

SERVES 4 (serving size: 1 chicken cutlet and ¼ cup sauce) **ACTIVE** 20 min. **TOTAL** 30 min.

PER $2.10 SERVING

Cast-Iron Chicken Piccata

CRISPY RAMEN-CRUSTED CHICKEN WITH ASIAN SALAD

- 1 bunch kale (about 8 oz.), stems removed, chopped (about 6 cups)
- 1 bunch cilantro, chopped (about ⅓ cup)
- 3 green onions, thinly sliced diagonally
- 1¼ cups matchstick carrots
- 3½ Tbsp. fresh lime juice (about 2 limes)
- 2 Tbsp. soy sauce
- 1 tsp. honey
- 6 Tbsp. olive oil, divided
- 2 (3-oz.) pkg. chicken-flavored instant Asian ramen noodle soup mix
- 1 tsp. ground ginger
- ¼ tsp. cayenne pepper
- 4 (5- to 6-oz.) chicken cutlets
- 2 large eggs, lightly beaten
- ½ cup dry-roasted peanuts, chopped

1. Toss together kale, cilantro, green onions, and carrots. Whisk together lime juice, soy sauce, honey, and 1 tablespoon olive oil in a small bowl; pour over kale mixture, and toss to coat. Set aside while preparing chicken, tossing occasionally.

2. Break ramen noodles into pieces. Process ramen noodles, seasoning mixtures from ramen packages, ginger, and cayenne pepper in a food processor until combined, 1 minute. Transfer mixture to a shallow dish, and set aside.

3. Place each chicken cutlet between two sheets of heavy-duty plastic wrap, and flatten to ¼-inch thickness, using a rolling pin or flat side of a meat mallet. Dip each cutlet in eggs, and dredge in ramen mixture, pressing to adhere.

4. Cook half of chicken in 2½ tablespoons hot olive oil in a large skillet over medium until golden brown and done, 2 to 3 minutes on each side. Place on a wire rack in a rimmed baking sheet, and keep warm in a 200°F oven. Repeat procedure with remaining chicken and olive oil.

5. Sprinkle peanuts over kale mixture, and serve with cutlets.

SERVES 4 (serving size: 1 chicken cutlet and 1½ cups salad) **ACTIVE** 25 min. **TOTAL** 30 min.

KICKIN' ORANGE-GLAZED CHICKEN

- **4** (5- to 6-oz.) chicken cutlets
- **1/2** tsp. kosher salt
- **1/4** tsp. black pepper
- **1** Tbsp. salted butter
- **1** Tbsp. olive oil
- **1/2** cup orange marmalade
- **4** tsp. Dijon mustard
- **1** tsp. lemon zest, plus 2 tsp. fresh lemon juice
- **1/4** tsp. red pepper flakes
  Garnish: lemon strips, lemon wedges

1. Preheat broiler. Sprinkle both sides of cutlets with salt and pepper. Melt butter with oil in a large ovenproof skillet over medium-high. Cook cutlets in butter mixture until lightly browned, 1 to 2 minutes on each side. Tilt pan; add marmalade and next 3 ingredients to drippings, and stir until combined. Spoon sauce over cutlets.
2. Broil 8 inches from heat until chicken is glazed and cooked through, about 6 minutes, turning cutlets every minute and basting with pan sauce. Spoon sauce over chicken.

Lemon-Sautéed Green Beans

Microwave 1 (12-oz.) package **fresh green beans** according to package directions for 3 minutes. Sauté beans, 1 teaspoon **lemon zest,** 1/2 teaspoon **kosher salt,** and 1/4 teaspoon black **pepper** in 2 teaspoons hot **olive oil** in a large nonstick skillet over medium-high until beans are hot and cooked crisp-tender, 2 to 3 minutes. Squeeze a lemon half over beans, and serve immediately.

SERVES 4 (serving size: 1 chicken cutlet and 3 oz. beans) **ACTIVE** 15 min. **TOTAL** 20 min.

PER $2.02 SERVING

SOUTHWEST CHICKEN CUTLET RICE BOWL

- 2 tsp. kosher salt, divided
- 1 1/2 tsp. ground cumin, divided
- 3/4 tsp. ground coriander, divided
- 1/2 tsp. black pepper, divided
- 1/8 tsp. cayenne pepper
- 4 (5- to 6-oz.) chicken cutlets
- 2 tsp. olive oil
- 2 (8.8-oz.) pkg. microwaveable long-grain white rice
- 3 Tbsp. olive oil, divided
- 1 medium poblano chile, seeds removed, chopped
- 1 small jalapeño chile, seeds removed, finely chopped
- 1/4 cup finely chopped red onion
- 1 cup fresh or frozen, thawed corn kernels
- 2 garlic cloves, minced
- 3 Tbsp. chopped fresh cilantro
- 1 tsp. lime zest plus 1 1/2 Tbsp. fresh lime juice

1. Stir together 1 teaspoon salt, 1 teaspoon cumin, 1/2 teaspoon coriander, 1/4 teaspoon black pepper, and 1/8 teaspoon cayenne pepper in a small bowl. Rub chicken cutlets with 1/2 teaspoon olive oil. Rub cutlets evenly with salt mixture. Chill 1 to 24 hours.
2. Cook rice according to package directions. Cook chicken cutlets in 1 tablespoon hot oil in a large nonstick skillet over medium-high until done and golden brown, 4 to 6 minutes on each side. Transfer to a platter, and cover with aluminum foil.
3. Add 1 tablespoon olive oil to skillet. Cook chiles and onions until tender, about 4 minutes. Sprinkle mixture with remaining 1 teaspoon salt, 1/2 teaspoon cumin, 1/4 teaspoon coriander, and 1/4 teaspoon black pepper. Add corn kernels and garlic, and cook 1 minute. Add remaining 1 tablespoon olive oil, and stir in rice; cook, stirring until thoroughly heated, about 3 minutes. Remove from heat, and stir in cilantro, lime zest, and lime juice. Serve with cooked chicken.

SERVES 4 (serving size: 1 chicken cutlet and 1 cup rice) **ACTIVE** 25 min. **TOTAL** 1 hour, 30 min.

GRILLED CHICKEN AND TOASTED COUSCOUS SALAD WITH LEMON-BUTTERMILK DRESSING

MARINADE

- 3 Tbsp. olive oil
- 2 garlic cloves, minced
- 1 Tbsp. lemon zest plus 2 tsp. fresh lemon juice
- 3 tsp. chopped fresh thyme
- 1/2 tsp. kosher salt
- 1/2 tsp. black pepper
- 4 (5- to 6-oz.) chicken cutlets

DRESSING

- 3/4 cup buttermilk
- 1/2 cup mayonnaise
- 3 Tbsp. finely chopped chives
- 1 Tbsp. fresh lemon juice
- 1 garlic clove, pressed
- 1/2 tsp. finely chopped fresh thyme
- 1/2 tsp. kosher salt
- 1/2 tsp. black pepper

COUSCOUS

- 1 cup uncooked pearl couscous
- 2 (3- x 1-inch) lemon peel strips
- 1 Tbsp. olive oil
- 2 cups water
- 1/4 tsp. kosher salt

VEGETABLES

- 1 lb. fresh asparagus, trimmed
- 2 Tbsp. olive oil, divided
- 1/2 tsp. kosher salt
- 1/4 tsp. black pepper
- 3 (1/2-inch-thick) red onion slices

1. Make Marinade: Whisk together olive oil, garlic cloves, lemon zest and juice, chopped thyme, salt, and black pepper in a small bowl. Place chicken cutlets in a 1-gallon zip-top plastic freezer bag, and add marinade. Seal bag, and turn to coat. Chill 30 minutes to 1 hour, turning occasionally. Remove chicken from bag and marinade; discard marinade.
2. Make Dressing: Whisk together buttermilk, mayonnaise, chives, lemon juice, pressed garlic clove, thyme, salt, and black pepper in a small bowl; cover and chill.
3. Make Couscous: Cook couscous and lemon peel strips in heated olive oil in a medium saucepan over medium, stirring often, until mostly golden, 7 to 8 minutes. Add water and salt; bring to a boil. Cover, reduce heat to low, and simmer until barely tender, 8 to 10 minutes. Drain and discard lemon peel strips.
4. Make Chicken and Vegetables: Coat cold cooking grate of grill with cooking spray, and place on grill. Preheat grill to medium (350° to 400°F). Toss asparagus with 1 tablespoon olive oil, and sprinkle with salt and black pepper. Brush both sides of onion slices with remaining olive oil. Grill chicken, asparagus, and onions until chicken is done and vegetables are tender and charred, about 3 minutes on each side.
5. Slice chicken; cut asparagus into 2-inch pieces, and roughly chop onions. Toss together couscous, chicken, asparagus, onions, and 1/2 cup dressing. Serve salad with remaining dressing.

SERVES 4 (serving size: 1 chicken cutlet and about 1 cup salad) **ACTIVE** 25 min. **TOTAL** 1 hour, 20 min.

PER **$3.35** SERVING

Grilled Chicken and Toasted Couscous Salad with Lemon-Buttermilk Dressing

MEET YOUR NEW FAVORITE APPETIZER...

Spinach-and-Vidalia Dip

Sweet Vidalia onions add an unexpected twist to the creamy, crowd-pleasing spinach dip.

- **3** Tbsp. (1 1/2 oz.) salted butter
- **4** cups chopped Vidalia or other sweet onions (about 2 large)
- **1** (5-oz.) pkg. fresh baby spinach, coarsely chopped
- **1** tsp. kosher salt, divided
- **1/2** tsp. black pepper, divided
- **1** (16-oz.) container sour cream
- **2** Tbsp. chopped fresh chives
  Potato chips and medley of veggies like cucumbers, radishes, and bell peppers

1. Melt butter in a large nonstick skillet over medium; add onions, and cook, stirring often, until golden and very tender, 20 to 30 minutes. Gradually add spinach, stirring just until wilted, about 1 minute. Sprinkle with 1/2 teaspoon salt and 1/4 teaspoon pepper. Remove from heat, and let stand 30 minutes.
2. Stir together onion-and-spinach mixture, sour cream, and chives in a medium bowl. Stir in the remaining 1/2 teaspoon salt and 1/4 teaspoon pepper. Cover and chill 30 minutes or up to 2 days. Serve with chips and veggies.

SERVES 12 (serving size: 1/4 cup)
ACTIVE 25 min. **TOTAL** 1 hour, 25 min.

Spice Up Your Night

LAYER BEANS, SAUSAGE, POTATOES, AND SEASONAL VEGGIES INTO ONE POT
FOR A FIX-AND-FORGET SOUP

WHITE BEAN AND CHORIZO SOUP

Fresh chorizo sausage gives this soup its vibrant red-orange hue and fiery flavor.

- 1 lb. fresh chorizo link sausage, casing removed
- 2 Tbsp. olive oil
- 1 large yellow onion, chopped (about 2 cups)
- 2 medium carrots, chopped (about 1 cup)
- ½ lb. small red potatoes, chopped
- 3 garlic cloves, minced
- 1 tsp. paprika
- 1 tsp. kosher salt
- 1 Tbsp. tomato paste
- 2 (15-oz.) cans great Northern beans, drained and rinsed
- 1 (32-oz.) container reduced-sodium chicken broth
- ½ cup fresh parsley leaves, chopped

1. Cook chorizo in a Dutch oven over medium-high, stirring constantly, until browned and crumbled, about 8 minutes. Drain well on paper towels. Wipe Dutch oven clean.
2. Heat oil in Dutch oven over medium-high. Add onions and next 5 ingredients, and sauté until tender, about 5 minutes. Stir in tomato paste, and cook 1 minute, stirring often.
3. Increase heat to high. Add beans, chicken broth, and chorizo, and bring to a boil. Reduce heat to medium-low, and simmer, stirring occasionally and skimming off any fat from top, 20 minutes. Stir in parsley, and serve immediately.

SERVES 6 (serving size: about 1⅓ cups)
ACTIVE 20 min. **TOTAL** 40 min.

TEST KITCHEN TIP
....
Choose Mexican chorizo, which cooks like ground beef when casings are removed.

THE *SL* TEST KITCHEN ACADEMY

BLONDE ONIONS
15-20 minutes

BEST FOR:
Soups, dips,
pasta sauce,
frittatas

GOLDEN ONIONS
30-40 minutes

BEST FOR:
Pizzas, salads,
bruschetta

DEEP BROWN ONIONS
45-60 minutes

BEST FOR:
Burgers, tacos,
sandwiches

3 DELICIOUS KINDS OF CARAMELIZED ONIONS

SOUTHERNERS HAVE A SAYING about things that take a while: slower than molasses running uphill in the winter. While caramelizing onions doesn't take *that* long, it does take time. To achieve the rich, browned, candy-sweet slices meant for stacking on burgers, topping on salads, and piling on baguettes, you'll need about an hour. And we think it's worth every minute. There are three kinds of caramelized onions—blonde, golden, deep brown—each with its own purpose and cooking time. Start by following our go-to technique below.

INGREDIENTS: 2 or 3 yellow onions (sliced ⅛ inch thick), canola oil (2 Tbsp. for every sliced onion)

MASTER TECHNIQUE: Place oil and onions in a large, wide pot or skillet so the moisture in the onions evaporates, instead of steams. Cook over medium-low, stirring occasionally. Resist the urge to bump up the heat, which will scorch slices.

Add a splash of water every 15 minutes to keep onions from burning and to help deglaze the brown bits.

TIP: You can use butter, but a neutral oil, like canola, is better for browning 20 minutes or more. It can go the distance without burning or breaking down.

HOW TO MAKE A CUTLET FROM A CHICKEN THIGH

Easy to prepare, quick to defrost, fast-cooking, and versatile (see recipes starting on page 102), the chicken cutlet is a busy cook's best friend. But grocery store cutlets cost more than value packs of bone-in thighs. Follow these simple steps for making your own cutlets.

Remove skin:
If your chicken thigh has skin on, pull it off. (Save that skin for frying up later as an appetizer.) Make sure to trim off any excess fat.

Find the bone:
Flip the thigh rough-side up, and locate the bone. **Use the tip of your knife to score a deep line along the bone.** Grasp one end of the bone with your free hand, and make short, scraping cuts to remove all meat from the bone.

Flatten it out:
Place the meat between two sheets of plastic wrap, and using a meat mallet or rolling pin, flatten each piece to about ½ inch in thickness.

Give It a Twirl

LIGHTEN UP THIS CREAMY FETTUCCINE WITH FRESH, SEASONAL ASPARAGUS

FETTUCCINE ALFREDO WITH ASPARAGUS

- 8 oz. uncooked fettuccine
- 1 tsp. olive oil
- 1 lb. fresh asparagus spears, trimmed and cut into 2-inch pieces
- 3/4 tsp. kosher salt
- 1/2 tsp. black pepper
- 1 tsp. lemon zest
- 2 tsp. fresh lemon juice
- 1 Tbsp. butter
- 1 Tbsp. vodka or water
- 4 garlic cloves, minced
- 2 oz. 1/3-less-fat cream cheese
- 1/4 cup fat-free milk
- 6 Tbsp. (1 1/2 oz.) grated Parmesan cheese
- 1 Tbsp. chopped fresh chives

1. Cook pasta according to package directions. Drain in a colander over a large bowl. Reserve 1/4 cup cooking water.

2. Heat a large skillet over medium-high. Add oil; swirl to coat. Add asparagus, 1/4 teaspoon of the salt, and 1/4 teaspoon of the pepper; sauté until crisp-tender, about 6 minutes. Remove from heat. Add lemon zest and juice; toss. Keep warm.

3. Melt butter in a medium saucepan over medium. Add vodka and garlic; cook 1 minute. Add cream cheese, stirring until smooth. Stir in milk, Parmesan cheese, and remaining 1/2 teaspoon salt and 1/4 teaspoon pepper. Stir in reserved cooking water, pasta, and asparagus; toss. Sprinkle with chives.

NUTRITIONAL INFORMATION *(per serving)*

CALORIES 365; FAT 11.2g (SATURATED FAT 5.9g); PROTEIN 16g; FIBER 4g; CARBOHYDRATES 50g; SODIUM 609mg

Chocolate Matzo Madness

TAKE A CRACK AT THIS SOUTHERN SPIN ON A TRADITIONAL PASSOVER TREAT

SALTED CHOCOLATE MATZO TOFFEE

- 1 **cup (8 oz.) salted butter, plus butter to grease pan**
- 4 **to 5 sheets lightly salted matzos**
- 1 **cup packed dark brown sugar**
- 1 **(12-oz.) package semisweet chocolate chips**
- 1 **cup chopped toasted pecans**
- 1/4 **tsp. Maldon sea salt, if desired**

1. Preheat oven to 350°F. Line an 18- x 12-inch rimmed baking sheet with heavy-duty aluminum foil. Grease foil with butter. Arrange matzos in prepared pan, breaking as necessary to fit and completely cover bottom.

2. Bring 1 cup butter and brown sugar to a boil in a heavy saucepan over medium, whisking occasionally. Boil, whisking constantly, 3 minutes. Carefully pour mixture over matzos; spread over matzos.

3. Bake in preheated oven until bubbly all over, 8 to 10 minutes. Carefully remove baking sheet from oven to a wire rack. Let stand 1 minute. Sprinkle chocolate chips over top; let stand until chips soften, about 2 minutes. Spread chocolate over brown sugar mixture. Sprinkle with pecans; sprinkle with salt, if desired. Let stand at room temperature 30 minutes. Chill toffee until firm, about 30 minutes. Break or cut into about 36 pieces. Store in an airtight container up to 1 week in refrigerator.

Note: We tested with Lightly Salted Streit's Matzos.

SERVES 18 (serving size: 2 pieces)
ACTIVE 15 min. **TOTAL** 1 hour, 25 min.

Community Cookbook

BUILD A BETTER LIBRARY, ONE GREAT BOOK AT A TIME

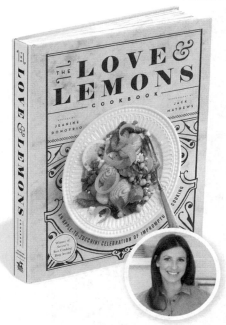

This month, vegetarians and meat-lovers alike will dig into the more than 100 fresh, seasonal recipes in the first cookbook by Love & Lemons, the popular lifestyle blog by husband-and-wife duo Jack Mathews and **Jeanine Donofrio**. This Austin-based couple has created a delicious lineup of surprising, plant-based dishes, which includes everything from avocado breakfast tacos to double chocolate zucchini muffins.

SPRING POLENTA WITH RADISHES AND GARLIC SCAPES

- 3 cups water
- 1 cup polenta
- 1 garlic clove, minced
- 2 Tbsp. extra-virgin olive oil or unsalted butter
  Sea salt and freshly ground black pepper
- 4 Tbsp. grated pecorino cheese (optional)
- 1 tsp. extra-virgin olive oil
- 12 radishes, sliced in half
- 1 cup cooked chickpeas, drained and rinsed
- 3 garlic scapes, sliced into 1-inch pieces (about 1 cup)
- 2 cups Broccolini
  Radish sprouts
  Sea salt

1. Make the polenta: In a medium saucepan, bring the 3 cups water to a boil over medium-high heat. Add a few generous pinches of salt. Gradually whisk in the polenta and bring back to a boil. Reduce the heat and continue cooking until the polenta is tender, 20 to 30 minutes, whisking often. Turn off the heat and whisk in the garlic, 2 tablespoons olive oil or butter, pinches of salt and pepper, and cheese, if using. Taste and adjust seasonings. Cover to keep warm.
2. In a large skillet, heat 1 teaspoon olive oil over medium heat. Add the radishes, chickpeas, and a pinch of salt, and sauté for 5 minutes. Stir; then add the garlic scapes and Broccolini and cook until the vegetables are tender but still have a vibrant bite, about 5 more minutes. Season with salt and pepper. Spoon the polenta into bowls; season with sea salt. Top with the vegetables and radish sprouts.

SERVES 4

MISO-BRAISED MUSTARD GREENS

- 1 tsp. white miso paste
- 1/4 cup warm water
  Several bunches of Asian mustard greens or baby bok choy, about 20 leaves
- 1 tsp. extra-virgin olive oil
- 1/2 tsp. rice wine vinegar
- 1/2 tsp. maple syrup or honey
  Toasted sesame oil, for drizzling
  Sesame seeds, for sprinkling

1. In a small bowl, whisk together the miso paste and water.
2. Trim off the rough bottoms of the mustard greens, separate the leaves, and rinse under running water. Pat dry.
3. In a large skillet, heat the oil over medium heat. Add the mustard greens and cook about 2 minutes, turning occasionally. Add half the miso water, cover, and let cook until the stems start to soften, about 2 more minutes. If the skillet is getting dry, add more miso water.
4. Add the rice wine vinegar and maple syrup, and toss. Transfer to a serving plate, drizzle with sesame oil, and sprinkle with sesame seeds.

SERVES 4 as a side

To purchase *The Love & Lemons Cookbook,* visit your local bookstore or *amazon.com.*

May

Dinner on the Half shell

THIS MONTH, OUR SPIRITED ENTERTAINING COLUMNIST SHARES EXCLUSIVELY WITH US
A FAVORITE CHAPTER FROM HER COOKBOOK *JULIA REED'S SOUTH*

I SWEAR I THINK I owe the evolution of this menu to my friend Christopher Gow and his vast offerings of silvered seashells at least as much as I do to the actual shellfish. I began collecting Christopher's magical wares in the early 1990s, when his business was called Ruzzetti and Gow and operated out of a third-floor walk-up in Manhattan's dingy West 30s. These days his partner is Jamie Creel, and their shop (now Creel and Gow) on East 70th Street is a dazzling cabinet of curiosities, but those shells are still as popular as ever. My own collection includes starfish and sea urchin candleholders, ingenious cockleshell place-card holders, burgus shell salts, and lots more specimens to sprinkle about the table.

Such gorgeous props demand a menu like this one, and to complete the look, I encrusted vases (with the help of a glue gun) with natural shells, inspired by an ancient Ralph Lauren lamp that was a gift from my generous friend Bobby Harling. This particular dinner took place in my mother's lovely dining room, and, as luck would have it, her silver pattern is Fiddle, Thread, and Shell. For the hors d'oeuvres course, we let guests help themselves to both fried and baked oysters from our combined collections of oyster plates on the sideboard. The theme continued on the outside bar, where a giant clamshell served as a wine cooler and an enormous shell-encrusted bowl (another gift from Bobby) served as a receptacle for the cocktail's citrus.

My favorite wine with oysters is always a Muscadet. We served a Chablis with the soup course. The vivid acidity of the Grüner Veltliner from Austria's Weingut Knoll (one of the most versatile wines ever) made it the perfect match for the shrimp, which contains a healthy dose of curry.

Green Goddess Soup with Jumbo Lump Crabmeat

I made the vases myself with terra-cotta pots, seashells, and a glue gun.

A SEAFOOD SUPPER

THE RECIPES

GREEN GODDESS SOUP WITH JUMBO LUMP CRABMEAT

At her popular Los Angeles dinner parties, my good friend Suzanne Rheinstein, an interior designer and New Orleans native, often serves a first course consisting of a generous scoop of jumbo lump blue crab napped with green goddess dressing. The pale green-and-white color combo is gorgeous, and the Californians, used to flaky Dungeness crab, always swoon. The first time I tasted the combo, I was struck not by the crab (which I'm blessedly used to) but by how perfect the tart, herby dressing was with the lush crabmeat. I now serve what I think of as "Suzanne's Green Goddess Crabmeat" a lot, but for this dinner, which features an embarrassment of shellfish riches, an entire serving of crab would be too much. Instead, I inverted the dish by making a soup out of green goddess ingredients and using a few lumps of crab as garnish only. Even without the crab, the soup (inspired by a recipe from another pal, Nora Etheridge) is pretty great.

SERVES 8 as a first course

- 1 medium cucumber, peeled, seeded, and roughly chopped
- 1 ripe medium avocado, peeled, pitted, and quartered
- 6 scallions, including about 1 inch of the green stem, roughly chopped (about 1 cup)
- 1/4 cup Italian parsley leaves, roughly chopped
- 1 tablespoon tarragon leaves, plus 1 tablespoon minced for garnish
- 1 tablespoon chives, roughly chopped, plus 1 tablespoon minced for garnish
- 1 cup unsalted chicken stock
- 1 cup sour cream
- 3 tablespoons fresh lemon juice
- 1 teaspoon salt
  Pinch of cayenne pepper
- 1 pound jumbo lump crabmeat

1. Place the cucumber, avocado, scallions, parsley, tarragon leaves, and chopped chives into a food processor. Process for about 10 seconds. Add the chicken stock, sour cream, lemon juice, salt, and cayenne. Process for another 10 seconds, until the mixture is smooth and well blended.

2. Pour the soup into a large bowl, cover with plastic wrap, and chill for at least 2 hours. When ready to serve, ladle into soup bowls or plates, garnish with a couple of lumps of the crabmeat, and sprinkle with the minced tarragon and minced chives.

NOTE: I like to serve this soup accompanied by thin slices of baguette brushed with melted butter, toasted, and sprinkled with sea salt. Make enough to offer with the Shrimp Malacca.

SHRIMP MALACCA WITH RICE

I found this recipe by Maurice Moore-Betty in a late-1970s issue of House & Garden *while I was still in college, and I've been making it ever since. Moore-Betty was an Irish-born author, cooking teacher, and all-around lovely man who advised many a prominent Manhattan hostess. This dish is essentially shrimp Creole with the addition of curry powder, which elevates it by a surprising degree. Serve over rice, accompanied by a simple green salad.*

SERVES 8

- 1/3 cup vegetable or canola oil
- 2 medium yellow onions, finely diced
- 1 large green bell pepper, seeded, stemmed, and finely diced
- 2 celery ribs, peeled and diced (about 1/2 cup)
- 1 16-ounce can whole peeled Italian plum tomatoes
- 1 cup tomato puree
  Generous pinch of cayenne pepper
  Generous pinch of dried basil
- 2 garlic cloves, mashed with 1 teaspoon kosher salt
- 2 bay leaves
  Salt and freshly ground black pepper
- 2 tablespoons curry powder
  Boxed or canned seafood stock. (If available, use homemade shrimp stock.)
- 3 pounds (36 to 40 count) shrimp, peeled
  Cooked white rice for serving

Justine's Pineapple-Mint Ice Cream

1. Heat the vegetable oil over medium in a large heavy saucepan. Add the onions, bell pepper, and celery, and cook until soft, stirring occasionally.
2. Add the tomatoes, tomato puree, cayenne, basil, garlic, bay leaves, and salt and black pepper to taste. Bring to a boil over high, and add the curry powder. Turn down the heat, and simmer the mixture, covered, for about 25 minutes. If the sauce seems too thick, thin it with a little seafood stock or water. Add the shrimp, and simmer for about 10 minutes, until just cooked through. Remove the bay leaves.

3. Serve over cooked white rice. (I love Uncle Ben's Original Converted rice.)
Recipe adapted from Julia Reed's South

JUSTINE'S PINEAPPLE-MINT ICE CREAM

Justine's, the Memphis restaurant housed in an ivy-covered 19th-century mansion on the banks of the Mississippi River, was the first "fine dining" restaurant in which I ever ate. Long before anyone had ever heard the phrase "farm to table," the garden at Justine's provided both fresh produce and old roses, and the food was so good we made the two-and-a-half-hour trek north from Greenville, Mississippi, with astonishing frequency. Famous for its buttery Crabmeat Justine, the restaurant always featured at least one or two homemade ice creams for dessert, often served in scoops piled high in silver bowls on the antique sideboards.

MAKES about 3 quarts **SERVES** 10 to 12

1¼	cups sugar
1¼	cups water
2	cups lightly packed mint leaves
½	cup light corn syrup
2	cups canned crushed pineapple in its own juice
1½	cups canned pineapple juice
2	cups whole milk
2	cups heavy cream
¼	cup white crème de menthe
1	cup fresh lemon juice Shortbread cookies for garnish

1. Combine the sugar and water in a medium saucepan, and bring to a boil over medium-high, cooking until the sugar has dissolved. Boil without stirring for about 10 minutes, until it reaches the soft-ball stage (234° to 240°F on a candy thermometer), when a drop forms a soft ball in a cup of cold water. Stir in the mint, and simmer over medium for 10 minutes more. Remove from the heat, and let cool.

2. Pour the mint syrup into a blender, and puree. Strain into a large bowl. Stir in the corn syrup.

3. Rinse the blender, add the pineapple and pineapple juice, and puree. Add the pineapple puree to the mint syrup mixture along with the milk, cream, crème de menthe, and lemon juice.

4. Chill for at least 4 hours or overnight. (In a pinch, I put it in the freezer for an hour.) Transfer the chilled mixture to an ice-cream maker, and freeze according to the manufacturer's directions.

5. Scrape the ice cream into a large bowl. Cover with plastic wrap, and place in the freezer until ready to serve. When ready to serve, scoop into dessert bowls or cups, and garnish with shortbread cookies.

Get your copy at *amazon.com* **or follow @juliaevansreed on Instagram to find out when she will be in your area for a book signing.**

Home for Mother's Day

BIRMINGHAM CHEF **JOHN HALL** OWES HIS CULINARY SUCCESS TO THE WOMEN IN HIS FAMILY.
THIS HOLIDAY, HE CELEBRATES WITH A SPECIAL HOMEMADE BRUNCH.

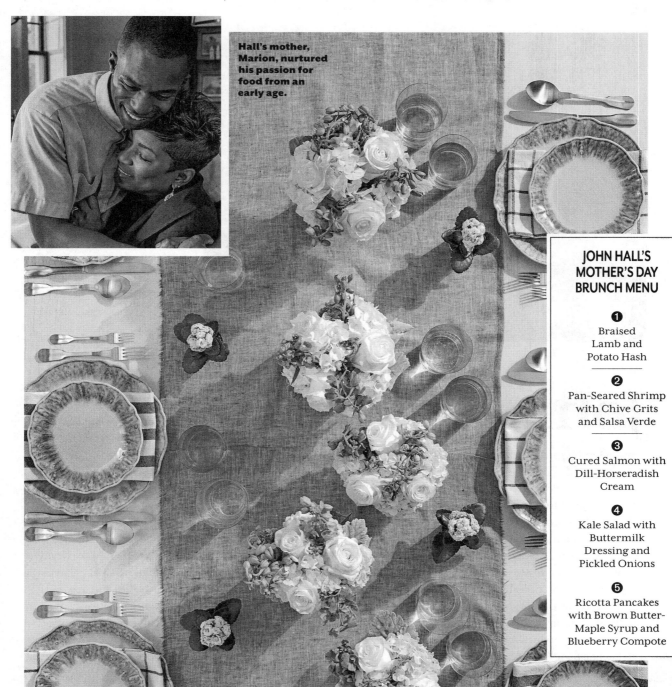

Hall's mother, Marion, nurtured his passion for food from an early age.

JOHN HALL'S MOTHER'S DAY BRUNCH MENU

❶
Braised
Lamb and
Potato Hash

❷
Pan-Seared Shrimp
with Chive Grits
and Salsa Verde

❸
Cured Salmon with
Dill-Horseradish
Cream

❹
Kale Salad with
Buttermilk
Dressing and
Pickled Onions

❺
Ricotta Pancakes
with Brown Butter-
Maple Syrup and
Blueberry Compote

His grandmother Louellen Wilkins (pictured above) taught Hall how to cook with the seasons.

John Hall's

Birmingham pizzeria, Post Office Pies, is a favorite name to drop when describing the city's cultural renaissance. Mentioned in national travel magazines and "best-of" lists for its wood-fired pies, house-made meatballs, and seasonal salads, many credit its success to John's prior experience cooking in the lauded New York kitchens of Gramercy Tavern, Momofuku Ssäm Bar, and Per Se.

But Hall will tell you the real credit goes to his mother and grandmother. These matriarchs not only nurtured his early excitement and curiosity for food but also taught him the skills he needed to succeed in those major-league line-cooking gigs, which eventually led him to opening his own kitchen doors at just 32 years old.

Hall grew up down the street from where his restaurant sits in Birmingham's Avondale neighborhood, then known more as a working-class community than the trendy, restaurant-rich area it is today.

As a kid, he was enthralled with the vegetables and herbs his grandmother Louellen Wilkins tended in her small garden and how they manifested on the family's table. Peppers, tomatoes, okra, collard greens, rosemary—anything she could grow herself, she did. "This was way before all the farm-to-table hoopla," says Hall. "She cooked with the seasons, and she pickled and canned damn near everything. She really embodied that special Southern spirit." Cooking together, Wilkins taught her grandson the fundamentals: how to work clean in the kitchen; how to learn from his mistakes; and how to enjoy the process even when it gets frustrating.

As he was growing up, his mother, Marion, a single mom with a full-time job and a shoestring budget, made sure there was always a home-cooked weeknight meal on the table for Hall and his two brothers. But he always looked forward to the weekends when he would help flip pancakes on Saturdays and set out soul food spreads on Sundays. "Our family meals were geared around comfort in good times and bad," he says. "That was the thing that made me interested in cooking: Food brought people together and made them happy."

Marion recognized the joy that putting dinner on the table brought Hall and recalled the day she asked her son if he wanted to be a cook. He replied, "No, Mom. A chef."

After high school, Hall went on to culinary training in Charleston and Rhode Island and cooked abroad in Luxembourg. He built up his résumé in Birmingham with chef Frank Stitt, then moved on to New York. Between working rigorous shifts, he ran a side business called Insomnia Pizza out of his tiny Brooklyn apartment, making and delivering late-night pies on his bike.

Then, in 2013, the opportunity arose for Hall to start a restaurant of his own, one not just in Birmingham but in his old neighborhood. This meant being closer to his family—especially his grandmother. He could have opened a hipper spot with a tasting menu and the requisite white subway tile, but instead he made the decision to plant a local pizza joint inspired by the ones he saw in Brooklyn. "It doesn't matter who you are or where you come from," Hall says. "Everyone loves pizza."

He moved into the house next door to Louellen and began remodeling the old vacant post office down the street, which inspired the restaurant's name. When he wasn't overseeing construction of the kitchen, he mowed his grandmother's lawn.

As soon as Post Office Pies opened in 2014, customers crowded in front of the restaurant's colorful, 10-foot-high chalkboard menu, with lines spilling beyond the front doors.

Sadly, Louellen passed away just a month before the restaurant opened. Knowing that her heartfelt approach meant cooking done right, Hall still prepares everything the way she and his mother taught him, from the scratch-made tomato sauce to the market salads with locally grown greens.

And the lessons Marion and Louellen passed down to him are apparent in more than just the tomato sauce. Hall's restaurant has become a community center where everyone is welcome to take a seat. It's a place where watching the game with a beer doesn't clash with the artfully arranged beet salad or basil-topped Margherita pizza; most of all, it's a hometown gem brimming with homegrown love. "I use what they taught me as guideposts," he says. "To open a place where I grew up means everything to me."

CURED SALMON WITH DILL-HORSERADISH CREAM
"People don't think salmon is a Southern thing, but my mom made salmon croquettes every Sunday before church."

KALE SALAD WITH BUTTERMILK DRESSING
"My grandmother always had a bottle of buttermilk in the fridge, and I love how it adds acidity and creaminess to this dressing."

BRAISED LAMB AND POTATO HASH

Active 30 min. - Total 4 hours, 45 min.

SERVES 4

- 3 Tbsp. vegetable oil
- 4 lamb shanks (about 14 oz. each), trimmed
- 1 Tbsp. plus ½ tsp. kosher salt
- 1¼ tsp. black pepper, divided
- 1 yellow onion, quartered
- 1 large carrot, cut into 2-inch pieces
- 4 garlic cloves, smashed
- 1 cup dry red wine
- 1 (14.5-oz.) can crushed tomatoes
- 1½ cups chicken broth
- ¼ cup chopped fresh flat-leaf parsley
  Potato Hash (recipe follows)

1. Preheat oven to 300°F. Heat oil in a large roasting pan over medium-high. Season lamb with 1 tablespoon salt and 1 teaspoon pepper. Brown lamb in hot oil, 5 to 7 minutes on each side. Remove from pan. Add onion, carrot, and garlic cloves. Cook until slightly softened, 5 to 6 minutes. Add wine; cook 2 minutes, stirring and scraping bottom of pan. Stir in tomatoes and broth; cook 2 minutes. Return lamb to pan; bring to a boil. Place parchment paper directly on lamb; cover pan tightly with aluminum foil.
2. Bake at 300°F for 3 ½ hours. Remove foil, and bake until meat falls off the bone or when a meat thermometer inserted in thickest portion registers 200°F, about 30 more minutes, turning halfway through.
3. Transfer lamb to a platter; cover with foil. Strain cooking liquid into a medium saucepan; discard solids. Add remaining ½ teaspoon salt and ¼ teaspoon pepper, and cook over medium-high until reduced to about 3 cups, 5 to 7 minutes. Spoon 1 cup sauce over lamb, and serve with remaining sauce. Top with parsley, and serve with Potato Hash.

BRAISED LAMB WITH POTATO HASH

"I love braises for brunch. They're so easy. You can make one ahead of time and warm it up right beforehand. The potato hash reminds me of the classic hash browns Mom used to make for breakfast."

Potato Hash

Active 30 min. - Total 1 hour

SERVES 4

- 1 cup crème fraîche or sour cream
- 2 Tbsp. water
- 1 tsp. lemon zest plus 1 tsp. fresh lemon juice (1 lemon)
- 2½ tsp. kosher salt, divided
- ¾ tsp. black pepper, divided
- 1½ lb. Yukon Gold potatoes, cut into ½-inch dice
- 5 Tbsp. olive oil, divided
- 1 large yellow onion, thinly sliced
- 1 red bell pepper, cut into ½-inch dice
- 1 Tbsp. roughly chopped fresh flat-leaf parsley

1. Whisk together first 3 ingredients, ½ teaspoon salt, and ½ teaspoon pepper. Set in fridge to chill.
2. Preheat the oven to 325°F. Place potatoes on baking sheet; add 1 tablespoon oil and ¾ teaspoon salt, and toss to coat.
3. Bake in preheated oven, about 30 minutes, stirring once halfway through.

4. Heat a large cast-iron skillet over medium. Add 1 tablespoon oil; swirl to coat. Add onion and 1/2 teaspoon salt, and cook, stirring, about 5 minutes. Add bell pepper, and cook, stirring, 5 minutes. Remove onion and bell pepper.

5. Increase heat to medium-high. Add remaining 3 tablespoons oil to skillet. Add potatoes; cook until golden brown, 4 minutes. Stir and cook 2 more minutes. Add bell pepper mixture, remaining 3/4 teaspoon salt, and 1/4 teaspoon pepper, and cook 1 minute. Remove from heat; stir in chopped parsley. Serve with crème fraîche mixture.

KALE SALAD WITH BUTTERMILK DRESSING AND PICKLED ONIONS

Active 20 min. - Total 1 hour, 10 min.

SERVES 6

- 1 cup water
- 1 Tbsp. granulated sugar
- 1/2 cup plus 1 Tbsp. apple cider vinegar, divided
- 2 1/4 tsp. kosher salt, divided
- 1 red onion, thinly sliced
- 1 small red beet, sliced into 4 rounds
- 1/2 cup buttermilk
- 1/3 cup mayonnaise
- 2 Tbsp. olive oil
- 1 Tbsp. chopped fresh flat-leaf parsley
- 1 Tbsp. chopped chives
- 1 small garlic clove, minced
- 1/4 tsp. black pepper
- 1 bunch (about 12 oz.) curly kale, stems removed, torn into bite-size pieces
- 3 hard-cooked eggs, each cut into 8 pieces
  Whole parsley leaves, chopped chives, Buttery French Bread Croutons (recipe follows)

1. Bring water, sugar, 1/2 cup vinegar, and 1 1/2 teaspoons salt to a boil in a small saucepan over high. Boil, whisking until sugar and salt dissolve, about 1 minute. Remove from heat.

2. Place onions and beets in a glass bowl; add vinegar mixture. Let stand at room temperature 1 hour. Drain and serve, or chill up to 2 weeks.

3. Whisk together buttermilk, mayonnaise, and olive oil in a bowl until smooth. Whisk in parsley, chives, garlic, and remaining 1 tablespoon vinegar. Stir in pepper and remaining 3/4 teaspoon salt.

4. Toss together kale, onion mixture, and 1/2 cup dressing. Top with eggs, parsley, chives, and croutons. Serve with remaining dressing.

Buttery French Bread Croutons

Active 5 min. - Total 30 min.

MAKES ABOUT 5 CUPS

Preheat oven to 350°F. Combine 5 cups 1-inch cubed **French bread** (about 5 ounces), 3 tablespoons melted salted **butter,** and 1/2 teaspoon **kosher salt.** Bake in preheated oven until golden, about 15 minutes. Let cool completely.

CURED SALMON WITH DILL-HORSE-RADISH CREAM

Active 15 min. - Total 36 hours, 15 min.

SERVES 6

- 2 cups kosher salt
- 1 cup granulated sugar
- 1 Tbsp. lemon zest
- 1 Tbsp. lime zest
- 1 Tbsp. orange zest
- 1 (2-lb.) skin-on salmon fillet (about 1 inch thick)
  Dill-Horseradish Cream (recipe follows)
  Sourdough bread slices, toasted

1. Stir together first 5 ingredients in a medium bowl. Rub half of mixture (about 1 1/2 cups) on both sides of salmon. Place in a 13- x 9-inch baking dish, skin side down, and cover flesh of salmon with remaining salt mixture.

Cover with plastic wrap, and chill 36 hours.

2. Rinse salmon under cold water. Pat dry, and remove and discard skin. Thinly slice salmon, and serve with Dill-Horseradish Cream and toasted sourdough bread slices.

Dill-Horseradish Cream

Active 5 min. - Total 5 min.

MAKES 1¼ CUPS

- 1 cup sour cream
- 2 Tbsp. fresh dill, finely chopped
- 1 tsp. lemon zest plus 1 1/2 Tbsp. fresh lemon juice (about 1 lemon)
- 1 1/2 Tbsp. prepared horseradish
- 2 tsp. granulated sugar
- 1/2 tsp. kosher salt
- 1/2 tsp. black pepper

Whisk together all ingredients in a bowl. Serve immediately, or refrigerate up to 48 hours.

PAN-SEARED SHRIMP WITH CHIVE GRITS AND SALSA VERDE

Active 25 min. - Total 40 min.

SERVES 6

- 3 cups water
- 1 cup whole milk
- 3 tsp. kosher salt, divided
- 1 cup yellow stone-ground grits
- 6 Tbsp. salted butter, divided
- 2 lb. jumbo raw shrimp, peeled and deveined, divided
- 1/2 tsp. black pepper, divided
- 1 Tbsp. lemon juice, divided
- 2 Tbsp. chopped chives
- 1 pt. cherry tomatoes, halved
  Salsa Verde (recipe follows)

1. Bring 3 cups water, milk, and 2 teaspoons salt to a boil in a large heavy saucepan over high. Whisk in grits, and cook, whisking constantly, 45 seconds, scraping bottom and sides as needed. Return to a boil; cover and reduce heat to medium-low. Cook grits until tender, 20 to 25 minutes. (For a looser texture, whisk in 2 to 4 tablespoons water halfway through cooking.)
2. Meanwhile, melt 2 tablespoons butter in a large skillet over medium-high. Add half of the shrimp, 1/2 teaspoon salt, and 1/4 teaspoon pepper. Sauté until shrimp are almost pink, 5 to 6 minutes. Toss with 1/2 tablespoon lemon juice, and transfer to a plate. Repeat with 2 tablespoons butter and remaining shrimp, salt, pepper, and lemon juice.
3. Add chives and remaining 2 tablespoons butter to grits. Top with shrimp, tomatoes, and Salsa Verde.

Salsa Verde

Active 10 min. - Total 30 min.

MAKES 1 CUP

- 1 cup roughly chopped fresh flat-leaf parsley leaves and small stems
- 1 cup roughly chopped fresh cilantro leaves and small stems
- 1 cup roughly chopped fresh basil leaves
- 3/4 tsp. kosher salt
- 1/4 tsp. red chile flakes
- 2 garlic cloves
- 1 Tbsp. lemon zest plus 2 Tbsp. fresh lemon juice, divided
- 1/2 cup olive oil

Pulse first 6 ingredients plus 1 tablespoon lemon zest in a food processor until roughly chopped. With processor running, pour olive oil through food chute, until smooth. Transfer to a bowl; let stand 20 minutes. Before serving, stir in lemon juice.

RICOTTA PANCAKES WITH BROWN BUTTER-MAPLE SYRUP AND BLUEBERRY COMPOTE

Active 25 min. - Total 40 min.

SERVES 4

- 1 1/2 cups (6 oz.) all-purpose flour
- 2 Tbsp. granulated sugar
- 1 tsp. baking soda
- 1/2 tsp. table salt
- 1 1/2 cups buttermilk
- 2 large eggs, separated
- 1 Tbsp. lemon zest
- 1/3 cup whole milk ricotta cheese
  Butter for greasing griddle
- 4 oz. (1/2 cup) salted butter, diced
- 1/4 cup maple syrup
  Blueberry Compote (recipe follows)

1. Prepare Pancakes: Stir together first 4 ingredients in a large bowl. Whisk buttermilk, egg yolks, and zest in a medium bowl. Stir buttermilk mixture into flour mixture. Gently stir in ricotta cheese.
2. Beat egg whites at high speed with an electric mixer until soft peaks form. Gently fold egg whites into batter.
3. Heat a nonstick griddle or 12-inch nonstick skillet over medium. When hot (350°F), coat lightly with butter. Drop batter by 1/2 cupfuls onto griddle, and cook until pancakes are browned on the bottom and edges begin to look dry, about 4 minutes. Turn with a wide spatula, and cook until set in the middle, about 4 more minutes. Wipe griddle clean; coat with more butter, and repeat with remaining batter. Keep warm in a single layer on a baking sheet in a 200°F oven for up to 15 minutes.
4. Prepare Brown Butter-Maple Syrup: Heat 1/2 cup butter in a small saucepan over medium, stirring often, about 10 minutes. (The butter will foam; when the foam subsides, little brown flakes will appear.) Remove from heat, and whisk in maple syrup. Serve with pancakes and Blueberry Compote.

Blueberry Compote

Active 10 min. - Total 20 min.

MAKES 1¾ CUPS

- 3 cups fresh blueberries (about 14 oz.)
- 1/4 cup granulated sugar
- 1 tsp. lemon zest plus 1 Tbsp. fresh lemon juice (about 1 lemon)
- 1 Tbsp. water

Combine ingredients in a small saucepan; bring to a boil over medium-high. Boil, stirring often, until blueberries soften, 8 to 10 minutes. Serve warm.

PAN-SEARED SHRIMP WITH CHIVE GRITS AND SALSA VERDE

"My mom made shrimp and grits way before it became such an overwhelmingly popular dish. Here, it's made her way but I added a bright, herbaceous salsa verde, which I learned from my days at Gramercy Tavern."

RICOTTA PANCAKES WITH BROWN BUTTER-MAPLE SYRUP AND BLUEBERRY COMPOTE

"Pancakes were a Saturday staple for us growing up. I elevated these a bit by using ricotta for a fluffier, richer pancake. I also infused the syrup with nutty brown butter."

Sweet Sensations

SLICED, DICED, OR STRAIGHT FROM THE PATCH, OUR FAVORITE SPRINGTIME FRUIT IS RIPE FOR THE PICKING

JUICY, PLUMP STRAWBERRIES are what Mother Nature serves at spring's coming out party. When allowed to ripen fully in the field under the sparkling sun, strawberries reward our patience for waiting on their arrival. They lure us with their perfume and collapse into sweet pulp in our mouths. It's tempting to buy a box of the enormous berries that flood the produce aisle during winter, but the out-of-season picks make promises they can't keep. They might be brightly colored, but they are often as hard and tasteless as pebbles. Strawberries harvested before they ripen might turn a bit more red after they are picked, but they will never get any sweeter. The key to the fruit's deliciousness is time in the warm fields to ripen from cap to tip and develop its unmistakable scent. Aroma, not color, is a sure sign of good flavor, so follow your nose to find tasty berries.

Beyond buying them by the flat at farmers' markets and roadside stands, strawberries are easy pickings for most Southerners at a local pick-your-own berry patch. With a gentle tug, the berries slip right off the plants and into a waiting pail—or into your mouth. It's been suggested that when a preschool class invades a patch for their very first picking, the farmer would be wise to weigh the children before and after, instead of their buckets. Who can blame the eager eaters? No recipe, not even shortcake, can beat a candy-sweet berry still warm from the sun. Anyone who emerges from a patch without a strawberry-stained smile has missed out.

It's easy to grow strawberries at home in the South, from an entire garden to a little patio pot. When planted in a sunny, fertile spot, these perennials produce more plants and berries each year without your having to do a thing besides wait and watch.

We call strawberries "berries," of course, but actually they aren't berries, because they wear their seeds on the outside. Strawberries are the only fruit to do so, and each one sports around 200 tiny golden seeds, like a bedazzled party dress. To put an even finer point on this curious characteristic, each strawberry seed is technically a separate fruit, botanically speaking.

Peak season for strawberries is fleeting, only three or four weeks in most cases, so feast while you can. Eat the delectable berries. Preserve any overripe berries. Pickle any underripe berries. Then eat more delicious ones, as many as you can hold. It'll be awhile before the chance comes around again.

Mini Strawberry Tarts

MINI STRAWBERRY TARTS

Active 30 min. - Total 5 hours, 15 min., including 4 hours, 30 min. chilling

SERVES 8

- 1 cup (4.5 oz.) all-purpose flour
- 1/3 cup powdered sugar
- 1/4 cup chopped pistachios
- 6 Tbsp. (3 oz.) salted butter, cubed
- 1 (8-oz.) package cream cheese, softened
- 2 tsp. lemon zest plus 1 Tbsp. fresh juice (1 lemon)
- 1/2 cup granulated sugar
- 1 cup heavy whipping cream, whipped
- 2 cups sliced fresh strawberries
- 1 Tbsp. granulated sugar

1. Preheat oven to 350°F. Lightly grease 8 (3 1/2-inch) round, 1-inch-deep mini fluted tart pans with removable rims, and place on a large rimmed baking sheet. Process the flour, powdered sugar, and pistachios in a food processor until nuts are finely ground, about 1 minute. Add the cubed butter to processor, and pulse 6 to 8 times or until mixture resembles coarse meal. Press about 4 1/2 tablespoons of the flour mixture on bottom and up sides of each tart pan.

2. Bake at 350°F until lightly browned, 15 to 20 minutes. Remove tart pans to a wire rack, and cool completely (about 30 minutes).

3. Beat the cream cheese with an electric mixer at medium speed until smooth. Add the lemon zest, lemon juice, and 1/2 cup granulated sugar, and beat until well blended. Gently fold the whipped cream into cream cheese mixture until incorporated. Spoon about 5 tablespoons of the cream cheese mixture into each tart shell. Cover tarts with plastic wrap, and chill 4 to 24 hours.

4. Toss together the sliced strawberries and 1 tablespoon granulated sugar, and spoon on tarts just before serving.

Strawberry Dream Cake, page 126

Tangy Strawberry Barbecue Sauce, page 127

Grilled Chicken Cutlets with Strawberry Salsa, page 126

Strawberry Salad with Warm Goat Cheese Croutons, page 127

Strawberry-Poppy Seed Vinaigrette, page 127

STRAWBERRY DREAM CAKE

Active 30 min. - Total 2 hours, 10 min.

SERVES 12

CAKE LAYERS
Shortening
Flour for pans
1 cup (8 oz.) salted butter, softened
2 cups granulated sugar
4 large eggs, separated
3 cups (about 12 oz.) all-purpose flour
1 Tbsp. baking powder
1/4 tsp. table salt
1 cup whole milk
1 tsp. vanilla extract
1/2 tsp. almond extract
2 (16-oz.) containers fresh strawberries

DREAMY WHIPPED FROSTING
1 (8-oz.) container mascarpone cheese, softened
2/3 cup granulated sugar, divided
2 cups heavy whipping cream
1/2 tsp. vanilla extract
1/2 tsp. almond extract

1. Make the Cake Layers: Preheat oven to 350°F. Grease, with shortening, and flour 2 (9-inch) round, 2-inch-deep cake pans. Beat the butter with a heavy-duty stand mixer at medium speed until fluffy; gradually add the sugar, beating well. Add the egg yolks, 1 at a time, beating just until blended after each addition.

2. Whisk together the flour, baking powder, and salt; add to butter mixture alternately with milk, beginning and ending with flour mixture. Beat at low speed just until blended after each addition. Stir in the vanilla and almond extracts.

3. Beat the egg whites at high speed with an electric mixer until stiff peaks form. Fold about one-third of the egg whites into batter; fold in remaining egg whites in 2 batches. Spoon batter into prepared cake pans.

4. Bake at 350°F until a wooden pick inserted in center comes out clean, 28 to 32 minutes. Cool in pans on a wire rack 10 minutes; remove from pans, and cool completely on wire rack, about 1 hour.

5. Meanwhile, cut a thin slice from stem end of each of 20 to 25 whole strawberries to form a flat base; set strawberries aside.

6. Make the Dreamy Whipped Frosting: Gently stir together the mascarpone cheese and 1/3 cup sugar in a medium bowl. Beat whipping cream and vanilla and almond extracts with an electric mixer at medium speed until foamy; increase speed to medium-high, and slowly add remaining 1/3 cup sugar, beating until stiff peaks form. Fold one-third of the whipped cream mixture into cheese mixture; gently fold in remaining whipped cream mixture in 2 batches.

7. Place 1 cooled cake layer on a cake plate or serving platter; spread top with 3/4 cup of the frosting. Working from the outer edge of cake layer toward middle, place strawberries, flat base sides down and pointed tops up, on top of frosted bottom layer.

8. Spoon about 1 1/2 cups frosting into a zip-top plastic freezer bag; snip 1 corner to make a small hole. Pipe frosting between strawberries, filling in spaces completely. Gently spread about 3/4 cup of the frosting on top of berries.

9. Place second cake layer on berry layer; spread remaining frosting over top and sides of cake. Garnish with whole and sliced strawberries, if desired.

GRILLED CHICKEN CUTLETS WITH STRAWBERRY SALSA

Active 20 min. - Total 1 hour, including salsa

SERVES 6

We also love to drizzle Tangy Strawberry Barbecue Sauce (page 127) over the chicken.

1 (6-oz.) can pineapple juice (about 3/4 cup)
2 Tbsp. apple cider vinegar
2 Tbsp. olive oil
1 Tbsp. ground cumin
1 tsp. ground ancho chile pepper
1 1/2 tsp. kosher salt
1/2 tsp. black pepper
2 lb. chicken breast cutlets
Strawberry Salsa (recipe follows)

1. Whisk together the pineapple juice, vinegar, oil, cumin, ground ancho chile, salt, and pepper. Place the chicken cutlets in a large zip-top plastic freezer bag; pour marinade over chicken, turning to coat. Seal bag, and chill 30 minutes. Remove chicken from marinade, discarding marinade. Pat chicken dry.

2. Coat cold cooking grate of grill with cooking spray, and place on grill. Preheat grill to 350° to 400°F (medium-high). Place chicken on grate, and grill cutlets until grill marks appear and cutlets are done, 4 to 5 minutes on each side. Serve with Strawberry Salsa.

SEASONAL KNOW-HOW

EAT SOME NOW, SAVE SOME FOR LATER

STORING

Ripe berries taste best when stored at room temperature up to two days; they keep five to seven days when placed in the fridge crisper drawer. Remove berries from their original containers, and arrange in a single layer on a tray or plate lined with paper towels. Discard bad berries daily because mold spreads like wildfire.

WASHING

Strawberries soak up water like small sponges, and wet berries will quickly turn mushy; wash them right before using under cool running water, and then pat dry. Remove the caps after washing.

FREEZING

To keep whole frozen strawberries separated, spread washed, capped, and dried berries in a single layer on a baking sheet or other shallow container that will fit on your freezer shelf. Once they're frozen solid, transfer them into freezer bags or other airtight containers, and keep stored in the freezer. This allows you to pull out as many berries as needed rather than having to thaw an entire bag.

Strawberry Salsa

Active 10 min. - Total 10 min.

MAKES 3 CUPS

Toss together 2 cups diced fresh **strawberries**, 2 thinly sliced **scallions**, 1/2 cup thinly sliced **baby radishes**, 2 Tbsp. finely chopped **chives**, 2 Tbsp. fresh **lime juice**, 1/2 tsp. **kosher salt**, and 1/4 tsp. **black pepper** in a bowl. Gently toss in 1 diced ripe **avocado** just before serving.

Tangy Strawberry Barbecue Sauce

Active 10 min. - Total 10 min.

MAKES 3 CUPS

Process 4 cups sliced fresh **strawberries**, 1/2 cup **chili sauce**, 2 Tbsp. **apple cider vinegar**, 2 Tbsp. **Worcestershire sauce**, 1/2 tsp. **lemon zest** plus 2 Tbsp. fresh **juice** (about 1 lemon), 1 large minced **garlic clove**, 1 Tbsp. **light brown sugar**, 1/2 tsp. **kosher salt**, and 1/2 tsp. **cayenne pepper** in a food processor until smooth, 15 to 20 seconds.

STRAWBERRY SALAD WITH WARM GOAT CHEESE CROUTONS

Active 20 min. - Total 50 min., including vinaigrette

SERVES 6

- 2 (4-oz.) goat cheese logs
- 1/3 cup (about 1 oz.) all-purpose flour
- 1 large egg
- 2 Tbsp. whole milk
- 1/2 cup panko (Japanese-style breadcrumbs)
- 1/2 tsp. kosher salt
- 1/4 tsp. black pepper
- 1/4 cup vegetable oil
- 5 oz. mixed baby greens
- 1 1/2 cups sliced fresh strawberries
- 1 cucumber, peeled, halved lengthwise, seeds removed, cut crosswise into 1/2-inch slices
- 1/4 red onion, thinly sliced

**Strawberry-Poppy Seed Vinaigrette (recipe follows)
Garnish: dill sprigs**

1. Cut each goat cheese log into 4 rounds. Gently press each round to 1/2-inch thickness on a baking sheet, and freeze 20 minutes.
2. Place the flour in a small bowl. Whisk together the egg and milk in a second small bowl. Combine the panko, salt, and pepper in a third small bowl. Dredge goat cheese rounds in flour, dip in egg mixture, and dredge in panko mixture until coated. Place on a plate, and chill until all goat cheese rounds are breaded.
3. Heat the vegetable oil in a large skillet over medium until hot. Add goat cheese rounds to skillet, and cook until golden brown on each side, 3 to 4 minutes total. Remove to a paper towel-lined plate.
4. To serve, arrange salad greens on a serving platter; top with strawberries, cucumber, onion, and goat cheese croutons. Drizzle with vinaigrette, and garnish with dill sprigs.

Strawberry-Poppy Seed Vinaigrette

Active 5 min. - Total 20 min.

MAKES 1½ CUPS

Toss together 1 cup quartered fresh **strawberries**, 2 Tbsp. **granulated sugar**, 5 Tbsp. **white wine vinegar**, 1 tsp. **kosher salt**, and 1/4 tsp. **black pepper** in a bowl; let stand 15 minutes. Transfer the strawberry mixture to a blender, and process until smooth, about 30 seconds. Turn blender on low, and gradually add 1/3 cup **extra virgin olive oil** in a slow, steady stream. Return mixture to bowl, and whisk in 1 Tbsp. **poppy seeds**. Whisk vinaigrette just before serving.

STRAWBERRY BISCUITS

Active 20 min. - Total 45 min.

SERVES 12

- 1/2 cup (4 oz.) salted butter, frozen
- 2 1/2 cups (11 oz.) self-rising flour
- 1/4 cup granulated sugar
- 1/4 tsp. baking powder
- 1 cup chilled heavy whipping cream
- 1 cup chopped fresh strawberries
- 2 Tbsp. salted butter, melted Basil-Honey Butter (recipe follows)

1. Preheat the oven to 475°F. Line a rimmed baking sheet with parchment paper. Grate the frozen butter using large holes of a box grater. Toss together grated butter, flour, sugar, and baking powder in a large bowl. Chill 10 minutes.
2. Make a well in the center of the butter mixture. Add the heavy cream, and stir 10 times. Add the strawberries, and stir 5 times. (Dough will be loose and flaky.)
3. Turn the dough out onto a lightly floured surface, and gently knead 3 to 4 times. Lightly sprinkle flour over top of dough. Using a lightly floured rolling pin, roll dough into a 3/4-inch-thick rectangle (about 9 x 5 inches). Starting at 1 short end, fold dough in half so short ends meet. Repeat rolling and folding procedure 4 more times.
4. Roll the dough to 1-inch thickness. Cut dough with a floured 2 1/2-inch round cutter, and place on prepared baking sheet, rerolling dough scraps and flouring as needed.
5. Bake at 475°F until lightly browned, about 15 minutes. Brush warm biscuits with melted salted butter, and serve with Basil-Honey Butter.

BASIL-HONEY BUTTER

Active 5 min. - Total 5 min.

MAKES ¼ CUPS

Stir together 1/2 cup (4 oz.) **salted butter**, softened; 2 Tbsp. chopped fresh **basil;** 1 tsp. **lime zest;** and 1 tsp. **honey.** Serve with Strawberry Biscuits.

Your Spring Vegetable Cookbook

FRESH AND FABULOUS RECIPES FOR THE SEASON'S BEST PRODUCE

I WAS A LUCKY CHILD.
Vegetables seemed to be everywhere. If there weren't plump tomatoes on the vine, there were mustard greens swishing in the sink or huge Vidalia onions being carefully loaded into the legs of pantyhose. I may not have been high off the ground when I started to take note of the vegetables in my life, but I was drawn in by their vivid colors, the range of aromas, and the way they seemed to bring everyone together.

Growing up in a farming community, I had vegetables coming into our home in bushels rather than grocery store bags. It was fresh produce that drew my parents and my grandmothers to the screened porch to shuck, shell, string, or snap. My hometown was small, but crops seemed to be plentiful. It was an ideal setting to learn the value of the journey from seed to plate.

Although you can now find nearly every type of produce year-round in supermarkets, a new respect for vegetables is emerging as we Southerners recommit to the standards that our grandparents lived and farmed by. Eat what's in season, put up for when it's not, cook what grows nearby, and be thankful for the Southern soil, rain, and sun.

Georgia Shrimp and Radish Salad, page 131

"It was fresh produce that drew my parents and my grandmothers to the screened porch to shuck, shell, string, or snap."

REBECCA LANG,
author of *The Southern Vegetable Book: A Root-to-Stalk Guide to the South's Favorite Produce*

Spring Pea Orzo,
page 131

If you can't find haricots verts, use regular green beans instead.

LEMONY GREEN BEAN PASTA SALAD

Lemon and shallots marry for a bright taste that's ideal for a ladies' lunch or light supper.

- 12 oz. casarecce (or penne) pasta
- 1/2 lb. haricots verts (French green beans), cut in half lengthwise
- 1 Tbsp. fresh thyme
- 5 tsp. lemon zest, divided
- 1/4 cup finely chopped roasted salted pistachios, plus more for topping
- 2 Tbsp. Champagne vinegar
- 1 Tbsp. minced shallots
- 1 garlic clove, minced
- 1 tsp. table salt
- 1/2 tsp. freshly ground black pepper
- 5 Tbsp. olive oil
- 1 1/2 cups loosely packed arugula
  Grated Parmesan cheese, for topping

1. Cook pasta according to package directions, adding green beans to boiling water during last 2 minutes of cooking time; drain. Rinse pasta and green beans with cold water; drain well.
2. Place pasta mixture, thyme, and 3 tsp. lemon zest in a large bowl; toss gently to combine.
3. Whisk together 1/4 cup pistachios, next 5 ingredients, and remaining 2 tsp. lemon zest in a small bowl. Add oil in a slow, steady stream, whisking constantly until blended. Drizzle over pasta mixture. Add arugula, and toss gently to coat. Top the pasta with chopped pistachios and Parmesan.

SERVES 4 to 6 **ACTIVE** 15 min. **TOTAL** 30 min.

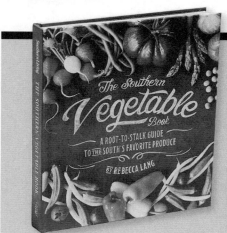

GET THE BOOK!

Let your farmers' market bounty—tomatoes, corn, zucchini, and more—shine in the 100 fresh and seasonal recipes you'll find in Rebecca Lang's cookbook *The Southern Vegetable Book.*

SKIRT STEAK WITH FENNEL SLAW

This raw fennel and celery salad brings light and bright flavor to grilled marinated skirt steak. Throw corn tortillas on the grill to make impromptu tacos, a favorite weeknight dinner.

STEAK

- 1/3 cup red wine vinegar
- 1/3 cup extra virgin olive oil
- 4 garlic cloves, minced
- 1/2 tsp. Dijon mustard
- 1/2 tsp. table salt
- 1/2 tsp. freshly ground black pepper
- 1 1/2 lb. skirt steak

FENNEL SLAW

- 1 1/4 cups thinly sliced fennel bulb
- 1/4 cup sliced green onions
- 2 Tbsp. thinly sliced celery
- 1 Tbsp. mayonnaise
- 2 Tbsp. fresh lime juice
- 1 Tbsp. chopped fresh cilantro
- 1 tsp. diced jalapeño pepper
- 1 tsp. red wine vinegar
- 1/8 tsp. table salt
- 1/8 tsp. freshly ground black pepper

1. Prepare the Steak: Preheat grill to 350° to 400°F (medium-high). In a large zip-top plastic bag, combine the vinegar, olive oil, garlic, mustard, salt, and pepper. Shake to combine. Add steak to the bag, seal bag, and marinate 30 minutes. Remove steak from marinade, discarding marinade.
2. Grill steak, turning once, 10 minutes total for medium-rare (or until desired doneness). Let steak rest for 10 minutes before slicing.
3. Prepare the Fennel Slaw: Combine all ingredients in a large bowl, and toss together. Chill until ready to serve.
4. Slice each strip of steak in half to make 2 shorter strips. Slice down the long side (across the grain) of each strip to create 1/2-inch-thick slices. Serve steak with Fennel Slaw.

SERVES 4 (serving size: about 1 cup)
ACTIVE 30 min. **TOTAL** 1 hour

Skirt Steak with Fennel Slaw

SPRING PEA ORZO

Add the dressing to the orzo while it's still warm, which allows the flavor to soak fully into the pasta. This salad tastes even better the next day, so make it ahead.

- 3 to 4 lemons
- 8 oz. orzo pasta
- 1/4 cup minced shallot or red onion
- 2 Tbsp. extra virgin olive oil
- 1 Tbsp. Dijon mustard
- 1/2 tsp. table salt
- 1/2 tsp. freshly ground black pepper
- 1 1/2 cups cooked fresh or frozen peas
- 1 cup snow peas or sugar snap peas, blanched and chopped
- 1 cup assorted chopped fresh herbs (like mint, chives, and parsley)
- 1/2 cup sliced almonds, toasted

1. Grate zest from lemons to equal 2 tsp.; set aside. Cut lemons in half; squeeze juice to equal 1/2 cup.
2. Prepare pasta according to package directions. Whisk together shallots, olive oil, mustard, salt, pepper, and lemon juice in a large bowl. Toss together cooked, drained pasta and shallot mixture. Cover with plastic wrap, and chill 1 to 48 hours.

3. Add peas, snow peas, herbs, almonds, and lemon zest to the pasta-shallot mixture just before serving. Toss together, and add salt, pepper, and additional lemon juice to taste.

SERVES 6 (serving size: about 1 cup)
ACTIVE 20 min. **TOTAL** 1 hour, 30 min.

GEORGIA SHRIMP AND RADISH SALAD

Radishes at the farmers' market can seem as varied and abundant as the colors of Easter eggs. Two different varieties give this salad vibrant color, texture, and flavor.

- 2 lb. unpeeled, large raw shrimp
- 2 Tbsp. extra virgin olive oil
- 1 tsp. table salt, divided
- 3/4 tsp. freshly ground black pepper, divided
- 1 (4-oz.) watermelon radish, cut into fourths and thinly sliced
- 4 oz. D'avignon (French breakfast) radishes, thinly sliced
- 4 green onions, sliced
- 1/2 cup diced fennel bulb
- 1/4 cup fresh orange juice
- 1 tsp. honey
- 2 Tbsp. mayonnaise
- 1/4 cup chopped fresh mint, plus a few sprigs for garnish

1. Peel and devein shrimp, and pat dry. Sauté in a very hot cast-iron grill pan over medium-high 4 minutes.
2. Combine shrimp, olive oil, 1/2 tsp. salt, 1/2 tsp. pepper, and next 4 ingredients in a large bowl.
3. Whisk together orange juice, next 3 ingredients, and remaining 1/2 tsp. salt and 1/4 tsp. pepper. Pour over shrimp mixture, and toss. Serve chilled.

SERVES 4 (serving size: about 1 cup)
ACTIVE 20 min. **TOTAL** 50 min.

Mediterranean Medley

A ZESTY MARINADE LIVENS UP THIS PORK-AND-VEGGIE SHEET PAN SUPPER

GREEK PORK CHOPS WITH SQUASH AND POTATOES

- 4 (1-inch-thick) frenched pork loin chops
- 1/2 cup fresh lemon juice
- 4 Tbsp. olive oil
- 3 garlic cloves, minced
- 3 Tbsp. chopped fresh oregano
- 1 tsp. black pepper
- 3 tsp. kosher salt, divided
- 2 medium yellow squash, sliced 1/2 inch thick
- 1 large zucchini, sliced 1/2 inch thick
- 1/2 lb. small red potatoes, quartered

1. Place pork chops in a 13- x 9-inch baking dish. Whisk together lemon juice, oil, garlic, oregano, pepper, and 2 1/2 teaspoons salt; reserve 2 tablespoons marinade. Pour remaining marinade over pork, turning to coat. Chill 1 to 8 hours.

2. Preheat the oven to 425°F. Combine squash, zucchini, potatoes, and reserved marinade. Spread squash mixture in an even layer on a heavy-duty aluminum foil-lined rimmed sheet pan.

3. Remove pork from marinade. Pat dry with paper towels, and place on top of squash mixture.

4. Bake at 425°F for 25 minutes. Increase temperature to broil, and broil until a meat thermometer inserted into thickest portion registers 140°F, about 5 minutes. Transfer pork to a serving platter, and cover with foil. Return pan to oven, and broil squash mixture until slightly charred, 3 to 4 minutes. Transfer squash mixture to a serving bowl; toss with remaining 1/2 teaspoon salt, and serve with pork.

SERVES 4 (serving size: 1 pork chop and about 1 cup vegetables) **ACTIVE** 20 min.
TOTAL 1 hour, 40 min.

Dressed-Up Chicken Salad

LEFTOVER CHICKEN GETS A FRESH MAKEOVER WITH CRISP LETTUCE LEAVES, TOASTED WALNUTS, AND DRIED CHERRIES

ONLY
343 CAL
SL

CHICKEN SALAD IN LETTUCE CUPS

- ¼ cup chopped walnuts
- ¼ cup light mayonnaise
- ¼ cup plain fat-free Greek yogurt
- 2 tsp. sherry vinegar
- ¼ tsp. kosher salt
- ¼ tsp. freshly ground black pepper
- 2 cups shredded skinless, boneless rotisserie chicken breast
- 2 Tbsp. chopped fresh flat-leaf parsley
- 6 green onions, white and light green parts, chopped
- 6 Bibb lettuce leaves
- ⅓ cup tart dried cherries

1. Preheat the oven to 350°F.
2. Spread walnuts in a single layer on a baking sheet; bake in preheated oven until nuts are toasted, about 5 minutes. Cool.
3. Stir together mayonnaise, yogurt, vinegar, salt, and pepper in a bowl.
4. Place chicken, toasted walnuts, parsley, and green onions in a large bowl; toss to combine. Add the dressing, stirring well to coat.
5. Place 1 lettuce leaf in each of 6 bowls. Divide chicken salad evenly among the bowls; top with cherries.

SERVES 6 (serving size: 1 lettuce cup)
ACTIVE 20 min. **TOTAL** 25 min.

NUTRITIONAL INFORMATION
(per serving)
CALORIES: 343; FAT 12.2g
(SAT FAT: 6.5g); PROTEIN: 26g;
FIBER 2g; CARBOHYDRATES
31g; SODIUM: 647mg

Veggie Lessons

LEARN HOW TO MAKE THE MOST OF YOUR FARMERS' MARKET BOUNTY

BEETS

PICK WISELY: The smaller the beet, the more tender it will be. Bright greens are also better.

EASY PREP: Wrap in foil, and bake at 350°F for 1 hour, or until tender when pricked. Rub off the skins with paper towels.

SAVE THE TOPS: Add chopped beet greens to salads, or thinly slice and garnish on soups.

GREEN BEANS

PICK WISELY: Select crisp, slender pods. Avoid brown spots.

EASY PREP: Instead of snapping each bean like Grandma did, line up the pods and remove stems with a chef's knife.

BLANCH THEM: For crisp, tender beans, blanch in boiling water 4 to 5 minutes; then plunge into an ice bath for 4 to 5 minutes more.

EGGPLANT

PICK WISELY: No matter the size, color, or shape, choose a firm eggplant with shiny skin and green top.

EASY PREP: Small, young eggplants can be used as is; larger, older ones should be peeled.

ADD A PINCH: Curb bitterness in large eggplants by sprinkling with salt. Slice, salt, and let sit for 30 minutes. Rinse before cooking.

RADISHES

PICK WISELY: Choose plump, firm radishes with fresh green leaves. Bigger isn't always better: The larger the radish, the less crisp it will be.

EASY PREP: Trim—don't toss—leaves. The greens are great for sautéing or garnishing dishes.

SOAK AND SERVE: Prefer extra-crunchy radishes? Soak in ice water before serving.

THE RIGHT WAY TO HULL A STRAWBERRY

Rest your thumb on the flat spine of a paring knife. Hold the berry in your other hand, and insert the knife at a 45-degree angle into the center of the fruit.

Keeping your thumb in the same position, twist the strawberry so the knife makes a circular cut around the stem. Remove the leaves and core.

MEET YOUR NEW FAVORITE APPETIZER...

Party Poppers

Satisfy hungry houseguests with a spicy two-bite appetizer stuffed with chicken-cream cheese filling and wrapped in some hickory-smoked bacon

- **12** medium jalapeño chiles
- **1** (8-oz.) pkg. cream cheese, softened
- **1** cup finely chopped cooked chicken
- **2** Tbsp. finely chopped fresh cilantro
- **1** Tbsp. fresh lime juice
- **3/4** tsp. kosher salt
- **12** hickory-smoked bacon slices, cut in half
- **24** wooden picks

1. Preheat the oven to 400°F. Cut each chile in half lengthwise; remove seeds and membranes.

2. Stir together the cream cheese, chicken, cilantro, lime juice, and salt. Spoon 1 1/2 to 2 teaspoons chicken mixture into each chile half, spreading to fill cavity. Wrap each half with a bacon piece, and secure with a wooden pick. Place poppers on a lightly greased wire rack in an aluminum foil-lined rimmed baking sheet.

3. Bake at 400°F until bacon begins to crisp and chiles are softened, about 25 minutes. Increase oven temperature to broil, and broil until bacon is crisp, 2 to 3 minutes. Let stand 5 minutes before serving.

SERVES 6 (serving size: 4 poppers)
ACTIVE 20 min. **TOTAL** 35 min.

For those who don't like it hot, swap mini sweet peppers for spicy jalapeños.

Banana Pudding with a Twist

THIS TAKE ON THE SOUTHERN CLASSIC OFFERS A TASTE OF THE TROPICS

COCONUT-BANANA PUDDING

The recipe below feeds a crowd, family style, but can be halved and served in individual bowls.

6   **large egg yolks**
1   **cup (7 oz.) granulated sugar**
½   **cup (2.25 oz.) all-purpose flour**
¼   **tsp. table salt**
3   **cups half-and-half**
2   **Tbsp. (1 oz.) salted butter**
¼   **tsp. coconut extract**
3   **tsp. vanilla extract, divided**
3   **cups heavy cream**
½   **cup (2 oz.) powdered sugar**
1   **(11-oz.) package vanilla wafers**
6   **small ripe bananas, sliced ¼ to ½ inch**

1. Whisk egg yolks in a medium bowl until thick and lemon colored (about 1 minute).

2. Stir together sugar, flour, and salt in a large heavy saucepan; gradually whisk in half-and-half. Whisking constantly, bring mixture just to a boil over medium (about 8 to 10 minutes). Remove from heat.

3. Gradually whisk about one-fourth of hot sugar mixture into yolks; gradually add yolk mixture to remaining hot sugar mixture, whisking constantly. Return to heat; cook over medium, whisking constantly, 1 minute. Remove from heat, and whisk in butter, coconut extract, and 2 teaspoons vanilla. Transfer to a medium bowl, and place plastic wrap directly on warm filling to prevent a film from forming; cool completely (about 2 hours).

Keep banana slices from turning brown by tossing with 2 tablespoons lemon juice.

4. Beat cream and remaining 1 teaspoon vanilla at medium-high speed with an electric mixer until foamy; gradually add powdered sugar, and beat until medium peaks form.

5. Reserve 12 vanilla wafers. Arrange half of remaining wafers in 1 layer in the bottom of a 3 ½- to 4-quart bowl.

Top with half of banana slices, half of custard, and half of whipped cream. Repeat layers once. Top with crumbled reserved wafers.

SERVES 16 (serving size: about 1 cup) **ACTIVE** 30 min. **TOTAL** 2 hours, 30 min., including 2 hours cooling

June

Slice of SUMMER

FROM A SALAD PILED HIGH WITH HEIRLOOMS TO A CHARRED RELISH, THERE'S NO MATCH
FOR THE SOUTH'S SUN-RIPENED TOMATOES

A LINE FROM *Steel Magnolias* might tell you that I don't meet the definition of a Southern lady. I don't grow tomatoes. Sorry, Ouiser. I'm getting older, and I make my own rules.

My avoidance is not a lack of tomato love. It's the opposite: I adore them too much to subject them to my indifferent skills as a gardener. When I was young and foolish, I tried valiantly to grow juicy tomatoes and eventually learned a bitter lesson: The greatest by-product of the Southern summer is a terrible thing to waste on blossom end rot, uneven watering, and squirrel battles.

Instead, I saved my money for my favorite tomato tables at the local farmers' market. I'd rather pay a farmer to grow a great tomato and spend my time making good use of their labors.

I have plenty of those good uses, from the endless bags of roasted-tomato sauce I tuck in my freezer to the summer-long parade of Caprese salads and tomato gratins to those tomato slices buried under browned mozzarella on homemade pizza dough.

Out of all those, though, I'd like to suggest that the highest achievement of the summer is no recipe at all. It's the tomato sandwich: white bread, mayonnaise, tomato slices, salt, and pepper.

It sounds simple, but the subject is fraught with controversy, with every step leading to argument. Bread choice. Mayonnaise loyalty. Lack of lettuce and bacon. And heaven help you if you equate the plain tomato sandwich with Southernness. People will react like you hurled rotten tomatoes at Fort Sumter.

For once, let's put aside our invectives and consider the exquisiteness that is the tomato sandwich.

A friend recently told me about her perfect tomato sandwich moment—a day at the beach when she was 13, stumbling inside in the middle of the afternoon, salty, oily, and sweaty; starving as only a teenager can be after a day plunging through the waves.

Spying a ripe tomato in the kitchen, she grabbed her father's favorite white bread so squishy you could barely handle it without thumb prints. She sliced the tomato, smeared Duke's mayonnaise, and seasoned with salt and pepper. That first bite stays with her 30 years later, the moment by which all tomato moments are measured.

Listening to her, I recalled a moment of my own 13-year-old hunger, when I was too empty even to consider the bread and mayonnaise. I grabbed a ripe tomato from my mother's kitchen windowsill and prepared to eat it like the love apple of its name.

I already knew enough to know that salt is absolutely required. When I sprinkled it on the skin, though, it just bounced off. I solved my problem by licking the tomato so just enough salt would stick until I could bite through the skin.

I still remember the delight: sweet enhanced by salt, acidity filling my mouth, juice running down my arm. I ate it bite by bite, pausing only to shake a little more salt on the wet, exposed flesh.

Tomato love, born in each of us however we come to it.

Blossom end rot, drought, and squirrels be damned, Ouiser. Nothing comes between me and a summer full of tomatoes.

—KATHLEEN PURVIS

MOUTHWATERING MARINATED TOMATOES

ACTIVE 5 MIN. - TOTAL 1 HOUR, 50 MIN.

MAKES ABOUT 4 CUPS

This makes a flavorful Tomato Vinaigrette for adding to all types of salads.

Gently stir together 2 lb. assorted **tomatoes,** roughly chopped; 1 small minced **shallot;** 3 crushed **garlic** cloves; 1/2 cup **red wine vinegar;** 3 Tbsp. **extra virgin olive oil;** 1 1/2 tsp. kosher **salt;** and 1/2 tsp. freshly ground black **pepper,** and set aside for 1 hour and 45 minutes, tossing occasionally. Stir in 1 cup loosely packed fresh **basil** leaves and 1/4 cup loosely packed Italian **parsley** leaves. Serve immediately.

SPAGHETTI WITH MARINATED TOMATOES AND MOZZARELLA

ACTIVE 6 MIN. - TOTAL 20 MIN.

SERVES 4 TO 6

Cook 8 ounces thin **spaghetti** according to package directions; drain and return to pot. Spoon in **Marinated Tomatoes** (recipe left) and desired amount of vinaigrette; add ½ cup small **mozzarella balls.** Serve immediately.

SESAME, TOMATO, AND CUCUMBER SALAD

ACTIVE 10 MIN. - TOTAL 10 MIN.

SERVES 6

- 1 lb. tomatoes, thinly sliced crosswise
- 1/2 cup thinly sliced English cucumber
- 1 Tbsp. soy sauce
- 1 Tbsp. rice vinegar
- 2 tsp. olive oil
- 1 1/2 tsp. granulated sugar
- 2 medium scallions, dark green parts only, thinly sliced
- 1 medium serrano or jalapeño chile, thinly sliced crosswise
- 2 tsp. toasted sesame seeds
- 1/4 tsp. flaky sea salt (such as Maldon)
- 1/4 tsp. black pepper

Arrange tomato and cucumber slices on a platter. Whisk together soy sauce, vinegar, olive oil, and sugar in a small bowl until sugar dissolves. Drizzle 2 tablespoons of dressing over tomatoes and cucumbers, and top with scallions, chile, and sesame seeds. Sprinkle with salt and pepper. Serve immediately with remaining dressing.

OPEN-FACED TOMATO SANDWICHES WITH CREAMY CUCUMBER SPREAD

ACTIVE 20 MIN. - TOTAL 20 MIN.

SERVES 6

- 1 (8-oz.) pkg. cream cheese, softened
- 2 cucumbers, seeds removed, diced (about 2 cups)
- 1/4 cup finely chopped red onion
- 2 1/2 tsp. chopped fresh dill
- 2 1/2 tsp. chopped fresh mint
- 2 tsp. fresh lemon juice
- 1 tsp. white wine vinegar
- 1 tsp. kosher salt, plus more for serving
- 1/2 tsp. black pepper, plus more for serving

- 6 Texas Toast slices or other thick white bread slices, toasted
- 1 1/2 to 1 3/4 lb. assorted fresh tomatoes (about 3 large), cut into 1/2-inch-thick slices
- 2 Tbsp. extra-virgin olive oil Thinly sliced chives

1. Stir together cream cheese, cucumbers, red onion, dill, mint, lemon juice, vinegar, salt, and pepper in a medium bowl until well combined.
2. Spread about 1/4 cup of the cucumber mixture onto each slice of the toasted bread. Top each with 2 to 3 tomato slices, and drizzle each with 1 teaspoon olive oil. Sprinkle tomatoes with chives, salt, and pepper. Serve immediately.

GRILLED FLAT IRON STEAK WITH CHARRED TOMATO RELISH

ACTIVE 20 MIN. - TOTAL 20 MIN.

SERVES 4

- 6 medium-size plum or Campari tomatoes, halved lengthwise
- 3 Tbsp. olive oil, divided
- 2 tsp. kosher salt, divided
- 1 1/4 tsp. black pepper, divided
- 1 1/2 lb. flat iron steak
- 1/4 cup firmly packed fresh flat-leaf parsley leaves, coarsely chopped
- 1 Tbsp. red wine vinegar
- 1 garlic clove, finely chopped
- 1 tsp. granulated sugar
- 1/4 tsp. crushed red pepper

1. Preheat grill to 350° to 400°F (medium-high) or heat a grill pan over medium-high. Toss together tomatoes, 1 tablespoon of the oil, 1/2 teaspoon of the salt, and 1/4 teaspoon of the black pepper in a medium bowl. Rub steak with 1 tablespoon of the oil and remaining 1 1/2 teaspoons salt and 1 teaspoon black pepper.
2. Grill tomatoes, turning often, until charred and softened, 4 to 6 minutes.

Remove from grill, and let cool until ready to use. Grill steak, turning occasionally, until lightly charred and medium-rare, 8 to 10 minutes. Transfer to a board, and let rest, 5 to 10 minutes.
3. Coarsely chop tomatoes, and transfer to a medium bowl. Add parsley, vinegar, garlic, sugar, crushed red pepper, and remaining 1 tablespoon olive oil, and toss to combine.
4. Slice steak against the grain, and spoon tomato relish over top.

BLT SALAD WITH BUTTERMILK-PARMESAN DRESSING AND BUTTERY CROUTONS

ACTIVE 15 MIN. - TOTAL 20 MIN.

SERVES 6

- 2 1/2 cups cubed white bread
- 3 Tbsp. butter, melted
- 1 tsp. kosher salt
- 1/4 tsp. freshly ground black pepper
- 1 Tbsp. minced shallot
- 1/4 cup cider vinegar
- 1/2 cup buttermilk
- 3/4 cup mayonnaise
- 1/2 cup grated Parmesan cheese
- 1/2 tsp. kosher salt
- 1/4 tsp. freshly ground black pepper
- 1/8 tsp. sugar
- 12 oz. romaine lettuce hearts, chopped
- 1 1/2 lb. assorted fresh tomatoes, sliced
- 6 slices cooked bacon, chopped Flat-leaf parsley and torn basil leaves to garnish

1. Preheat oven to 375°F.
2. Prepare Croutons: Toss together bread, melted butter, salt, and pepper in a medium mixing bowl. Place on a baking sheet, and bake 7 to 8 minutes. Remove from oven, and set aside.
3. Prepare Dressing: Combine shallot and vinegar in a medium mixing bowl, and let stand for 5 minutes. Whisk in buttermilk and next 5 ingredients.

Sesame, Tomato, and Cucumber Salad

Open-Faced Tomato Sandwiches with Creamy Cucumber Spread

Grilled Flat Iron Steak with Charred Tomato Relish

BLT Salad with Buttermilk-Parmesan Dressing and Buttery Croutons

THE *SL* BLT

ACTIVE 35 MIN. - TOTAL 35 MIN.

SERVES 1

Cook 4 strips of **bacon** in a large skillet over medium, turning occasionally, until golden and crisp, 5 to 7 minutes. Transfer to a plate lined with paper towels, and drain. Stir together 2 Tbsp. **mayonnaise,** grated **garlic** to taste, and a pinch of **black pepper** in a small bowl. Spread evenly on 2 slices lightly toasted **white sandwich bread.** Top 1 slice of bread with 1 large **green leaf lettuce** leaf (or Bibb, romaine, or iceberg), breaking to fit if necessary, and about 2 ¼-inch-thick beefsteak **tomato** slices. Sprinkle tomatoes with **kosher salt** and pepper. Top with bacon and remaining bread slice. Slice sandwich in half before serving.

4. Make Salad: Arrange romaine lettuce hearts on a serving platter. Top with sliced tomatoes and chopped bacon, and drizzle with 3 Tbsp. of dressing. Add croutons, parsley, and basil. Serve immediately with remaining dressing on the side.

FRIED GREEN TOMATOES WITH BUTTERMILK-FETA DRESSING

ACTIVE 36 MIN. - TOTAL 1 HOUR, 6 MIN.

SERVES 4

- 3 **green tomatoes, sliced ½ inch thick**
- 1¼ **tsp. kosher salt, divided, plus more for serving**
- ½ **cup (2 oz.) all-purpose flour**
- 2 **large eggs, beaten**
- ⅓ **cup plain yellow cornmeal**
- ⅓ **cup fine, dry breadcrumbs**
- 3 **cups vegetable oil**
- 2 **Tbsp. buttermilk**
- 2 **Tbsp. mayonnaise**
- 2 **Tbsp. sour cream**
- 1 **Tbsp. fresh dill, chopped, plus more for serving**
- 1 **Tbsp. fresh lemon juice**
- ¼ **tsp. black pepper**
- 4 **oz. (1 cup) feta cheese, crumbled, divided**

1. Set a wire rack in a rimmed baking sheet. Place tomato slices on wire rack, and sprinkle with ½ teaspoon of the salt. Turn slices over, and sprinkle with another ½ teaspoon of the salt. Let stand 30 minutes. Blot tomatoes dry with paper towels.

2. Place flour in a shallow dish. Place eggs in a second shallow dish. Stir together cornmeal and breadcrumbs in a third shallow dish. Working with 1 slice at a time, dredge tomato slices in flour; dip in eggs, shaking off excess. Dredge slices in breadcrumb mixture, pressing gently to adhere. Place tomatoes in a single layer on wire rack.

3. Heat oil in a large heavy skillet, preferably cast-iron, over medium-high. (When a few breadcrumbs dropped in the oil sizzle, it's ready for frying.) Fry tomatoes, in batches, until golden brown and crisp, turning halfway through, about 2 minutes per side. (Be careful not to overcrowd the skillet.) Transfer to wire rack to drain. Top each tomato with a pinch of salt.

4. Whisk together buttermilk, mayonnaise, sour cream, dill, and lemon juice in a small bowl. Whisk in black pepper, ½ cup of the feta, and remaining ¼ teaspoon salt. Spoon about 3 tablespoons of the dressing onto each plate; add 3 or 4 tomato slices. Sprinkle with dill and remaining ½ cup feta.

Fried Green Tomatoes with Buttermilk-Feta Dressing

Quicker Chicken Suppers

THE SECRET TO MAKING A
DELICIOUS DINNER IN LESS THAN
30 MINUTES? ROTISSERIE CHICKEN

CHICKEN STIR-FRY

Whisk together 1 (14-oz.) can
low-sodium **chicken broth,**
¼ cup lite **soy sauce,** 1 to 2
tablespoons **chili-garlic sauce,**
2 tablespoons **cornstarch,**
1 tablespoon **brown sugar,** and
1 teaspoon **ground ginger.** Heat
2 tablespoons **dark sesame oil**
in a large skillet or wok over
medium-high 2 minutes. Add
3 cups shredded **rotisserie
chicken** and 1 (16-oz.) package
frozen stir-fry vegetables;
stir-fry 1 to 2 minutes. Add broth
mixture, and cook until sauce
thickens and vegetables are
tender. Serve with steamed **rice.**

SERVES 4 to 6 **ACTIVE** 10 min.
TOTAL 10 min.

CHICKEN NOODLE BOWL WITH PEANUT-GINGER SAUCE

PEANUT-GINGER SAUCE

- 1/2 cup creamy peanut butter
- 4 1/2 Tbsp. fresh lime juice
- 3 Tbsp. soy sauce
- 3 Tbsp. honey
- 2 Tbsp. peeled and chopped fresh ginger
- 1 1/2 tsp. sesame oil
- 1/4 tsp. crushed red pepper
- 3 Tbsp. rice vinegar
- 1/4 tsp. kosher salt

CHICKEN NOODLE BOWL

- 8 cups water
- 2 Tbsp. rice vinegar
- 1 Tbsp. kosher salt
- 6 oz. rice noodles or bean threads
- 3 cups shredded cooked chicken
- 3 cups shredded napa cabbage
- 1 1/2 cups halved and thinly sliced seedless cucumber
- 1 1/2 cups matchstick carrots
- 1 1/2 cups thinly sliced red bell pepper
- 6 Tbsp. chopped lightly salted dry-roasted peanuts

1. Prepare the Sauce: Process all 9 ingredients in a blender or food processor until smooth.

2. Prepare the Chicken Noodle Bowl: Microwave water in a large bowl on HIGH 10 minutes. Stir vinegar and salt into boiling water. Add noodles, and let stand until softened, about 5 minutes. Drain noodles.

3. Divide noodles, chicken, cabbage, cucumber, carrots, and bell pepper among 6 bowls. Top each bowl with 1 tablespoon peanuts and 2 tablespoons Peanut-Ginger Sauce. Serve remaining sauce on the side.

SERVES 6 **ACTIVE** 20 min. **TOTAL** 20 min.

Chicken Noodle Bowl with Peanut-Ginger Sauce

HEIRLOOM TOMATO AND CHICKEN TOSS

Serve this fresh summer salad with plenty of crusty bread to soak up the flavorful tomato juices.

- 4 Tbsp. white wine vinegar
- 3 Tbsp. extra-virgin olive oil
- 2 1/2 tsp. granulated sugar
- 1 1/2 tsp. kosher salt
- 1/2 tsp. black pepper
- 3 cups shredded cooked chicken
- 2 lb. heirloom tomatoes, cut into 1/2- to 1-inch wedges
- 1/2 cup thinly sliced red onion
- 2 Tbsp. chopped fresh basil
- 2 Tbsp. finely chopped fresh chives
- 2 Tbsp. chopped fresh flat-leaf parsley leaves
- 1 Tbsp. chopped fresh thyme

Whisk together vinegar, olive oil, sugar, salt, and pepper in a small bowl. Gently toss together chicken, tomatoes, onion, basil, chives, parsley, and thyme in a large bowl. Add vinegar mixture, and gently toss until thoroughly combined. Serve immediately, or cover and let stand at room temperature for up to 1 hour.

SERVES 6 (serving size: 1 3/4 cups)
ACTIVE 20 min. **TOTAL** 20 min.

DIY PANINI PRESS

You can make hot sandwiches with two heavy cast-iron skillets—no panini press required. While you're cooking a sandwich in one skillet, heat the second one on a separate burner. Once hot, place the second skillet on top of the sandwich for 1 to 2 minutes. Repeat on the flip side, cooking for 1 to 2 minutes more.

CHICKEN AND FONTINA PANINI

Crusty on the outside, gooey on the inside, this sandwich requires little effort and makes a satisfying lunch or light dinner.

- 1 (8-oz) loaf ciabatta bread, cut in half horizontally
- 3 Tbsp. pesto sauce
- 2 plum tomatoes, sliced
- 1 cup shredded rotisserie chicken
- 2 slices fontina cheese

1. Preheat panini press.

2. Spread bottom half of bread with pesto. Top with tomato slices, chicken, and cheese. Top with bread.

3. Place sandwich in panini press; cook 3 to 4 minutes or until cheese melts and bread is toasted. Cut into quarters, and serve hot.

SERVES 2 servings **ACTIVE** 7 min.
TOTAL 10 min.

CHICKEN AND WHITE BEAN SALAD WITH CITRUS VINAIGRETTE

This vibrant salad is quick to toss together and travels well, which makes it ideal for summer picnics and potlucks.

- 3 Tbsp. fresh orange juice
- 2 Tbsp. white wine vinegar
- 2 tsp. country Dijon mustard
- 2 tsp. honey
- 2 Tbsp. minced shallot
- 1 tsp. kosher salt
- 1/4 tsp. black pepper
- 1/2 cup olive oil
- 3 cups chopped cooked chicken
- 1 (15.5-oz.) can cannellini beans, drained and rinsed
- 1 (6-oz.) bag microwave steam-in-bag snow peas, steamed according to package directions and sliced into 1-inch pieces
- 3 cups shredded purple cabbage
- 2 oranges, sectioned
- 6 Tbsp. roasted sliced almonds with salt

1. Whisk together orange juice, vinegar, Dijon mustard, honey, shallot, salt, and pepper in a large bowl; slowly whisk in olive oil.

2. Add the chicken, cannellini beans, snow peas, purple cabbage, and oranges to the bowl. Toss the salad in the dressing until all the ingredients are thoroughly coated. Divide salad among 6 plates, and top each plate with 1 Tbsp. sliced almonds.

SERVES 6 (serving size: 2 cups)
ACTIVE 20 min. **TOTAL** 20 min.

SOUTHWEST CHICKEN TORTILLAS

- 1 (8.5-oz.) pouch microwaveable basmati rice
- 3/4 cup mayonnaise
- 1/3 cup buttermilk
- 1/4 cup chopped fresh cilantro
- 1 canned chipotle chile in adobo sauce, seeded
- 2 Tbsp. fresh lime juice
- 1 tsp. granulated sugar
- 1/2 tsp. canned adobo sauce
- 1/2 tsp. ground cumin
- 1/2 tsp. table salt
- 2 cups chopped cooked chicken
- 1 (15-oz.) can black beans, drained and rinsed
- 1/4 cup chopped scallions
- 6 to 12 corn tortillas, grilled or warmed
- 3/4 cup salsa
- 3 oz. shredded Mexican 4-cheese blend (3/4 cup)

1. Microwave rice according to package directions. Transfer to a large bowl, and fluff with a fork. Set aside.

2. Process mayonnaise, buttermilk, cilantro, chipotle chile, lime juice, sugar, adobo sauce, cumin, and salt in a blender or food processor until smooth.

3. Gently stir chicken, beans, scallions, and 3/4 cup mayonnaise mixture into rice. Spoon about 1/2 cup chicken mixture into each tortilla. Top each with 1 tablespoon salsa and 1 tablespoon cheese. Serve with additional mayonnaise mixture.

SERVES 6 (serving size: 2 tortillas)
ACTIVE 20 min. **TOTAL** 30 min.

Chicken and White Bean Salad with Citrus Vinaigrette

Southwest Chicken Tortillas

MEET YOUR CROWD-PLEASING SIDE

Field Pea and Pasta Salad

Farfalle and fresh veggies make a delicious summer side.

SALAD

- 4 cups fresh or frozen field peas, cooked, drained, and cooled
- 8 oz. mini farfalle pasta, cooked, rinsed with cold water, and drained
- 1/2 cup chopped red bell pepper
- 1/2 cup chopped yellow bell pepper
- 1/2 cup chopped orange bell pepper
- 1/4 cup chopped fresh flat-leaf parsley
- 2 Tbsp. chopped fresh basil
- 2 Tbsp. chopped fresh dill
- 2 Tbsp. chopped fresh mint
- 3 cups chopped cooked chicken (optional)

DRESSING

- 1/4 cup white wine vinegar
- 1 Tbsp. country-style Dijon mustard
- 1 Tbsp. fresh lemon juice
- 2 tsp. honey
- 3/4 tsp. kosher salt
- 1/4 tsp. black pepper
- 1/2 cup olive oil

1. Make the Salad: Toss together field peas, pasta, bell peppers, parsley, basil, dill, mint, and, if desired, chicken.

2. Make the Dressing: Whisk together white wine vinegar, mustard, lemon juice, honey, salt, and pepper in a small bowl. Gradually whisk in olive oil until incorporated. Pour dressing over the salad, and gently toss until coated.

SERVES 8 (serving size: 1 1/4 cups)
ACTIVE 15 min. **TOTAL** 15 min.

Foods Even Better on the Grill

THINK BEYOND THE BURGER WHEN COOKING OVER A FIRE

ROOT VEGGIES

Wrap beets, carrots, and onions in aluminum foil, and roast on a hot grill 15 to 25 minutes until tender. Unwrap and grill a few minutes more to add char marks.

HERBS

Grill woody herbs—thyme, rosemary, tarragon—in a small cast-iron skillet away from direct flames. Their smoky flavor will enhance dry rubs and marinades.

CITRUS

Charred orange, lemon, and lime slices add an extra burst of flavor to iced tea, sangria, seafood, and vinaigrettes.

BERRIES

Place raspberries, blueberries, or blackberries on a perforated grill sheet or in a foil packet; grill 3 to 5 minutes or until hot. Serve with pound cake or ice cream.

SALAD

Drizzle olive oil on quartered or halved heads of endive, cabbage, romaine, or radicchio, and season with salt and black pepper. Grill on all sides, turning every 1 to 2 minutes, until lightly charred. Top with salad dressing or a squeeze of lemon.

A SMART WAY TO CUT CHERRY TOMATOES

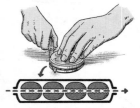

❶

Start with two rimmed plastic lids of matching size, such as the tops of cream cheese containers. Place bottom lid rim side up.

❷

Add as many tomatoes as will fit in the bottom lid (about 10). Cover with second lid, rim side down.

❸

With one hand, press gently on the top lid, and, using a serrated knife, slice tomatoes between lids.

"**When buying field peas, look for lady cream peas. They're a bit more expensive but their flavor—and clear potlikker—is worth it.**"

PAM LOLLEY
SL Test Kitchen Professional

Peach Cobbler on the Grill

THE FIRE GIVES THIS CLASSIC AN EXTRA-SMOKY, CARAMELIZED FLAVOR

GRILLED PEACH COBBLER

Serve hot off the grill or at room temperature.

COBBLER

- 7 cups ½-inch fresh peach slices or 2 (20-oz.) bags frozen sliced peaches, thawed and drained
- ¾ cup granulated sugar
- 2 Tbsp. all-purpose flour
- 1 tsp. ground cinnamon
- ¼ tsp. kosher salt
- ⅛ tsp. ground nutmeg
- 2 Tbsp. butter

BISCUIT TOPPING

- 1 cup all-purpose flour
- ¼ cup granulated sugar
- 1½ tsp. baking powder
- ½ cup heavy cream
- ¼ cup butter, melted

1. Heat 1 side of grill to medium-high (350° to 400°F). Place peaches in a large bowl. Stir together sugar and next 4 ingredients in a small bowl. Sprinkle mixture over peaches, and stir gently to combine. Spoon peach mixture into a buttered 10-inch cast-iron skillet. Cut 2 tablespoons butter into small pieces over peaches. Cover skillet tightly with aluminum foil.

2. Place skillet over lit side of grill, and grill, covered, until bubbling and hot, about 15 minutes.

3. Biscuit Topping: Stir together flour and next 2 ingredients in a small bowl. Make a well in the center, and add cream and melted butter. Stir just until mixture comes together. Uncover grill, and discard foil; dollop peaches with dough mixture. Cover with grill lid, and grill until biscuits are browned, about 15 more minutes. Remove skillet from grill, and let stand 10 minutes before serving.

ACTIVE 15 min. **TOTAL** 40 min.

July

RIPE FOR THE PICKING

SIX DELICIOUS DESSERTS STARRING SUMMER'S FRESHEST FRUIT

Plum-Berry Cornmeal Sheet Cake, page 155

Top it with ice cream or sour cream mixed with vanilla extract and light brown sugar.

Berry Cobbler with Pecan
Sandie Streusel, page 155

This cobbler is delicious with any fresh combination of berries. We mixed it up with four kinds.

Arrange slices in a single layer so they bake evenly. Leave a 1 1/2-inch border around the edges.

Spiced Peach Galette, page 155

PLUM-BERRY CORN-MEAL SHEET CAKE

Active 20 min. - Total 2 hours
SERVES 12

Bake and take this easy-to-transport, fruit-filled dessert to any summer gathering.

3/4 cup (6 oz.) salted butter, softened
1 1/2 cups granulated sugar
4 large eggs
1 1/2 cups (about 6 3/8 oz.) all-purpose flour
1 cup fine yellow cornmeal
2 tsp. baking powder
1 tsp. kosher salt
3/4 cup sour cream
1 Tbsp. orange zest plus 1/2 cup fresh juice (about 2 oranges)
2 tsp. vanilla extract
2 1/2 cups mixed fresh berries
2 red plums, sliced

1. Preheat oven to 350°F. Line the bottom and sides of a lightly greased 13- x 9-inch pan with parchment paper. Beat butter and sugar with an electric mixer at medium speed until light and fluffy, 3 to 4 minutes, stopping to scrape sides of bowl as needed. Add eggs, 1 at a time, beating well after each addition and stopping to scrape sides of bowl as needed.
2. Whisk together the flour, cornmeal, baking powder, and salt in a medium bowl. Whisk together the sour cream, orange zest, orange juice, and vanilla in a separate bowl. Add flour mixture to butter mixture alternately with sour cream mixture, beginning and ending with flour mixture. Beat at low speed just until blended after each addition. Spread batter into prepared baking pan, and scatter berries and plum slices over batter.
3. Bake in preheated oven until a wooden pick inserted in center comes out clean, 55 minutes to 1 hour and 5 minutes. Cool on a wire rack 20 minutes. Cut into squares, and serve warm or at room temperature.

BERRY COBBLER WITH PECAN SANDIE STREUSEL

Active 25 min. - Total 1 hour, 45 min.
SERVES 8

The toasty, nutty streusel topping is a surprising twist on the classic berry cobbler.

---

1 3/4 cups (about 7 1/2 oz.) plus 5 Tbsp. all-purpose flour, divided
2/3 cup granulated sugar, divided
3/4 tsp. kosher salt, divided
1/2 cup (4 oz.) plus 2 Tbsp. cold salted butter, diced, divided
1 1/4 cups lightly toasted chopped pecans
1/2 cup heavy cream
1 1/2 tsp. vanilla extract, divided
2 cups fresh blackberries
2 cups fresh blueberries
2 cups fresh raspberries
2 cups fresh strawberries, halved
2 tsp. lemon zest
1/4 tsp. ground nutmeg
1 Tbsp. turbinado sugar

1. Whisk together 1 3/4 cups of the flour, 1/3 cup of the granulated sugar, and 1/2 teaspoon of the salt in a medium bowl. Using a pastry blender, cut 1/2 cup of the butter into flour mixture until well blended and mixture resembles small peas. Stir in toasted pecans.
2. Stir together cream and 1/2 teaspoon of the vanilla in a small bowl; add cream mixture to flour mixture, stirring with a fork until mixture is combined but still crumbly. Chill until ready to use.
3. Preheat oven to 400°F. Gently toss together blackberries, blueberries, raspberries, strawberry halves, lemon zest, nutmeg, and remaining 5 tablespoons flour, 1/3 cup granulated sugar, 2 tablespoons butter, 1 teaspoon vanilla extract, and 1/4 teaspoon salt in a large bowl. Transfer to a lightly greased 10-inch cast-iron skillet. Place skillet in an aluminum foil-lined rimmed baking sheet.
4. Bake in preheated oven until bubbly around the edges, 20 to 22 minutes. Remove from oven. Crumble chilled streusel over hot filling, and sprinkle with turbinado sugar. Return to oven, and bake until golden, 25 to 28 more minutes. Serve warm.

SPICED PEACH GALETTE

Active 45 min. - Total 4 hours
SERVES 8 TO 10

You can make a flavor swap by substituting the cardamom in the peach filling for 1 teaspoon each of cinnamon and nutmeg.

CRUST
2 3/4 cups (about 11 3/4 oz.) all-purpose flour
2 Tbsp. granulated sugar
1 tsp. kosher salt
3/4 cup cold butter, cubed
1/4 cup frozen shortening, cubed
8 to 10 Tbsp. ice water
FILLING
1/2 cup granulated sugar
2 tsp. ground cardamom
1 Tbsp. cornstarch
6 medium peaches, ripe yet still firm
1 tsp. fresh lemon juice
1 tsp. vanilla extract
1 Tbsp. grated fresh ginger
2 Tbsp. heavy cream
1 Tbsp. turbinado sugar (optional)

1. Prepare the Crust: Place first 3 ingredients in the large bowl of a food processor; pulse 5 times to combine. Add the cubed butter and shortening. Pulse 12 to 15 times until mixture resembles small peas. Evenly sprinkle 8 tablespoons of the ice water over the top of the flour and butter mixture. Pulse 5 times to combine. Pinch dough; if it does not stick together, add up to 2 tablespoons ice water, 1 tablespoon at a time, pulsing 3 to 5 times to combine after each addition. Turn dough out onto a work surface, and knead 4 to 5 times to bring together. Shape into a 1-inch-thick oval. Wrap with plastic wrap, and chill 1 to 24 hours.
2. Preheat oven to 425°F. Let dough stand at room temperature 15 minutes to slightly soften. Place on a lightly floured sheet of parchment paper, and roll into a 12- x 16-inch oval about 1/8 inch thick. Transfer dough and parchment to a large baking sheet; chill until ready to use.
3. Prepare the Filling: Stir together the sugar, cardamom, and cornstarch in a large bowl. Cut each peach into 8

wedges, and add to sugar mixture. Gently toss to coat. Add the lemon juice, vanilla, and ginger; gently toss to combine.

4. Remove peaches from the bowl, reserving 4 tablespoons of the liquid. Arrange the peaches in a single layer on the dough, overlapping slightly, leaving a 1 ½-inch border along each edge. Cut the pastry border every 4 inches, and fold each piece up over the fruit. Brush crust with heavy cream, and, if desired, sprinkle with turbinado sugar. Drizzle reserved 4 tablespoons liquid from bowl over the peaches.

5. Bake in preheated oven 15 minutes. Reduce heat to 350°F, and bake until golden brown, about 40 minutes. Cool 10 minutes on baking sheet; transfer galette to a wire rack, and cool 1 hour.

CHERRY-PLUM PIE WITH CORNMEAL CRUST

Active 40 min. - Total 6 hours, 50 min.
SERVES 8

If you don't have a cherry pitter, try inserting a wooden chopstick through the stem end of each cherry to remove the pits.

CRUST

- 2 **cups (about 8 ½ oz.) all-purpose flour, plus more for dusting dough**
- ½ **cup plus 1 Tbsp. fine yellow cornmeal**
- 2 **Tbsp. granulated sugar**
- 1 **tsp. kosher salt**
- ¾ **cup cold butter (6 oz.), cubed**
- ¼ **cup chilled shortening, cubed**
- 8 **to 10 Tbsp. ice water**

FILLING

- 1 **lb. cherries, pitted and halved**
- 1 ½ **lb. red plums, diced into 1-inch pieces**
- 2 **tsp. vanilla extract**
- ¾ **cup granulated sugar**
- 2 **tsp. ground cinnamon**
- 2 **Tbsp. cornstarch**
- 1 **Tbsp. heavy cream**
- 1 **Tbsp. turbinado sugar**

1. Prepare the Crust: Place first 4 ingredients in the large bowl of a food processor; pulse 5 times to combine. Add the butter and shortening. Pulse 12 to 15 times until mixture resembles small peas. Evenly sprinkle 8 tablespoons ice water over the flour and butter mixture. Pulse 5 times to combine. Pinch dough; if it does not stick together, add up to 2 additional tablespoons, 1 tablespoon at a time, and

pulse 3 to 5 more times after each addition to combine. Turn dough out onto a smooth surface, and knead 4 to 5 times to bring together. Divide in half, and form into 2 rounds, about ½ inch thick. Wrap in plastic wrap, and refrigerate 1 to 24 hours.

2. Preheat oven to 425°F. Remove dough from the refrigerator; let rest 15 minutes. Place 1 round on a lightly floured piece of wax paper; sprinkle dough with flour. Top with another sheet of wax paper. Roll dough to ⅛-inch thickness and 13 inches wide. Place on a baking sheet, and return to refrigerator.

3. Repeat the rolling process with the second round of dough. Remove and discard top sheet of wax paper. Starting at 1 edge, wrap dough around rolling pin, separating dough from bottom sheet of wax paper as you roll. Discard bottom sheet of wax paper. Unroll dough onto a 9-inch pie pan; gently press dough into pie pan. Chill until ready to use.

4. Prepare the Filling: Combine the cherries, plums, and vanilla in a large bowl. Mix the sugar, cinnamon, and cornstarch in a small bowl. Combine the dry ingredients with the fruit, and transfer to the prepared pie pan.

5. Remove the reserved crust from the refrigerator. Cut second dough round into 16 (½-inch-wide) strips. Arrange in a

Fine yellow cornmeal gives this crust a slightly crunchy and flaky texture.

Cherry-Plum Pie with Cornmeal Crust, above

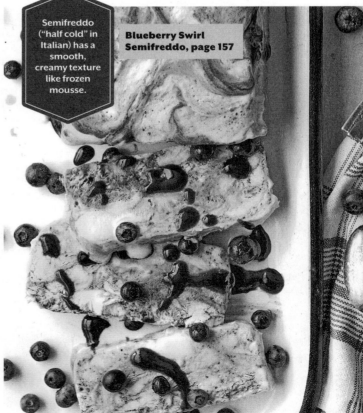

Semifreddo ("half cold" in Italian) has a smooth, creamy texture like frozen mousse.

Blueberry Swirl Semifreddo, page 157

lattice design over pie filling. Place pie on a baking sheet. Brush dough with heavy cream, and sprinkle with turbinado sugar. Bake in preheated oven 20 minutes; reduce oven temperature to 350°F, and bake until crust is browned and filling is cooked through, 45 to 50 minutes. Cool to room temperature before serving, about 4 hours.

BLACKBERRY COBBLER WITH ALMOND-GINGER BISCUITS

Active 20 min. - Total 1 hour
SERVES 6

Pockets of spicy crystallized ginger and sweet almonds are a surprising addition to this biscuit topping.

FILLING
- 7 **cups fresh blackberries**
- 1/3 **cup granulated sugar**
- 1/4 **tsp. almond extract**
- 1/4 **tsp. kosher salt**
- 1/4 **cup (about 1 1/8 oz.) all-purpose flour**
- 2 **Tbsp. salted butter, diced**

ALMOND-GINGER BISCUITS
- 2 **tsp. baking powder**
- 1/2 **tsp. kosher salt**
- 1 3/4 **cups (about 7 1/2 oz.) all-purpose flour**
- 1/4 **cup turbinado sugar, divided**
- 1/2 **cup (4 oz.) cold salted butter, diced**
- 2/3 **cup sliced almonds, lightly toasted**
- 3 **Tbsp. minced crystallized ginger**
- 2/3 **cup buttermilk**
- 1 **large egg, lightly beaten Vanilla ice cream**

1. Prepare the Filling: Preheat oven to 400°F. Stir together the blackberries, sugar, almond extract, salt, flour, and butter in a large bowl. Place 6 lightly greased 8-ounce ramekins in an aluminum foil-lined rimmed baking sheet. Divide berry mixture among ramekins. Bake in preheated oven until mixture just begins to bubble, 12 to 14 minutes.
2. Prepare the Almond-Ginger Biscuits: Whisk together baking powder, salt, flour,

and 3 tablespoons of the turbinado sugar in a large bowl. Cut 1/2 cup butter into flour mixture using a pastry blender until mixture resembles small peas. Add almonds and crystallized ginger, and toss to combine. Add buttermilk, stirring just until dry ingredients are moistened. Turn dough out onto a lightly floured surface, and knead 3 to 4 times. Pat into a 3/4-inch-thick rectangle (about 7 by 5 inches). Cut into 6 pieces, about 3 by 2 1/2 inches.
3. Remove ramekins from oven, and carefully place 1 dough piece over hot filling in each ramekin. Brush dough with egg, and sprinkle with remaining 1 tablespoon turbinado sugar. Return to oven, and bake until fruit is bubbly and biscuits are golden, 22 to 25 minutes. Let stand 20 minutes. Top with vanilla ice cream.

BLUEBERRY SWIRL SEMIFREDDO

Active 20 min. - Total 6 hours, 55 min.
SERVES 6 TO 8

This soft and creamy dessert calls for store-bought ice cream. For the smoothest texture, choose a premium ice cream, such as Häagen-Dazs brand.

- 4 **cups fresh blueberries, divided**
- 1/2 **cup water**
- 1 1/2 **cups granulated sugar**
- 1/2 **tsp. lemon zest**
- 2 **Tbsp. fresh lemon juice**
- 1 **tsp. vanilla extract**
- 1 **pt. vanilla ice cream**
- 1 **cup heavy cream**

1. Combine 3 cups blueberries, water, sugar, lemon zest and juice, and vanilla in a medium saucepan. Bring to a boil over high; reduce to medium-low, and simmer until slightly thickened, about 20 minutes. Pour mixture through a fine wire-mesh strainer into a bowl, pressing gently on solids; discard solids. Let cool to room temperature. Reserve 1/2 cup blueberry sauce for Step 4.
2. Remove the vanilla ice cream from the freezer, and thaw at room temperature 20 minutes. Stir together the cooled

For the right berry-to-biscuit ratio, bake the cobbler in individual ramekins.

Blackberry Cobbler with Almond-Ginger Biscuits, left

blueberry sauce and partially thawed ice cream in a large bowl, leaving some large pieces of frozen ice cream.
3. Whip the heavy cream to stiff peaks. Gently fold whipped cream into blueberry mixture, and swirl gently with a knife. Pour into a 9- x 5-inch loaf pan. Cover and freeze 6 hours or overnight.
4. To serve, run each side of loaf pan under hot water. Run a knife around the edge of the loaf pan, and turn out onto a cutting board. Cut into 3/4-inch-thick slices; place on serving plates. Top with remaining 1 cup blueberries and reserved 1/2 cup sauce; serve immediately.

The New Cookout Classics

SEVEN SIZZLING SPINS ON THE ALL-AMERICAN SUMMER MENU

Colorful Collard Slaw, page 196

Buttermilk-Hot Sauce Brined Chicken, page 194

Street Corn Salad, page 194

Corn-off-the-Cob Bread,
page 196

Rum Baked
Beans,
page 196

Colorful
Collard Slaw,
page 196

Sesame, Tomato, and Cucumber
Salad, page 140

clockwise from top left:

- Mouthwatering Marinated Tomatoes (page 138)
- Grilled Flat Iron Steak with Charred Tomato Relish (page 140)
- The *SL* BLT (page 142)
- Chicken Noodle Bowl with Peanut-Ginger Sauce (page 145)

Southwest Chicken
Tortillas, page 147

Blackberry Cobbler with Almond-Ginger Biscuits, page 157

clockwise from top left:

• Cherry-Plum Pie with
Cornmeal Crust (page 156)
• Spiced Peach Galette
(page 155)
• Berry Cobbler with
Pecan Sandie Streusel
(page 155)
• Plum-Berry Cornmeal
Sheet Cake (page 155)

Buttermilk-Hot Sauce Brined Chicken, page 194; Street Corn Salad, page 194; Colorful Collard Slaw, page 196

Corn-off-the-Cob Bread,
page 196

clockwise from top:

- Berry Swirl Gelato Cake
  (page 200)
- Pear and Golden Raisin
  Ginger Chutney (page 209)
- Cherry Pie Bars (page 217)

Gibson Martini with Pickled
Pearl Onions, page 206

clockwise from top left:
- Pickled Cremini Mushrooms (page 208)
- Pickled Plums (page 209)
- Bread 'n' Butter Zucchini, (page 209)
- Pickled Turnips (page 209)

Arugula Salad with
Smoked Almonds, page 211

Charred Summer Vegetable
Salad, page 212

Gulf Shrimp Orzo, page 216

Skirt Steak Sandwiches, page 203

Apple-Spice Bundt Cake with
Caramel Frosting, page 227

Pecan Praline Deep-Dish Skillet Cookie, page 246

Strawberry Shortcake Deep-Dish Skillet Cookie, page 246

Grasshopper Deep-Dish Skillet Cookie, page 246

Hummingbird Deep-Dish Skillet Cookie, page 246

Mississippi Mud Deep-Dish Skillet Cookie, page 246

Praline Layer Cake, page 226

Garlicky Roasted Spatchcock
Chicken, page 238

Brown Butter Apple Pie,
page 243

clockwise from top left:

- Spaghetti with Shrimp and Roasted Cherry Tomatoes (page 221)
- Grilled Italian Spareribs (page 221)
- Fig Dutch Baby Pancake (page 241)

Roasted Pumpkin Soup,
page 258

Classic Beef Chili, page 258

Skillet Chicken Pot Pie,
page 251

Sweet Tea-Brined Chicken,
page 255

Hugh's Southern Mac and Cheese,
page 252

clockwise from top left:
- Maple Peanut Pie (page 281)
- Pumpkin-Lemon Cream Cheese Chess Pie (page 282)
- Green Tomato Mincemeat Pie (page 280)
- German Chocolate-Pecan Pie (page 280)

Sweet-and-Spicy Roast Chicken, page 268

Skillet Squash Blossom,
page 269

Goat Cheese Mashed
Potatoes, page 274

Smashed Baby Red
Potatoes, page 274

Brussels Sprouts with Cornbread Croutons, page 269

Honey-Glazed Spiced Carrots, page 270

Slow-Cooker Green Beans, page 270

Sweet Potato Bread with
Buttermilk-Lime Icing,
page 278

Buttermilk-Hot Sauce
Brined Chicken,
page 194

Sour Cream Potato
Salad, page 194

GRILLED TOMATOES ON THE VINE

- 2 lb. cherry tomatoes on the vine
- 2 tsp. olive oil
- 1 tsp. kosher salt
- 1/2 tsp. black pepper
- 1 Tbsp. torn basil, thyme, or oregano leaves or 1 rosemary sprig
  Coarse sea salt

1. Heat grill to medium (300°F to 350°F). Place tomatoes (attached to vine) in the center of an 18- x 18-inch piece of heavy-duty aluminum foil. Drizzle with olive oil, and sprinkle with salt and pepper. Sprinkle with desired herb. Seal foil to make a packet.
2. Grill tomatoes, covered, 10 minutes; open packet slightly, and grill until tomatoes soften and are heated through, 5 to 10 minutes. Sprinkle with sea salt, and serve.

SERVES 8 (serving size: 1/2 cup)
ACTIVE 5 min. **TOTAL** 15 min.

STREET CORN SALAD

- 1/2 cup chopped fresh cilantro
- 3 Tbsp. fresh lime juice
- 1 tsp. kosher salt
- 1/2 tsp. black pepper
- 2 Tbsp. olive oil
- 4 cups fresh corn kernels
- 1 cup thinly sliced radishes
- 1 cup cherry tomato halves
- 1/3 to 1/2 cup crumbled Cotija cheese (or feta cheese)

1. Combine first 4 ingredients; whisk in olive oil.
2. Stir together corn, radishes, and tomatoes in a medium bowl. Gently stir in dressing; spoon mixture onto a serving platter, and sprinkle with cheese.

SERVES 8 (serving size: 3/4 cup)
ACTIVE 20 min. **TOTAL** 20 min.

BUTTERMILK-HOT SAUCE BRINED CHICKEN

- 2 cups buttermilk
- 2 cups cold water
- 1/4 cup kosher salt
- 1 Tbsp. black pepper
- 1/2 cup plus 3 Tbsp. hot sauce
- 1/4 cup firmly packed plus 2 tsp. light brown sugar, divided
- 1 lime, thinly sliced
- 4 garlic cloves, smashed
- 4 to 5 lb. skin-on, bone-in chicken breasts and leg quarters
- 1/4 cup ketchup
- 2 Tbsp. melted salted butter
- 1 Tbsp. apple cider vinegar

1. Whisk together buttermilk, water, salt, pepper, 1/2 cup of the hot sauce, and 1/4 cup of the brown sugar in a large bowl until sugar is dissolved; stir in lime slices and garlic.
2. Place buttermilk mixture and chicken in a large zip-top plastic freezer bag; seal bag, and chill 24 hours. Remove chicken from marinade, discarding marinade; pat dry with paper towels.
3. Heat a grill to medium (300°F to 350°F) with an area cleared of coals (for charcoal grill) or a burner turned off (for gas) to make an indirect heat area. Place chicken, skin side up, over indirect heat, and grill, covered, until a meat thermometer inserted in thickest portion registers 165°F, about 1 hour and 15 minutes.
4. Whisk together ketchup, butter, vinegar, and remaining 3 tablespoons hot sauce and 2 teaspoons brown sugar.
5. Brush ketchup mixture onto both sides of chicken; transfer, skin side down, to direct side of grill, and grill, uncovered, 1 to 2 minutes or until skin is browned and crispy; turn and grill, uncovered, 1 to 2 more minutes. Let rest 5 minutes before serving.

SERVES 6 **ACTIVE** 25 min.
TOTAL 25 hours, 25 min., plus 24 hours for brining

SOUR CREAM POTATO SALAD

- 3 lb. small russet potatoes, thinly sliced (about 1/4 inch thick)
- 6 thick-cut bacon slices, cooked crisp and crumbled
- 3/4 cup sour cream
- 1/2 cup mayonnaise
- 1 Tbsp. chopped fresh flat-leaf parsley
- 1 Tbsp. finely chopped fresh chives
- 1 Tbsp. white vinegar
- 1 1/2 tsp. table salt
- 1 tsp. granulated sugar
- 1/4 tsp. garlic powder
- 1/8 tsp. white pepper
- 1 scallion, finely chopped

1. Place potato slices in a Dutch oven, and cover with cold water; bring to a boil over medium-high. Reduce heat to medium-low, and simmer until tender, about 15 minutes. Drain and cool. Place potatoes in a large bowl; gently stir in bacon.
2. Whisk together remaining 10 ingredients in a small bowl. Add sour cream mixture to potato mixture, and stir gently to incorporate.

SERVES 8 (serving size: 1 cup) **ACTIVE** 20 min.
TOTAL 1 hour, 40 min.

Street Corn
Salad, page 194

Grilled Tomatoes
on the Vine,
page 194

COLORFUL COLLARD SLAW

- 1/2 cup white wine vinegar
- 5 Tbsp. granulated sugar
- 2 Tbsp. fresh lime juice
- 2 tsp. prepared horseradish
- 1/4 tsp. dried crushed red pepper
- 2 tsp. kosher salt, divided
- 1/2 cup olive oil
- 1 bunch collard greens (about 1 3/4 lb.)
- 2 cups matchstick carrots
- 1 sweet apple (such as Braeburn, Pink Lady, or Honey Crisp), diced (about 2 cups)

1. Whisk together first 5 ingredients and 1 1/2 teaspoons of the salt in a small bowl until sugar is completely dissolved; slowly whisk in olive oil until completely incorporated.
2. Trim and discard tough stems from collard greens; thinly slice leaves, and place in a large bowl. Sprinkle with remaining 1/2 teaspoon salt, and gently massage into greens 1 to 2 minutes. (This helps tenderize them and remove any bitterness.) Pour off any liquid.
3. Add carrots, apple, and 2 tablespoons of the dressing to collards; stir gently to combine, and let stand 30 minutes. Add 1/4 cup of the dressing to slaw, and toss. Serve remaining dressing on the side.

SERVES 10 (serving size: 1 cup) **ACTIVE** 20 min. **TOTAL** 50 min.

CORN-OFF-THE-COB BREAD

- 1/2 cup (4 oz.) salted butter
- 1 1/2 cups self-rising white cornmeal mix
- 1/2 cup (2 oz.) all-purpose flour
- 1 1/2 cups buttermilk
- 1 cup fresh corn kernels
- 2 large eggs

1. Preheat oven to 425°F. Place butter in a 10-inch cast-iron skillet, and heat in oven until butter has melted and skillet is hot, about 5 minutes.
2. Meanwhile, whisk together cornmeal and flour in a large bowl. Whisk together buttermilk, corn kernels, and eggs in a medium bowl. Stir buttermilk mixture into cornmeal mixture. Add melted butter from skillet to cornmeal mixture, and stir just until blended. Pour into hot skillet.
3. Bake until golden brown, 25 to 30 minutes. Remove from oven, and immediately turn out onto a platter.

SERVES 8 **ACTIVE** 15 min. **TOTAL** 45 min.

RUM BAKED BEANS

- 6 thick-cut bacon slices, chopped
- 1 cup chopped sweet onion
- 2 garlic cloves, minced
- 1 (28-oz.) can baked beans with bacon and brown sugar
- 1 (16-oz.) can navy beans, drained and rinsed
- 1 (16-oz.) can dark red kidney beans, drained and rinsed
- 1 (16-oz.) can light red kidney beans, drained and rinsed
- 1 (15-oz.) can black beans, drained and rinsed
- 1/2 cup firmly packed dark brown sugar
- 1/2 cup ketchup
- 1/2 cup gold rum
- 1/4 cup apple cider vinegar

1. Preheat oven to 350°F. Cook bacon in a large skillet over medium until crisp; remove, reserving 2 tablespoons drippings in skillet. Add onion, and cook, stirring often, until tender, about 5 minutes; add garlic, and cook 1 minute.
2. Stir together bacon, onion mixture, baked beans, and next 8 ingredients in a large bowl. Spoon into a lightly greased 13- x 9-inch baking dish.
3. Bake, covered with aluminum foil, 30 minutes; uncover and bake 30 more minutes.

SERVES 10 (serving size: 3/4 cup) **ACTIVE** 20 min. **TOTAL** 1 hour, 20 min.

TWO-BITE APPETIZERS

Muffin Pan Tomato Tarts

Our new twist on the classic summer pie starts with puff pastry sheets.

- 1 (17.3-oz.) pkg. frozen puff pastry sheets, partially thawed
- 1/2 cup mayonnaise
- 2 tsp. kosher salt
- 1 tsp. black pepper
- 10 oz. sharp Cheddar cheese, finely shredded (2 1/2 cups)
- 11 oz. multicolored cherry tomatoes (about 3 cups), halved
- 2 Tbsp. torn fresh basil

1. Preheat oven to 400°F. Gently unfold both pastry sheets. Spread 1/4 cup mayonnaise on each pastry sheet; sprinkle each with 1 teaspoon salt and 1/2 teaspoon pepper.
2. Cut each pastry sheet into 9 (3-inch) squares. Gently press squares into 2 lightly greased muffin pans. Divide cheese and tomatoes among tarts.
3. Bake in preheated oven until pastry is golden brown, about 20 minutes. Let cool in pans on a wire rack 5 minutes. Top with torn fresh basil. Serve immediately.

MAKES 18 tarts **ACTIVE** 20 min.
TOTAL 50 min.

Flat-Out Delicious

Hold the tomato sauce and try this flavorful take on sheet pan pizza

SHEET PAN WHITE PIZZA WITH SALAMI AND PEPPERS

- 1 lb. store-bought pizza dough
- 8 oz. ricotta cheese (about 1 cup)
- 1 oz. shredded mozzarella cheese (about 1/4 cup)
- 1 garlic clove, minced
- 1 tsp. kosher salt
- 1/4 tsp. black pepper
- 3 Tbsp. extra-virgin olive oil, divided
- 8 slices salami, cut into strips
- 1 small yellow bell pepper, thinly sliced
- 1 small red bell pepper, thinly sliced
- 1/3 cup thinly sliced red onion
- 3 cups fresh arugula
- 1 tsp. fresh lemon juice
- 1/4 tsp. dried crushed red pepper

1. Place a large rimmed baking sheet (at least 17 x 11 inches) in oven. Preheat oven to 450°F. Place pizza dough on a lightly floured surface, and cover with plastic wrap. Let stand 20 minutes.

2. Stir together cheeses, garlic, salt, pepper, and 2 tablespoons of the olive oil.

3. Roll out dough on a floured surface to a 17- x 11-inch rectangle. Transfer to a large piece of lightly greased parchment paper; carefully place in hot baking sheet. Top with ricotta mixture, salami, bell peppers, and red onion. Brush edges with 1/2 tablespoon of the olive oil.

4. Bake in preheated oven until dough is golden brown and crisp, 15 to 18 minutes.

5. Toss together arugula, lemon juice, remaining 1/2 tablespoon olive oil, and salt and pepper to taste. Top pizza with arugula mixture; sprinkle with red pepper.

SERVES 6 **ACTIVE** 30 min. **TOTAL** 48 min.

PEACH PEELING POINTERS

FOUR SIMPLE STEPS TO GETTING THAT FUZZY SKIN TO SLIDE RIGHT OFF

1. Score ripe peaches with a paring knife by making an X on the pointed side of the fruit. (Cut through the skin, not the flesh.)

2. Submerge the peaches in boiling water for 40 to 60 seconds, longer if the fruit is underripe.

3. Dunk the peaches in an ice bath. Let cool completely.

4. Remove the skin by gently pulling back or rubbing off the scored marks. The skin should slide off quickly and easily.

1.

2.

3.

4.

HOW TO

TAKE CORN OFF THE COB

WHAT YOU'LL NEED: Bundt pan and knife

1. Place the cob on the center of the Bundt pan.

2. Using knife, slice downward along the sides of the cob to remove kernels.

3. Scrape the back of the knife along the cob to release juices.

SLICE AND SEASON

Just a pinch of salt (kosher or sea salt) can be your best summer seasoning. It will enhance the natural sweetness of ripe melons, strawberries, and pineapple, and reduces bitterness in underripe fruit.

Red, White & Berries

A FROZEN FOURTH OF JULY DESSERT TOPPED WITH SWEET SEASONAL FRUIT

BERRY SWIRL GELATO CAKE

For this recipe, we like Talenti brand gela-to for its softer, easy-to-spread texture.

- 2 cups fresh blackberries
- 2 cups fresh raspberries
- 5 cups waffle cone pieces (about 1 [7-oz.] pkg. waffle cones)
- ⅓ cup cocktail peanuts
- 2½ Tbsp. granulated sugar
- ½ tsp. kosher salt
- 7 Tbsp. salted butter, melted
- ⅓ cup malted milk powder
- 2 (1-qt.) containers vanilla bean gelato
- 2 to 3 cups assorted fresh berries Powdered sugar (optional)

1. Process blackberries and raspberries in a food processor until very smooth. Pour through a fine wire-mesh strainer, using the back of a spoon to press as much pulp through as possible; discard solids. Cover and chill 2 hours to 2 days.
2. Preheat oven to 350°F. Pulse waffle cone pieces, peanuts, sugar, and salt in a food processer until coarsely ground. Add butter, and pulse until well combined. Using a straight-sided glass, press the mixture into the bottom and all the way up the sides of a 9-inch springform pan.
3. Bake in preheated oven until fragrant, 10 to 12 minutes. Cool about 30 minutes. Freeze 30 minutes.
4. Beat malt powder and 1 quart of gelato with an electric mixer at low speed until smooth and soft, about 1 minute. In a separate bowl, beat chilled berry puree and remaining quart of gelato at low speed until blended, about 1 minute.
5. Spoon some of the berry-gelato mixture into prepared pan. Top that with some of the malted gelato. Repeat layers, ending with the berry-gelato mixture. Using a wooden skewer, swirl layers together. Cover and freeze 24 hours. Remove sides of pan. Just before serving, top cake with berries and, if desired, a sprinkling of powdered sugar.

SERVES 10 **ACTIVE** 30 min. **TOTAL** 25 hours, including 24 hours freezing

August

Let's Eat Out

JULIA REED SHARES AN IDEA-PACKED PICNIC THAT'S READY FOR THE LAKE OR PARK

I LOVE A PICNIC. The great American food writer James Beard called picnics "one of the supreme pleasures of outdoor life," and I wholeheartedly concur. The most elegant versions call for china and crystal, candelabra and fine linens, as with many of the feasts laid out in The Grove, the storied tailgating destination at Ole Miss. During an adolescent summer in France, I didn't learn a lick of French, but I discovered the joys of a rather more simple outdoor repast: a hunk of cheese and/or pâté, a baguette, and a bottle of wine.

Our picnic here on the dock at Lake Washington, near where I grew up in the Mississippi Delta, lies somewhere in between. After a day of swimming and boating, I offer up a platter of sandwiches made with

grilled skirt steak from a recipe I adapted from my pal, the writer and talented cook Ellen Stimson. To go with the sandwiches, I resurrected the curried rice salad with marinated artichoke hearts that was a summer staple in the 1970s. The recipe, which appears in countless Junior League cookbooks (and which can still be found online), was a combination of chicken-flavored rice, marinated artichoke hearts, sliced green olives, chopped scallions and bell pepper, plus a sauce made of the artichoke marinade, commercial mayonnaise, and curry powder. I lightened it up by using plain converted rice, adding minced celery, and using more marinade than mayo. It's still delicious and holds up well. For dessert, I usually make a lemon loaf cake because it's so easy to transport.

For drinks, I fill a cooler with beer and wine and tote along a big jar of lemonade sweetened with

mint-infused simple syrup. (Boil a cup of sugar with a cup of water until the sugar is just dissolved, throw in a bunch of mint, and strain when cool.) Kids love it, and grown-ups should feel free to add vodka or rum! The good news is that none of this food requires super refrigeration. Just layer the sandwiches and container of rice salad on top of the ice in which you've packed the beer and wine. Everything else can go in the hamper with the forks and linens. For this occasion, our linen cloth—made with fabric by designer Peter Fasano— is a stylish riff on the Hudson's Bay blankets often used for picnics. I love the bold stripes, but you could also use an Indian bedspread or even an old quilt. Either way, I highly recommend linen or cotton napkins. It's just as easy to pack them up and take them home as it is to throw away a lot of trash—plus guests will feel a whole lot more pampered.

TO START OFF, I offer a crock of yummy smoked catfish pâté from The Crown Restaurant in Indianola, Mississippi (available at *tasteofgourmet.com*). **For years, I've collected enamel bowls, plates, and cups, which are far more festive than their paper counterparts. Likewise, inexpensive wooden forks (from** *justartifacts.net*) **are preferable to plastic.**

THE RECIPES

SKIRT STEAK SANDWICHES

I like to crisp the cut surfaces of the brioche rolls by brushing both sides lightly with melted butter and placing them, cut sides down, in a hot skillet for a few minutes.

- 18 small brioche rolls or slider buns, split
  Horseradish Mayonnaise
  Coffee and Brown Sugar-Encrusted Skirt Steak
  Lettuce leaves
  Thinly sliced red onion

Spread cut sides of rolls with Horseradish Mayonnaise. Top each bottom half with skirt steak slices, lettuce, and slices of red onion.

MAKES 18 sandwiches
ACTIVE 20 min. **TOTAL** 20 min.

COFFEE AND BROWN SUGAR-ENCRUSTED SKIRT STEAK

- 2 1/2 to 3 lb. skirt steak
- 3/4 cup packed dark brown sugar
- 1/4 cup finely ground dark-roast coffee
- 2 Tbsp. kosher salt
- 1 Tbsp. dry mustard
- 2 tsp. black pepper
- 1 Tbsp. olive oil

1. Thoroughly pat steak dry with paper towels. Cut steak into thirds.
2. Place sugar, coffee, salt, mustard, and pepper in a small bowl; using your hands, mix until combined and sugar is broken down into fine crystals. Coat steak generously with sugar mixture, pressing to adhere. Wrap each steak piece tightly in plastic wrap; chill 1 hour.
3. Heat grill to high (450°F to 550°F). Unwrap steak pieces; pat dry with paper towels. Drizzle with olive oil. Grill, uncovered, until medium-rare, about 2 minutes per side. Transfer meat to a cutting board; cut across the grain into thin slices.

Note: For variety, I like to offer chicken sandwiches as well. Roast a chicken (or buy one already cooked), and slice the breast meat. Make the same sandwich, but omit the red onion and instead of adding horseradish and Creole mustard to the mayo, add chopped fresh tarragon or basil with a little minced scallion.

MAKES 1 steak **ACTIVE** 20 min.
TOTAL 1 hour, 20 min.

HORSERADISH MAYONNAISE

A trick I learned from the very talented Suzanne Goin of Lucques, A.O.C., and Tavern (three Los Angeles restaurants) is to drape a dishtowel over a small saucepan and set a metal bowl on it. This holds the bowl containing the mayonnaise in place and gives you the height you need for easy whisking. You can also use a hand mixer for this step, in which case, you will likely need to loosen up the mixture periodically with a few drops of warm water.

- 1 large pasteurized egg yolk, at room temperature
- 2 tsp. fresh lemon juice
- 1 tsp. Dijon mustard
- 1/4 tsp. table salt
- 3/4 cup vegetable or canola oil
- 3 tsp. prepared horseradish
- 2 tsp. Creole mustard (such as Zatarain's) or other whole-grain mustard
  Pinch of cayenne pepper

1. Whisk together egg yolk, lemon juice, Dijon mustard, and salt in a medium bowl until smooth. Slowly dribble in oil, whisking constantly. When mixture starts to thicken, add oil in a thin stream until completely incorporated. (If mayonnaise gets too thick, add 1 teaspoon water.)
2. Add horseradish, Creole mustard, and cayenne, and whisk until incorporated. Cover with plastic wrap, and chill until ready to use.

MAKES about 1 cup
ACTIVE 10 min. **TOTAL** 10 min.

Skirt Steak Sandwiches

WRAP SANDWICHES in old-fashioned wax paper and tie with jute twine for a better look and eco-friendlier choice than plastic bags.

PUTTING UP

GEORGIA CHEF AND CANNING ENTHUSIAST
HUGH ACHESON SHOWS US HOW HE CELEBRATES—
AND PRESERVES—HIS SUMMER BOUNTY

Pimiento Cheese with Pickled Okra on Toast, page 208

PLANTING THAT EXTRA OKRA SOUNDED like a good idea at the time. Saturday morning's trip to the farmers' market resulted in 10-too-many pounds of zucchini or an orchard's worth of plums now sitting on your counter. Sound familiar?

Don't get overwhelmed. With a little help from your friends and a set of canning jars, you can turn a bumper crop into a bumpin' shindig—or what we Southerners like to call a "put-up" party. Not only will you put all of that ripe produce to good use, but also your pals will think highly of your generous spirit when you send them home with jars of summer's bounty.

Canning in a group setting might sound like a hot mess waiting to happen, but chef and author of *Pick a Pickle* Hugh Acheson says put-up parties shouldn't be high-stress entertaining. All it takes is a little prep work, the right equipment, and a few easy recipes to pull off a laid-back preserving soiree. "Pickling is a fun way to

share an important Southern foodway with each other," he says. "Anyone, regardless of skill, can put up, and it's endless in creativity and possibility."

We asked Acheson to invite a few of his hometown friends over for an afternoon get-together in Athens, Georgia, to show us how it's done.

To up the fun factor and keep the hard work to a minimum, Acheson shared his go-to put-ups that will keep in the refrigerator so you can skip the hot and bothersome water bath. Plus, he gives us the scoop on his favorite theme-appropriate nibbles for your guests and suggestions for how to use your post-party creations. So what are you waiting for? Those fresh fruits and veggies aren't getting any younger. Call up your friends—preferably the ones with the prolific pear trees—and use our handy guide for setting up your own put-up party.

Gibson Martini with Pickled Pearl Onions

GIBSON MARTINI WITH PICKLED PEARL ONIONS

2 1/2 oz. (5 Tbsp.) gin (such as Beefeater)
1/2 oz. (1 Tbsp.) dry vermouth (such as Dolin)
3 Pickled Pearl Onions

Combine gin and vermouth in an ice-filled cocktail glass. Stir gently to cool. Strain into an ice-cold martini glass; garnish with Pickled Pearl Onions.

MAKES 1 (3-oz.) martini **ACTIVE** 5 min. **TOTAL** 5 min.

Pickled Pearl Onions

1 1/4 cups apple cider vinegar
1 1/4 cups water
2 Tbsp. granulated sugar
1 1/2 Tbsp. pickling salt
6 dried allspice berries
6 black peppercorns
1 whole clove
3 (10-oz.) pkg. fresh pearl onions, peeled according to package directions

1. Combine vinegar, water, sugar, pickling salt, allspice berries, peppercorns, and clove in a nonreactive saucepan; bring to a boil over high. Add onions; reduce heat to low, and simmer 5 minutes.
2. Transfer onions into 1 (1-quart) canning jar or 2 (1-pint) canning jars, leaving 1/2 inch of room at the top, reserving liquid in saucepan.
3. Carefully ladle hot vinegar mixture over onions in jars, leaving 1/2 inch of room at the top of each. Discard any remaining liquid. Wipe jar rims. Cover at once with metal lids; screw on bands. Cool jars to room temperature. Onions will keep up to a month in refrigerator.

MAKES 1 quart **ACTIVE** 10 min. **TOTAL** 20 min.

Pickled Cremini Mushrooms,
page 208

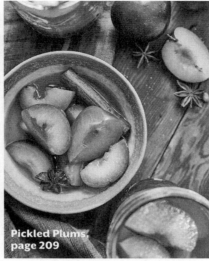
Pickled Plums,
page 209

Pickled Turnips,
page 209

Pear and Golden Raisin Ginger Chutney,
page 209

Bread 'n' Butter Zucchini,
page 209

HUGH ACHESON'S

PUT-UP PARTY TIPS

KEEP THE GUEST LIST SHORT

Invite up to eight guests; any more will cramp the kitchen.

PLAN AHEAD

Coordinate with your guests to figure out who is bringing vinegar, pounds of produce, or that extra bottle of wine.

PREP JARS

Sterilize canning jars right before guests arrive by boiling them for 10 minutes, then let them air dry.

DELEGATE DUTIES

Assign each guest a task, like chopping up zucchini or measuring out spices, so everyone has a part in the process.

FORM AN ASSEMBLY LINE

Once the ingredients are prepped, everyone can assume a role: packing jars, adding brine, or sealing lids.

MAKE LABELS

Be sure every jar is labeled with its contents, packing date, and how long it keeps.

PICKLED OKRA

- 2 lb. fresh okra
- 3 jalapeño chiles, seeds removed, thinly sliced
- 3 garlic cloves, halved
- 3 fresh dill sprigs, halved
- 1 qt. apple cider vinegar
- 1 1/2 cups water
- 1/4 cup kosher salt
- 1 Tbsp. yellow mustard seeds

1. Divide and pack okra, jalapeño slices, garlic, and dill evenly among 6 (1-pint) canning jars.
2. Combine vinegar, water, salt, and mustard seeds in a stockpot, and bring to a boil over high. Remove from heat. Carefully ladle hot vinegar mixture over okra mixture in jars, leaving 1/2 inch of room at the top of each. Wipe rims. Cover with lids; screw on bands. Cool jars to room temperature. Okra will keep up to 2 months in the refrigerator.

MAKES 6 pints **ACTIVE** 10 min.
TOTAL 10 min.

PIMIENTO CHEESE WITH PICKLED OKRA ON TOAST

- 1 lb. sharp white Cheddar cheese, grated (4 cups)
- 2 large red bell peppers, roasted, peeled, seeds removed, and diced
- 1/2 cup mayonnaise
- 1 tsp. Dijon mustard
- 1/2 tsp. smoked paprika
- 1/2 tsp. kosher salt
  Pinch of cayenne pepper
- 1 baguette
- 2 Tbsp. olive oil
  Pickled Okra

1. Preheat oven to 400°F. Stir together Cheddar, bell peppers, mayonnaise, mustard, paprika, salt, and cayenne in a large bowl.
2. Diagonally cut baguette into 1/2-inch slices. Brush both sides of baguette slices with olive oil, and place slices on a baking sheet. Bake for 3 minutes. Turn bread slices, and bake until toasted, about 3 minutes. Remove

from oven, and cool. Serve toast with pickled okra and pimiento cheese.

MAKES 3 cups pimiento cheese
ACTIVE 15 min. **TOTAL** 15 min.

PICKLED CREMINI MUSHROOMS

- 6 qt., plus 1 1/2 cups water, divided
- 4 lb. fresh cremini mushrooms
- 4 cups white wine vinegar
- 6 Tbsp. yellow or white miso (optional)
- 2 Tbsp. kosher salt
- 1 1/2 tsp. crushed red pepper
- 1 tsp. smoked paprika
- 3/4 cup finely chopped fresh flat-leaf parsley
- 3 Tbsp. finely chopped fresh rosemary
- 3 Tbsp. minced fresh garlic
- 3 tsp. finely chopped fresh thyme

1. Bring 6 quarts of the water to a boil in a large stockpot over high. Trim 1/4 inch away from each mushroom stem. Quarter mushrooms. Add mushrooms to water; cook 45 seconds. Drain and transfer mushrooms to a large bowl.
2. Combine vinegar, miso (if desired), salt, red pepper, paprika, and remaining 1 1/2 cups water in a medium saucepan; bring to a boil over high.
3. Drain mushrooms again. Add parsley, rosemary, garlic, and thyme to mushrooms; toss to combine.
4. Add boiling vinegar mixture to mushrooms in bowl. Let stand at room temperature 5 minutes. Carefully ladle mushroom mixture evenly into 6 (1-pint) canning jars. Wipe rims. Cover at once with lids; screw on bands. Cool jars to room temperature. Refrigerate 2 days before serving. Pickled mushrooms will keep up to 1 week in refrigerator.

MAKES 6 pints **ACTIVE** 30 min.
TOTAL 2 days, 30 min., including 2 days chilling

6 CANNING ESSENTIALS

LADLE
For pouring hot brine into jars

PICKLING SALT
Free of iodine or anti-caking agents that might make your put-ups cloudy. Diamond Crystal Kosher Salt also works.

FUNNEL
Helps make ladling brine into jars easier and neater

HEINZ APPLE CIDER VINEGAR AND DISTILLED WHITE VINEGAR
Reliable, affordable staples

CLEAN JARS WITH NEW LIDS
Recycle old jars, as long as you properly sterilize them. For safety's sake, buy new lids.

NONREACTIVE BOWLS AND PANS
Put-ups can pick up a metallic taste or change color if they're prepared in certain metal or copper vessels. Use plastic, stainless steel, ceramic, and glass where noted.

BREAD 'N' BUTTER ZUCCHINI

7 1/2   cups 1/4-inch-thick zucchini slices
2   medium-size sweet onions, thinly sliced
2 1/2   Tbsp. pickling salt, divided
3/4   cup firmly packed fresh celery leaves, torn
2 1/2   cups apple cider vinegar
2   cups water
3/4   cup granulated sugar
1 1/2   tsp. yellow mustard seeds
3/4   tsp. curry powder
3/4   tsp. celery seeds
1/2   tsp. crushed red pepper
1/2   tsp. fennel seeds
6   dried allspice berries

1. Combine zucchini and onions in a large nonreactive bowl. Add 1 1/4 tablespoons of the pickling salt; toss well to coat. Let stand at room temperature 1 hour.
2. Transfer zucchini mixture to a colander, and rinse thoroughly to remove pickling salt. Drain and transfer to a medium bowl. Stir in celery leaves.
3. Divide and pack mixture evenly into 6 (1-pint) canning jars, leaving 1/2 inch of room at the top of each.
4. Combine vinegar and next 8 ingredients with remaining 1 1/4 tablespoons pickling salt in a medium saucepan; bring to a boil over high. Reduce heat to low, and simmer 5 minutes. Remove from heat.
5. Carefully ladle hot vinegar mixture over zucchini mixture in jars, leaving 1/2 inch of room at the top of each. Wipe rims. Cover at once with lids; screw on bands. Cool jars to room temperature. Pickles will keep up to a month in refrigerator.

MAKES 6 pints **ACTIVE** 20 min. **TOTAL** 20 min.

PICKLED PLUMS

2 1/2   cups rice vinegar
2 1/2   cups apple cider vinegar
2   cups water
1/2   cup plus 2 Tbsp. light brown sugar
5   Tbsp. pickling salt
5   tsp. ground ginger
5   lb. firm black plums (18 to 24 plums), quartered
8   pieces whole star anise
4   cinnamon sticks, broken in half

1. Combine rice vinegar and next 5 ingredients in a stockpot. Bring to a boil over high; reduce heat to medium, and simmer 5 minutes.
2. Divide and pack plum quarters evenly into 8 (1-pint) canning jars. Add 1 piece star anise and 1 cinnamon stick half to each jar. Carefully ladle hot vinegar mixture over plums in jars, leaving 1/2 inch of room at the top of each. Wipe rims. Cover at once with lids; screw on bands. Let stand 2 hours. Chill 1 week before serving. Plums will keep up to 2 months in refrigerator.

MAKES 8 pints **ACTIVE** 20 min.
TOTAL 1 week, 2 hours, 20 min., including 1 week chilling

PEAR AND GOLDEN RAISIN GINGER CHUTNEY

2   Tbsp. olive oil
1   shallot, minced
2   lb. Bartlett pears (about 4 pears), cored and diced
1   Tbsp. fresh lemon juice
1/2   cup white wine vinegar
1/3   cup golden raisins
1/4   cup packed light brown sugar
1   Tbsp. finely chopped fresh ginger
1   tsp. kosher salt
1/2   tsp. yellow mustard seeds
1/4   tsp. ground cinnamon
1/4   tsp. ground nutmeg
1/4   tsp. lemon zest
1/3   cup pine nuts, toasted

1. Heat olive oil in a Dutch oven over medium. Add shallot, and cook, stirring occasionally, 2 minutes. Add pears and lemon juice, and cook, stirring occasionally, until softened, about 5 minutes.
2. Add vinegar, raisins, brown sugar, ginger, salt, mustard seeds, cinnamon, nutmeg, and lemon zest; cook, stirring occasionally, until pears are softened, 20 to 25 minutes. Remove from heat. Fold in pine nuts.
3. Spoon pear mixture into 3 (1/2-pint) canning jars. Cool 15 minutes. Wipe jar rims. Cover at once with metal lids; screw on bands. Chill until ready to use. Chutney will keep up to 2 weeks in refrigerator.

MAKES about 3 cups **ACTIVE** 30 min. **TOTAL** 30 min.

PICKLED TURNIPS

3   lb. turnips
3   small red beets, halved
6   small garlic cloves
4   cups water
1 1/2   cups apple cider vinegar
6   Tbsp. pickling salt
1 1/2   tsp. ground sumac
6   bay leaves

1. Peel turnips, and remove tops. Cut turnips into 2-inch pieces. Divide turnip pieces evenly among 6 (1-pint) canning jars. Add 1 beet half and 1 garlic clove to each jar, leaving 1 inch of room at the top of each jar.
2. Combine water and next 4 ingredients in a medium saucepan, and bring to a boil.
3. Carefully pour vinegar mixture over turnip mixture in jars, leaving 1/2 inch of room at the top of each. Wipe jar rims. Cover at once with metal lids; screw on bands. Let stand at room temperature 1 week; chill. Turnips will keep in refrigerator up to 3 months.

MAKES 6 pints **ACTIVE** 20 min.
TOTAL 1 week, 25 min., including 1 week chilling

Romaine Salad with Pickled Beans, page 212

Arugula Salad with Smoked Almonds, page 211

SUMMER SALAD COOKBOOK

TOSSING AROUND DINNER IDEAS?
GET OUT OF THE ORDINARY
GREENS-AND-GRILLED-CHICKEN
RUT WITH THESE FAST,
FRESH, FLAVOR-PACKED RECIPES

Chopped Kale and Bacon Salad, page 211

Grilled Southern Garden Salad, page 213

Raspberry and Fig Salad, page 213

Charred Summer Vegetable Salad, page 212

ADD A PROTEIN
Thinly sliced grilled flank steak complements this salad's spicy and smoky flavor.

ARUGULA SALAD WITH SMOKED ALMONDS

Heirloom tomatoes and spicy peppers pair well with this salad's tangy dressing.

Reserve 2 tablespoons **Honey-Cider Vinegar Dressing** (recipe, page 214) in a small bowl. Combine 5 ounces **baby arugula** and remaining dressing in a large bowl; toss to coat, and arrange on a large platter. Top with 8 ounces **small yellow heirloom tomatoes** cut into wedges; ¼ cup **smoked almonds,** chopped; and, if desired, 10 **pickled sport peppers,** sliced.

SERVES 4 **ACTIVE** 15 min. **TOTAL** 15 min.

ARUGULA
These strong peppery greens can stand up to bold salad dressings— best drizzled on just before serving to avoid wilting.

CHOPPED KALE AND BACON SALAD

Since kale can be tough, it's best to tear leaves into bite-size pieces.

Cook 4 thick-cut **bacon slices** in a skillet until crisp. Drain the bacon, chop it, and set aside, reserving the bacon drippings in the pan. Chop 2 large **hard-cooked eggs,** and combine with **Buttermilk Dressing** (recipe, page 214) in a large bowl. Slice 2 more hard-cooked eggs in half, and reserve. Combine ¾ cup chopped **tomato** and 2 tablespoons hot **bacon drippings;** toss to coat. Add 6 cups chopped curly **kale** to Buttermilk Dressing-egg mixture; toss to coat. Divide salad among 4 bowls. Top with the chopped bacon, tomato mixture, ¼ cup thinly sliced **red onion,** ¼ cup thinly sliced **radishes,** and reserved egg halves.

SERVES 4 **ACTIVE** 20 min. **TOTAL** 20 min.

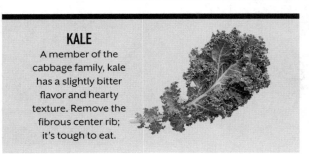

KALE
A member of the cabbage family, kale has a slightly bitter flavor and hearty texture. Remove the fibrous center rib; it's tough to eat.

ADD A PROTEIN
Cubes of grilled chicken pair deliciously with sweet corn and smoky okra.

CHARRED SUMMER VEGETABLE SALAD

Charred okra is the surprising star of this warm and hearty salad. As the okra cooks, allow it to brown in the pan and don't be tempted to stir it too much.

Preheat oven to 400°F. Add 2 cups halved baby heirloom **tomatoes** to a lightly greased rimmed baking sheet. Bake in preheated oven until tomatoes begin to wilt, about 13 minutes. Heat 1 tablespoon **oil** in skillet over medium-high. Add 2 cups **okra,** halved lengthwise; cook 2 minutes, stirring once. Add 1 cup fresh **corn** kernels and ¼ teaspoon table **salt;** cook, stirring occasionally, until okra is well charred and corn is tender, about 1 minute. Toss together 5 ounces fresh **baby spinach** and **Buttermilk Dressing** (recipe, page 214) in a large bowl until coated; top with okra mixture and tomatoes.

SERVES 4 **ACTIVE** 30 min. **TOTAL** 30 min.

BABY SPINACH
These greens are harvested before they are fully grown, so they have a tender texture and slightly sweet flavor.

ROMAINE SALAD WITH PICKLED BEANS

This crisp salad is a real crowd-pleaser on a hot summer night.

Whisk together ¼ cup **mayonnaise,** 1 tablespoon **Old Bay** seasoning, and 2 large **eggs** in a medium bowl until well combined. Add 1 lb. fresh **lump crabmeat,** drained, and ⅔ cup **panko** (Japanese-style breadcrumbs) to bowl, stirring gently until just combined. Divide crab mixture into 8 equal portions; shape each into a 3-inch patty. Heat 3 tablespoons **olive oil** in a large skillet over medium-high. Add patties to pan; cook until well browned, about 4 minutes on each side. Remove from pan. Arrange 2 chopped **romaine** lettuce hearts in 4 bowls. Top evenly with 1 cup sliced **dilly beans** (pickled green beans) and ½ cup sliced **radishes.** Combine **Buttermilk Dressing** (recipe, page 214) and 1 tablespoon chopped fresh **dill** in a small bowl. Drizzle dressing over each serving.

SERVES 4 **ACTIVE** 30 min. **TOTAL** 30 min.

ROMAINE
These long lettuce leaves are crisp and slightly bitter. Their sturdy texture is a good match for thick salad dressings.

ADD A PROTEIN
Crispy crab cakes, grilled salmon, or shrimp makes this a light and summery dish.

ADD A PROTEIN
For a more satisfying meal, add slices of pork tenderloin.

RASPBERRY AND FIG SALAD

Figs and blue cheese are made for each other, especially when topped with a tangy lemon-thyme dressing.

Divide 1 head **Bibb lettuce** (about 8 ounces), torn into bite-size pieces, evenly among 4 bowls. Sprinkle with 1 (6-ounce) container fresh **raspberries;** 4 medium **figs,** quartered; 3 ounces **blue cheese,** crumbled; and ¼ cup toasted and roughly chopped **pecans.** Drizzle with **Lemon-Thyme Dressing** (recipe, page 214).

SERVES 4 **ACTIVE** 25 min. **TOTAL** 25 min.

BIBB
These soft, ruffled leaves look pretty in a salad and have a delicate, buttery flavor that works best with bright, fruity ingredients.

GRILLED SOUTHERN GARDEN SALAD

This dish was inspired by the bounty of summertime produce in Southern gardens and farmers' markets.

Preheat grill to medium-high (350°F to 400°F). Brush both sides of 4 fresh **Texas toast** bread slices with 2 tablespoons **olive oil.** Grill bread, uncovered, until toasted on each side. Cut 2 medium **zucchini** in half crosswise, then in half lengthwise. Cut 1 large **eggplant** in half crosswise into ½-inch-thick slices. Brush zucchini, eggplant, and 8 sweet **mini bell peppers** with ¼ cup olive oil; sprinkle with 1 teaspoon table **salt** and ¼ teaspoon black **pepper.** Grill vegetables, covered, until slightly charred and tender, 4 to 5 minutes on each side. Cut toasted bread into 2-inch pieces. Divide vegetables and bread among 4 bowls; top with 8 ounces (1 cup) torn **burrata cheese.** Drizzle with **Honey-Cider Vinegar Dressing** (recipe, page 214), and sprinkle with ½ cup **fresh herb leaves** such as basil, flat-leaf parsley, or chives.

SERVES 4 **ACTIVE** 15 min. **TOTAL** 30 min.

ADD A PROTEIN
Burrata is mozzarella filled with luscious cream. If you can't find it, simply use fresh mozzarella.

DRESS APPROPRIATELY

WITH THESE THREE BLENDS, YOU COULD ENJOY A DIFFERENT SALAD EVERY DAY

BUTTERMILK DRESSING

Whisk together 1/4 cup **mayonnaise,** 3 tablespoons **buttermilk,** 1 tablespoon chopped fresh **chives,** 1 1/2 teaspoons **apple cider vinegar,** 1/2 teaspoon table **salt,** 1/2 teaspoon black **pepper,** and 1 minced **garlic** clove in a medium bowl until smooth.

SERVES 4 **ACTIVE** 5 min.
TOTAL 5 min.

HONEY-CIDER VINEGAR DRESSING

Whisk together 2 tablespoons **apple cider vinegar,** 1 tablespoon **whole-grain mustard,** 2 teaspoons **honey,** 1 teaspoon minced **garlic,** 1/2 teaspoon table **salt,** and 1/2 teaspoon black **pepper** in a medium bowl until smooth. Add 1/4 cup **extra-virgin olive oil** in a slow, steady stream, whisking constantly until smooth.

SERVES 4 **ACTIVE** 5 min.
TOTAL 5 min.

LEMON-THYME DRESSING

Whisk together 2 tablespoons fresh **lemon juice,** 1 1/2 tablespoons chopped fresh **thyme,** 2 teaspoons **Dijon mustard,** 1/2 teaspoon table **salt,** and 1/2 teaspoon black **pepper** in a medium bowl until smooth. Add 1/4 cup **extra-virgin olive oil** in a slow, steady stream, whisking constantly until smooth.

SERVES 4 **ACTIVE** 5 min.
TOTAL 5 min.

20-MINUTE APPETIZER

5 Quick Twists on Crostini

Layer fresh, flavorful toppings on crisp, butter-brushed toast for a sensational party starter.

Preheat oven to 375°F. Arrange 24 (1/2-inch-thick) diagonally cut **baguette slices** in a single layer on a baking sheet. Brush tops with 1/4 cup melted **unsalted butter.** Bake in preheated oven until slices are just beginning to brown at edges, about 12 minutes. Remove from oven, and cool to room temperature. Top as desired.

SERVES 8 **ACTIVE** 6 min. **TOTAL** 20 min.

Lemony Buttermilk Cream Cheese

Process 8 ounces softened **cream cheese,** 6 tablespoons whole **buttermilk,** 2 teaspoons **lemon zest,** 1/2 teaspoon kosher **salt,** and 1/2 teaspoon black **pepper** in a food processor until smooth. Spread 1 1/2 teaspoons on each crostini.

SERVES 1 1/4 cups **ACTIVE** 8 min. **TOTAL** 8 min.

SHAVED RADISH
Thinly sliced radishes + flaky sea salt + black pepper + thyme leaves

PESTO AND CORN
Jarred pesto + fresh corn kernels + sugar + salt

SMOKED TROUT
Smoked trout + dill sprig

TOMATO AND BLACK-EYED PEA RELISH
Quartered cherry tomatoes + black-eyed peas + olive oil + apple cider vinegar + salt + black pepper + chopped chives

HAM AND MUSTARD
Thinly sliced prosciutto or ham + jarred mustard-mayonnaise sauce + chive sprigs

One-Skillet Shrimp and Orzo

TOSS TOGETHER A LATE-SUMMER SEAFOOD SUPPER IN UNDER AN HOUR

GULF SHRIMP ORZO

- 3 Tbsp. olive oil, divided
- 1 medium-size yellow onion, chopped
- 1 pt. grape tomatoes, halved
- 3 garlic cloves, minced
- 2 tsp. chopped fresh oregano
- 1 1/4 tsp. kosher salt, divided
- 1/2 tsp. black pepper, divided
- 3 1/4 cups chicken broth
- 12 oz. uncooked orzo pasta
- 1 lb. large raw Gulf shrimp, peeled and deveined
- 1/2 cup panko (Japanese-style breadcrumbs)
- 1 oz. Parmesan cheese, grated (1/4 cup)
- 2 Tbsp. salted butter, melted
- 2 tsp. lemon zest
  Torn fresh flat-leaf parsley
  Lemon wedges

1. Preheat oven to 400°F with oven rack 5 to 6 inches from heat source. Heat 2 tablespoons of the oil in a large ovenproof skillet (with a lid) over medium-high. Add onion, and cook until translucent, about 5 minutes. Add tomatoes, garlic, oregano, 3/4 teaspoon of the salt, and 1/4 teaspoon of the pepper; cook until tomatoes are softened, about 2 minutes. Stir in broth and orzo; bring to a boil, stirring occasionally. Cover and bake until orzo is tender and liquid is mostly absorbed, about 15 minutes. Remove from oven; increase temperature to broil.

2. Toss shrimp with remaining 1 tablespoon oil, 1/2 teaspoon salt, and 1/4 teaspoon pepper; arrange shrimp on orzo. Combine panko, Parmesan, butter, and lemon zest; sprinkle over shrimp and orzo. Return to oven; broil, uncovered, until shrimp are opaque, 4 minutes. Garnish with parsley and lemon wedges.

SERVES 4 (serving size: 2 cups)
ACTIVE 20 min. **TOTAL** 40 min.

Sweet As Pie

A CLASSIC CHERRY DESSERT BAKED INTO CROWD-PLEASING TREATS

CHERRY PIE BARS

Make and store these fruity desserts, wrapped in aluminum foil, for up to three days.

- 3 cups (12 oz.) all-purpose flour
- 3/4 cup granulated sugar
- 1/2 tsp. table salt
- 1 1/2 cups (12 oz.) cold butter, cubed
- 3 cups canned cherry pie filling (about 1 1/2 [21-oz.] cans)
- 3/4 cup chopped pecans
- 1 cup powdered sugar
- 4 to 5 tsp. whole milk
- 1/4 tsp. almond extract

1. Preheat oven to 350°F. Line bottom and sides of a 13- x 9-inch pan with heavy-duty aluminum foil, allowing 2 to 3 inches to extend over sides; lightly grease foil with cooking spray.

2. Pulse flour, granulated sugar, and salt in a food processor until combined. Add butter cubes, and pulse until mixture is crumbly. Reserve 1 cup flour mixture. Press remaining flour mixture onto bottom of prepared pan.

3. Bake in preheated oven until lightly browned, 25 to 30 minutes. Spread cherry pie filling over crust in pan. Toss together reserved 1 cup flour mixture and pecans. Sprinkle pecan mixture evenly over filling.

4. Bake in preheated oven until golden brown, 40 to 45 minutes. Cool completely in pan on a wire rack, about 1 hour. Lift baked bars from pan, using foil sides as handles.

5. Stir together powdered sugar, 4 teaspoons milk, and almond extract. Add additional milk, if needed, to reach desired consistency. Drizzle over pecan mixture. Cut into 48 bars.

SERVES 24 (serving size: 2 bars)
ACTIVE 15 min. **TOTAL** 2 hours, 15 min.

SUMMER PEPPER PRIMER

A HANDY GUIDE FOR KNOWING THE SWEET BELLS FROM THE SCORCHING-HOT SCOTCH BONNETS

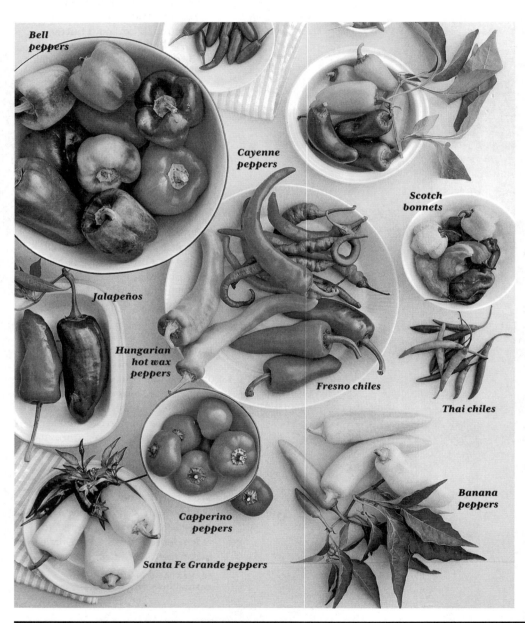

Bell peppers

Cayenne peppers

Scotch bonnets

Jalapeños

Hungarian hot wax peppers

Fresno chiles

Thai chiles

Capperino peppers

Banana peppers

Santa Fe Grande peppers

PICK AND PREP LIKE A PRO

TASTE THE RAINBOW
All red, yellow, and orange bell peppers start green. As color changes, their sweetness increases depending on how long they ripen on the vine.

SIZE MATTERS
Peppers of the same variety can vary in terms of heat. In general, the larger the pepper, the less spicy it will be.

TOO HOT TO HANDLE Hot varieties (jalapeño, cayenne, chili, Scotch bonnet) contain oils that can burn skin. Pick them up by the stem and wear gloves to cut.

BURN NOTICE
The seeds aren't the real source of a chile's spice: The spongy white vein-like ribs they dangle from hold the most heat. Remove with a paring knife or small melon baller.

HOW TO

CHOP A SALAD

1. Assemble all ingredients in a large bowl.
2. Add desired amount of dressing; toss.
3. Turn mixture onto cutting board. If you don't have a mezzaluna, use two knives to finely chop all ingredients to a uniform shape.

September

A Late Summer Supper

JULIA REED ENTERTAINS WITH AN ITALIAN-INSPIRED MENU THAT TAKES ADVANTAGE OF
WARM-WEATHER PRODUCE AND A SIMPLE, RUSTIC SETTING

WHEN I WAS A KID, everything I knew about Italian food was learned over countless meals at the Venetian Cafe in my hometown of Greenville, Mississippi, and at Perri's Italian Restaurant—a festive trattoria in Fort Walton Beach, Florida, near Destin, where we vacationed. Both featured red-and-white checked tablecloths, dripping candles in straw-covered bottles, lasagna, pizza, and a whole lot of long-simmered red sauce. I loved it all, but I had no idea what I'd been missing until Marcella Hazan published *The Classic Italian Cook Book* in 1973. It was the first of six tomes that would change the way Americans thought about Italian food in much the same way that Julia Child had introduced us to the glories of French cuisine a little more than a decade earlier.

Long before "farm to table" became a thing, Hazan stressed the importance of fresh ingredients and uncomplicated technique. Her own—exquisite—tomato sauce is enriched with nothing more than butter, onion, and salt. Her spareribs, which inspired the ones featured here, are marinated in just olive oil, garlic, rosemary, salt, and pepper.

I most often make like Marcella in the waning days of summer, when eggplant and zucchini are plentiful and late tomatoes are just coming in. It's still too hot to linger long over a stove or grill, but a porch outfitted with a ceiling fan can make the weather bearable and foreshadow

the fall months ahead. For a late lunch or early supper, I start with spaghetti tossed with a tomato sauce different from those of my childhood. Roasting cherry tomatoes intensifies their flavor without a lot of fuss. When fresh shrimp is available, I add it too. The aforementioned ribs are grilled for no more than 30 or 35 minutes—a fact that always stuns the guests who insist on parboiling or prebaking prior to grilling and then saucing them to death before serving. They are truly a revelation and can be paired with Italian sausages that require little time on the grill.

To accompany the meat, I love a clean and bright zucchini salad. Hazan's version calls for boiling the zucchini whole in salted water until just tender before slicing and tossing with olive oil and lemon juice. Jacques Pépin slices and roasts his in a 400° oven for five minutes before tossing with oil and vinegar. You can't go wrong with either one, though in both cases chopped fresh mint is a welcome addition. For dessert, I take the easy route and buy gelato or lemon sorbet at the grocery store.

Though I have no objection to a red-and-white cloth, a softer palette is more in keeping with both the season and the menu. Here I use the hand-printed Argus linen by my talented friend, fabric designer Elizabeth Hamilton. When she first showed it to me, I couldn't believe how well it complemented the McCartys pottery

I've long collected. Now Elizabeth and her husband, Peter Fasano (also a fabric designer), are McCartys collectors too. I love the literal earthiness of the pottery pieces in combination with the rustic Italian food. We may be dining on plates made from Mississippi mud near my hometown, but we are a long way in spirit from the Venetian Cafe.

JULIA'S ITALIAN CLASSICS

THE RECIPES

GRILLED ITALIAN SPARERIBS

- 1   Tbsp. fennel seeds
- 1   tsp. crushed red pepper
- 2   Tbsp. kosher salt
- 1   (4- to 5-lb.) slab pork spareribs
- 1/4   cup extra-virgin olive oil
- 2   Tbsp. fresh lemon juice
- 2   Tbsp. finely chopped fresh rosemary
- 1   Tbsp. minced garlic
- 1   tsp. freshly ground black pepper

1. Grind together fennel seeds and crushed red pepper in a spice grinder. (If you don't have a spice grinder, use a heavy knife to mince the seeds and red pepper.) Combine ground spices and salt; rub mixture all over the ribs. Cover ribs, and refrigerate 8 hours or overnight, if possible. (If not, rub the ribs a minimum of 2 hours ahead of time.)
2. Stir together olive oil, lemon juice, rosemary, garlic, and black pepper in a small bowl. Remove the ribs from the refrigerator. Place the ribs on a platter or broiler pan, and pour the marinade from the bowl over the meat, rubbing

it in with your fingers. Let stand at room temperature for at least 1 hour, turning the ribs at least once.
3. Preheat the broiler or gas grill to high (450°F to 550°F) 15 minutes before you are ready to cook. (If using charcoal, allow it time to form a full coating of white ash.) Place the broiler pan (or the grilling rack, if it's adjustable) about 8 inches from the source of heat. Place spareribs on the pan or grill, and brush with any remaining marinade. Cook for 30 to 35 minutes, turning rack 3 or 4 times.

SERVES 6 **ACTIVE** 45 min.
TOTAL 1 hour, 50 min. (plus 8 hours chilling)

SPAGHETTI WITH SHRIMP AND ROASTED CHERRY TOMATOES

- 3   pt. cherry tomatoes, halved
- 1/4   tsp. crushed red pepper
- 1/2   cup extra-virgin olive oil, divided
- 3   Tbsp. chopped garlic, divided
- 4 1/2   tsp. kosher salt, divided
- 1   lb. uncooked spaghetti
- 1   lb. medium-size raw shrimp, peeled and deveined
- 2   Tbsp. chopped fresh flat-leaf parsley
- 1   cup loosely packed basil leaves, torn

1. Preheat oven to 325°F. Toss together tomatoes, crushed red pepper, 4 tablespoons of the oil, 2 tablespoons of the garlic, and 1 teaspoon of the salt in a 13- x 9-inch baking dish. Bake in preheated oven until tomatoes soften and release their juices, about 45 minutes. (You can do this step a few hours ahead of time. Let tomatoes stand at room temperature until ready to use.)

2. Bring a large pot of water and 1 tablespoon of the salt to a boil over high. Add spaghetti, and cook until al dente, 9 to 11 minutes. Drain spaghetti, reserving 1 cup cooking water.
3. Meanwhile, heat 2 tablespoons of the oil in a large skillet over medium. Add remaining 1 tablespoon garlic, and cook, stirring constantly, until just beginning to brown, about 1 minute. Add shrimp, and cook, stirring constantly, until shrimp begin to turn pink and are cooked through, about 2 minutes. Add reserved cooking water to shrimp mixture; reduce heat, and cook, stirring occasionally, 2 minutes. Stir in parsley.

4. Transfer drained pasta to a large serving bowl. Add shrimp mixture, tomatoes, basil, and remaining 2 tablespoons oil and 1/2 teaspoon salt, and gently toss. Serve immediately.

NOTE: You can make this without the shrimp. Sauté garlic in the skillet as directed, and add the pasta water and parsley, omitting shrimp. When I do it this way, I also toss in 1/2 cup grated Parmesan or pecorino cheese.

SERVES 6 (serving size: about 1 3/4 cups)
ACTIVE 25 min. **TOTAL** 1 hour

ANY WAY YOU SLICE IT

SEVEN GORGEOUS FALL DESSERTS WITH
DELICIOUS SURPRISES INSIDE, FROM
DECADENT CHOCOLATE LAYERS
TO FRESH AND FLAVORFUL
SEASONAL INGREDIENTS

CHOCOLATE-COCONUT LAYER CAKE

Layers of chocolate cake and coconut cream are covered in dark chocolate frosting for a striking dessert that tastes every bit as good as it looks. The cake layers can be baked and frozen up to two weeks in advance to cut down on hands-on time.

CAKE

- 1 1/2 cups boiling water
- 1/2 cup unsweetened cocoa
- 4 oz. unsweetened chocolate, finely chopped
- 1/4 tsp. instant coffee (optional)
- 3 cups (about 12 3/4 oz.) all-purpose flour
- 1 Tbsp. baking powder
- 1/2 tsp. table salt
- 1 cup salted butter
- 1 cup packed dark brown sugar
- 1 cup granulated sugar
- 3 large eggs
- 1/2 cup sour cream or plain yogurt
- 1 tsp. vanilla extract

COCONUT CREAM FILLING

- 1 3/4 cups half-and-half
- 1/2 cup sweetened shredded coconut
- 5 Tbsp. granulated sugar
- 3 Tbsp. cornstarch
- 3 large egg yolks
- 2 Tbsp. salted butter
- 1 1/2 Tbsp. rum
- 1 tsp. vanilla extract
- 1/2 tsp. coconut extract
- 1/2 cup heavy cream

CHOCOLATE FROSTING

- 2 cups heavy cream
- 2 Tbsp. powdered sugar
- 1 lb. 60% to 64% bittersweet chocolate, finely chopped
- 2 cups unsweetened flaked coconut, lightly toasted

1. Prepare the Cake: Preheat oven to 350°F. Combine boiling water, cocoa, unsweetened chocolate, and, if desired, instant coffee in a bowl. Let stand 2 minutes; whisk until smooth. Let cool completely.

2. Whisk together flour, baking powder, and salt in a bowl. Beat butter with an electric mixer at medium speed until smooth, about 1 minute. Add brown sugar and 1 cup granulated sugar; beat until light and fluffy, about 2 minutes. Add eggs, 1 at a time, beating well after each addition. Beat in sour cream and 1 teaspoon vanilla. Add flour mixture to butter mixture alternately with cocoa mixture, in 5 additions, beginning and ending with flour mixture. Beat at medium speed until smooth, about 1 minute. Divide batter evenly between 2 (9-inch) greased and floured round cake pans. Bake in preheated oven until a wooden pick inserted in the center comes out clean, 28 to 32 minutes. Cool in pans on a wire rack 10 minutes. Remove cake from pans; cool completely, about 30 minutes.

3. Prepare the Coconut Cream Filling: Stir together half-and-half and shredded coconut in a small saucepan over medium; bring just to a boil.

Remove pan from heat; let stand 30 minutes. Pour mixture through a fine wire-mesh strainer into a bowl, pressing on solids; discard solids. Return coconut liquid to pan; bring to a simmer. (Coconut liquid should just begin to bubble around the edges of pan.) Whisk together 5 tablespoons granulated sugar, cornstarch, and egg yolks in a medium bowl until smooth. Gradually add hot coconut liquid to egg mixture, whisking constantly. Return mixture to pan. Cook, whisking constantly, over medium until thick and bubbly, 5 to 6 minutes. Remove pan from heat. Whisk in 2 tablespoons butter, rum, 1 teaspoon vanilla, and coconut extract. Pour mixture into a shallow dish; refrigerate until completely cold, about 2 hours. Transfer chilled custard to a medium bowl.

4. Beat 1/2 cup heavy cream until stiff peaks form. Gently fold whipped cream into custard in 2 batches. Refrigerate until ready to use.

CHOCOLATE-COCONUT LAYER CAKE

5. Prepare Chocolate Frosting: Combine 2 cups heavy cream and powdered sugar in a medium saucepan. Bring to a simmer over medium. (Do not boil.) Place bittersweet chocolate in a medium bowl; pour hot cream mixture over chocolate. Let stand 1 minute; gently stir until all of the chocolate melts and mixture is smooth. Chill until mixture thickens to spreading consistency, 30 to 40 minutes, stirring every few minutes.

6. To assemble cake, slice cake layers in half horizontally using a serrated knife; place 1 layer, cut side up, on a plate. Spread about ¼ cup Chocolate Frosting over top. Top with one-third of Coconut Cream Filling, leaving a ½-inch border. Top with another cake layer; repeat layers twice, beginning with frosting and ending with a cake layer. Spread remaining Chocolate Frosting on top and sides of cake. (If chocolate gets too thick to spread, microwave at HIGH until spreadable, 5 to 7 minutes.) Press unsweetened flaked coconut around sides of cake.

SERVES 10 (serving size: 1 slice)
ACTIVE 30 min. **TOTAL** 3 hours, 30 min.

CINNAMON ROULADE WITH ROASTED APPLE-CREAM CHEESE FILLING

The secret to making a roulade: Line your baking pan with parchment paper. Use the paper as a guide to roll the cake when it is still slightly warm. After the cake has cooled, unroll it, add the filling, and reroll it back into a spiral.

APPLE-CREAM CHEESE FILLING

- 2   large Fuji apples, peeled and cut into ½-inch cubes
- 1   Tbsp. granulated sugar
- 2   (8-oz.) pkg. cream cheese, softened
- 3   Tbsp. salted butter, softened
- 1   tsp. vanilla extract
- ⅛   tsp. table salt
- 1½ cups (about 6 oz.) powdered sugar

CREAM CHEESE STUDDED WITH **ROASTED APPLES** IS ROLLED BETWEEN LAYERS OF CINNAMON-SPICED CAKE

CINNAMON ROULADE

CAKE

- 4   large eggs, separated
- ¾   cup granulated sugar, divided
- 1   tsp. vanilla extract
- ¾   cup (about 2 ⅞ oz.) bleached cake flour
- 2   tsp. ground cinnamon
- ¾   tsp. baking powder
- ¼   tsp. table salt
- 6   Tbsp. powdered sugar, divided

1. Prepare the Apple-Cream Cheese Filling: Preheat oven to 400°F. Place apples and 1 tablespoon granulated sugar in a bowl; toss well to coat. Spread apples in a single layer on a baking sheet coated with cooking spray. Bake in preheated oven until tender and well browned, about 20 minutes, stirring after 10 minutes. Remove apples from pan, and cool completely.

2. Meanwhile, beat cream cheese, butter, 1 teaspoon vanilla, and ⅛ teaspoon salt with an electric mixer at medium speed until smooth, about 1 minute. Add 1½ cups powdered sugar; beat until smooth, about 1 minute. Fold in roasted apples. Refrigerate until ready to use.

3. Prepare the Cake: Preheat oven to 400°F. Coat a 17- x 12-inch rimmed

baking sheet with cooking spray; line with parchment paper. Coat parchment with cooking spray.

4. Beat egg yolks and ½ cup granulated sugar at high speed until thick and pale, about 5 minutes. Beat in 1 teaspoon vanilla.

5. Using clean, dry beaters, beat egg whites in a separate bowl at medium speed until foamy. Increase speed to high, and beat until soft peaks form. Add remaining ¼ cup granulated sugar, 1 tablespoon at a time, beating at high speed until medium peaks form. Stir one-fourth of egg white mixture into egg yolk mixture; gently fold in remaining three-fourths egg white mixture.

6. Sift together cake flour, cinnamon, baking powder, and ¼ teaspoon salt. Sift cake flour mixture over egg mixture, ¼ cup at a time, folding in until blended after each addition. Spread batter in prepared baking sheet.

7. Bake at 400°F until puffed and lightly browned on top, 8 to 10 minutes. Cool 5 minutes. Sprinkle 4 tablespoons powdered sugar over top of cake. Invert cake onto a parchment paper-lined surface. Peel off top layer of parchment paper from cake. Starting at 1 short side, roll cake and bottom parchment together. Transfer to a wire rack, and cool completely, about 30 minutes.

8. Unroll cake onto a flat surface. Spread Apple-Cream Cheese Filling over top, leaving a 1-inch border on all sides. Starting at 1 short side and using parchment paper as a guide, roll up cake in jelly-roll fashion. Place cake on a platter, seam side down. Sprinkle top and sides with remaining 2 tablespoons powdered sugar. Serve immediately.

SERVES 10 (serving size: 1 slice)
ACTIVE 30 min. **TOTAL** 1 hour, 50 min.

PUMPKIN SPICE BATTENBERG

Coat your pan with cooking spray because that's what will keep the parchment paper divider in place for the pretty pumpkin and vanilla layers.

- 2/3 **cup (about 5 1/4 oz.) salted butter, softened**
- 2/3 **cup granulated sugar**
- 1 **tsp. vanilla extract**
- 2 **large eggs**
- 1 **large egg yolk**
- 1 3/4 **cups (about 7 1/2 oz.) all-purpose flour**
- 1/2 **tsp. baking powder**
- 1/2 **tsp. table salt**
- 1/4 **cup canned pumpkin**
- 1 **tsp. ground pumpkin pie spice**
- 3 **Tbsp. apricot jam**
- 1 **(7-oz.) pkg. marzipan**
- 3 **Tbsp. powdered sugar, sifted**

1. Preheat oven to 325°F. Coat an 8-inch square baking pan with cooking spray. Cut a 25- x 8-inch piece of parchment paper. Fold parchment rectangle in half (short end to short end), pressing firmly on folded end to make a crease. Fold creased end over about 3 inches, pressing firmly to make another crease in parchment paper. Unfold entire piece, and turn over. Pinch and pick up middle crease, creating a 3-inch-tall divider in middle of rectangle. Place in greased pan, pressing paper onto bottom of pan to fit as tightly as possible, and making sure divider is in the middle. Allow excess paper to extend over sides to use as handles. Coat top of parchment paper with cooking spray.

2. Beat butter, granulated sugar, and vanilla with an electric mixer at medium speed until well combined, about 1 minute. Beat in eggs and egg yolk. Add flour, baking powder, and salt to egg mixture; beat at medium speed until smooth, about 2 minutes. Remove 1 1/4 cups batter to another bowl, and stir in canned pumpkin and pumpkin pie spice. Spoon plain batter into 1 side of the parchment paper divider in prepared pan; spread until smooth. Spoon pumpkin batter into the empty side of the parchment paper divider of the prepared pan; spread until smooth.

3. Bake in preheated oven until a wooden pick inserted in center comes out clean, 30 to 33 minutes. Cool in pan 10 minutes. Lift cakes from pan, using paper sides as handles, and place on wire rack. Cool completely, about 30 minutes.

4. Remove cakes from parchment paper; trim the edges and tops of both cakes, as needed. Cut each loaf in half lengthwise, creating 4 equal strips.

5. Place jam in a microwave-safe bowl; microwave at HIGH just until warm, about 30 seconds. Spread jam on tops and sides of cake strips. Gently press 1 strip of each color together at long sides; top with remaining 2 strips, alternately stacking to create a checkerboard pattern.

6. Roll marzipan on a surface sprinkled with sifted powdered sugar into a 12- x 8-inch rectangle. Place cake loaf, top jam-side down, in center of marzipan rectangle with the short ends of loaf facing the long sides of rectangle. Brush remaining 3 sides of cake with jam. Wrap marzipan around cake loaf, and gently press to adhere. Trim ends and where seam meets. Place cake loaf on platter, seam side down. Brush surface of cake lightly to remove excess powdered sugar. Lightly score top of cake in a diamond pattern with the edge of a sharp knife.

SERVES 10 (serving size: 1 slice)
ACTIVE 30 min. **TOTAL** 2 hours, 10 min.

PUMPKIN SPICE BATTENBERG

PRALINE LAYER CAKE

The "cooked" buttercream in this cake is an old-fashioned method that yields delicious results.

CANDIED PECANS

- 2 Tbsp. light brown sugar
- 1 Tbsp. granulated sugar
- 1/4 tsp. table salt
- 1 large egg white
- 2 cups pecan halves

CAKE

- 3 cups (about 12 3/4 oz.) all-purpose flour
- 1 Tbsp. baking powder
- 3/4 tsp. table salt
- 2 cups granulated sugar
- 1 cup (8 oz.) unsalted butter, softened
- 3 large eggs
- 2 large egg yolks
- 1 1/4 cups whole milk
- 1 Tbsp. pecan liqueur
- 1 tsp. vanilla extract

FILLING

- 3/4 cup packed dark brown sugar
- 6 Tbsp. (3 oz.) unsalted butter
- 1/4 cup heavy cream
- 1 1/2 cups (about 6 oz.) powdered sugar
- 1/4 tsp. vanilla extract
- 1/2 cup finely chopped toasted pecans

BUTTERCREAM

- 1 cup packed light brown sugar
- 1 cup whole milk
- 1/2 cup (about 2 1/8 oz.) all-purpose flour
- 1/4 tsp. table salt
- 1 cup (8 oz.) unsalted butter, softened
- 1 1/2 tsp. vanilla extract

1. Prepare the Candied Pecans: Preheat oven to 300°F. Whisk together 2 tablespoons light brown sugar, 1 tablespoon granulated sugar, 1/4 teaspoon salt, and 1 egg white in a medium bowl until foamy. Add pecan halves; toss well to coat. Spread pecan halves in a single layer on a baking sheet lined with parchment paper. Bake in preheated oven until browned, 25 to 28 minutes, stirring after 15 minutes. Cool completely, about 30 minutes. (Pecans will become crisp when cool.)

2. Prepare the Cake: Increase oven temperature to 350°F. Whisk together 3 cups flour, 1 tablespoon baking powder, and 3/4 teaspoon salt in a bowl. Beat 2 cups granulated sugar and 1 cup butter in a large bowl of a stand mixer at medium speed until light and fluffy, about 4 minutes. Add eggs and egg yolks, 1 at a time, beating well after each addition. Add flour mixture to butter mixture alternately with milk, in 5 additions, beginning and ending with flour mixture. Beat at low speed after each addition. Beat in pecan liqueur and 1 teaspoon vanilla. Divide batter evenly between 2 (9-inch) greased and floured round cake pans.

3. Bake in preheated oven until a wooden pick inserted in the center comes out clean, 28 to 30 minutes. Cool in pans on a wire rack 10 minutes. Remove cakes from pans; cool completely on wire rack, about 30 minutes.

4. Prepare the Filling: Combine 3/4 cup dark brown sugar, 6 tablespoons butter, and 1/4 cup heavy cream in a small saucepan over medium-low, and cook, stirring occasionally, until butter melts; bring to a boil. Cook, stirring constantly, 1 minute. Remove pan from heat; add powdered sugar and 1/4 teaspoon vanilla. Beat at low speed until mixture thickens to spreading consistency, about 1 minute. Stir in chopped toasted pecans.

5. Prepare the Buttercream: Whisk together 1 cup light brown sugar, 1 cup milk, 1/2 cup flour, and 1/4 teaspoon salt in a small saucepan until smooth. Place pan over medium-high, and cook, whisking constantly, until mixture is very thick and bubbly, 4 to 5 minutes. Spoon mixture into a bowl; place bowl in freezer, uncovered, until mixture is cold, about 20 minutes, stirring every 5 minutes.

6. Beat 1 cup butter with an electric mixer at medium speed, using whisk

PRALINE LAYER CAKE

WE TURNED ONE OF THE SOUTH'S MOST HUMBLE SWEETS—**THE PRALINE**— INTO A SHOWSTOPPING DESSERT.

attachment, until creamy and smooth, about 2 minutes. Add cold brown sugar mixture, 1 tablespoon at a time, beating well after each addition. Add 1 1/2 teaspoons vanilla, and beat at high speed until light and fluffy, about 5 minutes.

7. Place 1 cake layer on a serving plate; spread Filling evenly over top, leaving a 1/2-inch border. Place remaining cake layer on top, pressing lightly. Spread Buttercream on top and sides of cake. Arrange Candied Pecans over top.

SERVES 10 (serving size: 1 slice)
ACTIVE 1 hour, 10 min. **TOTAL** 2 hours, 55 min.

CRANBERRY-APPLE GRANOLA MUFFINS

These caramel- and granola-topped muffins may look and taste like a fancy coffeehouse treat, but they're easy to whip up any fall morning.

1 1/2	**cups** (about 6 3/8 oz.) **all-purpose flour**
1/2	**cup sweetened dried cranberries**
1 1/2	**tsp. baking powder**
1 1/2	**tsp. apple pie spice**
1	**tsp. kosher salt**
1/2	**tsp. baking soda**
1	**cup cinnamon granola** (such as Nature Valley), **divided**
3/4	**cup unsweetened applesauce**
1/2	**cup packed light brown sugar**
1/2	**cup unsalted butter, melted**
2	**large eggs**
1	**tsp. vanilla extract**
12	(5-inch) **parchment paper squares**
1	**large Pink Lady apple** (about 8 oz.), **cut into 1/2-inch pieces** **Sticky Maple-Caramel Sauce** (optional)

1. Preheat oven to 375°F. Stir together flour, cranberries, baking powder, apple pie spice, salt, baking soda, and 3/4 cup of the granola in a large bowl. Whisk together applesauce, brown sugar, butter, eggs, and vanilla in a medium bowl. Add applesauce mixture to flour mixture, stirring until just combined.

2. Fit 1 parchment square into each of the lightly greased cups of a 12-cup muffin pan, pressing folds into paper as needed. Divide muffin batter evenly among prepared muffin cups in pan. Lightly press apple pieces into tops of batter, and sprinkle with remaining 1/4 cup granola. Bake in preheated oven until a wooden pick inserted in center comes out clean, 22 to 27 minutes. Cool in pans on wire racks 5 minutes. Remove from pans to wire racks, and cool completely (about 30 minutes). Drizzle with Sticky Maple-Caramel Sauce before serving, if desired.

SERVES 12 (serving size: 1 muffin)
ACTIVE 20 min. **TOTAL** 1 hour, 20 min.

Sticky Maple-Caramel Sauce

Place 12 **caramel candies,** 2 Tbsp. **heavy cream,** 2 Tbsp. pure **maple syrup,** and 1/4 tsp. kosher **salt** in a small microwave-safe bowl, and microwave on HIGH just until smooth, 1 minute to 1 minute and 30 seconds, stirring at 30-second intervals. Cool, stirring occasionally, until thickened, about 10 minutes.

MAKES about 1/2 cup **ACTIVE** 5 min. **TOTAL** 15 min.

APPLE-SPICE BUNDT CAKE

APPLE-SPICE BUNDT CAKE WITH CARAMEL FROSTING

We updated an old-fashioned Southern cake with the warm spice of chai, an Indian tea.

CREAM CHEESE FILLING

1	(8-oz.) **pkg. cream cheese, softened**
1/4	**cup granulated sugar**
1	**large egg**
2	**Tbsp. all-purpose flour**
1	**tsp. vanilla extract**

APPLE-SPICE BATTER

1	**cup packed light brown sugar**
1	**cup vegetable oil**
1/2	**cup granulated sugar**
3	**large eggs**
2	**tsp. vanilla extract**
2	**tsp. baking powder**
2	**tsp. pumpkin pie spice**
1 1/2	**tsp. ground cardamom**
1	**tsp. kosher salt**
1/2	**tsp. baking soda**
1/2	**tsp. ground coriander**
3	**cups** (about 12 3/4 oz.) **all-purpose flour**
3	**large Granny Smith apples** (about 1 1/2 lb.), **peeled and grated** **Caramel Frosting** (page 228)
2/3	**cup roughly chopped toasted pecans**

1. Prepare the Cream Cheese Filling: Preheat oven to 350°F. Beat cream cheese, 1/4 cup granulated sugar, 1 egg, 2 tablespoons flour, and 1 teaspoon vanilla with an electric mixer on medium speed until smooth.

2. Prepare the Apple-Spice Batter: Beat brown sugar, oil, and 1/2 cup granulated sugar with an electric stand mixer on medium speed until well blended. Add 3 eggs, 1 at a time, beating well after each addition. Stir in 2 teaspoons vanilla. Whisk together baking powder, pumpkin pie spice, cardamom, salt, baking soda, coriander, and 3 cups flour. Gradually add to brown sugar mixture, beating on low speed until just blended. Add apples, and beat on low speed just until combined.

3. Spoon half of the batter into a greased and floured 14-cup Bundt pan. Dollop Cream Cheese Filling over the apple mixture, leaving a 1-inch border around edges of pan. Swirl filling through batter using a knife. Spoon remaining batter over filling.

4. Bake in preheated oven until a long wooden pick inserted in center comes out clean, 50 minutes to 1 hour. Cool cake in pan on a wire rack 20 minutes; remove from pan to wire rack, and cool completely (about 2 hours). Spoon frosting immediately over cooled cake; sprinkle with pecans.

SERVES 12 (serving size: 1 slice)
ACTIVE 25 min. **TOTAL** 3 hours, 45 min

Caramel Frosting

- 1/2 **cup packed light brown sugar**
- 1/4 **cup heavy cream**
- 1/4 **cup salted butter**
- 1 **tsp. vanilla extract**
- 1 1/4 **cups (about 5 oz.) powdered sugar, sifted**

1. Bring brown sugar, cream, and butter to a boil in a 2-quart heavy saucepan over medium, whisking constantly; boil, whisking constantly, 1 minute.

2. Remove pan from heat; stir in vanilla. Gradually whisk in powdered sugar until smooth. Gently stir until mixture begins to cool and thicken, 4 to 5 minutes. Use immediately.

MAKES about 1 cup **ACTIVE** 10 min.
TOTAL 10 min.

BANANA CUPCAKES WITH PEANUT BUTTER BUTTERCREAM

Filled with banana cream, topped with peanut butter buttercream, and drizzled with chocolate, these are outrageously rich.

BANANA CREAM FILLING

- 1 1/4 **cups mashed ripe banana (about 2 small)**
- 1 **tsp. fresh lemon juice**
- 1/4 **cup powdered sugar**
- 3 **oz. cream cheese, softened**
- 2 **Tbsp. heavy cream**

CUPCAKES

- 1 1/2 **cups (about 6 3/8 oz.) all-purpose flour**
- 1 **tsp. baking powder**
- 1/2 **tsp. baking soda**
- 1/2 **tsp. ground nutmeg**
- 1/4 **tsp. table salt**
- 1/2 **cup granulated sugar**
- 1/4 **cup packed light brown sugar**
- 1/2 **cup (4 oz.) salted butter, softened**
- 1/4 **cup whole milk**
- 2 **large eggs**
- 1/2 **tsp. vanilla extract**

PEANUT BUTTER BUTTERCREAM

- 6 **Tbsp. creamy peanut butter**
- 1/4 **cup salted butter, softened**
- 3 **Tbsp. cream cheese, softened**
- 1/4 **tsp. vanilla extract**
- 1/8 **tsp. table salt**
- 3 **cups (about 12 oz.) powdered sugar**
- 3 **to 4 Tbsp. heavy cream**
- 2 **oz. bittersweet chocolate, melted**

1. Prepare the Banana Cream Filling: Stir together banana and lemon juice in a small bowl. Beat 1/4 cup powdered sugar, 3 ounces cream cheese, and 2 tablespoons heavy cream in a medium bowl with an electric mixer at low speed until smooth. Stir in 1/2 cup of the banana-lemon mixture, reserving the remaining 3/4 cup banana-lemon mixture for the batter.

2. Prepare the Cupcakes: Preheat oven to 350°F. Place baking cup liners in a 12-cup muffin pan; lightly coat liners with cooking spray. Whisk together flour, baking powder, baking soda, nutmeg, and 1/4 teaspoon salt in a bowl. Beat granulated sugar, brown sugar, and 1/2 cup butter at medium speed in a large bowl until well combined, about 3 minutes. Add milk, eggs, and 1/2 teaspoon vanilla; beat at low speed until combined, about 2 minutes. (Mixture may look curdled.) Gradually add flour mixture, beating at medium-low speed until smooth, about 3 minutes. Stir reserved 3/4 cup banana-lemon mixture into batter.

3. Spoon about 1 tablespoon cupcake batter into each muffin cup; top evenly with Banana Cream Filling. Top evenly with remaining cupcake batter, and bake in preheated oven until tops are golden brown and cupcakes spring back when lightly touched, 18 to 20 minutes. Cool in pan 5 minutes. Remove cupcakes to a wire rack, and cool completely, about 30 minutes.

4. Prepare the Peanut Butter Buttercream: Beat peanut butter, 1/4 cup butter, 3 tablespoons cream cheese, 1/4 teaspoon vanilla, and 1/8 teaspoon salt in a medium bowl at medium-low speed until smooth, about 2 minutes. Add 3 cups powdered sugar alternately with 3 tablespoons of the cream, beating at low speed until smooth after each addition. Add the remaining 1 tablespoon of the cream, 1 teaspoon at a time, if needed, to reach desired consistency. Spoon frosting into a zip-top plastic freezer bag. Snip 1 corner of bag to make a small hole. Pipe about 3 tablespoons buttercream onto each cupcake. Drizzle melted chocolate evenly over buttercream.

SERVES 12 (serving size: 1 cupcake)
ACTIVE 20 min. **TOTAL** 1 hour, 35 min.

Bon Temps On the Bayou

IN SOUTHWEST LOUISIANA, A FISH-CAMP FEAST
CELEBRATES THE LOCAL BOUNTY AND THE FAMILY
HISTORY OF TWO PASSIONATE CAJUN COOKS

YOU CAN'T GET TO THIS PARTY WITH-OUT A BOAT, so the fun begins at Don's Boat Landing just outside of Abbeville, where it's never too early for a Bloody Mary and a bag of Zapp's. From this fishing town in southwest Louisiana, it's a 30-minute ride through Boston Canal, a man-made waterway, past grazing horses, endless cattails, and gators sunning on the banks. After passing various intriguing inlets, you'll cross the Intracoastal Waterway, dotted with massive barges, until a "no wake zone; dead slow" sign and scattering of stilt houses announce that you're close. There, near the mouth of Vermilion Bay, is Camp Peace. It's best to arrive hungry.

Chef David Guas grew up in New Orleans, and the beloved flavors of his childhood inspired Bayou Bakery—his cafés in Arlington, Virginia, and Washington, D.C. Guas trained at several high-end restaurants, but he learned the fundamentals of Cajun cooking from his feisty Aunt Boo, aka Janice Bourgeois Macomber. The daughter of a shrimper father and a Sicilian mother, Boo has always been a force to be reckoned with—especially in the kitchen.

Boo began cooking in the seventies, when she lived in the French Quarter. After she was widowed

CRAB FOR A CROWD: Chef David Guas helps his Aunt Boo (aka Janice Bourgeois Macomber) prepare a crab-artichoke spread at her Louisiana fish shack.

at 36, she returned to her hometown of Abbeville to raise her two young daughters. These days, when she's not catching flying beads at Mardi Gras or sipping beer at Jazz Fest, she's at home in Abbeville or in a boat pointed toward Camp Peace, her bayou refuge and happy place. The rustic shack was the only one in the area that survived Hurricane Rita, hence its name. (Boo credits this to divine intervention.)

Whenever Guas returns to Louisiana to visit his aunt, they head to Camp Peace to stock crab traps, fish, and do what they do best: cook. "The key to cooking on the Boston Canal with Aunt Boo is to have just the right amount of cold beer and bourbon to make it to the end of the trip," David says, "'cause once you're on da canal, *cher*, you out there!" Today is that sort of gathering; friends and family have come together to sip cold beer and feast on the Gulf's bounty as they honor the history that stitches them together. This is the kind of meal that kicks off early (with grilled oysters and spiked sun tea) and lasts through every last drop of daylight.

While Guas may have gone on to run two restaurants, author two cookbooks, and host a television show, when he's at Camp Peace, Boo tells her nephew how it's done: the correct way to score redfish for easy serving, for instance, or how to brown a roux. (In his restaurants, Guas relies on the steady heat of his oven, which prompts Boo to shake her head in disbelief.) Today, Guas has been scolded several times for buying the wrong cut of frozen chicken for the crab traps. "I still want to be the boss in the kitchen," she confesses, although she's clearly pleased with her protégé. "He found his passion at a young age, and I am so proud that he stuck with it."

Guas doesn't mind deferring. "At the end of the day I yield, because there's the deepest amount of love and respect for that woman. If she says it's done a certain way, then that's how it's done."

Grilled Banana "Pirogues" with Pecan Pralines, page 233

COUNTRY BOY ON THE ROCKS

SERVES 10 (serving size: 1 [16-oz.] cocktail)
ACTIVE 5 min. **TOTAL** 5 min.

Made with strong tea that's typically steeped on the dock in the morning sun, this refreshing elixir is dangerously easy to sip, and can be made with your favorite bourbon.

- 32 oz. (1 qt.) unsweetened brewed black tea (such as Luzianne or Lipton)
- 32 oz. (1 qt.) lemonade
- 20 oz. (2 1/2 cups) bourbon
- 1 bunch (or 1 [4-oz.] pkg.) fresh mint sprigs
- 2 lemons, sliced into rounds

Stir together tea and lemonade in a pitcher, and chill until very cold, about 1 hour. To assemble each drink, fill a 16-ounce glass two-thirds full with ice. Add 2 ounces bourbon, and fill glass with tea mixture. Place 3 or 4 fresh mint leaves and 2 or 3 lemon slices in a cocktail shaker. Pour contents of glass into shaker; cover and shake vigorously for 10 seconds. Pour cocktail into same glass. Repeat process to make 9 cocktails.

CRAB C'EST SI BON!

MAKES 5 cups
ACTIVE 15 min. **TOTAL** 35 min.

This dish was born when Boo found herself with artichokes and lots of leftover boiled crab. As the name implies (Crab—It's So Good!), the luxurious sauté of lump crab and artichokes is delicious.

- 1 lb. fresh lump crabmeat, drained
- 1/2 cup extra-virgin olive oil, divided
- 1/2 cup panko (Japanese-style breadcrumbs)
- 1/4 cup (2 oz.) salted butter
- 1 medium onion, chopped
- 1 (14-oz.) can artichoke hearts, drained and chopped
- 1/3 cup loosely packed fresh oregano leaves, chopped
- 8 garlic cloves, minced

Country Boy on the Rocks

- 1 Tbsp. Worcestershire sauce
- 1 bay leaf
- 1/2 tsp. cayenne pepper
- 1/2 tsp. kosher salt
- 1/4 tsp. black pepper
- 1/2 cup dry white wine
- 2 Tbsp. fresh lemon juice
- 1/2 cup thinly sliced scallions
- 1/2 cup chopped fresh flat-leaf parsley
- 1 baguette or crusty French bread loaf, thinly sliced

1. Pick crabmeat, removing any bits of shell.
2. Heat 2 tablespoons of the oil in a small skillet over medium. Add breadcrumbs, and cook, stirring often, until toasted and golden brown, 2 to 3 minutes. Remove from heat, and set aside.
3. Heat butter and remaining 6 tablespoons oil in a large, deep skillet over medium-high. When butter starts to sizzle, add onion, artichoke hearts, oregano, garlic, Worcestershire sauce, bay leaf, cayenne, salt, and pepper, and cook, stirring often, until vegetables are slightly softened, about 5 minutes. Add wine and lemon juice, and cook until liquid reduces slightly, about 5 minutes. Add crabmeat, scallions, and parsley, and cook, stirring often, until crabmeat is warm and wine is mostly evaporated, 2 to 3 minutes. Remove from heat; taste and add seasonings as desired. Remove bay leaf. Cover and let stand 5 minutes.

Transfer warm crab mixture to a serving dish, and top with toasted breadcrumbs. Serve immediately with bread slices.

GRILLED OYSTERS WITH LEMON-GARLIC BUTTER

MAKES 24 oysters
ACTIVE 30 min. **TOTAL** 35 min.

This is a great appetizer to kick off a party, because oysters tend to draw a crowd—it's fun to watch (and smell) them sizzling over the heat. Prep the lemon-garlic butter and cheese topping in advance, then shuck and grill the oysters in batches. They're best eaten soon after they come off the grill, with slices of bread to sop up any remaining sauce.

- 1 cup (1/2 lb.) unsalted butter
- 1/4 cup chopped fresh flat-leaf parsley
- 2 Tbsp. fresh lemon juice
- 3 garlic cloves, minced
- 1 tsp. kosher salt
- 1/4 cup (1 oz.) grated Parmesan cheese
- 1/4 cup (1 oz.) grated Romano cheese
- 24 large Gulf oysters
- 1 loaf French bread

1. Melt butter in a small saucepan over medium. Stir in parsley, lemon juice, garlic, and salt. Remove from heat, and place saucepan next to grill to keep butter warm.

2. Heat grill to medium (about 400°F). Stir together Parmesan and Romano cheeses in a bowl.

3. Shuck oysters, and discard top shell. Using an oyster knife, disconnect the oyster from the bottom shell, keeping the oyster in the shell. Place the raw oysters on the half shell on the grill, and top each oyster with about 1 tablespoon of the butter mixture. Grill, uncovered, until juices start to bubble and the edges of the oysters begin to curl, about 2 minutes. Top each oyster with a generous pinch of the cheese mixture. Continue grilling, uncovered, until the edges of the shells start to brown, about 2 minutes. Using tongs, transfer oysters from grill to a serving platter. Top with any remaining butter mixture. Serve with grilled or baked French bread.

NOTE: Large oysters are important here, because they stand up better on the grill and cradle more of the buttery sauce.

SHRIMP NANA

MAKES 12 1/2 cups **ACTIVE** 35 min.
TOTAL 2 days, 35 min., including 2 days marinating

Shrimp Nana, a recipe from Boo's Sicilian mother, Theresa Russo, is a party staple. Boo marinates the shrimp a few days in advance so that by the time she arrives at Camp Peace, they have become instant appetizers to be eaten in between beers.

- 7 qt. water
- 2 Tbsp. plus 1 tsp. kosher salt, divided
- 5 lb. unpeeled, medium-size or large, raw Gulf shrimp
- 2 medium-size yellow onions, thinly sliced (about 5 cups)
- 1 cup extra-virgin olive oil
- 1 cup fresh lemon juice
- 1/4 cup brined capers with juice
- 2 Tbsp. prepared horseradish
- 1 Tbsp. Worcestershire sauce
- 2 tsp. garlic powder
- 2 tsp. paprika

Crab C'est Si Bon!, page 231

- 2 tsp. celery salt
- 1/2 tsp. cayenne pepper
  Hot sauce
  Lemon wedges

1. Bring 7 quarts water and 2 tablespoons of the salt to a rolling boil in a large stockpot over high. Carefully add shrimp, and cook until the shrimp turn pink and are just cooked through, 1 to 2 minutes. Drain shrimp in a colander, and rinse with cold water. When shrimp are cool enough to handle, peel and devein. (Save shells for stock, if desired.)

2. Layer shrimp and onion slices in alternating layers in a large, sealable storage container.

3. Whisk together olive oil, lemon juice, capers, horseradish, Worcestershire sauce, garlic powder, paprika, celery salt, cayenne, and remaining 1 teaspoon salt in a large bowl. Pour marinade over shrimp; cover and chill 2 hours. Toss mixture (or invert container), and chill 2 to 3 days, tossing occasionally. Taste shrimp before serving, and add salt, heat, or lemon juice as desired. Serve as an appetizer, with toothpicks, hot sauce, and lemon wedges. Shrimp will keep for an additional 3 days in the refrigerator.

NOTE: This recipe can be enhanced with any fresh herbs you have on hand. Feel free to add a few fresh bay leaves to the marinade, or toss marinated shrimp with chopped fresh flat-leaf parsley just before serving.

REDFISH COURT-BOUILLON

SERVES 6 **ACTIVE** 25 min.
TOTAL 1 hour, 25 min.

Court-bouillon is a classic French broth used for poaching seafood and infusing it with flavor. For the Cajun version (pronounced roughly "KORR-boo-yawn"), a whole Gulf fish such as redfish or catfish is cooked in rich tomato gravy. Boo's long-simmered sauce has plenty of personality. This dish is a fish-camp favorite because it cooks while everyone snacks and sips and enjoys the party down below.

- 1/2 cup extra-virgin olive oil
- 3 medium-size yellow onions, chopped
- 4 celery stalks, chopped
- 1 large green bell pepper, chopped
- 1 cup button mushrooms, stems removed, sliced
- 6 garlic cloves, minced
- 2 bay leaves
- 1 cup dry white wine
- 2 (15-oz.) cans tomato sauce
- 1 (10-oz.) can diced tomatoes and green chiles (such as Rotel), undrained
- 1 cup shrimp stock or water
- 1/2 cup Italian olive salad
- 1/2 cup thinly sliced scallions (green parts only)
- 1/2 cup chopped fresh flat-leaf parsley
- 1 whole 3- to 5-lb. redfish or similar Gulf fish (such as grouper or drum), scaled, gutted, and trimmed
- 1 1/2 tsp. kosher salt
- 1 lemon, thinly sliced
- 1 lb. raw shrimp, peeled and deveined
  Steamed rice

1. Heat oil in a large, heavy saucepan over medium-high. Add onions, celery, bell pepper, mushrooms, garlic, and bay leaves, and cook until vegetables have softened, about 7 minutes. Add wine, and cook, stirring once or twice, until liquid is slightly reduced, 3 to 4 minutes. Stir in tomato sauce, tomatoes and chiles, and shrimp stock, and bring to a boil. Reduce heat

Shrimp Nana, page 232

6 to 7 minutes on each side. Remove from heat, and cool 5 minutes. Cut a slit lengthwise through each banana peel from stem to end without cutting through banana. Gently open the slit. Place each banana in a shallow bowl. Top each with ice cream and about ¼ cup crumbled Pecan Pralines.

NOTE: To help your "pirogue" sit upright in the bowl, slice a strip of peel off the base to create a flat bottom.

Pecan Pralines

MAKES about 3 dozen pralines
ACTIVE 20 min. **TOTAL** 20 min.

- 4 **Tbsp. unsalted butter**
- 1¼ **cups packed light brown sugar**
- 1 **cup granulated sugar**
- ½ **cup plus 2 to 4 Tbsp. heavy cream, divided**
- 2 **cups chopped pecans**

1. Line 2 rimmed baking sheets with parchment paper. Melt butter in a medium saucepan over medium-low. Add brown sugar, granulated sugar, and ½ cup of the cream; stir until sugar dissolves. Increase heat to medium, and simmer, using a heatproof rubber spatula to stir gently occasionally, until a candy thermometer reads 240°F to 250°F. (If mixture begins to crystallize, add 2 tablespoons of the cream, and cook, stirring, until it liquefies.) Stir in chopped pecans. Turn off heat, and give the mixture a final gentle stir, making sure to scrape the bottom and corners of the pan.

2. Using a wooden spoon, scoop about 2 tablespoons of the hot praline mixture onto the prepared baking sheets, leaving at least 1 inch between pralines. If mixture begins to crystallize in pan, add remaining 2 tablespoons of the cream, heat over medium, and stir until mixture looks creamy. Cool pralines on pans until solid, about 30 minutes. Transfer to an airtight container. (Pralines may be kept in the airtight container up to 3 days.)

Redfish Court-Bouillon

with aluminum foil, and bake in preheated oven, basting occasionally with pan sauce, until fish is cooked through and flakes easily with a fork, about 45 minutes. Remove pan from oven, and stir shrimp into pan sauce. Cover with foil, and return to oven. Cook until shrimp turn pink, about 15 minutes. Remove from oven, discard foil, and let fish rest 5 to 10 minutes. Serve with steamed rice.

GRILLED BANANA "PIROGUES" WITH PECAN PRALINES

SERVES 8 **ACTIVE** 30 min. **TOTAL** 35 min.

For this rich, playful, and fun-to-eat preparation, grilled bananas masquerade as pirogues (Cajun flat-bottomed boats). Making the pralines in advance—they'll keep for 3 days in a sealed container— helps this dessert come together quickly.

- 8 **ripe bananas, unpeeled**
  Vanilla ice cream
- 2 **cups crumbled Pecan Pralines**

Heat grill to medium (350°F to 450°F). Grill bananas, uncovered, turning once, until they soften and blacken,

to low, and simmer, uncovered, stirring occasionally, about 15 minutes. Stir in olive salad, scallions, and parsley. Remove from heat.

2. Preheat oven to 350°F. Rinse redfish. Make 4 parallel cuts on each side of fish, slicing into the flesh at an angle and down to the bone, to create 4 fairly even portions. Sprinkle salt evenly on fish, rubbing some salt into the cuts. Place fish in a large roasting pan, and pour half of the sauce over fish. Layer lemon slices on fish, and cover with remaining sauce. Cover

The Modern Casserole

TAKE COMFORT IN THESE FIVE CROWD-PLEASING DISHES STARRING
SOME OF OUR FAVORITE SEASONAL INGREDIENTS

**Skillet-Baked Ziti
with Andouille,
Tomatoes, and
Peppers**

ANDOUILLE

This spicy, heavily smoked pork sausage is seasoned slowly and cooked over pecan wood and sugar-cane to achieve its distinctive flavor and firm texture.

SHOP SMART: Andouille is sold ready-to-eat, with or without heating. Although it is fully cooked, it must be refrigerated.

COOKING TIP: Commonly associated with jambalaya and gumbo, andouille can be used in place of any spicy sausage, like hot Italian sausage or pepperoni.

SKILLET-BAKED ZITI WITH ANDOUILLE, TOMATOES, AND PEPPERS

An Italian-American classic gets a dose of Southern flavor. Other than cooking the pasta, you can pull this casserole together in a single skillet, making it ideal for busy weeknights.

12	oz. uncooked ziti pasta
1	Tbsp. olive oil
1	lb. andouille sausage, cut into 1/2-inch slices
1/2	small red bell pepper, cut into thin strips
1/2	small yellow or orange bell pepper, cut into thin strips
1/2	cup chopped sweet onion
2	tsp. minced garlic
2	(14.5-oz.) cans fire-roasted diced tomatoes
1	(8-oz.) can tomato sauce
2	tsp. granulated sugar
1	tsp. kosher salt
1/2	tsp. black pepper
3	oz. Parmesan cheese, shredded (about 3/4 cup)
4	oz. mozzarella cheese, shredded (about 1 cup)
	Basil leaves, for topping

1. Preheat oven to 350°F. Prepare pasta according to package directions, reducing boiling time to 8 minutes.

2. Cook sausage, peppers, onion, and garlic in hot oil in a 12-inch cast-iron skillet over medium-high, stirring often, until vegetables are soft and sausage has begun to brown slightly, 7 to 8 minutes. Stir in tomatoes, tomato sauce, sugar, salt, and pepper. Bring mixture to a simmer over medium, and add 1/2 cup of the Parmesan, stirring until melted. Stir in cooked pasta. Remove from heat, and

sprinkle with mozzarella and remaining 1/4 cup Parmesan.

3. Bake in preheated oven until mixture is bubbly and cheese is golden, 25 to 30 minutes. Let stand 10 minutes before serving.

SERVES 8 (serving size: about 2 cups)
ACTIVE 20 min. **TOTAL** 50 min.

CREAMY CHICKEN AND COLLARD GREEN ENCHILADAS

Collards pair well with this chile sauce, but you can substitute other hearty greens too, like kale.

- 2 Tbsp. salted butter
- 1 (16-oz.) pkg. fresh chopped collards, coarsely chopped
- 1/2 cup chopped onion
- 1 garlic clove, minced
- 4 oz. cream cheese, cubed (about 1/2 cup)
- 1/2 cup whole milk
- 1 tsp. granulated sugar
- 1 tsp. kosher salt
- 1/2 tsp. black pepper
- 1 (8-oz.) block Monterey Jack cheese, shredded and divided
- 2 cups shredded cooked chicken
- 2 (8-oz.) pouches green chile enchilada sauce
- 1/2 cup sour cream
- 12 (6-inch) corn tortillas
  Sliced radishes, sliced jalapeño chiles, cilantro leaves

1. Preheat oven to 375°F. Lightly coat a 13- x 9-inch baking dish with cooking spray; set aside. Melt butter in a large skillet over medium. Add collards, onion, and minced garlic; cook, stirring often, until collards are cooked to desired degree of tenderness, 10 to 15 minutes. Stir in cream cheese, milk, sugar, salt, pepper, and 1 cup of the cheese; cook, stirring constantly, until heated through, about 4 minutes. Remove from heat, and stir in chicken.

2. Whisk together enchilada sauce and sour cream in a small bowl. Spoon 1 cup sauce mixture into prepared baking dish.

3. Wrap tortillas in damp paper towels, and tightly wrap with plastic wrap. Microwave at HIGH until tortillas are softened, about 1 minute. (Softening the tortillas prevents them from tearing.)

4. Spoon about 1/3 cup collard green mixture just below the center of each tortilla. Fold opposite sides of tortilla over filling, and roll up. Place enchiladas, seam side down, on sauce mixture in baking dish. Top with remaining sauce mixture and remaining 1 cup cheese.

5. Bake in preheated oven until light brown and bubbly, 25 to 30 minutes. Garnish with sliced radishes and jalapeños and cilantro leaves.

SERVES 6 (serving size: 2 enchiladas)
ACTIVE 35 min. **TOTAL** 1 hour

SAVORY SWEET POTATO BREAD PUDDING

Cubes of French bread are baked in a rich Parmesan custard with smoky bacon, spinach, and chunks of roasted sweet potatoes. Serve this comforting casserole with a green salad for dinner or as a company-worthy brunch.

2 1/2   lb. sweet potatoes, peeled and cut into 1 1/2- to 2-inch cubes
1   Tbsp. olive oil
1 1/2   tsp. kosher salt, divided
1/2   tsp. black pepper, divided
8   thick-cut bacon slices
1/2   cup chopped sweet onion
1   (5-oz.) pkg. baby spinach
1   (8-oz.) French bread loaf, cut into 1-inch cubes
6   large eggs
2 1/2   cups half-and-half
2   oz. Parmesan cheese, grated (about 1/2 cup)

1. Preheat oven to 400°F. Lightly coat an aluminum foil-lined baking sheet with cooking spray. Toss together sweet potatoes, olive oil, 1/2 teaspoon of the salt, and 1/4 teaspoon of the pepper on the prepared baking sheet. Bake in preheated oven until sweet potatoes are just tender, 20 to 25 minutes, stirring halfway through.
2. Meanwhile, cook bacon, in batches, in a large skillet over medium until crisp, 10 to 12 minutes; remove bacon, and drain on paper towels, reserving 2 tablespoons drippings in skillet. Crumble bacon.
3. Remove potatoes from oven, and set aside. Reduce oven temperature to 350°F.
4. Cook onion in hot drippings over medium until just tender, 2 to 3 minutes. Add spinach, and cook until spinach begins to wilt, about 1 minute. Add bread cubes and crumbled bacon to spinach mixture, stirring to completely incorporate.
5. Whisk together eggs, half-and-half, Parmesan, and remaining 1 teaspoon salt and 1/4 teaspoon pepper in a large bowl. Stir in bread cube mixture, stirring gently to completely incorporate. Gently stir in roasted potatoes.

Lightly coat a 13- x 9-inch baking dish with cooking spray; spoon mixture into prepared dish.
6. Bake at 350°F until golden brown and set in the middle, 45 to 50 minutes. Let stand 10 minutes before serving.

SERVES 8 (serving size: 1 1/2 cups)
ACTIVE 40 min. **TOTAL** 1 hour, 30 min.

OKRA AND RICE CASSEROLE

This dish is simple to make, but it packs a surprising amount of flavor from tender sautéed okra, sweet corn, Cajun spices, and buttery garlic breadcrumbs.

3   Tbsp. canola oil
2   Tbsp. all-purpose flour
1/2   cup chopped yellow onion
1/2   cup chopped celery
1/2   cup chopped green bell pepper
2   tsp. minced garlic
1   (14.5-oz.) can diced tomatoes
3   cups vegetable broth
1 1/2   lb. fresh okra, trimmed and cut into 1 1/2- to 2-inch pieces
1   cup fresh corn kernels (from 2 ears)
2   tsp. Cajun seasoning
1/4   tsp. black pepper
1/4   cup (2 oz.) salted butter, melted
2   garlic cloves, pressed
8   (1-inch-thick) French bread slices
2   (8.5-oz.) pouches microwavable basmati rice

1. Preheat oven to 350°F. Lightly grease a 13- x 9-inch baking dish. Whisk together oil and flour in a Dutch oven; cook over medium-high, whisking, until mixture is golden brown, 5 to 7 minutes. Stir in onion, celery, bell pepper, and minced garlic, and cook, stirring, until vegetables begin to soften, about 3 minutes.
2. Stir in tomatoes, broth, okra, corn, Cajun seasoning, and pepper, and bring to a boil over medium-high. Reduce heat to medium, and cook, stirring, until slightly thickened, 10 minutes.
3. Meanwhile, combine melted butter and pressed garlic. Brush both sides of French bread slices with garlic butter, and bake in preheated oven until lightly golden, about 3 minutes

OKRA

These green pods are delicious deep-fried, but they are more versatile than you might think.

SHOP SMART: The smaller pods are the most tender, so look for ones 3 to 4 inches long. Refrigerate and cook within a few days.

EASY PREP: Okra "slime" (called mucilage) naturally thickens soups and stews. This substance is released as you cut the pods, so we suggest cutting them into larger chunks, rather than thin slices.

per side. Remove from oven, and process in a food processor until coarsely crumbled.

4. Squeeze rice pouches to separate grains. Tear a 2-inch vent in each pouch. Microwave both pouches at the same time at HIGH for 2 minutes. (The rice will be slightly undercooked.) Spoon into prepared baking dish. Top with okra mixture and breadcrumbs.

5. Bake in preheated oven until breadcrumbs are golden brown, 25 to 30 minutes. Let stand 10 minutes before serving.

SERVES 8 (serving size: 1 1/2 to 2 cups)
ACTIVE 45 min. **TOTAL** 1 hour, 10 min.

CHEESY HAM, CORN, AND GRITS BAKE

This impressive-looking casserole bakes up puffy and golden with pockets of fresh corn and savory ham. Think of it as a soufflé without the work.

- 2 Tbsp. salted butter
- 1/4 cup finely chopped yellow onion
- 2 tsp. minced garlic
- 4 1/2 cups water
- 1 tsp. table salt
- 1 1/2 cups uncooked yellow stone-ground grits
- 2 (8-oz.) pkg. cubed boneless ham, drained and patted dry with paper towels
- 1 (8-oz.) pkg. shredded sharp Cheddar cheese
- 1 (8-oz.) pkg. shredded extra-sharp Cheddar cheese
- 1 cup whole milk
- 1 cup fresh corn kernels (from about 2 ears)
- 1 1/2 tsp. chopped fresh thyme
- 1/4 tsp. black pepper
- 4 large eggs, lightly beaten

1. Lightly grease a 3-quart baking dish. Preheat oven to 350°F.

2. Melt butter in a Dutch oven over medium; stir in onion and garlic, and cook, stirring constantly, 2 minutes. Stir in water and salt, increase heat to medium-high, and bring to a boil. Whisk in grits, and stir in ham; return to a boil. Reduce heat to medium-low, and simmer, whisking occasionally, until thickened and grits are almost tender, 15 to 20 minutes. Remove from heat; add both cheeses, stirring until completely melted. Stir in milk, corn, thyme, pepper, and eggs. Spoon mixture into prepared baking dish.

GRITS

Made from ground dried corn, this pantry staple is a delicious addition to your breakfast, lunch, or dinner menu.

SHOP SMART: Look for "stone-ground" for the most tooth-some texture—but prepare for a long cooking time. Quick grits will cook in about half the time but have less flavor and texture because they are more processed.

STORE WISELY: Stone-ground grits are perishable, so keep them in the refrigerator or freezer for maximum freshness.

3. Bake in preheated oven until golden and cooked through, 50 minutes to 1 hour. Let stand 15 minutes before serving.

SERVES 8 (serving size: about 2 cups)
ACTIVE 25 min. **TOTAL** 1 hour, 15 min.

A Cut Above

THE BEST AND FASTEST WAY TO ROAST A CHICKEN REQUIRES SIMPLE KNIFE SKILLS

GARLICKY ROASTED SPATCHCOCK CHICKEN

Removing a chicken's backbone—called spatchcocking (or butterflying)—ensures juicy meat and golden crisp skin in less time than roasting a whole bird.

1	(5-lb.) whole chicken
4	garlic cloves, chopped
1	tsp. kosher salt
6	Tbsp. (3 oz.) salted butter, softened
1	Tbsp. chopped fresh thyme
2	Tbsp. lemon zest, plus 3 Tbsp. fresh juice, divided
3/4	tsp. black pepper, divided
12	oz. small red new potatoes, halved
8	oz. small carrots with tops, trimmed
8	oz. Brussels sprouts, trimmed and halved

1. Preheat oven to 450°F. Rinse chicken, and pat dry. Place chicken, breast side down, on a cutting board. Using poultry shears, cut along both sides of backbone, and remove backbone. (Discard or reserve for stock.) Turn chicken breast side up, and open the underside of chicken like a book. Using the heel of your hand, press firmly against breastbone until it cracks. Place chicken in a large rimmed baking pan. Tuck wing tips under chicken so they don't burn.

2. Combine garlic and salt on a cutting board. Using the flat edge of a knife, mash into a paste. Combine garlic paste, butter, thyme, zest, and pepper in a bowl. Set aside 2 tablespoons of the garlic mixture. Rub remaining garlic mixture under skin of chicken breasts and thighs.

3. Bake chicken in preheated oven 10 minutes. Remove pan from oven. Reduce heat to 400°F. Arrange potatoes and carrots around chicken; return to oven, and bake 20 minutes. Arrange Brussels sprouts around chicken, and spread remaining 2 tablespoons garlic mixture on breasts; return to oven, and bake until a meat thermometer inserted in thickest portion registers 165°F, about 20 minutes. Drizzle with lemon juice, and let stand 10 minutes. Carve chicken, and serve with pan juices.

SERVES 4 **ACTIVE** 30 min. **TOTAL** 1 hour, 40 min.

cooking ◆SL◆ school

HOW TO SPATCHCOCK A CHICKEN

SOUNDS FUNNY BUT THIS SERIOUS TECHNIQUE WILL HELP ROAST A CHICKEN FASTER AND MORE EVENLY

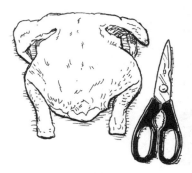

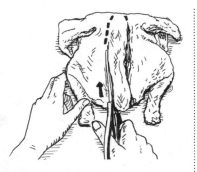

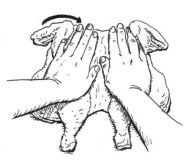

1 Place a whole chicken, breast side down, on a cutting board.

2 Starting at the thigh end, cut along one side of the backbone with kitchen shears. Repeat on the other side to remove the backbone. Freeze and reserve for stock.

3 Flip the chicken over so that it's cut-side down. Then firmly press on the breastbone with your hands to flatten it.

DEB WISE
SL Test Kitchen Professional

"Sometimes a layer cake's filling can leak over the sides. To keep it contained, pipe icing around the top edge of the bottom cake layer. Spread the filling inside your icing; then add the top layer, and frost the entire cake."

MAKE-AHEAD TIP
BEST WAY TO FREEZE A CASSEROLE

Want to win at weeknight meals? Stock up on a stack of freezer-friendly casseroles with this simple storage trick.

1. Line baking dish with aluminum foil, leaving enough excess foil on all sides to cover the entire pan.

2. Prepare casserole in the dish, and bake as normal. Let cool. Wrap casserole with excess foil; freeze.

3. Once frozen solid, remove foil-wrapped casserole from pan; put back in freezer. Tip: Label it so you know what's inside (and date it).

1

2

Fig-and-Kale Salad

Falling for Figs

IN HER NEW COLUMN, ATLANTA-BASED CHEF AND COOKBOOK AUTHOR VIRGINIA WILLIS SHARES HER FAVORITE WAYS TO USE PEAK-OF-SEASON SOUTHERN INGREDIENTS

FRESH FIGS ARE THE TENNESSEE WILLIAMS play of Southern fruit, prized for their undercurrent of sensuality. When ripe, these luscious fruits burst to reveal sweet, crimson flesh. It's enough to make you reach for your smelling salts.

My family did not grow figs on our property; however, my grandmother's neighbor had a giant, sweeping fig tree to the side of her front porch. Miz Jackson (as she was called by my grandmother despite the fact that they'd been dear friends for 50 years) would phone and say the figs were ripe. With promptly issued baskets neatly lined with paper towels, my grandfather and I would drive down the road that very afternoon to harvest the goodness.

The real attraction of this fruit is its preciousness. Ripe figs won't keep, and they are only in season for a few short weeks in late summer and early fall. Classic recipes for preserving include fig jam and preserves, both often made with citrus to counter their sweetness. My grandmother would add thinly sliced lemons so that as they cooked with the figs they would candy, becoming translucent wagon wheels.

While I do love "putting up" the fruit for later, there is little that is as straightforward and pleasurable as a perfectly ripe fig. If eaten in any way other than out of hand, a fig's honeyed sweetness is best accented with salt or acidity for balance. Figs pair wonderfully with cheese, ham, and crisp, bitter greens such as arugula and baby kale. Like a real Southern beauty, these tantalizing delicacies need little to no embellishment to shine.

FIG-AND-KALE SALAD

- 5 oz. baby kale, arugula, or a combination of both
- 3 bacon slices, cut into strips
- 12 medium-size fresh figs, halved lengthwise
- 1 shallot, chopped (about ¼ cup)
- 3 Tbsp. extra-virgin olive oil, divided
- 1 tsp. finely chopped fresh ginger
- 1 cup pecan halves
- 1 Tbsp. balsamic vinegar
- ¼ tsp. kosher salt
- ¼ tsp. black pepper
- 3 oz. blue cheese, crumbled

1. Place the kale in a large bowl. Set aside. Heat a large skillet over medium-high. Add bacon, and cook, stirring occasionally, until crisp, about 6 minutes. Remove with a slotted spoon, and drain on paper towels, reserving 1 teaspoon drippings in skillet.
2. Increase the heat to high, and place the figs, cut side down, in the skillet. Cook until just seared, 1 to 2 minutes. Remove figs to a plate, and cover to keep warm. Reduce heat to medium-low.
3. Add shallots and 1 tablespoon of the olive oil to skillet. Cook over medium-low, stirring occasionally, until softened, 2 minutes. Add ginger, and cook, stirring occasionally, until tender, about 1 minute. Add pecans, and cook, stirring often, until pecans are lightly toasted, about 5 minutes. Stir in vinegar, salt, pepper, and remaining 2 tablespoons oil.
4. Pour the warm pecan mixture over the greens, scraping all the bits from the pan, and toss gently to coat. Top with the warm figs, blue cheese, and bacon. Serve immediately.

SERVES 4 (serving size: about 1 cup)
ACTIVE 25 min. **TOTAL** 25 min.

Fig Dutch Baby Pancake

Ham-Wrapped Figs

FIG DUTCH BABY PANCAKE

Feel free to use ½ teaspoon pure vanilla extract in place of vanilla bean seeds.

- 2 Tbsp. unsalted butter
- ½ vanilla bean
- ¾ cup 2% reduced-fat milk
- 2 large eggs, lightly beaten
- ¼ tsp. fine sea salt
- ½ cup (2.13 oz.) all-purpose flour
- 6 fresh figs, halved lengthwise
- 2 to 3 Tbsp. powdered sugar

1. Preheat oven to 400°F. Place the butter in a 10-inch cast-iron skillet or ovenproof stainless-steel skillet, and place in preheating oven to melt the butter and heat the skillet.

2. Meanwhile, split vanilla bean pod, and scrape seeds into a small bowl. (Reserve pod for another use.) Add milk, eggs, and salt, whisking until smooth. Place flour in a medium bowl; slowly add milk mixture to flour, whisking until smooth. Remove the hot skillet from the oven. Add the melted butter to the batter, and whisk to combine. Quickly place the figs, cut side up, in the skillet, and pour the batter over the figs. Bake until puffed and brown, 25 to 30 minutes.
3. Remove from oven, and sprinkle with powdered sugar. Cut into 4 wedges, and serve immediately.

SERVES 4 (serving size: 1 wedge)
ACTIVE 10 min. **TOTAL** 40 min.

HAM-WRAPPED FIGS

Trim the stem end of 24 fresh **figs.** Quarter the figs, but don't cut all the way through the bottom. Gently separate pieces of fig, leaving bottom connected. Fill the center of each fig with about ½ teaspoon crumbled **goat cheese** or blue cheese. (If the fig is large, simply cut it in half.) Wrap each stuffed fig with 1 (¾-inch-wide) thin strip of **country ham,** securing the ham with a wooden pick. Serve immediately, or, if desired, warm in a 350°F oven until the figs are heated through and the cheese has softened, 4 to 5 minutes.

SERVES 8 (serving size: 3 figs)
ACTIVE 20 min. **TOTAL** 20 min.

APPLE PICKING
For the best flavor and texture, mix it up: We chose Granny Smith for tartness and Honeycrisp for sweetness.

The Ultimate Apple Pie

BAKE UP A NEW TRADITION WITH OUR DELICIOUS TWIST ON AN OLD-FASHIONED FAVORITE

BROWN BUTTER APPLE PIE

Browned butter adds a subtle nutty flavor to the crust, and the filling gets a sweet makeover from two types of apples, rich brown sugar, and just the right amount of warming spices.

BROWN BUTTER CRUST

- 1 cup (8 oz.) plus 2 Tbsp. salted butter
- 3 cups (about 12 ¾ oz.) all-purpose flour
- 1 ½ tsp. kosher salt
- 1 large egg
- 5 to 6 Tbsp. ice-cold water

APPLE FILLING

- ¼ cup salted butter, divided
- 2 lb. Granny Smith apples, peeled and cut into about ⅓-inch-thick slices
- 2 lb. Honeycrisp apples, peeled and cut into about ⅓-inch-thick slices
- ⅓ cup packed dark brown sugar
- 1 ½ tsp. ground cinnamon
- ½ tsp. ground nutmeg
- 1 Tbsp. all-purpose flour
- ½ tsp. kosher salt
- 1 Tbsp. heavy cream
- 1 large egg
- 1 Tbsp. granulated sugar
  Butter pecan or vanilla ice cream (optional)

1. Prepare the Brown Butter Crust: Line a small bowl with aluminum foil. Melt 1 cup plus 2 tablespoons butter in a small heavy saucepan over medium, and cook, stirring constantly, until butter begins to turn golden brown, 6 to 8 minutes. Remove pan from heat, and immediately pour butter into prepared bowl. Freeze until butter is cool and begins to solidify, about 1 hour. Lift foil from bowl; remove butter from the foil, and cut it into small pieces.

2. Pulse 3 cups flour and 1 ½ teaspoons salt in a food processor until combined, 3 to 4 times. Add browned butter pieces, and pulse until mixture resembles coarse meal. Stir together 1 egg and 1 tablespoon ice-cold water. With processor running, gradually add egg mixture and up to 5 tablespoons ice-cold water, 1 tablespoon at a time, and process until dough begins to come together. Turn dough out on a lightly floured surface, and knead 3 to 4 times. Divide dough in half. Shape each half into a ball; flatten each ball into a disk, and wrap tightly in plastic wrap. Chill 30 minutes or up to 2 days.

3. Prepare the Apple Filling: Melt 2 tablespoons of the butter in a large skillet over medium. Add apples, and cook, gently stirring, until apples are just tender, 10 to 15 minutes. Spread apples on a rimmed baking sheet, and cool 30 minutes. Toss together apples, brown sugar, cinnamon, nutmeg, 1 tablespoon flour, and ½ teaspoon salt in a large bowl.

4. Preheat oven to 425°F. Unwrap 1 dough disk, and place on a lightly floured surface. Roll to ⅛-inch thickness. Fit dough into a lightly greased 9-inch deep-dish pie plate or pie pan. Spoon apple mixture into piecrust, spreading and pressing into an even layer. Chop remaining 2 tablespoons butter, and sprinkle over filling.

5. Repeat rolling procedure with remaining dough disk; cut dough into about 8 (1-inch-wide) strips. Arrange about half of the piecrust strips vertically over the filling (*Step 1*). Fold down every other strip, and place 1 strip horizontally across the top of the pie (*Step 2*). Unfold the folded strips, and fold up the remaining strips. Lay another strip horizontally across the pie (*Step 3*). Continue weaving the remaining strips to form a lattice. Trim excess dough from pie plate, and crimp the edges of the pie (*Step 4*). Whisk together cream and 1 egg. Brush entire pie with egg mixture. Sprinkle with granulated sugar. Freeze 30 minutes or until dough is firm. Place pie on an aluminum foil-lined baking sheet.

6. Bake on lower oven rack of preheated oven 20 minutes. Reduce oven temperature to 375°F, and bake 40 to 45 minutes, shielding pie with foil to prevent overbrowning after 20 minutes, if needed, until crust is golden and filling is bubbly. Remove from baking sheet to a wire rack; cool at least 1 hour before serving. Serve with ice cream, if desired.

SERVES 8 (serving size: 1 piece)
ACTIVE 45 min. **TOTAL** 3 hours, 30 min.

MAKE A LATTICE PIE CRUST

Step 1

Step 2

Step 3

Step 4

Pimiento Cheese Dip

Microwave 4 oz. **processed cheese** (such as Velveeta) in a microwave-safe bowl at HIGH until melted, about 1 minute, stirring after 30 seconds. Whisk in ¼ cup whole **milk,** 3 Tbsp. diced **pimientos,** well drained, ½ tsp. **paprika,** and ½ tsp. black **pepper.** Serve immediately.

SERVES 4 **ACTIVE** 5 min.
TOTAL 5 min.

Let's Do the Twist

KICK OFF TAILGATE SEASON WITH HOMEMADE PRETZELS AND A TRIO OF QUICK-FIX DIPS

HOMEMADE SOFT PRETZELS

1 ¼ cups warm water (105°F to 115°F)
  1 Tbsp. granulated sugar
  1 (¼-oz.) pkg. active dry yeast
2 ¼ cups (about 9.5 oz.) bread flour
2 ¼ cups (about 9.5 oz.) all-purpose flour
  3 Tbsp. kosher salt, divided
  2 large eggs
 10 cups plus 1 Tbsp. water, divided
  6 Tbsp. baking soda

1. Stir together 1 ¼ cups warm water and sugar in the bowl of a stand mixer. Sprinkle yeast over mixture, and let stand 5 minutes. Fit mixer with paddle attachment. Add flours, 1 tablespoon of the salt, and 1 egg to yeast mixture, and beat at low speed, about 30 seconds. Replace paddle with dough hook, and beat on medium speed until dough is smooth and has pulled away from the bowl, 5 minutes.

2. Transfer dough to a lightly greased bowl, turning to grease top. Cover and let rise in a warm place until doubled in bulk, 1 hour.

3. Preheat oven to 450°F. Lightly grease 2 wire racks, placing each in a rimmed baking sheet. Bring 10 cups of the water to a boil.

4. Meanwhile, turn dough out onto a lightly greased surface; roll out to a 12- x 8-inch (about ¾-inch-thick) rectangle. Cut into 8 (12-inch-long) strips; cut each strip into 4 pieces.

5. To shape the pretzels, form 1 strip into a "U" with the ends of the strip pointing up (*fig. A*). Fold one end down, making a small loop (*fig. B*). Fold the other end down, making a second small loop (*fig. C*). Press the dough in place to secure. Repeat with remaining dough.

6. Add baking soda to water; stir to dissolve. Add 3 to 4 pretzels and cook 3 minutes, turning occasionally. Transfer to pans. Repeat with remaining pretzels.

7. Let pretzels rest until moisture evaporates, 15 minutes. Whisk together remaining egg and water. Brush egg wash over tops of pretzels, and sprinkle with remaining 2 tablespoons salt.

8. Bake until tops are golden, 7 to 10 minutes, rotating pans from top to bottom rack about halfway through bake time. Turn pretzels over and bake until tops are golden, 3 to 5 minutes.

SERVES 6 **ACTIVE** 1 hour **TOTAL** 2 hours, 10 min.

Buttermilk Ranch Dip

Whisk together ½ cup **buttermilk,** ¼ cup each **sour cream** and **mayonnaise,** and 2 Tbsp. each **cider vinegar,** finely chopped **dill,** and finely chopped **chives.** Chill until ready to serve.

SERVES 4 **ACTIVE** 5 min. **TOTAL** 5 min.

Creole Honey Mustard Dip

Whisk together ½ cup **Dijon mustard,** 3 Tbsp. **mayonnaise,** 1 Tbsp. **honey,** and 1 tsp. **Creole seasoning** until smooth. Chill until ready to serve.

SERVES 4 **ACTIVE** 5 min. **TOTAL** 5 min.

HOW TO

HOW TO SHAPE A PRETZEL
CREATE A CLASSIC TWIST IN 3 EASY STEPS

fig. A   *fig. B*   *fig. C*

Cookies for a Crowd

THERE'S SOMETHING FOR EVERYONE HERE: FROM A GOOEY, CHEWY CLASSIC CHOCOLATE CHIP TO A SURPRISING HUMMINGBIRD CAKE-INSPIRED TREAT

DEEP-DISH SKILLET COOKIE

- 1 cup packed light brown sugar
- 1/2 cup granulated sugar
- 1/2 cup (4 oz.) salted butter, softened
- 1 large egg
- 3 Tbsp. whole milk
- 1 1/2 tsp. vanilla extract
- 2 cups (about 9 oz.) all-purpose flour
- 1 tsp. baking soda
- 1/4 tsp. table salt
- 1 1/2 cups semisweet chocolate chips, divided
  Vanilla ice cream

1. Preheat oven to 325°F. Lightly coat a 10-inch cast-iron skillet with cooking spray. Beat brown sugar, granulated sugar, and butter with a heavy-duty electric stand mixer at medium speed until light and fluffy. Add egg, milk, and vanilla, beating until blended.
2. Whisk together flour, baking soda, and salt in a bowl. Add to butter mixture gradually, beating at low speed until combined.
3. Add 1 cup of the chocolate chips; beat until combined.
4. Spread mixture evenly in prepared skillet. Top with remaining 1/2 cup chocolate chips.
5. Bake in preheated oven until golden and set, about 50 minutes. Let stand 15 minutes; cut into wedges. Serve with vanilla ice cream.

SERVES 8 to 10 **ACTIVE** 15 min.
TOTAL 1 hour, 20 min.

FIVE SKILLET COOKIE MAKEOVERS

START WITH OUR CLASSIC CHOCOLATE CHIP COOKIE RECIPE, AND THEN GET CREATIVE WITH FUN, FLAVORFUL MIX-INS

PECAN PRALINE

Omit chocolate chips. Prepare recipe as directed, stirring in 1/2 cup chopped **pecans** and 1/2 cup **toffee** bits in Step 3, and topping mixture with 3/4 cup pecan halves and 3 tablespoons jarred **caramel sauce** in Step 4. Sprinkle with **sea salt** just before serving.

MISSISSIPPI MUD

Increase **milk** to 5 tablespoons. Prepare recipe as directed, whisking 3 tablespoons **unsweetened cocoa** into flour mixture in Step 2, and topping cookie with 1/4 cup **miniature marshmallows** during the last 30 minutes of baking in Step 5.

STRAWBERRY SHORTCAKE

Increase **milk** to 1/4 cup. Substitute **white chocolate chips** for semisweet chocolate chips. Prepare recipe as directed, beating 3/4 cup chopped **frozen pound cake** into mixture with white chocolate chips in Step 3. Top mixture with 1/4 cup chopped frozen pound cake in Step 4. Serve cookie wedges with **whipped cream** and sliced **strawberries.**

GRASSHOPPER

Omit milk and chocolate chips. Prepare recipe as directed, beating 3 tablespoons **bourbon** into mixture with egg and vanilla in Step 1, and stirring in 1 cup halved thin **crème de menthe chocolate mints** in Step 3. Top mixture with 1/4 cup halved thin crème de menthe chocolate mints in Step 4.

HUMMINGBIRD

Omit milk and vanilla extract. Substitute **white chocolate chips** for semisweet chocolate chips. Prepare recipe as directed, adding 1/4 cup mashed **banana** and 1 1/2 teaspoons **coconut extract** to butter mixture in Step 1 and 1/2 cup sweetened flaked **coconut** and 1/2 cup chopped **dried pineapple** in Step 3.

Hummingbird

October

50th ANNIVERSARY SPECIAL

RECIPE REVIVALS

If you ever want to time travel, all you have to do is take a look through our enormous recipe archives. The food pages of *Southern Living* have documented how Southerners have been cooking and eating for the past five decades. As the images in our issues moved from black and white to color, our tastes also evolved—from congealed salads in the 1960s to the heirloom tomato salads of today. To celebrate our 50th anniversary year, we took our most iconic dishes and reimagined them with inventive new flavors and preparations. Here's a taste of some of our past and present-day favorites.

▲ THEN

CHICKEN POT PIE

Chicken pot pie may have roots elsewhere in the world, but its soul-satisfying comforts are not lost in the South. Baked family-style in a shallow casserole dish, this old-fashioned favorite hits all the right notes with a rich and creamy chicken filling and golden egg-washed lattice crust.

◀ NOW

SKILLET CHICKEN POT PIE

A few well-chosen shortcuts trim the prep time but not the made-from-scratch flavor. Rotisserie chicken jump-starts the creamy filling. (One bird yields just the right amount of meat.) Frozen hash browns get meltingly tender when baked, and matchstick carrots add a crisp, fresh snap. Bonus: The steady heat of a cast-iron skillet beautifully browns the bottom crust.

▲ THEN
MACARONI AND CHEESE

For a brief and shining moment in the '80s, sour cream and cottage cheese were the go-to stir-ins—amping up the creamy comforts of classic Southern Cheddar-and-elbow macaroni blends. This deluxe twist, spiked with smoky bits of diced ham and topped with buttered breadcrumbs, appeared in our stellar collection of five-star recipes.

◄ NOW
HUGH'S SOUTHERN MAC AND CHEESE

Georgia chef Hugh Acheson swaps elbow macaroni for cavatappi pasta—a tubular twist that captures the creamy goodness of béchamel, bacon, and leeks bound in a gooey mix of aged Cheddar and Gruyère. Baking in a cast-iron skillet seriously ups the crispy edge factor.

CHICKEN POT PIE

- 1/3 cup unsalted butter
- 1/2 cup chopped celery
- 1/2 cup chopped yellow onion
- 1/3 cup (about 1 1/2 oz.) all-purpose flour
- 2 3/4 cups chicken broth
- 3 1/2 cups chopped cooked chicken
- 1 (10-oz.) pkg. frozen mixed vegetables, thawed
- 3 hard-cooked eggs, peeled and chopped
- 1/2 tsp. salt
- 1/2 tsp. black pepper
  Pastry (recipe below)
- 1 large egg, lightly beaten

1. Preheat oven to 400°F. Melt butter in a large heavy saucepan over medium-high. Add celery and onion, and cook, stirring often, until softened, about 6 minutes. Add flour, and cook, stirring constantly, 1 minute. Slowly stir in broth. Reduce heat to medium, and cook, stirring constantly, until mixture is thickened and bubbly. Stir in chicken, vegetables, hard-cooked eggs, salt, and pepper. Transfer mixture to a lightly greased 11- x 7-inch (2-quart) baking dish.
2. Place the Pastry on a lightly floured surface, and roll out into a 1/8-inch-thick rectangle. Cut Pastry into 3/4-inch-wide strips, and arrange strips in a lattice design over the top of the chicken mixture. Lightly brush Pastry strips with beaten egg.
3. Bake in preheated oven until golden brown and bubbly, 35 to 40 minutes.

SERVES 6 **ACTIVE** 25 min.
TOTAL 2 hours, 5 min., including pastry

Pastry

- 1 1/2 cups all-purpose flour
- 3/4 teaspoon salt
- 1/2 cup plus 1 1/2 tablespoons shortening
- 4 to 5 tablespoons ice-cold water

Combine the flour and salt; cut in the shortening with a pastry blender until mixture is crumbly. Sprinkle the cold water, 1 tablespoon at a time, over the surface of the mixture; stir with a fork until all ingredients are moistened. Shape the dough into a flat rectangle; wrap in plastic wrap, and chill 1 hour.

MAKES enough for 17- x 11-inch lattice crust

SKILLET CHICKEN POT PIE

- 1/3 cup (2 2/3 oz.) plus 2 Tbsp. unsalted butter, divided
- 1/3 cup (about 1 1/2 oz.) all-purpose flour
- 1 1/2 cups chicken broth
- 1 1/2 cups whole milk
- 1 1/2 tsp. Creole seasoning
- 1 large sweet onion, diced
- 1 (8-oz.) pkg. sliced mushrooms
- 4 cups shredded rotisserie chicken
- 2 cups frozen cubed hash browns
- 1 cup matchstick carrots
- 1 cup frozen small sweet peas
- 1/3 cup chopped fresh flat-leaf parsley
- 1 (14.1-oz.) pkg. refrigerated piecrusts
- 1 large egg white

1. Preheat oven to 350°F. Lightly grease a 10-inch cast-iron skillet.
2. Melt 1/3 cup of the butter in a large saucepan over medium; add flour, and cook, whisking constantly, 1 minute. Slowly whisk in the chicken broth and milk; cook, whisking constantly, until thickened and bubbly, 6 to 7 minutes. Remove from heat, and stir in Creole seasoning.
3. Melt remaining 2 tablespoons butter in a large Dutch oven over medium-high; add onion and mushrooms, and cook, stirring often, until tender, about 10 minutes. Stir in chicken, hash browns, carrots, peas, parsley, and sauce.
4. Place 1 piecrust in prepared skillet. Spread chicken mixture in piecrust; top with remaining piecrust. Whisk egg white until foamy; brush top of piecrust with egg white. Cut 4 or 5 small slits in the top of the pie to allow steam to escape.
5. Bake in preheated oven until golden brown and bubbly, 1 hour to 1 hour and 5 minutes.

SERVES 6 to 8 (serving size: about 1 1/4 cups)
ACTIVE 30 min. **TOTAL** 1 hour, 30 min.

MACARONI AND CHEESE

- 1 (8-oz.) pkg. uncooked elbow macaroni
- 8 oz. sharp Cheddar cheese, shredded (about 2 cups)
- 2 cups cottage cheese
- 1 (8-oz.) container sour cream
- 1 cup diced cooked ham
- 2 Tbsp. finely chopped onion
- 1/4 tsp. kosher salt
- 1/4 tsp. black pepper
- 1 large egg, lightly beaten
- 1 cup soft fresh breadcrumbs
- 2 Tbsp. unsalted butter, melted
- 1/4 tsp. paprika
  Sliced cherry tomatoes (optional)
  Flat-leaf parsley sprigs (optional)

1. Preheat oven to 350°F. Prepare macaroni according to package directions.
2. Gently stir together macaroni, Cheddar cheese, cottage cheese, sour cream, ham, onion, salt, pepper, and egg in a large bowl. Transfer to a 2-quart baking dish coated with cooking spray.
3. Stir together breadcrumbs, butter, and paprika in a small bowl. Sprinkle breadcrumb mixture diagonally across the top of the macaroni mixture, forming stripes.
4. Bake in preheated oven until golden brown, 30 to 35 minutes. Top with sliced tomatoes and parsley, if desired.

SERVES 6 (serving size: 1 1/2 cups)
ACTIVE 20 min. **TOTAL** 50 min.

HUGH'S SOUTHERN MAC AND CHEESE

- ¼ lb. thick-cut bacon slices (about 4 slices), diced
- 2 medium leeks, cut into ½-inch rounds (about 1 cup)
- ⅓ (16-oz.) package uncooked cavatappi pasta
- 1½ Tbsp. unsalted butter
- 1½ Tbsp. all-purpose flour
- 1 cup whole milk, warmed
- ½ tsp. dry mustard
- ¼ tsp. salt
- ¼ tsp. black pepper
  Pinch of crushed red pepper
- 4 oz. 2-year-old aged Cheddar cheese, grated (about 1 cup), divided
- 1 large egg yolk
- 2 oz. Gruyère cheese, grated (about ½ cup)
- 2 Tbsp. heavy cream
- ¼ cup soft, fresh breadcrumbs, toasted

1. Preheat oven to 375°F. Cook bacon, stirring often, in a skillet over medium until crisp, about 7 minutes. Transfer to a plate lined with paper towels to drain. Reserve bacon drippings for another use.
2. Cook sliced leeks in boiling water in a Dutch oven 5 minutes. Remove with a slotted spoon, reserving water. Plunge the leeks into ice water to stop the cooking process; drain.
3. Add the pasta to boiling water. Cook al dente, 10 minutes. Drain.
4. Melt the butter in a large skillet over medium. Reduce heat to medium-low, and whisk in flour until smooth. Cook, whisking constantly, 2 minutes or until golden brown. Slowly whisk in the milk. Cook, whisking constantly, 3 minutes or until thickened. Whisk in the dry mustard, salt, black pepper, red pepper, and ½ cup of the Cheddar cheese, stirring until melted. Remove from heat.
5. Gently stir together the pasta, cheese sauce, half each of the cooked bacon and leeks, and egg yolk. Stir in the Gruyère cheese and remaining ½ cup Cheddar cheese. Spoon the pasta mixture into a buttered 8-inch cast-iron skillet, and sprinkle with the remaining bacon and leeks. Drizzle

with the cream; sprinkle with the breadcrumbs.
6. Bake at 375°F for 35 minutes or until golden and bubbly. Let stand 15 minutes before serving.

SERVES 4 (serving size: 1½ cups)
ACTIVE 45 min. **TOTAL** 1 hour, 35 min.

HEAVENLY SMOKED BRISKET

Brisket is the legendary low-and-slow-cooked cut of the Lone Star State, but its fame extends far beyond Texas borders. This recipe came to us from a reader in Alexandria, Louisiana. Hickory-smoked with a bold brown sugar-Cajun spice rub, it topped our annual list of favorites in 1995. There's no barbecue sauce. None needed. The heavenly flavor of the brisket speaks for itself.

- ½ cup packed dark brown sugar
- 2 Tbsp. salt
- 2 Tbsp. Cajun seasoning
- 1 Tbsp. lemon-pepper seasoning
- 2 Tbsp. Worcestershire sauce
- 1 (5- to 6-lb.) beef brisket, trimmed

1. Stir together dark brown sugar, salt, Cajun seasoning, lemon-pepper seasoning, and Worcestershire sauce. Place brisket in a large shallow dish. Spread sugar mixture on both sides of brisket. Cover and chill 8 hours.
2. Combine hickory wood chunks with water to cover; let stand 1 hour. Prepare smoker according to manufacturer's instructions, bringing the internal temperature to 225°F to 250°F; maintain temperature for 15 to 20 minutes.
3. Drain wood chunks, and place on coals. Remove brisket from marinade, reserving marinade. Place brisket on lower cooking grate. Pour reserved marinade over brisket, and cover with smoker lid.
4. Smoke brisket, maintaining a low temperature inside smoker between 225°F and 250°F, until a meat thermometer inserted in thickest portion registers 180°F, about 5 hours. Remove from smoker; wrap brisket in aluminum foil, and let stand 10 to 15

minutes. Cut against the grain into thin slices.

SERVES 12 (serving size: about ½ lb. brisket)
ACTIVE 10 min. **TOTAL** 13 hours, 20 min., including chilling and smoking

SMOKED BEEF BRISKET

Champion Texas pitmaster Christopher Prieto opts for a whole brisket to feed a crowd and uses a fiery dry rub, a seductively sweet sauce, and a judicious use of smoke: Wait until the intense early smoke clears before adding the meat.

- 1 (12- to 14-lb.) beef brisket, trimmed
- ½ cup Worcestershire sauce
- 1 cup Beef Rub (page 254)
  El Sancho Barbecue Sauce (page 254), optional

1. Brush or rub beef brisket generously with Worcestershire sauce. Coat brisket with Beef Rub; cover and chill 1 to 4 hours.
2. Remove brisket from refrigerator, and let stand 1 hour.
3. Prepare a charcoal fire in a smoker according to manufacturer's instructions. Place 3 or 4 pecan, hickory, or oak wood chunks on coals. Place a water pan in the smoker; add water to fill line. Bring internal temperature to 250°F to 260°F; maintain temperature for 15 to 20 minutes.
4. Place brisket, fat side down, on top cooking grate; close the smoker. Smoke until a meat thermometer inserted in center where the point and flat meet registers 165°F, about 5 hours.
5. Remove brisket from smoker, and wrap tightly in wax-free butcher paper; return brisket to smoker. Cook, checking temperature each hour, until a meat thermometer inserted in thickest portion registers 200°F, 3 to 5 hours.
6. Remove brisket from smoker; open butcher paper, and let steam escape for 4 minutes. Close butcher paper, and let brisket stand 2 hours.
7. Remove brisket from butcher paper, reserving ¼ cup drippings in paper. Place brisket on a cutting board. Slice

▲ THEN

BURK'S FARM-RAISED CATFISH FRY

In 1980, Rome, Georgia, reader Bessie Burk won the National Catfish Fry with her buttermilk-marinated, cornmeal-crusted catfish fillets expertly fried two at a time in hot peanut oil. The ultimate cookware for such crisp golden-brown perfection? A deep cast-iron Dutch oven that evenly holds the heat and is wide enough to fry without overcrowding.

NOW ▶

FRIED CATFISH WITH PICKLED PEPPERS

Ready to move beyond the predictable catfish-and-tartar-sauce combo? We thought so. Our new condiment of choice: the addictive sweet-and-sour bite of pickled peppers. We used a mix of banana peppers and jalapeños, but feel free to sub in serranos, Fresno, Thai, or poblanos.

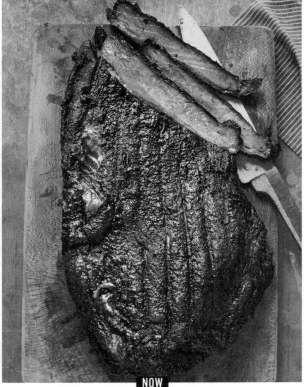

THEN

HEAVENLY SMOKED BRISKET

NOW

SMOKED BEEF BRISKET

meat across the grain into ¹/₄-inch-thick slices. Stir together reserved drippings and El Sancho Barbecue Sauce, if desired. Serve with brisket.

SERVES 14 (serving size: 8 oz.)
ACTIVE 40 min. **TOTAL** 12 hours, 45 min., including chilling and smoking

Beef Rub

- 1 cup kosher salt
- 1 cup ground Tellicherry black pepper
- 3 Tbsp. granulated garlic
- 2 tsp. crushed red pepper

Stir together all ingredients until well blended. Store in an airtight container up to 1 month.

MAKES 2¹/₄ cups **ACTIVE** 5 min.
TOTAL 5 min.

El Sancho Barbecue Sauce

To sauce or not to sauce? The debate rages on. Purists balk at sauces that blanket the flavorful crust or "bark" of smoked brisket, while other 'cue fans think sauceless brisket seems, well, naked. We say try it both ways.

- 1 cup apple cider vinegar
- ¹/₂ cup ketchup
- ¹/₃ cup tomato paste
- ¹/₄ cup yellow mustard
- ¹/₄ cup Worcestershire sauce
- 1 Tbsp. granulated onion
- 1 Tbsp. granulated garlic
- 1 Tbsp. kosher salt
- 1 Tbsp. hot sauce
- 1 tsp. ground Tellicherry black pepper
- 2 tsp. hickory liquid smoke
- 1 cup granulated sugar
- 1 cup honey

Stir together vinegar, ketchup, tomato paste, mustard, Worcestershire sauce, granulated onion, granulated garlic, salt, hot sauce, pepper, and liquid smoke in a saucepan over medium until well combined. Stir in sugar and honey, and bring to a boil over high. Reduce heat to medium-low; simmer, stirring occasionally, 30 minutes.

MAKES 3 cups **ACTIVE** 40 min.
TOTAL 40 min.

LEMONADE CHICKEN

Frozen lemonade concentrate was introduced in the late 1950s and soon became a favorite ingredient in both sweet and savory dishes. Here it teams up with soy sauce for a quick-fix basting sauce that amps up the smoky flavors of charcoal-grilled chicken. Feel free to substitute frozen limeade or orange juice concentrate.

- ¹/₂ (12-oz.) can frozen lemonade concentrate, thawed (about ³/₄ cup)
- ¹/₂ cup soy sauce
- 1 tsp. seasoned salt
- ¹/₂ tsp. celery salt
- ¹/₈ tsp. garlic powder
- 2 (2¹/₂- to 3-lb.) whole chickens, cut up
  Lemon slices

1. Preheat grill to medium (350°F to 400°F). Stir together concentrate, soy sauce, seasoned salt, celery salt, and garlic powder.
2. Grill chicken, covered, until skin begins to brown, 5 to 7 minutes. Brush with lemonade mixture, and grill, covered, turning and basting often, until a meat thermometer inserted in

thickest portion registers 165°F, 20 to 25 minutes. Serve with lemon.

SERVES 8 (serving size: ¼ chicken)
ACTIVE 15 min. **TOTAL** 40 min.

SWEET TEA-BRINED CHICKEN

It's a bold claim, but this just might be the finest chicken ever to come off our Test Kitchen grill. Embellished with fresh lemon, garlic, and rosemary, the tea creates a brine with remarkable flavor. Molasses-tinged brown sugar lends a subtle sweetness that caramelizes as the chicken slowly cooks over indirect heat.

- 4 cups water
- 2 family-size tea bags
- ½ cup packed light brown sugar
- ¼ cup kosher salt
- 1 Tbsp. black pepper
- 1 small sweet onion, thinly sliced
- 1 lemon, thinly sliced
- 3 garlic cloves, halved
- 2 rosemary sprigs
- 2 cups ice cubes
- 1 (3½- to 4-lb.) whole chicken, cut up

1. Bring water to a boil in a 3-quart heavy saucepan over medium-high; add tea bags. Remove from heat; cover and steep 10 minutes.
2. Discard tea bags. Add brown sugar, salt, pepper, onion, lemon, garlic, and rosemary sprigs; stir until sugar dissolves. Cool completely, about 45 minutes. Stir in ice.
3. Place chicken and tea mixture in a large zip-top plastic freezer bag; seal. Place bag in a shallow baking dish, and chill 24 hours, turning occasionally.
4. Preheat grill to low (300°F to 350°F) with an area cleared of coals or a burner turned off. Remove chicken from marinade; discard marinade. Pat chicken dry with paper towels. Grill chicken, covered, over indirect heat until done, 40 to 50 minutes. Transfer chicken, skin side down, to direct heat area, and grill until skin is crispy, 2 to 3 minutes. Let stand 5 minutes.

SERVES 6 to 8 (serving size: about ½ lb. chicken) **ACTIVE** 30 min. **TOTAL** 1 day, 2 hours, 35 min., including 1 day chilling

FRIED CATFISH WITH PICKLED PEPPERS

- 1½ cups (about 6 ³/₈ oz.) all-purpose flour
- 2¼ tsp. salt, divided
- 2 tsp. black pepper, divided
- 4 large eggs
- 2 Tbsp. water
- 1½ cups (about 6 ³/₈ oz.) plain yellow cornmeal
- 4 (6-oz.) catfish fillets
  Vegetable oil
  Pickled mild banana pepper rings
  Pickled jalapeño chile rings

1. Combine flour and 1 teaspoon each of the salt and pepper in a shallow dish. Whisk together eggs and water in a separate shallow dish. Combine cornmeal, 1 teaspoon of the salt, and remaining 1 teaspoon pepper in a third shallow dish. Sprinkle catfish with remaining ¼ teaspoon salt. Dredge fillets, 1 at a time, in the flour mixture, shaking off excess. Dip in the egg mixture, and dredge in the cornmeal mixture, shaking off excess. Place on a wire rack in a rimmed baking sheet.
2. Pour oil to a depth of 2 inches in a cast-iron Dutch oven. Heat over medium-high to 350°F. Fry fillets, 2 at a time, in the hot oil until golden, about 6 minutes. Drain on wire rack lined with paper towels. Serve with banana pepper and jalapeño rings.

SERVES 4 (serving size: 1 fillet)
ACTIVE 20 min. **TOTAL** 20 min.

BURK'S FARM-RAISED CATFISH FRY

- 6 (³/₄- to 1-lb.) farm-raised catfish fillets
- 1 cup buttermilk
- 1 Tbsp. black pepper
- 1½ tsp. salt
- 2 cups (about 8 ²/₃ oz.) self-rising cornmeal mix
- 1½ to 2 qt. peanut oil

1. Cut shallow diagonal slices 2 inches apart into thickest portion of both sides of fillets. Place fillets in a large shallow dish.
2. Stir together buttermilk, pepper, and salt; pour over fillets. Cover and chill 8 to 24 hours, turning fillets occasionally.
3. Remove fillets from marinade; discard marinade. Dredge fillets in cornmeal mix, pressing to adhere.
4. Pour peanut oil to a depth of 1½ inches in a large cast-iron Dutch oven or deep skillet; heat over medium-high to 370°F. Fry fish, 2 fillets at a time, until golden, about 6 minutes. Drain on wire rack lined with paper towels.

SERVES 6 (serving size: 1 fillet)
ACTIVE 25 min. **TOTAL** 8 hours, 25 min., including 8 hours chilling

What's Old Is New Again

Since our first issue, we've been the South's recipe box. And in our new cookbook, *Recipe Revival* (on sale October 18), we've given new delicious spins to the region's much-loved favorites.

You're Getting Warmer

NOTHING TAKES THE CHILL OFF A FALL EVENING LIKE A HEARTY BOWL OF CHILI, SOUP, OR STEW. DIG INTO THESE EIGHT SPECTACULAR CROWD-PLEASERS

Classic Beef Chili,
page 258

ONE-POT BEEF STEW

This dish gets zip from whole-grain mustard and richness from red wine. And leftover wine pairs beautifully with the stew.

---

1 ½ lb. beef chuck roast, trimmed and cut into ¾-inch cubes (about 1 lb. trimmed meat)
1 tsp. black pepper
1 ½ tsp. salt, divided
1 Tbsp. canola oil
3 medium carrots (about 7 oz.), cut diagonally into 1 ½-inch pieces
1 medium-size yellow onion (about 8 oz.), cut into 12 wedges
6 garlic cloves, chopped
1 cup dry red wine
2 Tbsp. all-purpose flour
4 cups beef broth
12 oz. baby new potatoes, cutting larger ones in half
2 Tbsp. whole-grain mustard
1 Tbsp. red wine vinegar
¼ cup loosely packed fresh flat-leaf parsley leaves

1. Sprinkle beef with pepper and 1 teaspoon salt. Heat oil in a Dutch oven over medium-high. Add beef to Dutch oven; cook, stirring occasionally, until brown on all sides, about 6 minutes. Transfer to a plate.
2. Add carrots and onions to Dutch oven; cook, stirring often, until carrots and onions start to soften, 4 to 6 minutes. Add garlic; cook, stirring occasionally, 1 minute. Add red wine; cook until liquid has almost evaporated, 10 to 12 minutes, stirring and scraping to loosen browned bits from bottom of Dutch oven.
3. Whisk together flour and ½ cup broth in a small bowl; add to Dutch oven. Stir in beef and remaining ½ teaspoon salt and 3 ½ cups broth; bring to a boil. Reduce heat to medium-low; cover and simmer 45 minutes. Add potatoes; cover and cook until potatoes are tender, about 20 minutes. Stir in mustard and vinegar. Sprinkle each serving with about 1 tablespoon parsley.

SERVES 4 (serving size: about 1 ½ cups)
ACTIVE 20 min. **TOTAL** 1 hour, 25 min.

WHITE BEAN-AND-PORK CHILI

Our white chili gets spice from green chiles, brightness from lime juice, and luscious texture from the last-minute addition of shredded cheese.

---

4 Tbsp. olive oil
2 lb. ground pork
1 medium-size white onion, chopped (about 2 cups)
1 poblano chile, seeded, chopped
3 garlic cloves, minced
2 (4.5-oz.) cans chopped green chiles, undrained
1 Tbsp. ground cumin
1 Tbsp. kosher salt
2 (15.5-oz.) cans white beans (such as cannellini or great Northern), drained and rinsed
3 ⅓ cups reduced-sodium chicken broth
6 oz. shredded Monterey Jack cheese (about 1 ½ cups)
2 Tbsp. fresh lime juice

1. Heat 2 tablespoons of the oil in a Dutch oven over medium-high. Add pork, and cook, stirring until crumbled and no longer pink, 6 to 8 minutes. Drain pork, and set aside. Wipe Dutch oven clean.
2. Heat remaining 2 tablespoons oil in Dutch oven over medium. Add onion, poblano, garlic, green chiles, cumin, and salt, and cook, stirring often, until vegetables are tender, 3 to 4 minutes.
3. Increase heat to high. Stir in beans, broth, and pork, and bring to a boil. Reduce heat to medium-low, and simmer, stirring occasionally, until heated through, about 40 minutes. Add cheese and lime juice, and stir until cheese is melted. Serve immediately.

SERVES 8 (serving size: about 1 cup)
ACTIVE 15 min. **TOTAL** 55 min.

CHICKEN CHILI

Packed with seasonal vegetables, spices, and shredded rotisserie chicken, this is a fresher alternative to a traditional beef chili.

---

1 (2-lb.) whole rotisserie chicken
2 (28-oz.) cans whole peeled plum tomatoes, undrained
2 Tbsp. olive oil
2 cups chopped yellow onions
4 garlic cloves, minced
2 green bell peppers, chopped
2 yellow bell peppers, chopped
2 ½ tsp. kosher salt
2 ½ tsp. chili powder
2 tsp. ground cumin
1 tsp. paprika
½ tsp. cayenne pepper
½ cup chopped fresh cilantro, plus more for topping
Sour cream, for topping

1. Remove skin from chicken, and discard; shred meat to about 4 cups, and set aside.
2. Pulse tomatoes in a food processor until slightly crushed.
3. Heat oil in a large Dutch oven over medium. Add onions and garlic, and cook, stirring occasionally, until tender, about 8 minutes. Add bell peppers, salt, chili powder, cumin, paprika, and cayenne pepper, and cook, stirring, 2 minutes.
4. Increase heat to high; stir in crushed tomatoes, and bring to a boil. Reduce heat to medium, and stir in chicken. Cover and simmer, stirring occasionally, until heated through, about 30 minutes. Stir in cilantro. Serve with additional cilantro and sour cream.

SERVES 8 (serving size: about 1 cup)
ACTIVE 15 min. **TOTAL** 50 min.

SPICY SAUSAGE-AND-CHICKPEA SOUP WITH GARLIC OIL

Spicy Italian pork sausage gives this soup a kick, but you can also substitute sweet Italian sausage.

- 1/4 **cup olive oil**
- 6 **garlic cloves, sliced**
- 1 **lb. spicy Italian pork sausage, casings removed**
- 1 **cup chopped yellow onion (about 1 onion)**
- 1/2 **cup chopped celery (about 2 stalks)**
- 1/2 **cup chopped carrots (about 2 large carrots)**
- 4 **cups chicken broth**
- 1 **(15-oz.) can crushed tomatoes**
- 1 **(15-oz.) can chickpeas (garbanzos), drained**
- 1/2 **tsp. black pepper**
- 4 **cups chopped Lacinato kale (about 3 1/2 oz.)**

1. Cook oil and garlic in a large saucepan over medium until garlic begins to brown, 4 to 5 minutes. Remove and discard garlic; reserve 3 tablespoons of the garlic oil.
2. Increase heat to medium-high. Add sausage to pan; cook, stirring often, until browned and crumbled, about 6 minutes. Remove sausage from pan; drain on paper towels. Add onion, celery, and carrots to pan; cook, stirring occasionally, until slightly tender, about 4 minutes. Stir in broth, tomatoes, chickpeas, and pepper; stir in sausage. Bring to a simmer; reduce heat to medium-low, and cook 20 minutes. Stir in kale; cook until wilted, about 5 minutes. Drizzle each serving with 1/2 tablespoon reserved garlic oil.

SERVES 6 (serving size: 1 1/2 cups)
ACTIVE 20 min. **TOTAL** 50 min.

CLASSIC BEEF CHILI

This is our latest take on traditional chili, and it comes together in just under an hour.

- 2 **Tbsp. olive oil**
- 2 **cups chopped yellow onion**
- 8 **garlic cloves, minced**
- 3 **lb. ground chuck**
- 1 **(6-oz.) can tomato paste**
- 1/3 **cup chili powder**
- 2 **Tbsp. ground cumin**
- 1 **Tbsp. kosher salt**
- 1 **tsp. black pepper**
- 1 **tsp. dried thyme**
- 1 **tsp. dried oregano**
- 2 **(15-oz.) cans pinto beans, drained and rinsed**
- 1 **(15-oz.) can dark red kidney beans, drained and rinsed**
- 1 **(28-oz.) can crushed tomatoes**
- 2 **cups reduced-sodium chicken broth**
- 1 **(12-oz.) bottle beer**

1. Heat oil in a large Dutch oven over medium-high. Add onions and garlic, and cook, stirring often, until tender, about 5 minutes. Add ground chuck, and cook, stirring until beef crumbles and is no longer pink, 8 to 10 minutes. Drain beef mixture well, and return to Dutch oven.
2. Add tomato paste, chili powder, cumin, salt, pepper, thyme, and oregano, and cook, stirring often, 2 minutes.
3. Increase heat to high. Stir in beans, tomatoes, chicken broth, and beer, and bring to a boil. Reduce heat to medium-low, and simmer, stirring occasionally, about 30 minutes.

SERVES 8 (serving size: about 1 1/4 cups)
ACTIVE 25 min. **TOTAL** 55 min.

ROASTED PUMPKIN SOUP

Pumpkins, carrots, onions—this is as close as you'll get to serving fall in a bowl.

- 1 **(3-lb.) sugar pumpkin, butternut squash, or kabocha squash**
- 4 **Tbsp. olive oil, divided**
- 1 1/2 **cups chopped yellow onion (about 1 large onion)**
- 1 1/2 **cups chopped celery (about 3 stalks)**
- 1/2 **cup chopped carrots (about 2 medium carrots)**
- 6 **garlic cloves, crushed**
- 4 **thyme sprigs, plus more for topping**
- 1 **sage sprig**
- 1 **oregano sprig**
- 3/4 **tsp. salt**
- 1/2 **tsp. ground turmeric**
- 6 **cups chicken broth**
- 2 **Tbsp. apple cider vinegar**
- 4 **Tbsp. sour cream**
- 3 **Tbsp. whole milk**
  Pomegranate seeds for topping (optional)
  Pumpkin seeds for topping (optional)

Roasted Pumpkin Soup

1. Preheat oven to 425°F. Cut pumpkin into quarters; discard seeds. Place on a baking sheet, and drizzle with 2 tablespoons of the olive oil. Bake in preheated oven until tender, 45 minutes to 1 hour. Cool until easy to handle. Remove skin, and discard. Set aside 1 1/2 cups (about 15 ounces) cooked pumpkin; reserve remaining pumpkin for another use.

2. Heat remaining 2 tablespoons olive oil in a large saucepan over medium. Add onion, celery, carrots, garlic, thyme, sage, and oregano; cook, stirring occasionally, until vegetables are very tender, 8 to 10 minutes. (Do not brown.) Add salt and turmeric; cook, stirring often, 1 minute. Stir in chicken broth and 1 1/2 cups cooked pumpkin; bring to a simmer. Cover and simmer 15 minutes. Remove and discard herb sprigs.

3. Place half of pumpkin mixture in a blender. Remove center piece of blender lid (to allow steam to escape); secure lid on blender, and place a clean towel over opening in lid. Process until mixture is very smooth, 1 to 2 minutes. Transfer to a large bowl. Repeat procedure with remaining pumpkin mixture. Stir in the apple cider vinegar.

4. Whisk together sour cream and milk in a small bowl. Divide soup evenly among 6 shallow bowls; drizzle with sour cream mixture, and sprinkle with pomegranate seeds and pumpkin seeds, if desired.

SERVES 6 (serving size: about 1 1/3 cups soup, about 1 Tbsp. sour cream mixture)
ACTIVE 25 min. **TOTAL** 1 hour, 40 min.

THREE SISTERS CHILI

This colorful chili is named for the three companion plants of American Indian agriculture: corn, beans, and squash.

- 2 (15-oz.) cans red kidney beans, drained and rinsed
- 2 Tbsp. olive oil
- 1 medium-size yellow onion, chopped
- 1 red bell pepper, chopped
- 2 jalapeño chiles, seeds removed, chopped

One-Pot Beef Stew, page 257

- 3 garlic cloves, minced
- 1 Tbsp. chili powder
- 1 Tbsp. kosher salt
- 1/2 tsp. ground cumin
- 1/2 tsp. smoked paprika
- 2 lb. butternut squash, peeled, seeds removed, chopped into 1/2-inch pieces
- 2 cups fresh corn kernels (about 3 ears)
- 1 (15-oz.) can diced tomatoes
- 4 cups vegetable broth

1. Mash 1/2 cup of the red kidney beans, and set aside with the remaining whole kidney beans.
2. Heat oil in a large Dutch oven over medium. Add onion, bell pepper, jalapeños, and garlic, and cook, stirring often, 5 minutes. Stir in chili powder, salt, cumin, and paprika, and cook, stirring constantly, 1 minute.
3. Increase heat to high; stir in butternut squash, corn, tomatoes, broth, whole beans, and reserved 1/2 cup mashed beans, and bring to a boil. Reduce heat to medium-low, and simmer, stirring occasionally, until squash is tender, 30 to 45 minutes.

SERVES 8 (serving size: about 1 1/4 cups)
ACTIVE 20 min. **TOTAL** 55 min.

SLOW-COOKER BRISKET CHILI

- 3 Tbsp. all-purpose flour
- 2 Tbsp. ancho chile powder
- 1 Tbsp. ground cumin
- 1 Tbsp. kosher salt
- 1 tsp. dried oregano
- 2 lb. beef brisket, trimmed and cut into 1-inch cubes

- 2 (15-oz.) cans black beans
- 1 (15-oz.) can fire-roasted diced tomatoes, drained
- 1 red bell pepper, chopped
- 1 medium-size red onion, chopped
- 3 garlic cloves, minced
- 3/4 cup beef broth
- 4 Tbsp. olive oil

1. Stir together flour, ancho chile powder, cumin, salt, and oregano in a small bowl. Sprinkle spice mixture evenly on each side of beef brisket cubes, and set aside.
2. Combine black beans, tomatoes, bell pepper, onion, garlic, and beef broth in a 6- to 7-quart slow cooker.
3. Heat 2 tablespoons of the oil in a large skillet over medium-high. Add half of brisket cubes; cook, stirring often, until browned on all sides, 5 to 7 minutes. Transfer beef to slow cooker. Repeat procedure with remaining oil and brisket.
4. Cover and cook on LOW 8 hours. Uncover and cook until slightly thickened, about 1 hour.

SERVES 10 (serving size: about 3/4 cup)
ACTIVE 20 min. **TOTAL** 9 hours, 20 min.

COOK WITH COZI

Get these spectacular fall recipes with Cozi, a free meal-planning app from Time Inc.

The Last Word on Cornbread

OUR CRUNCHY, BUTTERY CRUST COMES FROM BAKING IT IN A SCREAMING-HOT CAST-IRON SKILLET

SOUTHERNERS HAVE STRONG OPINIONS about their cornbread. It should be savory. It should be sweet. Make it in Grandma's skillet with bacon fat. Use only yellow stone-ground cornmeal. Or white. And while the debates go on, one thing everyone agrees with is the best cornbread is made at home. And you'll be hard-pressed to find another dish that's as universally beloved throughout the entire South in so many different ways. We have plenty of opinions about cornbread, too, but ours are based on exhaustive trials and tastings in our test kitchen. We've made countless batches of cornbread over the last 50 years, so we set out to devise the ultimate classic recipe. We tinkered with cornmeal, fats, buttermilk ratios, and baking times until we cracked the cornbread code: a moist and tender crumb, deep corn flavor, and beautifully golden brown crust. While we think this recipe truly lives up to the title "best ever," we realize it will inspire even more debate—ideally over a slab of cornbread with lots of butter. Or buttermilk, which is another discussion entirely.

GO FOR THE GOLD
Fine yellow cornmeal is best for its big corn flavor and golden color when baked.

BUTTER IS BEST
We tested bacon fat, butter, and short-ening. Butter adds the most flavor without overpowering the other ingredients.

A TOUCH OF SUGAR
Our recipe is decidedly savory, but a little sugar is needed to balance the other ingredients and help the bread caramelize in the pan.

CLASSIC SKILLET CORNBREAD

1 1/2 **cups (about 8 5/8 oz.) fine stone-ground yellow cornmeal**
1/4 **cup all-purpose flour**
2 **tsp. granulated sugar**
1 **tsp. baking powder**
1 **tsp. baking soda**
1 **tsp. kosher salt**
1 3/4 **cups buttermilk**
2 **large eggs**
3 **Tbsp. salted butter**

1. Place a 10-inch cast-iron skillet in the oven, and preheat oven to 450°F. Heat skillet 7 minutes.
2. Meanwhile, stir together the cornmeal, flour, sugar, baking powder, baking soda, and salt in a large bowl. Stir together the buttermilk and eggs in a medium bowl.
3. Add butter to hot skillet, and return to oven until butter is melted, about 1 minute. Stir buttermilk mixture into cornmeal mixture until just combined. Pour melted butter from skillet into cornmeal mixture, and quickly stir to incorporate. Pour mixture into hot skillet, and immediately place in oven.
4. Bake in preheated oven until golden brown and cornbread pulls away from sides of skillet, 18 to 20 minutes. Remove from skillet; cool slightly before serving.

SERVES 8 (serving size: 1 piece)
ACTIVE 10 min. **TOTAL** 30 min.

SKILLET SMARTS

We can't *really* stop you from adding more sugar or choosing white over yellow cornmeal, but one rule is firm: Use a cast-iron pan, and it must be super hot when you add the batter. That's our secret to cornbread with a crunchy crust.

ONLY
442 CAL
SL

Simple, Sizzling Hash

YOU CAN SUBSTITUTE LEFTOVER CHICKEN OR PORK FOR
STEAK IN THIS HEARTY DISH

MASTER HASH

- 2 whole garlic heads
- 6 Tbsp. canola oil, divided
- ¾ cup plus 2 Tbsp. half-and-half, divided
- 3 Tbsp. instant potato flakes (such as Hungry Jack)
- 1½ pounds Yukon Gold potatoes, cut into ½-inch cubes
   Cooking spray
- 1 cup chopped red bell pepper
- ½ cup finely diced carrot
- 1½ Tbsp. chopped fresh thyme
- 1½ tsp. kosher salt, divided
- 2 cups vertically sliced onion
- 6 ounces cooked steak (such as New York strip or flank steak), cubed
- ¼ cup chopped fresh flat-leaf parsley, divided
- ½ tsp. freshly ground black pepper, divided
- ¼ cup white vinegar (optional)
- 6 large eggs (optional)

1. Preheat oven to 325°F. Cut off top ¼ inch of garlic heads to expose cloves. Place garlic, cut side up, on a piece of foil. Drizzle with 1 tablespoon oil. Wrap garlic heads tightly in foil. Roast in preheated oven until very soft, about 1 hour and 15 minutes; cool slightly. Squeeze pulp from roasted garlic into a small saucepan; discard papery skins. Add ¾ cup half-and-half to pan. Bring just to a boil, stirring to mash garlic; remove from heat. Add potato flakes, stirring with a whisk.

2. Arrange potatoes on a foil-lined rimmed baking sheet coated with cooking spray; also coat potatoes with cooking spray. Roast at 325°F until thoroughly cooked, about 45 minutes, stirring every 15 minutes; set aside.
3. Heat a large skillet over medium-high. Add 1 tablespoon oil to pan; swirl to coat. Add bell pepper, carrot, thyme, and ¼ teaspoon salt to pan; cook 2 minutes, stirring frequently. Reduce heat to medium-low; cook until soft, about 12 minutes. Remove mixture from pan; set aside.
4. Wipe pan with paper towels; return heat to medium-high. Add 1 tablespoon oil to pan; swirl to coat. Add onion and ¼ teaspoon salt. Cook 3 minutes, stirring frequently. Reduce heat to medium-low. Cook until caramelized and soft, about 15 minutes, stirring occasionally. Set aside.
5. Heat a large cast-iron skillet over medium-high. Add remaining 3 tablespoons oil to pan. Add potatoes; cook until golden brown, about 4 minutes. Stir in bell pepper mixture, onion, steak, and ¾ teaspoon salt. Cook until thoroughly heated, about 1 minute. Stir in garlic cream mixture, 2 tablespoons parsley, and ¼ teaspoon pepper; remove pan from heat.
6. (Optional) Add water to a saucepan, filling two-thirds full; bring to a boil. Reduce heat; stir in vinegar. Break each egg into a custard cup. Gently pour eggs into pan; cook 3 minutes. Remove with a slotted spoon; place on a paper towel-lined plate.
7. Stir remaining 2 tablespoons half-and-half into hash to loosen. Divide hash among 6 plates. Top each serving with 1 egg, if desired; sprinkle evenly with remaining ¼ teaspoon salt and ¼ teaspoon pepper. Garnish with remaining 2 tablespoons parsley.

SERVES 6 (serving size: about ¾ cup hash and 1 poached egg)
ACTIVE 1 hour, 30 min. **TOTAL** 1 hour, 45 min.

NUTRITIONAL INFORMATION *(per serving)*
CALORIES: 442; FAT 25.4g (SATURATED FAT: 6.1g); PROTEIN: 20g; FIBER 4g; CARBOHYDRATES: 35g; SODIUM: 603mg

DIY Doughnuts

THREE DELICIOUS TWISTS ON A HOMEMADE SEASONAL TREAT

APPLE CIDER DOUGHNUTS

For the most robust apple flavor, use cider, not juice, and shake the jug before measuring.

- 2 cups apple cider
- 1/2 cup peeled grated apple (1 large apple)
- 1/2 cup apple butter
- 1 1/2 Tbsp. apple cider vinegar
- 1/2 tsp. vanilla extract
- 4 oz. (1/2 cup) unsalted butter, softened
- 1/2 cup granulated sugar
- 1 large egg
- 3 1/4 cups (about 13 7/8 oz.) all-purpose flour
- 1 Tbsp. baking powder
- 1/4 tsp. ground cinnamon
- 1/4 tsp. kosher salt
  Peanut oil
  Pumpkin-Cinnamon Spice, Buttermilk Glaze, or Maple-Vanilla Icing

1. Combine apple cider and grated apple in a small saucepan over medium-high, and cook, stirring occasionally, until reduced to about 1/2 cup, about 25 minutes. Transfer to a bowl, and cool to room temperature. Stir in apple butter, vinegar, and vanilla.
2. Beat butter and sugar with an electric stand mixer on medium until light and fluffy, about 1 minute. Add egg, and beat until combined. Whisk together flour, baking powder, cinnamon, and salt; add to butter mixture alternately with apple cider mixture, beginning and ending with flour mixture. Beat on low just until blended after each addition. Turn dough out onto a floured surface, and roll into a 12- x 9-inch rectangle, about 1/2 inch thick.
3. Pour 2 inches of oil into a large Dutch oven, and heat over medium-high to 350°F.
4. Cut dough using a 2 1/2-inch round

Pumpkin-Cinnamon Spice

Whisk together 1 cup granulated **sugar,** 1/2 tsp. ground **cinnamon,** and 1/2 tsp. **pumpkin pie spice** in a medium bowl.

MAKES 1 cup

Buttermilk Glaze

Whisk together 1 1/2 cups (about 6 oz.) **powdered sugar,** 3 Tbsp. **buttermilk,** and 1/8 tsp. **kosher salt** in a large bowl.

MAKES about 1 cup

Maple-Vanilla Icing

Whisk together 2 cups **powdered sugar,** 3 Tbsp. pure **maple syrup,** 1 Tbsp. whole **milk,** 1 tsp. **vanilla** extract, and 1/8 tsp. **kosher salt** in a large bowl.

MAKES about 1 1/2 cups

cutter. Use a 1-inch round cutter to cut out the middle of dough rounds, reserving the cutouts as doughnut holes. Reroll scraps once. Fry in batches until golden brown, about 1 minute per side for doughnuts and 45 seconds per side for holes. Transfer with a slotted spoon to a paper towel-lined baking sheet. Toss warm doughnuts in Pumpkin-Cinnamon Spice. Or cool to room temperature and dip in Buttermilk Glaze or Maple-Vanilla Icing.

SERVES 18 (serving size: 1 doughnut, 1 doughnut hole) **ACTIVE** 30 min. **TOTAL** 2 hours

cooking SL school

HOW TO CUT WINTER SQUASH

CURVY PRODUCE CAN BE TRICKY. FOLLOW OUR EASY SLICING STEPS

BUTTERNUT SQUASH

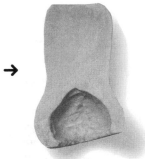

A
Place squash on its side, and, using a large knife, slice off the top and bottom ends.

B
Remove the thick outer skin with a peeler.

C
Cut the squash in half lengthwise, then spoon out and discard the seeds.

"**I always use a sharp Y-peeler to remove the squash skin.**"

PAM LOLLEY
SL *Test Kitchen Professional*

ACORN SQUASH

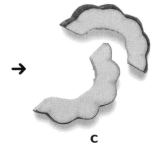

A
Position a knife blade between two middle grooves. Cut through the flesh to the center.

B
Continue slicing through the other half of the squash. Remove the seeds.

C
Slice the squash halves into half moons, if desired.

PANTRY PRIMER
5 FRESH IDEAS FOR CANNED PUMPKIN

1 Add to hot rice, mashed potatoes, or risotto for some extra nutrients.

2 Stir some pumpkin into waffle or pancake batter for a better fall breakfast.

3 Mix pumpkin, brown sugar, and cinnamon, and then top it with sweetened whipped cream and crushed gingersnaps.

4 Swirl pumpkin into your next batch of hummus. Top with roasted pumpkin seeds.

5 Spoon pumpkin into your favorite macaroni and cheese recipe for rich color and seasonal flavor.

Shrimp and Grits for the Win

THIS MEMPHIS TEEN BEAT THE COMPETITION WITH A TWIST ON A SOUTHERN CLASSIC

Watch the 13-year-old chef make his winning recipe at *southernliving.com/logan*.

WHEN WE SET OUT TO FIND ONE OF THE SOUTH'S greatest home cooks, we didn't know who or what to expect. And while we enjoyed diving into all of the entries, from the time-crunched mom with a quick and healthy make-ahead meal to the college kid with a mouthwatering barbecue sauce, it was Logan Guleff who captured our hearts and stomachs. Just 13 years old, he has been cooking since he was 2. "The first thing I ever made was Mom's coffee," the teenager admits. "Then we moved onto deviled eggs and pigs in a blanket, and it just went on from there." These days, Guleff is whipping up creative and delicious dishes like lobster cannoli and marinated flatiron steak. In addition to winning *MasterChef Junior* in 2014, he has been busy working on his own line of spice rubs, seasoning blends, and even a cookbook. The Memphis native is also a certified barbecue judge and calls Central BBQ one of his favorite spots. When we asked him if there's any food he doesn't

like, Guleff replied, "Onions, which is hard because they're a staple. But I still cook with them, because they go in everything." Spoken like a true Southern chef.

GULEFF'S SHRIMP AND GRITS

- 1/2 cup diced celery root (from 1 celery root)
- 1 tsp. olive oil
- 2 cups water
- 1 3/4 tsp. kosher salt, divided
- 1/2 cup uncooked stone-ground grits
- 2 oz. sharp Cheddar cheese, grated (about 1/2 cup)
- 3 Tbsp. salted butter, divided
- 3/4 cup diced yellow onion (from 1 onion)
- 1 cup frozen black-eyed peas
- 3 multicolored baby bell peppers, diced
- 1 large heirloom tomato, diced
- 1 garlic clove, minced
- 1 1/2 cups seafood stock, divided
- 12 large raw shrimp, peeled (about 3/4 lb.)
- 12 bay scallops, drained (about 1/2 lb.)
- 1/4 tsp. smoked paprika
- 1/8 tsp. black pepper
- 1 1/2 tsp. hot sauce, divided

1. Preheat oven to 450°F. Toss together diced celery root and oil on a rimmed baking sheet. Bake until tender, 10 to 15 minutes.

2. Bring water and 1/2 teaspoon of the salt to a boil in a saucepan over medium-high. Stir in grits, and simmer, stirring, until done, 20 to 25 minutes. Remove from heat; stir in cheese.

3. Melt 1 tablespoon of the butter in a large skillet over medium-high. Add onion; cook, stirring occasionally, until

caramelized, about 10 minutes. Add celery root, black-eyed peas, bell peppers, tomato, garlic, and 1 teaspoon of the salt; cook, stirring, until tender, 6 to 8 minutes. Add 1 cup of the stock, and cook, stirring occasionally, until liquid thickens, 20 to 25 minutes.

4. Melt remaining 2 tablespoons butter in a medium skillet over medium-high. Add shrimp and scallops; cook until shrimp turn pink and are almost done, 2 to 3 minutes. Add paprika, black pepper, 1 teaspoon of the hot sauce, and remaining 1/2 cup stock and 1/4 teaspoon salt; bring to a boil. Cook until shrimp and scallops are done, about 2 minutes. Transfer shrimp and scallops to a plate, and cover to keep warm. Increase heat to high, and cook stock mixture until thickened slightly, 5 to 6 minutes.

5. Divide cheese grits among 4 bowls. Top each with about 3/4 cup celery root mixture, 3 shrimp, 3 scallops, and a spoonful of sauce from each skillet. Sprinkle with remaining 1/2 teaspoon hot sauce.

SERVES 4 (serving size: 3/4 cup black-eyed pea mixture, 1/2 cup grits, 3 shrimp, 3 scallops) **ACTIVE** 30 min. **TOTAL** 50 min.

November

A Tale of
Two Turkeys

WHETHER YOU CHOOSE TO FLAVOR YOUR BIRD WITH OUR SWEET-AND-SPICY DRY RUB OR
AROMATIC HERB BUTTER, THIS WILL BE THE CENTERPIECE OF YOUR THANKSGIVING FEAST

ROASTED HERB TURKEY AND GRAVY

 3 Tbsp. salted butter
2 ½ Tbsp. kosher salt
 1 Tbsp. dried thyme
 2 tsp. dried sage
 2 tsp. black pepper
 1 tsp. dried fennel seeds, lightly crushed
 1 (12-lb.) fresh whole turkey
 2 Tbsp. canola oil
 4 cups coarsely chopped yellow onions (about 3 onions)
 3 cups coarsely chopped carrots (about 7 carrots)
 2 cups coarsely chopped celery (about 5 stalks)
 2 bay leaves
 3 cups water
 Turkey Gravy (recipe at right)

Roasted Herb Turkey and Gravy

THANKSGIVING TRADITIONALISTS, this turkey is for you. For crisp, golden skin and juicy meat, we coated this beautiful bird with an aromatic infused butter made with sage, thyme, and fennel seeds. And for the best gravy, we added onions, carrots, and celery to the roasting pan.

1. Melt butter in a small skillet over medium. Add salt, thyme, sage, pepper, and fennel seeds; cook, stirring often, until fragrant, about 1 minute. Remove from pan, and cool completely, about 10 minutes. Reserve 1 tablespoon of butter mixture.

2. Remove giblets and neck from turkey; reserve for another use. Pat turkey dry, and remove excess skin. Starting from neck, loosen and lift skin from turkey without completely detaching it. Spread butter mixture remaining in bowl evenly under skin. Carefully replace skin. Drizzle skin with oil, and rub with reserved 1 tablespoon butter mixture. Tie ends of legs together with kitchen twine; tuck wing tips under. Let stand at room temperature for 1 hour, or refrigerate 12 to 24 hours. (If refrigerated, let turkey stand at room temperature 1 hour before cooking.)

3. Preheat oven to 375°F. Place onions, carrots, celery, and bay leaves in bottom of a roasting pan; add a roasting rack. Coat rack with cooking spray. Place turkey on rack, and transfer to oven. Add water to pan. Bake in preheated oven until a meat thermometer inserted in thickest portion of thigh registers 165°F, about 1 hour and 45 minutes, rotating pan halfway (on same rack) after 55 minutes. Remove turkey from oven, and let stand at least 30 minutes.

Turkey Gravy

Transfer **drippings** and **vegetables** from roasting pan to a medium saucepan; add 3 ½ cups **chicken broth.** Bring to a boil over high. Reduce heat to medium, and simmer 20 minutes. Pour mixture through a wire-mesh strainer into a bowl, pressing on vegetables to extract juices. Discard vegetables. Return broth mixture to saucepan. Whisk together ¼ cup **all-purpose flour** and an additional ½ cup **chicken broth** in a small bowl; whisk into broth mixture. Bring to a boil over high; boil until reduced to about 4 cups, about 20 minutes. Serve turkey with 2 cups gravy, and reserve remaining 2 cups gravy for another use.

SERVES 8 (serving size: 10 oz. meat, about ¼ cup gravy) **ACTIVE** 45 min. **TOTAL** 4 hours

SWEET-AND-SPICY ROAST TURKEY

- 3 Tbsp. kosher salt
- 2 Tbsp. light brown sugar
- 1 Tbsp. onion powder
- 1 Tbsp. paprika
- 2 tsp. ground ginger
- 2 tsp. dry mustard
- 3/4 tsp. cayenne pepper
- 1 (12-lb.) fresh whole turkey
- 3 Tbsp. canola oil, divided
- 2 Tbsp. honey
- 1 Tbsp. hot sauce
- 3 cups water

1. Stir together salt, brown sugar, onion powder, paprika, ginger, dry mustard, and cayenne pepper in a small bowl. Reserve 2 tablespoons of salt mixture.

2. Remove giblets and neck from turkey; reserve for another use. Pat turkey dry, and remove excess skin. Starting from neck, loosen and lift skin from turkey without completely detaching it. Spread remaining salt mixture evenly under skin. Carefully replace skin. Drizzle skin with 2 tablespoons of the oil, and rub with reserved 2 tablespoons salt mixture. Tie ends of legs together with kitchen twine; tuck wing tips under. Let stand at room temperature 1 hour, or refrigerate 12 to 24 hours. (If refrigerated, let turkey stand at room temperature for 1 hour before cooking.)

3. Stir together honey, hot sauce, and remaining 1 tablespoon oil in a small bowl until well blended.

4. Preheat oven to 375°F. Place rack in a roasting pan; coat rack with cooking spray. Place turkey on rack, and transfer to oven. Add 3 cups water to pan. Bake in preheated oven 1 hour and 10 minutes. Rotate pan halfway (on same rack), brush with half of honey mixture, and continue baking until a meat thermometer inserted in thickest portion of thigh registers 165°F, about 25 more minutes. Remove turkey from oven, and brush with remaining honey mixture. Let stand at least 30 minutes.

Note: You may skip brushing the turkey with honey mixture when you rotate it if the turkey is already dark. Just brush the mixture on at the end.

SERVES 8 (serving size: 10 oz. turkey)
ACTIVE 20 min. **TOTAL** 3 hours, 25 min.

Sweet-and-Spicy Roast Turkey

GO BOLD with a turkey that's packed with heat—and a touch of sweetness. We dry-brined this bird with a fragrant spice rub and then roasted it with a honey-hot sauce glaze. This recipe might be a surprising new addition to your holiday table, but we think it will earn a repeat invitation.

Spectacular Sides

OF COURSE THE TURKEY IS THE MAIN EVENT, BUT EVERYONE KNOWS THE SIDES MAKE IT
A MEMORABLE FEAST. COUNT ON THESE 12 DISHES TO STEAL THIS YEAR'S SHOW

BRUSSELS SPROUTS WITH CORNBREAD CROUTONS

Toasty brown-butter croutons make simple roasted Brussels sprouts holiday-worthy fare.

- 2 lb. Brussels sprouts, trimmed and halved
- 1 1/2 Tbsp. olive oil
- 1 tsp. kosher salt
- 1/4 tsp. black pepper
- 2 cups cubed day-old cornbread (1/2-inch cubes)
- 1/4 cup salted butter
- 1 shallot, minced
- 1 Tbsp. fresh thyme leaves

1. Preheat oven to 425°F. Toss together first 4 ingredients in a large bowl; divide evenly between 2 rimmed baking sheets. Bake in preheated oven until golden brown, about 20 minutes. Reduce oven temperature to 350°F.
2. Spread cornbread cubes evenly on a baking sheet; bake at 350°F until browned and crispy, about 15 minutes.
3. Cook butter, stirring constantly, in a medium skillet over medium until foaming. Add shallot and thyme; cook, stirring often, 1 minute. Drizzle butter mixture over toasted cornbread. Arrange Brussels sprouts in a serving dish; top with cornbread mixture.

SERVES 8 to 10 (serving size: 3/4 cup)
ACTIVE 5 min. **TOTAL** 40 min.

Brussels Sprouts with Cornbread Croutons

SKILLET SQUASH BLOSSOM

The best part of this showstopping dish is the caramelized edges.

- 1 (1 1/2-lb.) butternut squash, peeled, halved lengthwise, seeds removed
- 3 center-cut bacon slices
- 1/2 cup diced yellow onion
- 2 Tbsp. olive oil
- 1 Tbsp. chopped fresh thyme
- 2 tsp. kosher salt
- 1/2 tsp. black pepper
- 4 tsp. pure maple syrup, divided

1. Preheat oven to 400°F. Place squash, cut side down, in an 8-inch square

to a serving platter. Sprinkle with chives.

SERVES 8 (serving size: about ³/₄ cup)
ACTIVE 5 min. **TOTAL** 35 min.

SLOW-COOKER GREEN BEANS

This recipe frees up precious stove-top space and reminds us of the traditional green beans our grandmothers used to make.

- 8 thick-cut bacon slices, divided
- 1 large yellow onion, sliced
- 2 lb. fresh green beans, trimmed
- ¼ cup reduced-sodium chicken broth
- 2 ½ tsp. kosher salt
- 1 tsp. black pepper
- 4 thyme sprigs

1. Cut 6 of the bacon slices into ¹/₂-inch pieces. Cook, stirring often, in a large skillet over medium-high until crispy, about 8 minutes. Transfer to a plate lined with paper towels to drain; reserve drippings in skillet. Crumble cooked bacon, and set aside. Add onion to skillet; cook, stirring occasionally, until just tender, about 3 minutes. Stir in green beans; cook, stirring often, 2 minutes.
2. Transfer green bean mixture to a 5-quart slow cooker. Stir in broth, salt, pepper, thyme sprigs, and 2 uncooked bacon slices. Cover and cook on HIGH until beans are tender, about 3 hours. Discard bacon and thyme; top with crumbled cooked bacon.

SERVES 8 (serving size: 1 cup)
ACTIVE 20 min. **TOTAL** 3 hours, 20 min.

ROOT VEGETABLE GRATIN

Assemble layers of veggies and cheese a day ahead to save on Turkey Day prep.

- 1 large rutabaga, peeled and cut into ¹/₈-inch-thick slices
- 2 large russet potatoes, peeled and cut into ¹/₈-inch-thick slices
- 3 large parsnips, peeled and cut into ¹/₈-inch-thick slices

Skillet Squash Blossom

baking dish; fill with 1 inch of water. Cover with plastic wrap, and microwave on HIGH 5 minutes. Thinly slice squash, and place in a large bowl.
2. Heat a 10-inch cast-iron skillet over medium. Cook bacon 5 minutes. Increase heat to medium-high, and cook until golden brown. Remove bacon, reserving drippings in skillet. Crumble bacon, and set aside. Reduce heat to medium; add onion to skillet, and cook until translucent, about 2 minutes. Stir in oil, thyme, salt, pepper, and 2 teaspoons of the maple syrup. Add mixture to squash slices; toss to combine.
3. Starting at the outer edge of the same skillet, arrange squash slices in slightly overlapping concentric circles to form a flower shape. Bake in preheated oven until squash is tender and edges begin to crisp, about 40 minutes. Drizzle with remaining 2 teaspoons maple syrup. Top with bacon.

SERVES 8 (serving size: ¹/₂ cup)
ACTIVE 10 min. **TOTAL** 50 min.

HONEY-GLAZED SPICED CARROTS

Spiced carrots will soon be your family's most requested Thanksgiving side.

- 4 Tbsp. unsalted butter, melted
- 3 Tbsp. honey
- 1 Tbsp. light brown sugar
- 1 ½ tsp. kosher salt
- ¹/₂ tsp. ground cinnamon
- ¹/₄ tsp. ground nutmeg
- ¹/₄ tsp. black pepper
- 2 lb. small carrots, peeled and trimmed
- 1 Tbsp. thinly sliced fresh chives

1. Preheat oven to 400°F. Stir together first 7 ingredients in a small bowl; reserve 2 tablespoons of mixture. Pour remaining butter mixture over carrots; toss to combine. Spread in a single layer on 2 baking sheets; bake in preheated oven 30 minutes.
2. Toss roasted carrots with reserved 2 tablespoons butter mixture; transfer

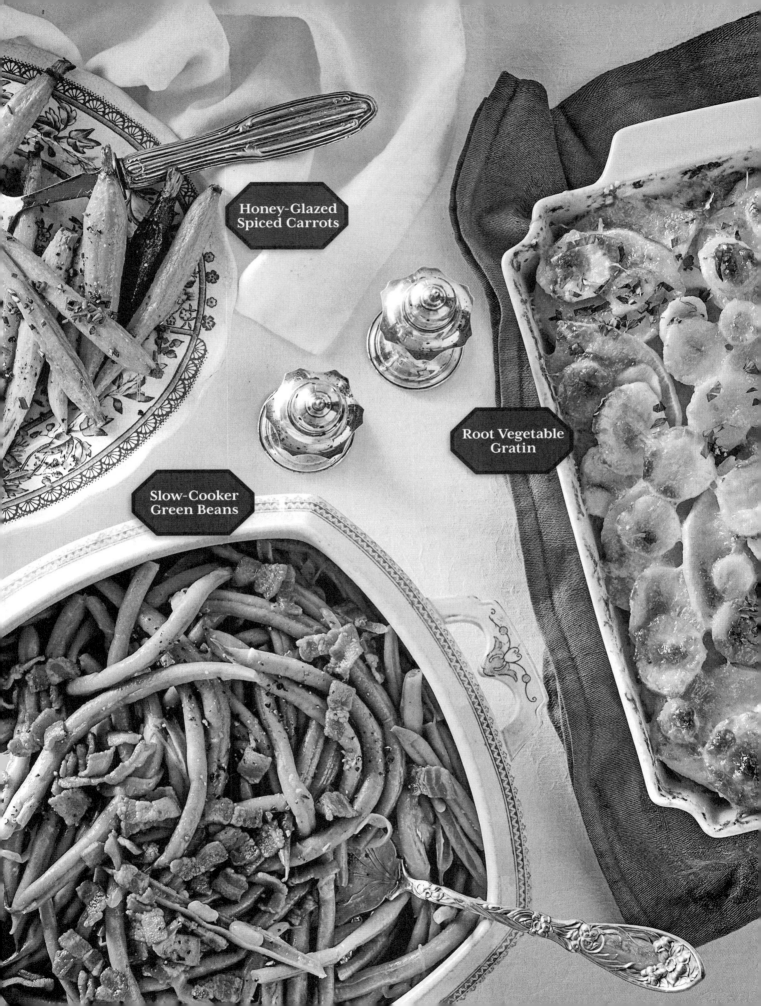

Honey-Glazed
Spiced Carrots

Root Vegetable
Gratin

Slow-Cooker
Green Beans

1 1/2 tsp. kosher salt
1 1/2 cups heavy cream, divided
   8 oz. Gruyère cheese, shredded
     (about 2 cups), divided

1. Preheat oven to 400°F. Toss together rutabaga, potatoes, parsnips, salt, and 3/4 cup of the cream in a large bowl. Spread one-third of the mixture evenly in a lightly greased 11- x 7-inch baking dish; top with 3/4 cup of the Gruyère. Layer one-third of the rutabaga mixture, 3/4 cup of the Gruyère, and remaining rutabaga mixture and 3/4 cup cream. Top with remaining 1/2 cup Gruyère.
2. Cover loosely with aluminum foil. Bake in preheated oven 45 minutes. Uncover and bake until vegetables are tender and cheese is golden brown, 20 to 25 minutes. Transfer to a wire rack; cool 5 minutes.

SERVES 8 (serving size: 1 cup)
ACTIVE 30 min. **TOTAL** 1 hour, 40 min.

CORNBREAD DRESSING WITH KALE AND BACON

Bacon adds smoky richness, and oven-baked kale makes a crispy topping.

1 1/2 cups (about 6 3/8 oz.) stone-ground yellow cornmeal
  1/4 cup all-purpose flour
    2 tsp. granulated sugar
    1 tsp. baking powder
    1 tsp. baking soda
    3 tsp. kosher salt, divided
1 3/4 cups buttermilk
    5 large eggs
    2 Tbsp. unsalted butter
    1 cup (8 oz.) melted unsalted butter, divided
    8 thick-cut bacon slices, cut into 1-inch pieces
  1/2 cup chopped celery (about 2 stalks)
    1 medium-size yellow onion, chopped
    2 garlic cloves, chopped
    2 bunches Lacinato kale, stems removed, chopped
    1 Tbsp. chopped fresh thyme
    1 tsp. black pepper
3 1/2 cups reduced-sodium chicken broth, divided

1. Place a 10-inch cast-iron skillet in oven; preheat oven to 450°F. (Do not remove skillet.) Heat skillet 7 minutes.
2. Meanwhile, stir together the first 5 ingredients and 1 teaspoon of the salt in a large bowl. Whisk together buttermilk and 2 eggs in a medium bowl.
3. Remove skillet from oven, and add 2 tablespoons butter to skillet. Return to oven. Stir buttermilk mixture into cornmeal mixture until just combined. Stir in 1/2 cup of the melted butter. Pour mixture into hot buttered skillet; return to oven. Bake until golden brown and cornbread pulls away from sides of skillet, 18 to 20 minutes. Transfer skillet to wire rack; cool 15 minutes. Crumble cornbread into a large bowl. Set aside. Reduce oven temperature to 400°F.
4. Cook bacon in a large skillet over medium-high until crispy, 8 to 10 minutes. Transfer to a plate lined with paper towels to drain; reserve 3 tablespoons drippings in skillet. Add celery and onion to skillet; cook, stirring occasionally, until tender, about 8 minutes. Stir in garlic; cook 30 seconds. Add kale, thyme, pepper, and remaining 2 teaspoons salt; cook, stirring often, until kale is crisp-tender, 8 to 10 minutes. Add 1/2 cup of the broth; cook, stirring, until evaporated.
5. Add kale mixture, bacon, and remaining 3 cups broth to cornbread mixture in bowl; gently stir to combine. Beat 3 eggs. Add beaten eggs and remaining 1/2 cup melted butter to cornbread mixture; gently stir to combine. Spoon mixture into a greased 13- x 9-inch baking dish. Bake at 400°F until golden brown, 35 to 40 minutes.

SERVES 8 (serving size: 1 1/4 cups)
ACTIVE 30 min. **TOTAL** 2 hours, 5 min.

Yeast Rolls

HERBED WILD RICE DRESSING

Wild rice, apples, and walnuts combine to make a dressing full of flavor and crunch.

    5 sourdough or white bread slices, cut into 1/2-inch cubes (about 3 cups)
    2 Tbsp. unsalted butter, melted
    2 Tbsp. extra-virgin olive oil
    1 cup chopped celery (about 3 stalks)
    1 medium-size red onion, diced
    2 Honeycrisp or Fuji apples, diced
    4 cups cooked wild rice
    1 cup toasted walnuts, roughly chopped
    2 Tbsp. chopped fresh flat-leaf parsley
    1 Tbsp. chopped fresh sage
    1 Tbsp. fresh lemon juice
    2 tsp. kosher salt
  1/2 tsp. black pepper
  1/4 cup firmly packed fresh flat-leaf parsley leaves

1. Preheat oven to 400°F. Toss bread cubes with melted butter in a medium bowl. Spread on a baking sheet, and bake until crispy and lightly browned, 5 to 8 minutes.
2. Heat oil in a skillet over medium-high. Add celery and onion; cook, stirring occasionally, until tender, about 8 minutes. Add apples; cook, stirring occasionally, until apples are crisp-tender and browned, 5 to 7

Goat Cheese Mashed Potatoes

Smashed Baby Red Potatoes

minutes. Stir in toasted bread cubes, rice, walnuts, chopped parsley, chopped sage, lemon juice, salt, and pepper. Cook until heated through, about 3 minutes. Spoon onto a serving platter. Top with parsley leaves.

SERVES 10 (serving size: 1 cup)
ACTIVE 15 min. **TOTAL** 40 min.

CORNBREAD DRESSING WITH SAUSAGE AND FENNEL

Use your favorite store-bought cornbread to make this crispy, golden dressing.

- 6 cups cubed day-old corn-bread (about 15 oz.)
- 1 lb. fresh mild Italian sausage, casings removed
- 1 fennel bulb, chopped
- 6 Tbsp. unsalted butter, divided
- 3 tsp. kosher salt, divided
- 1 1/2 tsp. black pepper, divided
- 1 1/2 cups chopped yellow onion (about 1 large onion)
- 1 cup chopped celery (about 3 stalks)
- 4 garlic cloves, minced
- 1 Honeycrisp apple, chopped
- 1 Tbsp. chopped fresh thyme
- 2 1/2 cups chicken broth
- 3 large eggs
- 2 tsp. pure maple syrup

1. Spread cubed cornbread on 2 rimmed baking sheets. Place in oven, and preheat to 400°F. Bake until cornbread is golden brown, about 15 minutes after oven preheats.
2. Heat a large nonstick skillet over high. Cook sausage, stirring occasionally, until browned, about 6 minutes. Transfer sausage to a large bowl, reserving drippings in skillet. Add fennel, 1 tablespoon of the butter, 1/2 teaspoon of the salt, and 1/4 teaspoon of the pepper to skillet. Reduce heat to medium-high; cook, stirring occasionally, until fennel is tender and slightly browned, about 8 minutes. Add fennel to bowl with sausage.
3. Add onion, celery, garlic, 1 tablespoon of the butter, 1/2 teaspoon of the salt, and 1/4 teaspoon of the pepper to skillet; cook, stirring occasionally, until tender, 12 to 15 minutes. Add to bowl with fennel and sausage. Add apple, thyme, and 1 tablespoon of the butter to skillet; cook, stirring often, until apples are slightly browned, 8 to 10 minutes. Add apple mixture and toasted cornbread to sausage mixture in bowl.
4. Whisk together chicken broth, eggs, and remaining 2 teaspoons salt and 1 teaspoon pepper. Pour over corn-bread mixture in bowl, and toss gently to combine. Let stand 10 minutes.
5. Grease a 13- x 9-inch baking dish with 1 tablespoon of the butter. Spread cornbread mixture in prepared dish. Cover with aluminum foil, and bake in preheated oven 30 minutes. Remove foil; dot dressing with remaining 2 tablespoons butter. Return to oven; bake until golden brown, 25 minutes. Drizzle with maple syrup before serving.

SERVES 8 to 10 (serving size: 1 cup)
ACTIVE 30 min. **TOTAL** 1 hour, 45 min.

CLASSIC BREAD DRESSING

Though cornbread dressing reigns supreme in the South, we love this sourdough version too.

- 1 Tbsp. olive oil
- 2 Tbsp. unsalted butter
- 2 cups sliced celery (about 6 stalks)
- 3 leeks, white parts only, thinly sliced
- 3 garlic cloves, chopped
- 1 1/2 Tbsp. chopped fresh thyme
- 1 1/2 tsp. kosher salt
- 1 tsp. black pepper
- 2 cups reduced-sodium chicken broth, divided
- 9 cups cubed sourdough bread (about 16 oz.), toasted
- 1/4 cup (2 oz.) melted unsalted butter
- 3 large eggs, lightly beaten
- 1 Tbsp. chopped fresh flat-leaf parsley

1. Preheat oven to 375°F. Heat oil and 2 tablespoons butter in a large nonstick skillet over high until butter melts. Stir in celery and leeks; cook, stirring occasionally, until tender, about 5 minutes. Add garlic; cook, stirring, 1 minute. Add thyme, salt, pepper, and 1/2 cup of the broth; cook, stirring, 1 minute.
2. Combine celery mixture and bread cubes in a large bowl. Add melted butter, eggs, and remaining 1 1/2 cups broth; stir to combine.
3. Spoon mixture into a lightly greased 11- x 7-inch baking dish; let stand 15 minutes. Bake in preheated oven until golden brown, 40 to 45 minutes. Sprinkle with parsley.

SERVES 8 (serving size: 1 1/4 cups)
ACTIVE 22 min. **TOTAL** 1 hour, 22 min.

YEAST ROLLS

- 1/2 cup warm water
- 1 (1/4-oz.) envelope active dry yeast
- 1/4 tsp. granulated sugar
- 1 cup warm (110°F) milk
- 1/4 cup honey
- 1 large egg, beaten
- 1/2 cup (4 oz.) plus 3 Tbsp. melted salted butter, divided
- 1 1/2 tsp. kosher salt
- 4 cups (about 17 oz.) all-purpose flour

1. Combine warm water, yeast, and sugar in a small bowl; let stand until mixture bubbles, about 5 minutes.
2. Beat warm milk, honey, egg, and 1/2 cup of the melted butter with a heavy-duty electric stand mixer on medium speed until well blended. Add yeast mixture and salt; beat until combined. With mixer running, gradually add flour until well combined.
3. Transfer dough to a bowl coated with cooking spray. Cover with plastic wrap, and chill 8 hours or overnight.
4. Lightly grease 2 (12-cup) muffin pans. Place chilled dough on a lightly floured surface; punch down dough into an 8-inch circle. Cut dough into quarters. Cut each quarter into 4 wedges; roll each wedge into an 8-inch-long rope. Starting at end, roll each rope into a spiral shape, and place in a prepared muffin cup. Cover pans with plastic wrap; let rise in a warm (80°F to 85°F) place, free from drafts, 45 minutes.
5. Preheat oven to 400°F. Brush rolls with 2 tablespoons of the melted butter; bake in preheated oven until golden brown, 15 to 18 minutes. Cool on a wire rack. Brush with remaining 1 tablespoon melted butter.

SERVES 16 (serving size: 1 roll)
ACTIVE 20 min. **TOTAL** 9 hours, 20 min., including 8 hours chilling

GOAT CHEESE MASHED POTATOES

- 4 lb. russet potatoes, peeled and cubed
- 8 oz. goat cheese (about 2 cups)
- 1 cup heavy cream
- 1/2 cup (8 oz.) salted butter
- 2 tsp. kosher salt
- 1/2 tsp. black pepper
- 1 Tbsp. chopped fresh chives

1. Place potatoes in a saucepan with cold water to cover by 1 inch. Bring to a boil over high; reduce heat to medium, and cook about 15 minutes.
2. Drain potatoes, and return to saucepan. Add goat cheese, cream, butter, salt, and pepper; using a potato masher, mash to combine. Top servings with chives.

SERVES 8 to 10 (serving size: 1 cup)
ACTIVE 30 min. **TOTAL** 30 min.

SMASHED BABY RED POTATOES

- 2 lb. baby red potatoes
- 4 rosemary sprigs
- 3 garlic cloves, smashed
- 1/4 cup plus 1/2 tsp. kosher salt, divided
- 1/4 cup extra-virgin olive oil, divided
- 2 Tbsp. unsalted butter, melted
- 1 Tbsp. chopped fresh flat-leaf parsley
- 2 tsp. chopped fresh thyme
- 1 tsp. chopped fresh rosemary
- 1 garlic clove, minced
- 1/4 tsp. black pepper

1. Preheat oven to 425°F. Place potatoes, rosemary sprigs, smashed garlic, 1/4 cup of the salt, and water to cover in a saucepan. Bring to a boil over high; reduce to medium, and simmer until potatoes are tender when pierced with a fork, 10 to 15 minutes. Drain; discard rosemary sprigs and garlic.
2. Brush a rimmed baking sheet with 2 tablespoons of the oil. Arrange potatoes on prepared baking sheet. Using the heel of your hand, lightly crush potatoes until they are about 1/2 inch thick. Brush with 1 tablespoon of the oil. Bake in preheated oven until golden brown and crisp, 25 minutes.
3. Stir together butter, chopped parsley, thyme, rosemary, minced garlic, pepper, and remaining 1 tablespoon oil and 1/2 teaspoon salt. Brush mixture over potatoes, and serve.

SERVES 8 (serving size: 3/4 cup)
ACTIVE 10 min. **TOTAL** 45 min.

Cornbread Dressing with Kale and Bacon

Cornbread Dressing with Sausage and Fennel

Herbed Wild Rice Dressing

Classic Bread Dressing

Sweet on Sweet Potatoes

APRIL MCGREGER, THE DAUGHTER AND SISTER OF MISSISSIPPI SWEET POTATO FARMERS, SHARES HER BEST RECIPES FOR THIS IN-SEASON SOUTHERN STAPLE

I WAS BORN IN Vardaman, Mississippi, the self-proclaimed "Sweet Potato Capital of the World." Since my current home state of North Carolina grows far more sweet potatoes—about as much as Mississippi and the other top-producing states of California and Louisiana combined—it seems that Vardaman should consider relinquishing this title. Locals maintain, however, that what they lack in quantity, they make up for in quality. In fact, one Vardaman farmer recently reported that visiting farmers from North Carolina State University went home with Mason jars filled with soil to decipher the secret to the silky sweet taste and the smoother, tighter skin of Vardaman sweet potatoes.

It's true that sweet potatoes are about the only thing happening in my hometown of about 1,300 people. In Vardaman, sweet potatoes are not just an iconic Southern food but a network of ties to community, economics, and identity. The annual Sweet Potato Festival, held on the first Saturday in November, kicks off a weeklong celebration of the harvest with cooking contests, tasting booths with everything from sweet potato sausage balls to sweet potato bonbons, and, in true Southern fashion, a Sweet Potato Queen.

In my family, we do not limit sweet potatoes to the usual Thanksgiving pie and casserole. Our Sunday roasts are cooked with them too. Our biscuits are often orange. We do not eat carrot cake so much as sweet potato cake.

Trust me, then, when I say that sweet potatoes can be prepared in countless ways. They're best when roasted low and slow, which allows ample time for the starches to be converted to sugars that bubble and caramelize. Follow my grandmother's lead and bake as many as your oven will hold; then freeze or refrigerate them, and save and savor these leftovers for later.

Brown Butter Sweet Potato Pie

3. Beat brown butter, sweet potatoes, condensed milk, sugar, eggs, vanilla, lemon juice, and salt with an electric mixer at medium speed until light and fluffy, 2 to 3 minutes. Divide mixture evenly between 2 piecrusts. Bake on middle rack in preheated oven until filling is slightly puffed and set, about 45 minutes. (If the crust gets too dark, loosely cover with aluminum foil.) Cool at least 1 hour before serving.

Note: If your sweet potatoes are at all stringy—which can happen sometimes, especially with larger sweet potatoes—you will need to pass them through a food mill or sieve.

MAKES 2 (9-inch) pies **ACTIVE** 15 min. **TOTAL** 3 hours, 15 min.

SWEET POTATO AND CHORIZO SAUSAGE BITES

In my hometown, you'll find a local twist on sausage balls, the ubiquitous Southern nibble. Sweet potato farmers' wives often mix a bit of roasted sweet potato into the dough. I've switched out breakfast sausage for peppery Mexican-style chorizo.

- 1 lb. fresh Mexican chorizo sausage, casings removed
- 2 1/4 cups all-purpose baking mix (such as Bisquick)
- 1 (8-oz.) pkg. preshredded extra-sharp Cheddar cheese
- 1/2 cup chilled mashed roasted sweet potato
- 1/8 tsp. ground cinnamon
- 1/8 tsp. kosher salt
- 6 Tbsp. plum jam or scuppernong jelly
- 2 Tbsp. Dijon mustard

1. Preheat oven to 350°F. Lightly grease a baking sheet.
2. Stir together sausage, baking mix, cheese, mashed sweet potato, cinnamon, and salt in a large bowl. Roll into 48 (1 1/2-inch) balls, and place about 1 inch apart on prepared baking sheet. Bake in preheated oven until sausage balls are cooked through and deep golden brown, about 20 minutes.

BROWN BUTTER SWEET POTATO PIE

Browning the butter with spices lends a deep, nutty flavor to this Southern classic.

- 1 (14.1-oz.) pkg. refrigerated piecrusts
- 1/2 cup (4 oz.) unsalted butter
- 1 cinnamon stick
- 2 whole cloves
- 4 cups mashed roasted sweet potatoes
- 1 (14-oz.) can sweetened condensed milk
- 1 cup granulated sugar
- 4 large eggs, beaten
- 2 tsp. vanilla extract
- 2 tsp. fresh lemon juice
- 1/2 tsp. kosher salt

1. Preheat oven to 350°F. Fit each piecrust into a 9-inch pie pan. Prick the bottoms of the piecrusts several times with a fork. Line piecrusts with parchment paper, and fill with pie weights or dried beans. Bake in preheated oven until slightly golden, about 15 minutes. Remove weights and parchment, and cool completely, about 1 hour.
2. Preheat oven to 350°F. Melt butter in a small saucepan over medium. Add cinnamon stick and cloves; cook, stirring occasionally, until foam subsides and butter begins to darken and smell fragrant, 3 to 4 minutes. Remove from heat, and pour through a fine wire-mesh strainer over a bowl. Discard cinnamon stick and cloves.

3. Stir together jelly and mustard in a small bowl until well blended. (If your jelly is too stiff to blend, microwave mixture at HIGH in 15-second increments until soft enough to stir.) Serve with sausage balls.

Note: Sausage balls can be frozen on baking sheet and transferred to zip-top plastic freezer bags for storage. Bake from frozen. (You may need to add 1 or 2 minutes to baking time.)

SERVES 12 (serving size: 4 sausage balls) **ACTIVE** 20 min. **TOTAL** 1 hour, 20 min.

TWICE-COOKED SWEET POTATOES WITH CITRUS AND HONEY

Tamari, a darker, richer soy sauce, is optional in this recipe, but its savory flavor makes the dish more interesting.

4	medium-size sweet potatoes, unpeeled
2	Tbsp. olive oil
1	tsp. black pepper
2 1/2	tsp. kosher salt, divided
4	Tbsp. salted butter, softened
2	Tbsp. heavy cream
1	tsp. orange zest
1/2	vanilla bean, split lengthwise, seeds scraped and reserved (or 1/2 tsp. vanilla extract)
2	Tbsp. honey, divided
1	tsp. tamari (optional)
2	large eggs
	Freshly grated nutmeg

1. Prick the sweet potatoes in a few places with a fork. Rub all over with the oil; sprinkle with pepper and 2 teaspoons of the salt. Place potatoes on a baking sheet lined with parchment paper or aluminum foil in a cold oven. Set oven temperature to 350°F, and bake sweet potatoes until the potato flesh has pulled away from the skins and potatoes are completely soft, 1 to 1 1/2 hours. Remove potatoes from the oven, and cool 15 minutes. Increase oven temperature to 400°F.
2. Cut sweet potatoes in half lengthwise. Carefully scoop pulp into a bowl, leaving shells with 1/4 inch of flesh intact. Place 6 shells in a single layer in a 13- x 9-inch baking dish; discard remaining 2 shells.
3. Process sweet potato pulp, butter, cream, orange zest, vanilla bean seeds, 1 tablespoon of the honey, remaining 1/2 teaspoon salt, and, if desired, tamari until smooth, about 1 minute. Add eggs, and process until blended, about 1 minute. Spoon filling into reserved skins.
4. Bake sweet potatoes at 400°F until filling is puffed and golden brown, 30 to 35 minutes. Drizzle sweet potatoes with remaining 1 tablespoon honey and a very light dusting of freshly grated nutmeg, and serve.

SERVES 6 (serving size: 1 potato boat) **ACTIVE** 15 min. **TOTAL** 2 hours

SWEET POTATO BREAD WITH BUTTERMILK-LIME ICING

Try this spicy treat as an alternative to pumpkin bread. Serve it unadorned for everyday or topped with this tangy icing for something extra special.

BREAD
	Salted butter, for greasing pan
1 3/4	cups (about 7 oz.) self-rising flour
1 1/2	tsp. ground cinnamon
1/2	tsp. ground nutmeg
1/2	tsp. ground ginger
1/2	tsp. baking powder
1/8	tsp. ground cloves
1/2	tsp. kosher salt
1 1/3	cups packed light brown sugar
1	cup mashed roasted sweet potato
3/4	cup vegetable oil
1	tsp. vanilla extract
3	large eggs, at room temperature

ICING
2 1/2	cups (about 8 1/2 oz.) sifted powdered sugar
2	Tbsp. buttermilk
1	Tbsp. fresh lime juice
1/2	tsp. vanilla extract
	Pinch of kosher salt
	Lime zest

Sweet Potato Bread with Buttermilk-Lime Icing

1. Prepare the Bread: Preheat oven to 350°F. Grease a 9-inch loaf pan with butter, and set aside. Combine flour, cinnamon, nutmeg, ginger, baking powder, cloves, and 1/2 teaspoon salt in a large bowl. Whisk together brown sugar, sweet potato, oil, and 1 teaspoon vanilla in a separate bowl until well blended. Add eggs, 1 at a time, to brown sugar mixture, whisking to combine after each addition. Slowly add brown sugar mixture to flour mixture, whisking constantly until well combined.
2. Transfer batter to prepared loaf pan. Bake on middle rack in preheated oven until a wooden pick inserted in center comes out clean, about 1 hour. Remove bread from oven; cool in pan on a wire rack 15 minutes.
3. Prepare the Icing: Whisk together powdered sugar, buttermilk, lime juice, 1/2 teaspoon vanilla, and pinch of salt in a medium bowl until smooth.
4. Remove bread from pan, and cool on wire rack. Drizzle bread with icing while bread is still warm. Top with zest.

SERVES 16 (serving size: 1 slice) **ACTIVE** 20 min. **TOTAL** 1 hour, 20 min.

SWEET POTATO-GINGER SCONES

In my years running a bakery stand at the Carrboro, North Carolina, farmers' market, customers clamored for the tender, apricot-hued scones studded with chunks of candied ginger. You can freeze the unbaked scones and bake them directly from the freezer; just add a few minutes to the baking time.

- 5 **cups (about 1 lb., 5 1/4 oz.) all-purpose flour, plus more for baking sheet**
- 2/3 **cup granulated sugar**
- 1 1/2 **Tbsp. baking powder**
- 1 **tsp. kosher salt**
- 1/8 **tsp. grated whole nutmeg**
- 5/8 **tsp. ground cardamom, divided**
- 1 1/2 **cups (12 oz.) very cold unsalted butter, cut into 1/2-inch pieces**
- 1/2 **cup chopped crystallized ginger**
- 2 **tsp. lemon zest**
- 1 **cup chilled mashed roasted sweet potato**
- 3/4 **cup cold buttermilk**
- 1/4 **cup plus 2 Tbsp. heavy cream, divided**
- 1/4 **cup turbinado sugar**

1. Preheat oven to 400°F. Line a baking sheet with parchment paper.

2. Sift together flour, sugar, baking powder, salt, nutmeg, and 1/2 teaspoon of the cardamom. Add butter; cut into the flour mixture with a pastry blender or a fork until butter pieces are the size of corn kernels. Stir in ginger and zest. Stir together sweet potatoes, buttermilk, and 1/4 cup of the cream in a small bowl. Make a well in the center of the flour mixture; place sweet potato mixture in well. Working quickly, stir until dough just comes together.

3. Sprinkle prepared baking sheet liberally with flour. Place dough on parchment, and divide dough in half. With floured hands, shape each dough half into a circle between 6 and 7 inches in diameter and about 1 inch thick. Brush circles evenly with remaining 2 tablespoons cream. Stir together turbinado sugar and remaining 1/8 teaspoon cardamom in a

Sweet Potato-Ginger Scones

small bowl, and sprinkle evenly over dough circles. Run a bread knife or bench scraper under cold water, and cut each circle into 8 wedges (like cutting a pie). Carefully pull wedges away from the center to separate them by about 3/4 inch. (Don't worry about any excess flour on your parchment paper.)

4. Bake on middle rack in preheated oven until golden brown and almost cooked through, about 30 minutes. Transfer baking sheet to lowest oven rack; bake until bottoms of scones are fully cooked, about 5 minutes. Serve warm or at room temperature.

MAKES 16 scones (serving size: 1 scone)
ACTIVE 20 min. **TOTAL** 55 min.

The South's Most Storied Pies

THE ROOTS OF OUR LOVE FOR ALL THINGS PIE RUN DEEP IN THE SOUTH AS THESE LUSCIOUS RECIPES PROVE

GREEN TOMATO MINCEMEAT PIE

MINCEMEAT FILLING

- 2 lb. Granny Smith apples (about 4 medium), peeled and chopped (about 5 1/4 cups)
- 1 1/2 lb. green tomatoes (about 3 medium), seeded and diced
- 1 (6-oz.) pkg. sweetened dried cranberries
- 1/4 cup bourbon
- 2 Tbsp. orange zest (from 3 small oranges)
- 1 Tbsp. apple pie spice
- 1 1/2 cups granulated sugar
- 1/2 tsp. salt
- 3/4 cup chopped pecans, toasted

CRUST

- 3 cups (about 12 3/4 oz.) all-purpose flour
- 1 Tbsp. granulated sugar
- 1 tsp. salt
- 1/2 cup (4 oz.) cold salted butter, cubed
- 1/2 cup cold shortening, cubed
- 8 to 10 Tbsp. ice water
- 1 large egg, lightly beaten
  Bourbon-Pecan Ice Cream

1. Prepare the Mincemeat Filling: Bring apples, tomatoes, cranberries, bourbon, zest, apple pie spice, 1 1/2 cups sugar, and 1/2 teaspoon salt to a boil in a 4-quart heavy saucepan over medium-high, stirring often. Reduce heat to medium, and cook, stirring often, until thickened, 30 to 35 minutes. Remove from heat, and cool completely, about 1 hour. Stir in pecans. (Mixture can be made and chilled up to 3 days ahead without pecans. Stir in toasted pecans just before spooning mincemeat into piecrust.)

2. Prepare the Crust: Stir together flour, 1 tablespoon sugar, and 1 teaspoon salt in a large bowl. Using a pastry blender, cut butter and shortening cubes into flour mixture until mixture resembles small peas. Using a fork, gradually stir in 8 tablespoons ice water, stirring until dry ingredients are moistened and dough begins to form a ball and pulls away from sides of bowl, adding up to 2 tablespoons more water, 1 tablespoon at a time, if necessary. Turn dough out onto a work surface; divide in half. Shape and flatten each dough half into a disk. Wrap each in plastic wrap, and chill 1 to 24 hours.

3. Preheat oven to 350°F. Unwrap 1 chilled dough disk, and place on a lightly floured surface. Let dough stand at room temperature until slightly softened, about 5 minutes. Sprinkle dough with flour, and roll into a 13-inch circle. Fit dough into a 9-inch glass pie plate. Spoon Mincemeat Filling into piecrust. Brush edge of piecrust with some of the beaten egg.

4. Unwrap remaining chilled dough disk, and place on a lightly floured surface. Sprinkle dough with flour, and roll into a 12-inch circle. Leaving a 3-inch border around edges, cut out and remove leaf shapes from middle of dough circle using a small (about 1 1/2-inch) maple leaf-shaped cutter. Brush top crust with some of the beaten egg, and carefully place over Mincemeat Filling. Press edges of bottom and top crusts together to seal, and trim excess even with rim of pie plate. Make small diagonal cuts into dough around piecrust edge at 1/2-inch intervals, making small tabs. Gently place every other tab on adjacent tab so that it slightly overlaps. Brush leaf cutouts with remaining beaten egg, and place decoratively on top of piecrust (as shown on page 281). Place pie on a rimmed baking sheet.

5. Bake in preheated oven on bottom oven rack until crust is golden brown and juices are bubbling, 1 hour and 20 minutes to 1 hour and 30 minutes, shielding with aluminum foil to prevent excessive browning, if necessary, and rotating pie halfway (on same rack) after 40 minutes. Transfer to a wire rack, and cool completely, about 3 hours. Serve with Bourbon-Pecan Ice Cream.

SERVES 8 (serving size: 1 slice, 1/2 cup ice cream) **ACTIVE** 1 hour, 15 min. **TOTAL** 7 hours, 55 min.

Bourbon-Pecan Ice Cream

Stir together 2 pints softened home-style vanilla ice cream, 1 cup chopped toasted pecans, and 1/4 cup bourbon until blended. Freeze 4 hours.

SERVES 8 (serving size: about 1/2 cup) **ACTIVE** 5 min. **TOTAL** 4 hours, 5 min.

GERMAN CHOCOLATE-PECAN PIE

CRUST

- 1 1/2 cups (about 6 3/8 oz.) all-purpose flour
- 1/2 Tbsp. granulated sugar
- 1/2 tsp. salt
- 1/4 cup cold salted butter, cubed
- 1/4 cup cold shortening, cubed
- 4 to 5 Tbsp. ice water

CHOCOLATE FILLING

- 1 (4-oz.) German's sweet chocolate baking bar, coarsely chopped
- 1/2 cup (4 oz.) salted butter
- 3/4 cup granulated sugar
- 3 Tbsp. all-purpose flour
- 1/8 tsp. salt
- 2 large eggs

Green Tomato Mincemeat Pie

German Chocolate-Pecan Pie

1 (5-oz.) can evaporated milk
1 tsp. vanilla extract
COCONUT-PECAN FILLING
1/2 cup packed light brown sugar
1/2 cup dark corn syrup
1/4 cup salted butter, melted
2 large eggs
1 tsp. vanilla extract
2 cups pecan halves and pieces, lightly toasted
2/3 cup sweetened flaked coconut
CHOCOLATE-COVERED PECANS
3/4 cup milk chocolate chips
35 toasted pecan halves

1. Prepare the Crust: Stir together 1 1/2 cups flour, 1/2 tablespoon granulated sugar, and 1/2 teaspoon salt in a large bowl. Using a pastry blender, cut butter and shortening cubes into flour mixture until mixture resembles small peas. Using a fork, gradually stir in 4 tablespoons ice water, stirring until dry ingredients are moistened and dough begins to form a ball and pulls away from sides of bowl, adding up to 1 more tablespoon of water, if necessary. Turn dough out onto a work surface; shape and flatten into a disk.

Wrap in plastic wrap, and chill 1 to 24 hours.
2. Preheat oven to 425°F. Unwrap chilled dough disk, and place on a lightly floured surface. Let dough stand at room temperature until slightly softened, about 5 minutes. Sprinkle dough with flour, and roll into a 13-inch circle. Fit dough into a 9-inch glass pie plate. Trim dough, leaving 1/2-inch overhang; fold edges under, and crimp. Prick bottom and sides 8 to 10 times with a fork. Freeze 20 minutes. Line piecrust with parchment paper, and fill with pie weights or dried beans. Bake in preheated oven 14 minutes. Remove weights and parchment paper, and bake until crust has lost its raw dough sheen, 5 to 7 minutes. Transfer to a wire rack, and cool completely, about 30 minutes. Reduce oven temperature to 350°F.
3. Prepare the Chocolate Filling: Microwave German's sweet chocolate and 1/2 cup butter in a microwave-safe bowl on HIGH until melted and smooth, 1 to 1 1/2 minutes, stirring at 30-second intervals. Whisk in 3/4 cup granulated sugar, 3 tablespoons flour, and 1/8 teaspoon salt. Add 2 eggs, 1 at a time, whisking just until blended

after each addition. Whisk in evaporated milk and 1 teaspoon vanilla until blended. Pour chocolate filling into prepared piecrust. Shield edges with aluminum foil to prevent excessive browning, and place on a rimmed baking sheet. Bake at 350°F for 30 minutes. (Pie will be partially baked.)
4. Prepare the Coconut-Pecan Filling: Whisk together brown sugar, corn syrup, 1/4 cup melted butter, 2 eggs, and 1 teaspoon vanilla until blended. Stir in pecans and coconut. Beginning at the outer edges of the partially baked chocolate filling, carefully spoon coconut-pecan filling over chocolate filling, and immediately return pie to oven. Bake until crust is golden and center is set, 35 to 40 minutes, shielding edges with aluminum foil to prevent excessive browning, if necessary. Cool pie completely on a wire rack, about 3 hours.
5. Prepare the Chocolate-Covered Pecans: Microwave chocolate chips in a small microwave-safe bowl on HIGH until melted, 30 to 45 seconds, stirring until smooth. Dip the lower half of each pecan into the melted chocolate, allowing excess chocolate to drip back into bowl, and place on a parchment paper-lined baking sheet. Chill until chocolate is firm, about 30 minutes. Arrange Chocolate-Covered Pecans decoratively around outer edge of pie. (You may have some left over.)

SERVES 8 (serving size: 1 slice)
ACTIVE 25 min. **TOTAL** 6 hours, 50 min.

MAPLE PEANUT PIE

CRUST
3 cups (about 12 3/4 oz.) all-purpose flour
1 Tbsp. granulated sugar
1 tsp. salt
1/2 cup (4 oz.) cold salted butter, cubed
1/2 cup cold shortening, cubed
8 to 10 Tbsp. ice water
1 large egg, lightly beaten
PEANUT FILLING
1/2 cup packed light brown sugar
2 tsp. all-purpose flour

Maple Peanut Pie

Tex-Mex Apple Pie

1/4 tsp. salt
1 cup Grade B pure maple syrup
1/2 cup creamy peanut butter
2 tsp. vanilla extract
1/2 cup (4 oz.) salted butter, melted
3 large eggs
1 1/2 cups coarsely chopped, lightly salted dry roasted peanuts
Flaky sea salt (optional)

1. Prepare the Crust: Stir together 3 cups flour, 1 tablespoon sugar, and 1 teaspoon salt in a large bowl. Using a pastry blender, cut cold butter and shortening cubes into flour mixture until mixture resembles small peas. Using a fork, gradually stir in 8 tablespoons ice water, stirring until dry ingredients are moistened and dough begins to form a ball and pulls away from sides of bowl, adding up to 2 tablespoons more water, 1 tablespoon at a time, if necessary. Turn dough out onto a work surface; divide in half. Shape and flatten each dough half into a disk. Wrap each in plastic wrap, and chill 1 to 24 hours.

2. Preheat oven to 425°F. Unwrap 1 chilled dough disk, and place on a lightly floured surface. Let the dough stand at room temperature until slightly softened, about 5 minutes. Sprinkle dough with flour, and roll into a 13-inch circle. Fit dough into a 9-inch glass pie plate. Trim dough, leaving 1/2-inch overhang; fold edges under. Prick bottom and sides 8 to 10 times with a fork.

3. Unwrap remaining chilled dough disk, and place on a lightly floured surface. Sprinkle with flour, and roll into a 12-inch circle. Cut dough with a 2-inch maple leaf-shaped cutter. Cut dough leaves in half lengthwise. Brush some of the beaten egg around edges of piecrust. Arrange dough half-leaf shapes around edge of crust, pressing to adhere, and brush with remaining beaten egg. Freeze 20 minutes. Line piecrust with parchment paper, and fill with pie weights or dried beans.

4. Bake in preheated oven 14 minutes. Remove weights and parchment paper, and bake until crust has lost its raw dough sheen, 5 to 7 minutes.

Transfer to a wire rack, and cool completely, about 30 minutes. Reduce oven temperature to 350°F.
5. Prepare Peanut Filling: Whisk together brown sugar, 2 teaspoons flour, and 1/4 teaspoon salt in a large bowl until blended. Add maple syrup, peanut butter, vanilla, and 1/2 cup melted butter; whisk until blended. Add 3 eggs, 1 at a time, whisking until blended after each addition. Stir in peanuts. Spoon peanut filling into prepared piecrust. Place pie on a rimmed baking sheet.
6. Bake at 350°F until center is set, 55 to 60 minutes, shielding edges with aluminum foil to prevent excessive browning, if necessary. Transfer to a wire rack, and cool completely, about 3 hours. Sprinkle pie with flaky sea salt, if desired.

Note: The intense flavor of Grade B maple syrup, usually tapped at the end of the sugaring season just before the maple trees bud, is perfect for piemaking.

SERVES 8 (serving size: 1 slice)
ACTIVE 20 min. **TOTAL** 6 hours, 10 min.

PUMPKIN-LEMON CREAM CHEESE CHESS PIE

CRUST

3 cups (about 12 3/4 oz.) all-purpose flour
1 Tbsp. granulated sugar
1 tsp. salt
1/2 cup (4 oz.) cold salted butter, cubed
1/2 cup cold shortening, cubed
8 to 10 Tbsp. ice water
1 large egg white, lightly beaten
PUMPKIN FILLING
1 (15-oz.) can pumpkin
1 tsp. pumpkin pie spice
1 1/2 cups granulated sugar
3 Tbsp. all-purpose flour
1/2 tsp. salt
1/2 cup (4 oz.) salted butter, melted
3 large eggs, lightly beaten
1 1/2 tsp. vanilla extract
1/2 cup heavy cream

LEMON-CREAM CHEESE FILLING

- 1/2 (8-oz.) pkg. cream cheese, softened
- 1 tsp. lemon zest (from 1 medium lemon)
- 1 large egg yolk
- 1/4 cup granulated sugar
- 2 Tbsp. heavy cream
  Sweetened whipped cream, for serving

1. Prepare the Crust: Stir together 3 cups flour, 1 tablespoon sugar, and 1 teaspoon salt in a large bowl. Using a pastry blender, cut butter and shortening cubes into flour mixture until mixture resembles small peas. Using a fork, gradually stir in 8 tablespoons ice water, stirring until dry ingredients are moistened and dough begins to form a ball and pulls away from sides of bowl, adding up to 2 tablespoons more water, 1 tablespoon at a time, if necessary. Turn dough out onto a work surface; divide in half. Shape and flatten each dough half into a disk. Wrap each in plastic wrap, and chill 1 to 24 hours.

2. Preheat oven to 425°F. Unwrap 1 chilled dough disk, and place on a lightly floured surface. Let stand at room temperature until slightly softened, about 5 minutes. Sprinkle dough with flour, and roll into a 13-inch circle. Fit dough into a 9-inch glass pie plate. Trim dough, leaving 1/2-inch overhang; fold edges under. Prick bottom and sides 8 to 10 times with a fork.

3. Unwrap remaining chilled dough disk, and place on a lightly floured surface. Lightly sprinkle with flour, and roll into a 12-inch circle. Cut dough with a 1/2-inch veined rose leaf-shaped cutter. Brush some of the beaten egg white around edges of piecrust. Arrange dough leaves, slightly overlapping, around edge of crust, and press to adhere. Brush dough leaves with remaining egg white. Freeze pie 20 minutes. Line piecrust with parchment paper, and fill with pie weights or dried beans.

4. Bake in preheated oven 14 minutes. Remove weights and parchment paper, and bake until crust has lost its raw dough sheen, 5 to 7 minutes. Transfer to a wire rack, and cool completely, about 30 minutes. Reduce oven temperature to 350°F.

5. Prepare the Pumpkin Filling: Whisk together pumpkin, pie spice, 1 1/2 cups sugar, 3 tablespoons flour, and 1/2 teaspoon salt until blended. Whisk in melted butter until blended. Whisk in eggs, vanilla, and 1/2 cup cream until blended. Spoon pumpkin mixture into prepared piecrust. (Piecrust will appear almost full, but there is just the right amount of room for the Lemon-Cream Cheese Filling.)

6. Prepare the Lemon-Cream Cheese Filling: Stir together cream cheese, zest, egg yolk, 1/4 cup sugar, and 2 tablespoons cream until blended. Spoon cream cheese filling, by rounded teaspoonfuls, over Pumpkin Filling; gently swirl with the tip of a knife.

7. Bake at 350°F until center is just set, 50 to 60 minutes, shielding edges with aluminum foil to prevent excessive browning, if necessary. Turn oven off. Let pie stand in oven, with door partially open, 20 minutes (to prevent cracks from forming in filling). Transfer pie to a wire rack, and cool completely, about 3 hours. Serve with sweetened whipped cream.

SERVES 8 (serving size: 1 slice)
ACTIVE 30 min. **TOTAL** 7 hours

TEX-MEX APPLE PIE

CREAM CHEESE PASTRY CRUST

- 1 1/4 cups (about 5 3/8 oz.) all-purpose flour
- 1/8 tsp. salt
- 1/2 cup (4 oz.) cold salted butter, cubed
- 1/2 (8-oz.) pkg. cold cream cheese, cubed

CREAM CHEESE STREUSEL

- 1 1/2 cups (about 6 3/8 oz.) all-purpose flour
- 1/2 cup packed light brown sugar
- 1/4 cup granulated sugar
- 1 tsp. ground cinnamon
- 1/4 tsp. salt
- 1/2 (8-oz.) pkg. cold cream cheese, cubed
- 1/4 cup cold salted butter, cubed
- 1 cup pecan pieces

APPLE FILLING

- 2 lb. Granny Smith apples (about 4 large)
- 2 lb. Braeburn or Fuji apples (about 4 large)
- 1/2 cup granulated sugar
- 1/4 cup salted butter
- 3 Tbsp. all-purpose flour
- 1/2 cup red pepper jelly (such as Braswell's)
- 1/2 cup packed light brown sugar
- 1/2 tsp. ground cinnamon

1. Prepare the Cream Cheese Pastry Crust: Pulse 1 1/4 cups flour and 1/8 teaspoon salt in a food processor until combined, about 3 or 4 times. Add 1/2 cup cold cubed butter and 4 ounces cold cubed cream cheese, and pulse until dough begins to clump together, about 10 to 12 times. Remove dough from processor, and gently shape into a flat disk. Wrap in plastic wrap, and chill 2 hours or up to 2 days.

2. Preheat oven to 425°F. Place cream cheese pastry disk on a lightly floured piece of parchment paper; sprinkle dough with flour. Top with another sheet of parchment paper. Roll dough into a 13-inch circle. Remove and discard top sheet of parchment. Starting at 1 edge of dough, wrap dough around rolling pin, separating dough from bottom sheet of parchment as you roll. Discard bottom sheet of parchment. Place rolling pin wrapped with dough over a 9-inch (1 1/2-inch-deep) glass pie plate. Unroll dough, and gently press it into pie plate. Trim dough, leaving 1/2-inch overhang; fold edges under, and crimp. Prick bottom and sides 8 to 10 times with a fork. Freeze until firm, about 20 minutes. Line pastry crust with parchment paper, and fill with pie weights or dried beans.

3. Bake in preheated oven 14 minutes. Remove weights and parchment paper, and bake until crust has lost its raw dough sheen, 5 to 7 minutes. Transfer to a wire rack, and cool completely, about 30 minutes. Reduce oven temperature to 375°F.

4. Prepare the Streusel: Stir together 1 1/2 cups flour, 1/2 cup brown sugar, 1/4 cup granulated sugar, 1 teaspoon cinnamon, and 1/4 teaspoon salt in a large bowl. Using a pastry blender, cut 4 ounces cold cubed cream cheese and ¼ cup cold cubed butter into flour mixture until mixture resembles peas; stir in pecans. Using your fingers, work pecans into crumb mixture, forming small clumps of streusel. Cover and chill 2 hours.

5. Meanwhile, prepare the Apple Filling: Peel and core apples; cut into ¹/₂-inch-thick wedges. Toss apple wedges with ¹/₂ cup granulated sugar in a large bowl. Arrange apple wedges in a single layer on 2 large parchment paper-lined rimmed baking sheets. Bake at 375°F until just tender, 20 to 25 minutes, switching pans top rack to bottom rack after 10 minutes. Remove from oven, and cool completely, about 15 minutes.

6. Melt ¼ cup butter in a small saucepan over medium. Whisk in 3 tablespoons flour, and cook, whisking constantly, 1 minute. Add pepper jelly, ¹/₂ cup brown sugar, and ¹/₂ teaspoon cinnamon, and cook, whisking constantly, until sugar and jelly are melted and mixture is smooth, about 1 to 2 minutes. Remove from heat, and toss with roasted apple wedges in a large bowl.

7. Spoon apple mixture into prepared crust, packing tightly and mounding slightly in center. Sprinkle streusel over apples, and gently press. (It will seem like a lot of streusel, but the streusel will compact considerably as the pie bakes.) Place pie on a rimmed baking sheet.

8. Bake at 375°F on bottom rack until juices are bubbling, 45 to 50 minutes, shielding with aluminum foil after 25 minutes to prevent excessive browning, if necessary. Transfer to a wire rack, and cool completely, about 3 hours.

SERVES 8 (serving size: 1 slice)
ACTIVE 25 min. **TOTAL** 7 hours, 45 min.

AMBROSIA PUDDING PIE

LEMON CURD

- 1 Tbsp. lemon zest, plus ¹/₂ cup fresh juice (from 4 lemons)
- ¼ cup salted butter, softened
- ¹/₂ cup granulated sugar
- 2 large eggs

CRUST

- 3 cups (about 12 ³/₄ oz.) all-purpose flour
- 1 Tbsp. granulated sugar
- 1 tsp. salt
- ¹/₂ cup (4 oz.) cold salted butter, cubed
- ¹/₂ cup cold shortening, cubed
- 8 to 10 Tbsp. ice water

COCONUT CUSTARD

- ¹/₂ cup granulated sugar
- 1 Tbsp. all-purpose flour
- ¹/₈ tsp. salt
- ¹/₂ cup heavy cream
- 2 tsp. vanilla extract
- 3 large eggs
- 1 cup sweetened flaked coconut

ADDITIONAL INGREDIENTS

- ¹/₂ cup sweet orange marmalade (such as Smucker's)
- 1 (8-oz.) can crushed pineapple in juice, well drained
- 1 large egg, lightly beaten

1. Prepare the Lemon Curd: Whisk together lemon zest, softened butter, and ¹/₂ cup sugar in a microwave-safe bowl until blended. Add 2 eggs, 1 at a time, whisking until blended after each addition. Gradually whisk in lemon juice until blended. (Mixture will look curdled.) Microwave on HIGH 2 minutes, whisking after 1 minute. Stir the mixture, and microwave on HIGH, stirring at 30-second intervals, just until mixture thickens and coats the back of a spoon, 1 to 2 minutes. Place plastic wrap directly on surface of warm curd (to prevent a film from forming), and chill 4 hours or up to 3 days.

2. Prepare the Crust: Stir together 3 cups flour, 1 tablespoon sugar, and 1 teaspoon salt in a large bowl. Using a pastry blender, cut cold butter and shortening cubes into flour mixture until mixture resembles small peas. Using a fork, gradually stir in 8 tablespoons ice water, stirring until dry ingredients are moistened and dough begins to form a ball and pulls away from sides of bowl, adding up to 2 tablespoons more water, 1 tablespoon at a time, if necessary. Turn dough out onto a work surface; divide in half. Shape and flatten each dough

half into a disk. Wrap each in plastic wrap, and chill 1 to 24 hours.

3. Preheat oven to 425°F. Unwrap 1 chilled dough disk, and place on a lightly floured surface. Let dough stand at room temperature until slightly softened, about 5 minutes. Sprinkle dough with flour, and roll into a 13-inch circle. Fit dough into a 9-inch glass pie plate. Trim dough, leaving ¹/₂-inch overhang; fold edges under, and crimp. Prick bottom and sides 8 to 10 times with a fork. Freeze 20 minutes. Line piecrust with parchment paper, and fill with pie weights or dried beans. Bake at 350°F oven 14 minutes. Remove weights and parchment paper, and bake until crust has lost its raw dough sheen, 5 to 7 minutes. Transfer to a wire rack, and cool completely, about 30 minutes. Reduce oven temperature to 350°F.

4. Prepare the Coconut Custard: Whisk together ¹/₂ cup sugar, 1 tablespoon flour, and ¹/₈ teaspoon salt in a medium bowl. Add cream, vanilla, and 3 eggs, and whisk until blended. Stir in coconut until blended.

5. Assemble the Pie: Spread orange marmalade over bottom of prepared piecrust; layer with crushed pineapple and Lemon Curd. Carefully pour Coconut Custard over Lemon Curd. Bake in preheated oven until center is set, 45 to 50 minutes, shielding edges with aluminum foil to prevent excessive browning, if necessary. Remove pie to a wire rack, and cool completely, about 3 hours.

6. Meanwhile, increase oven temperature to 425°F. Unwrap remaining chilled dough disk, and place on a lightly floured surface. Sprinkle dough with flour, and roll into a 12-inch circle. Cut dough with 2-inch and 1-inch maple leaf-shaped cutters. Place leaves on a parchment paper-lined baking sheet, and brush with beaten egg. Bake in preheated oven until golden brown, 7 to 9 minutes. Cool completely on a wire rack. Arrange pastry leaves around edge of pie.

SERVES 8 (serving size: 1 slice)
ACTIVE 25 min. **TOTAL** 9 hours

In Praise of Pecans

FOR VIRGINIA WILLIS, PECANS ARE MORE THAN A FAVORITE FALL INGREDIENT; THEY ARE A DELICIOUS CONNECTION TO HER PAST

GEORGIA MAY BE KNOWN AS "The Peach State," but the truth is that it's the perennial number one producer of pecans in the nation. The heart of the pecan belt is deeply rooted in the Georgia clay of the southwest corner of the state. I remember picking them growing up—it was as much a part of fall as football, and we all know that's nearly a religion. My grandmother had a tool that looked like an orange Slinky on a rod. She'd pop the Slinky end on the ground and it would "catch" the pecans. My sister and I would crawl about to fill our bags, the knees of our jeans damp in the wet earth. I can't say I always enjoyed it, but it did make powerful memories. The sound of the leaves rustling and twigs snapping is forever imprinted on my mind.

My grandfather had the best setup for cracking pecans. He had a handled nutcracker he attached to a two-by-four. With the nutcracker bridging two chairs on the back porch, he'd place an empty bucket underneath and sit in one of the chairs. Methodically, he'd reach into his gunnysack of the freshly foraged pecans and—whack, whack—he'd pull the handle and the shells would shatter. Over a few hours, he'd fill his bucket with the cracked delights. Then there was the tedious business of removing the meat from the shells with metal pincers and sticks with curved, pointed ends. The last step was brushing off any dust with a toothbrush. The intensive process resulted in a treasured bounty for holiday pies and cakes.

Pecans are less bitter than walnuts and more buttery than almonds, making them a very versatile nut. Every time I accidentally taste a rancid one I feel a twinge of sorrow for folks who have never had a really good pecan. Those poor people don't know what they are missing.

Cinnamon-Pecan Rolls

Farro Salad with Toasted Pecans, Feta, and Dried Cherries

Pecan-Crusted Rack of Lamb with Mint Dipping Sauce

CINNAMON-PECAN ROLLS

       3 Tbsp. granulated sugar
    1 1/2 tsp. baking powder
     1/2 tsp. baking soda
     1/2 tsp. kosher salt
    3 1/2 cups (about 14 7/8 oz.)
         all-purpose flour, divided
    1 1/2 cups buttermilk
       6 Tbsp. unsalted butter,
         melted, divided
    1 1/2 tsp. vanilla extract, divided
     1/4 cup packed dark brown sugar
    1 1/2 tsp. ground cinnamon
     3/4 cup coarsely chopped
         pecans, divided
       4 oz. cream cheese, softened
       1 cup (about 4 oz.) powdered
         sugar
     1/4 cup unsalted butter, softened
    1 to 2 tsp. whole milk

1. Preheat oven to 400°F. Line a rimmed baking sheet with parchment paper. Stir together granulated sugar, baking powder, baking soda, salt, and 3 cups of the flour in a medium bowl. Stir together buttermilk, 5 table-spoons of the melted butter, and 1 teaspoon of the vanilla in a small bowl. Add buttermilk mixture to flour mixture, and stir to combine.
2. Sprinkle 1/4 cup of the flour on work surface; turn out the dough, and sprinkle with remaining 1/4 cup flour. Knead lightly, using the heel of your hand to compress and push the dough away from you, and then fold it back over itself. Give the dough a small turn, and repeat 8 or so times. (It's not yeast bread; you want to activate the gluten just barely, not overwork it.)
3. Using a lightly floured rolling pin, roll dough into a 12-inch square about 1/4 inch thick. Brush dough with remaining 1 tablespoon melted butter. Sprinkle with brown sugar, cinnamon, and 1/2 cup of the pecans. Roll dough into a log, starting with edge closest to you. Pinch seam closed. (It'll be a bit messy, with filling spilling out. It might also stretch out a bit when you roll it, so push it back together at both ends to return it as close to 12 inches as possible.)
4. Using a very sharp or serrated knife, cut log into 1-inch-thick slices.

Transfer slices to prepared baking sheet. Bake in preheated oven until golden brown, 25 to 30 minutes. (Cover with aluminum foil at the end of baking if the exposed pecans start to darken too much.)
5. Meanwhile, stir together cream cheese, powdered sugar, softened butter, 1 teaspoon milk, and remaining 1/2 teaspoon vanilla in medium bowl. Beat with an electric mixer at medium speed until smooth and creamy. (Add up to 1 teaspoon more milk, 1/2 teaspoon at a time, and beat until desired consistency is reached.) Spread glaze over warm rolls. Top with remaining 1/4 cup pecans. Serve immediately.

SERVES 12 (serving size: 1 roll) **ACTIVE** 25 min. **TOTAL** 50 min.

PECAN-CRUSTED RACK OF LAMB WITH MINT DIPPING SAUCE

PECAN-CRUSTED LAMB

       1 frenched rack of lamb (about
         1 1/2 lb.)
     3/4 tsp. kosher salt
     3/4 tsp. black pepper
       1 tsp. olive oil
       3 Tbsp. Dijon mustard
     1/4 tsp. crushed red pepper
       2 garlic cloves, very finely
         chopped
     1/2 cup finely chopped pecans

MINT DIPPING SAUCE

       1 cup plain low-fat Greek
         yogurt
       2 Tbsp. chopped fresh mint,
         plus whole sprigs for garnish
       2 Tbsp. chopped fresh cilantro,
         plus whole sprigs for garnish
       2 garlic cloves, pressed
     1/4 tsp. kosher salt
     1/4 tsp. black pepper

1. Prepare the Lamb: Preheat oven to 375°F. Let lamb stand at room temperature 15 minutes. Sprinkle with 3/4 teaspoon each salt and black pepper. Heat oil in a large heavy-duty ovenproof skillet over high. When the oil is very hot, add lamb, and cook until browned, 3 to 5 minutes per side. Transfer to a cutting board, meat side up.

2. Stir together mustard, crushed red pepper, and finely chopped garlic in a small bowl. Place pecans in a large shallow dish.
3. Brush mustard mixture across the top of the rack until coated. Carefully dredge rack in pecans to coat evenly. Return lamb to skillet, pecan side up, and transfer to preheated oven. Bake until a thermometer inserted in thickest portion registers 145°F, 15 to 18 minutes. Increase heat to broil, and broil until pecans are lightly browned, about 2 minutes.
4. Meanwhile, prepare the Sauce: Stir together yogurt, mint, cilantro, and pressed garlic in a small bowl. Stir in 1/4 teaspoon each salt and black pepper.
5. Remove lamb from oven, and transfer lamb to a carving board, preferably with a moat. Cover with aluminum foil, and let rest about 5 minutes before slicing. Slice between the bones, forming either single or double chops. Place on a warmed serving platter, and garnish with mint and cilantro, if desired. Serve immediately with Mint Dipping Sauce.

SERVES 4 (serving size: 2 to 3 chops) **ACTIVE** 15 min. **TOTAL** 45 min.

FARRO SALAD WITH TOASTED PECANS, FETA, AND DRIED CHERRIES

Bring a large pot of **salted water** to a boil over high. Add 1 1/2 cups uncooked **farro,** and cook, stirring occasionally, until tender, about 15 minutes. Drain well in a fine wire-mesh strainer, and rinse under cold water. Shake to remove excess water, and transfer farro to a medium bowl. Stir in 1/2 cup toasted chopped **pecans,** 1/2 cup **dried cherries,** 1/3 cup chopped **scallions,** 1/4 cup chopped fresh flat-leaf **parsley,** 2 tablespoons fresh **lemon juice,** 2 tablespoons **olive oil,** and 1/4 teaspoon each of kosher **salt** and black **pepper.** Fold in 1/2 cup crumbled **feta** cheese. Serve at room temperature or chilled.

SERVES 6 (serving size: 3/4 to 1 cup) **ACTIVE** 15 min. **TOTAL** 30 min.

Best of What's Left

SIX SOUTHERN SPINS ON THE ICONIC DAY-AFTER-THANKSGIVING COMBO:
TURKEY SOUPS AND SANDWICHES

Italian

TURKEY PANINI

- 1/2 cup pepper jelly, divided
- 8 hearty white bread slices
- 8 oz. roast turkey, sliced
- 1/2 tsp. kosher salt
- 1/4 tsp. black pepper
- 2 cups loosely packed arugula
- 8 (1-oz.) mozzarella cheese slices
- 2 Tbsp. melted butter

1. Spread 1 tablespoon pepper jelly on each of 4 bread slices. Top each with 2 ounces turkey, and sprinkle evenly with salt and pepper. Divide arugula evenly among sandwiches, and top each with 2 mozzarella slices. Spread remaining 1/4 cup pepper jelly evenly on remaining 4 bread slices, and place, jelly side down, on each sandwich.

2. Brush a preheated panini press with melted butter, and cook sandwiches until golden, 2 to 3 minutes. Serve immediately.

SERVES 4 (serving size: 1 sandwich)
ACTIVE 15 min. **TOTAL** 15 min.

Turkey Panini

TURKEY TORTELLINI SOUP WITH GREENS

- 1 Tbsp. olive oil
- 1/2 cup chopped sweet onion (from 1 onion)
- 1/2 cup thinly sliced celery (from 2 stalks)
- 1/2 cup thinly sliced carrots (from 2 carrots)
- 2 tsp. minced garlic
- 6 cups Turkey Stock (page 289)
- 3 cups shredded roast turkey
- 1 (9-oz.) pkg. refrigerated three-cheese tortellini
- 1 (5-oz.) pkg. fresh spinach
- 1/2 tsp. kosher salt
- 1/2 tsp. black pepper
  Shaved Parmesan cheese

Heat oil in a Dutch oven over medium-high. Add onion, celery, and carrots; cook, stirring often, until vegetables begin to soften, 8 to 10 minutes. Add garlic; cook, stirring often, 1 minute. Add Turkey Stock and roast turkey, and bring to a boil. Reduce heat to low, and simmer 10 minutes. Add tortellini, and simmer until tortellini are cooked, about 6 minutes. Stir in spinach, salt, and pepper. Remove from heat. Top each serving with shaved Parmesan cheese.

SERVES 6 (serving size: about 1 1/2 cups)
ACTIVE 15 min. **TOTAL** 25 min.

Louisiana

GUMBO-STYLE TURKEY SOUP

- 1/2 lb. andouille sausage, cut into 1/4-inch-thick slices
- 1/2 cup canola oil
- 1/2 cup (about 2 1/8 oz.) all-purpose flour
- 1 cup chopped sweet onion (from 1 onion)
- 1 cup chopped green bell pepper (from 1 bell pepper)
- 1 cup chopped celery (from 3 stalks)

Gumbo-Style Turkey Soup

Thanksgiving Po'Boy

THANKSGIVING PO'BOY

- 2 (8-oz.) French bread loaves, warmed
- 3 Tbsp. mayonnaise
- 3 Tbsp. Creole mustard
- 9 oz. roast turkey, shredded
- 1/2 cup turkey gravy
- 1 1/2 cups cornbread dressing
- 3/4 cup cranberry sauce, divided

Cut each bread loaf lengthwise down the center, cutting almost but not quite all the way through the bread; cut each loaf crosswise into thirds. Stir together mayonnaise and mustard in a small bowl. Spread cut sides of bread evenly with mayonnaise mixture. Toss turkey and gravy together in a medium bowl. Divide turkey, dressing, and cranberry sauce evenly among sandwiches.

SERVES 6 (serving size: 1 sandwich)
ACTIVE 15 min. **TOTAL** 15 min.

Tex-Mex

TURKEY QUESADILLAS

- 8 (8-inch) fajita-size flour tortillas
- 2 Tbsp. salted butter, melted
- 8 oz. roast turkey, sliced
  Caramelized Onions and Red Peppers (recipe follows)
- 8 (3/4-oz.) pepper Jack cheese slices
- 2 Tbsp. roughly chopped cilantro
  Easy Guacamole (recipe follows)
- 1/2 cup sour cream

1. Preheat oven to 425°F. Brush 1 side of 4 tortillas evenly with 1 tablespoon melted butter, and place, buttered side down, on 2 baking sheets. Divide turkey, Caramelized Onions and Red Peppers, and cheese slices evenly among tortillas on baking sheet; top with remaining tortillas. Brush with remaining 1 tablespoon melted butter.

- 2 tsp. minced garlic
- 1 1/2 tsp. Creole seasoning
- 5 1/2 cups Turkey Stock (page 289)
- 4 cups shredded roast turkey
- 2 cups fresh or frozen cut okra
- 1 (14.5-oz.) can diced tomatoes
- 2 tsp. Worcestershire sauce
- 1 cup hot cooked rice

1. Cook sausage in a medium nonstick skillet over medium, stirring occasionally, until browned, 7 to 8 minutes. Remove from skillet, and drain on paper towels.
2. Heat oil in a large Dutch oven over medium-high; gradually whisk in flour, and cook, whisking constantly, until flour is a deep caramel color, 7 to 10 minutes. (Do not burn mixture.)
3. Reduce heat to medium. Stir in onion, bell pepper, celery, garlic, and Creole seasoning, and cook, stirring constantly, 5 minutes. Gradually stir in Turkey Stock, turkey, okra, tomatoes, Worcestershire sauce, and andouille sausage. Increase heat to medium-high, and bring to a boil. Reduce heat to low, and simmer, stirring occasionally, 30 minutes. Stir in cooked rice, and serve immediately.

SERVES 8 (serving size: 1 1/2 cups)
ACTIVE 30 min. **TOTAL** 1 hour

2. Bake in preheated oven until golden brown and cheese begins to melt, 12 to 15 minutes. Gently press quesadillas with a spatula; cut into wedges, and sprinkle with cilantro. Serve immediately with Easy Guacamole and sour cream.

SERVES 4 (serving size: 1 quesadilla, 2 Tbsp. guacamole, 2 Tbsp. sour cream) **ACTIVE** 45 min. **TOTAL** 45 min.

Caramelized Onions and Red Peppers

Cut 1 large **sweet onion** lengthwise into thin slices. Thinly slice 1 **red bell pepper.** Melt 2 Tbsp. **salted butter** in a large nonstick skillet over medium-high; add sliced **onion,** and sprinkle with 1 tsp. **granulated sugar.** Cook, stirring often, 15 minutes. Add **bell pepper** slices, and cook, stirring often, until onions are browned and tender and pepper slices are tender, about 10 minutes. Remove from heat, and sprinkle with ¼ tsp. **kosher salt** and ⅛ tsp. **black pepper.**

MAKES about 1 ½ cups **ACTIVE** 35 min. **TOTAL** 35 min.

Easy Guacamole

Mash together 1 large ripe **avocado,** chopped; 1 Tbsp. fresh **lime juice;** ½ tsp. **hot sauce;** and ¼ tsp. **kosher salt** in a bowl. Sprinkle with 2 Tbsp. chopped **cilantro.**

MAKES ½ cup **ACTIVE** 5 min. **TOTAL** 5 min.

GREEN CHILE-TURKEY SOUP WITH HOMINY

- 1 **Tbsp. olive oil**
- 1 **cup chopped yellow onion (from 1 onion)**
- ½ **cup chopped celery (from 2 stalks)**
- 2 **tsp. minced garlic**
- 2 **tsp. dried oregano**
- 2 **tsp. ground cumin**
- 1 **tsp. chili powder**
- 8 **canned tomatillos, drained and coarsely chopped**
- 6 **cups Turkey Stock**
- 2 **(15.5-oz.) cans white hominy, drained and rinsed**

Green Chile-Turkey Soup with Hominy

Turkey Quesadillas

- 1 **(4-oz.) can chopped green chiles**
- 4 **cups shredded roast turkey**
- ½ **cup chopped fresh cilantro**
- 2 **Tbsp. fresh lime juice**
- 1 **tsp. kosher salt**
- ¼ **tsp. black pepper**
     Toppings: thinly sliced radishes, lime wedges, fresh cilantro leaves

Heat olive oil in a Dutch oven over medium-high. Add onion, celery, garlic, oregano, cumin, and chili powder; cook, stirring constantly, 5 minutes. Add tomatillos; cook, stirring constantly, 1 minute. Add Turkey Stock, hominy, and green chiles; bring to a boil. Stir in roast turkey; reduce heat to low, and simmer until heated through, about 20 minutes. Remove from heat, and stir in cilantro, lime juice, salt, and pepper. Serve immediately with toppings.

SERVES 8 (serving size: 1 ½ cups) **ACTIVE** 20 min. **TOTAL** 45 min.

Our Best Turkey Stock

One delicious recipe that can be used with all three of our day-after soups

Place the carcass and skin of a roasted 12- to 14-lb. **turkey** in a very large stockpot. Add 2 qt. reduced-sodium **chicken broth;** 16 cups **water;** 2 chopped **celery stalks;** 2 chopped **carrots;** 1 **yellow onion,** quartered; and 1 Tbsp. **kosher salt.** Bring to a boil over high; reduce heat, and simmer until carcass falls apart and stock tastes very rich, 2 to 3 hours. Remove and discard large bones; pour liquid through a fine wire-mesh strainer, and discard solids. Cool completely, about 2 hours; cover and chill until ready to use. Skim and discard solidified fat before using. Refrigerate stock up to 1 week, or freeze up to 6 months.

MAKES about 17 cups **ACTIVE** 10 min. **TOTAL** 3 hours, 10 min.

cooking ◆SL◆ school

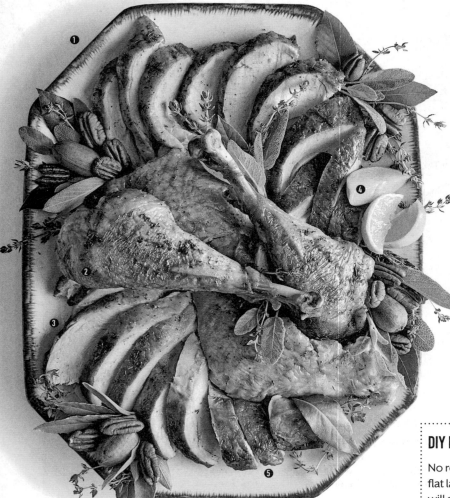

PLATE YOUR TURKEY LIKE A PRO

YOUR TURKEY SHOULD LOOK AS GOOD AS IT TASTES, EVEN WHEN IT'S ALL CARVED UP. FOLLOW THESE PRESENTATION POINTERS

1 PICK THE RIGHT SIZE PLATTER
Choose a "turkey platter" that is at least 16 inches and can accommodate the bird and garnishes.

2 TACKLE THE LEGS AND THIGHS
Using an electric knife, separate legs from the thighs and remove from turkey. Arrange in the middle of the platter.

3 SLICE THE BREAST MEAT
Remove the breasts, and slice the meat on the bias. (Don't tear the skin.) Fan out the slices on either side of the dark meat.

4 GARNISH THE MEAT
Surround the meat with edible trimmings: fresh herbs, nuts, whole or sliced produce.

5 FINISH WITH GRAVY
Brush the turkey skin with a little gravy.

> **DIY ROASTING RACK**
>
> No roasting rack? No problem. Place bird on a flat layer of carrots, celery, and parsnips, which will absorb turkey drippings.

DRESSING FACE-OFF: TO STUFF OR NOT TO STUFF

TWO OF OUR TEST KITCHEN PROS ANSWER THE ULTIMATE THANKSGIVING QUESTION: DOES THE DRESSING GO IN OR OUT OF THE BIRD?

"Growing up, we always stuffed our turkey. The dressing gets flavor and moisture from the bird itself, which makes it so delicious."

"Baking the dressing in a separate dish gives you a crispy brown top and edges, which I love. I fill my turkey with aromatic sage or citrus."

December

RAISE A GLASS to the holidays with a Christmas dinner menu that's impressive looking but so easy to make.

Peppercorn-Crusted Standing Rib Roast with Roasted Vegetables

HOLIDAY 2016

A Fabulous Holiday Feast

THIS CHRISTMAS, SIT DOWN TO A DAZZLING DINNER DESIGNED TO PLEASE THE ENTIRE FAMILY—AND THE COOK. THESE CLASSIC HOLIDAY DISHES LOOK AND TASTE AMAZING BUT DON'T REQUIRE MUCH FUSS IN THE KITCHEN.

BAKED BRIE BITES

This five-ingredient appetizer packs a whole lot of flavor and texture into one bite from the buttery pastry, spicy pepper jelly, and creamy melted brie.

24	frozen mini phyllo pastry shells, thawed
3	oz. Brie cheese, rind removed
2	Tbsp. red pepper jelly
24	toasted pecans
1	tsp. flaky sea salt

Preheat oven to 350°F. Arrange pastry shells on a rimmed baking sheet. Cut Brie into 24 very small pieces. Spoon ¼ teaspoon jelly into each shell; top evenly with Brie pieces and pecans. Bake in preheated oven until cheese is melted, 7 to 8 minutes. Sprinkle with salt; serve immediately.

SERVES 12 (serving size: 2 brie bites) **ACTIVE** 10 min. **TOTAL** 18 min.

SPARKLING POMEGRANATE PUNCH

3	cups cranberry juice, chilled
1	cup pomegranate juice, chilled
1	(750-milliliter) bottle prosecco, chilled
2	cups vodka
1 ½	cups chilled ginger ale
¼	cup Simple Syrup
1	Pomegranate Ice Ring

Stir together cranberry juice and pomegranate juice in a large serving bowl. Stir in prosecco, vodka, ginger ale, and Simple Syrup. Gently place ice ring in center; serve immediately.

SERVES 12 (serving size: 1 cup) **ACTIVE** 20 min. **TOTAL** 5 hours, 20 min., including 5 hours freezing

Simple Syrup

Bring 1 cup granulated **sugar** and 1 cup **water** to a boil in a small saucepan over medium, stirring occasionally. Boil until sugar dissolves, about 1 minute. Remove from heat, and cool 30 minutes. Refrigerate in an airtight container up to 2 weeks.

Pomegranate Ice Ring

Spread 3 cups **pomegranate** arils in an even layer in the bottom of a 12-cup Bundt pan. Pour 1 cup of ice-cold **distilled water** over arils. Place Bundt pan in freezer in a level position; freeze until frozen, about 1 hour. Add 7 more cups ice-cold distilled water; freeze until set, about 4 hours. Let stand at room temperature 10 minutes before removing Ice Ring from Bundt pan.

STUFFED ENDIVE WITH HERBED GOAT CHEESE

Red and green Belgian endive leaves make this edible "wreath" look even more festive for the holidays. Can't find endive? Serve this tangy spread with crackers.

- 1 oz. goat cheese, crumbled (about ¼ cup)
- 2 oz. cream cheese, softened (about ¼ cup)
- 1 tsp. lemon zest plus 1 Tbsp. fresh juice (from 1 lemon)
- ¼ tsp. kosher salt
- ¼ tsp. black pepper
- 2½ Tbsp. thinly sliced fresh chives, divided
- 1½ Tbsp. finely chopped fresh flat-leaf parsley, divided
- 2½ tsp. finely chopped fresh tarragon, divided
- 24 red and green Belgian endive leaves (about 2 heads)

1. Stir together goat cheese, cream cheese, zest, juice, salt, pepper, 2 tablespoons of the chives, 1 tablespoon of the parsley, and 2 teaspoons of the tarragon in a bowl. Spoon

mixture evenly into bottom halves of endive leaves.
2. Combine remaining ½ tablespoon each chives and parsley and ½ teaspoon tarragon. Sprinkle evenly over stuffed endive leaves. Serve immediately.

SERVES 12 (serving size: 2 stuffed endive leaves) **ACTIVE** 15 min. **TOTAL** 15 min.

PEPPERCORN-CRUSTED STANDING RIB ROAST WITH ROASTED VEGETABLES

Prepare for "oohs" and "aahs" when you place this showstopping roast on your holiday table. Although it looks impressive, it's simple to prepare—slather it with our special herbed butter the night before, then let your oven do all the work the next day.

- ½ cup (4 oz.) salted butter, softened
- 2 Tbsp. coarsely ground black pepper
- 2 Tbsp. kosher salt
- 1 Tbsp. chopped fresh rosemary
- 1 Tbsp. chopped fresh sage
- 1 Tbsp. chopped fresh thyme
- 1 Tbsp. extra-virgin olive oil
- 1 (8-lb.) 4-rib prime rib roast, chine bone removed

1. Stir together butter, pepper, salt, rosemary, sage, thyme, and oil in a small bowl. Spread evenly over roast. Chill, uncovered, 12 hours or up to 24 hours.
2. Remove roast from refrigerator; let stand at room temperature 1 hour.
3. Preheat oven to 450°F. Place roast on a lightly greased rack in a roasting pan. Bake in preheated oven on lowest oven rack 45 minutes. Reduce oven temperature to 350°F; bake until a meat thermometer inserted in thickest portion registers 120°F to 130°F for medium-rare or 130°F to 135°F for medium, about 1 hour and 30 minutes.
4. Let stand 30 minutes. Transfer roast to a serving platter, reserving ½ cup drippings for gravy.

SERVES 10 (serving size: 1 slice roast) **ACTIVE** 10 min. **TOTAL** 15 hours, 55 min., including 12 hours chilling

ROASTED VEGETABLES

Roasting the vegetables separate from the meat keeps them bright and colorful and from turning mushy.

- 1 lb. small carrots with tops, trimmed and peeled
- 1 lb. parsnips, peeled and cut lengthwise into 3-inch pieces
- 8 oz. golden beets, peeled and cut into 1-inch wedges
- 8 oz. Chioggia beets (candy cane beets), peeled and cut into 1-inch wedges
- 2 Tbsp. chopped fresh rosemary
- 2 Tbsp. olive oil
- 2 tsp. kosher salt
- 1 tsp. black pepper

Preheat oven to 400°F. Toss together all ingredients in a large bowl. Spread in a single layer in a 17- x 11-inch jelly-roll pan. Bake in preheated oven until tender, about 45 minutes, stirring every 15 minutes. Serve with roast.

SERVES 10 (serving size: about 1 cup) **ACTIVE** 13 min. **TOTAL** 1 hour

CLASSIC PAN GRAVY WITH SHERRY

A little bit of tangy sherry vinegar is the secret ingredient in this rich and flavorful gravy.

- ½ cup pan drippings from Peppercorn-Crusted Standing Rib Roast (recipe at left)
- ½ cup chopped yellow onion (from 1 onion)
- ½ cup (about 2 ⅛ oz.) all-purpose flour
- 4 to 5 cups beef broth
- 1½ Tbsp. sherry vinegar
- ¼ tsp. kosher salt
- ¼ tsp. black pepper

1. Heat pan drippings in a medium saucepan over medium. Add onions, and cook, stirring occasionally, until tender, about 5 minutes. Sprinkle flour over onions, stirring constantly; cook, stirring constantly, until flour is golden brown, about 2 minutes.
2. Gradually whisk in 4 cups of the broth. Cook, stirring often, just until mixture comes to a boil and is smooth and thick, about 5 minutes. If mixture is

too thick, add up to 1 cup broth, 1/4 cup at a time, until mixture reaches desired consistency. Stir in sherry vinegar, salt, and pepper. Serve with roast and vegetables.

SERVES 8 to 10 (serving size: 1/2 cup)
ACTIVE 15 min. **TOTAL** 15 min.

SAUTÉED MUSTARD GREENS WITH GARLIC AND LEMON

Here's a fast and fresh take on the usual long-simmered greens. Swap out kale, collards, or turnip greens for the mustard greens if you prefer.

- 2 Tbsp. olive oil
- 4 garlic cloves, thinly sliced
- 3 lb. mustard greens; washed, trimmed, and chopped (about 24 cups)
- 2 Tbsp. fresh lemon juice (from 1 lemon)
- 1/4 to 1/2 tsp. crushed red pepper
- 3/4 tsp. kosher salt
- 3/4 tsp. black pepper

Heat oil in a Dutch oven over medium. Add garlic; cook, stirring often, until garlic is golden brown and crispy, about 1 minute. Stir in greens, in batches; cook until wilted, 1 to 2 minutes, before adding more greens. Cover and cook, stirring occasionally, until tender-crisp, 10 to 12 minutes. Stir in lemon juice and 1/4 teaspoon crushed red pepper. Stir in an additional 1/4 teaspoon crushed red pepper, if desired. Sprinkle with salt and pepper.

SERVES 8 (serving size: about 1/2 cup)
ACTIVE 10 min. **TOTAL** 20 min.

Baby Hasselback Potatoes with Blue Cheese, Bacon, and Rosemary

BABY HASSELBACK POTATOES WITH BLUE CHEESE, BACON, AND ROSEMARY

Hasselback-style potatoes have thin, accordion-like slices that turn crisp in the oven. Blue cheese and bacon bring them over the top for the holidays.

- 10 (2 1/2-oz.) small Yukon Gold potatoes
- 1/2 cup (4 oz.) salted butter, melted
- 1 1/2 Tbsp. finely chopped fresh rosemary
- 1 1/2 tsp. kosher salt, divided
- 1 oz. blue cheese, crumbled (about 1/4 cup)
- 1/2 cup crumbled cooked bacon (about 6 slices)
- 1/4 cup chopped fresh chives

1. Preheat oven to 425°F. Slice each potato crosswise at 1/8-inch intervals, cutting to within 1/4 inch of the bottom of the potato. (Do not cut all the way through potatoes.) Arrange potatoes, cut side up, on a lightly greased baking sheet.
2. Combine melted butter, rosemary, and 1 teaspoon of the salt in a small bowl. Spoon 1/3 cup of the melted butter mixture evenly over potatoes.
3. Bake in preheated oven on middle oven rack until tender, 45 to 50 minutes. Spoon remaining butter mixture evenly over potatoes. Sprinkle with blue cheese and remaining 1/2 teaspoon salt. Bake until cheese is slightly melted and potatoes are golden brown, about 5 minutes.
4. Sprinkle with bacon and chives, and serve immediately.

SERVES 10 (serving size: 1 potato)
ACTIVE 35 min. **TOTAL** 1 hour, 20 min.

CORNMEAL POPOVERS

A basket of light, fluffy popovers goes hand-in-hand with a standing rib roast. Be sure not to peek at them while they are baking—keeping the oven door shut will help them rise higher in the pan.

- 1 1/2 cups (about 6 3/8 oz.) all-purpose flour
- 1/2 cup (about 2 7/8 oz.) fine white cornmeal
- 1 1/2 tsp. kosher salt
- 1 3/4 cups whole milk
- 4 large eggs
- 1/4 cup salted butter, melted

1. Place a 12-cup muffin pan in oven. Preheat oven to 450°F (do not remove pan while oven preheats).
2. Whisk together flour, cornmeal, and salt in a large bowl. Whisk together milk and eggs in a medium bowl. Gradually whisk milk mixture into flour mixture until well blended.
3. Remove muffin pan from oven. Spoon 1 teaspoon melted butter into each cup of hot muffin pan; return muffin pan to oven for 2 minutes.
4. Carefully remove muffin pan. Divide batter evenly among prepared muffin cups. Bake in preheated oven until popovers are puffed and golden brown, 18 to 20 minutes. (Centers still will be moist.) Serve immediately.

SERVES 12 (serving size: 1 popover)
ACTIVE 12 min. **TOTAL** 30 min.

Wine Pairings

A meal this special deserves the right bottle of wine. We asked Firstleaf, a new wine club, to select three bottles to pair with this menu. Sign up to get all three wines for $19.95; *firstleaf.wine/southernwine*

Sautéed Mustard Greens with Garlic and Lemon

Cornmeal Popovers

Coconut Cake with Rum
Filling and Coconut
Ermine Frosting, page 299

Cut to the Cakes

THE STORY BEHIND THE MOST BELOVED AND DELICIOUS CHRISTMAS
TRADITION AT *SOUTHERN LIVING*: THE WHITE CAKES ON OUR DECEMBER COVERS

OUR OBSESSION WITH WHITE CAKES began more than twenty years ago in the soft rolling hills of Northern Kentucky. We traveled to Longfield Farm, the childhood home of Louisville chef Kathy Nash Cary, to photograph a Christmas bluegrass celebration: a bountiful farm-to-table dinner that ended with a lemon-filled coconut layer cake crowned with fresh cranberries and greenery. This snowy-white Christmas dream of a coconut cake was too picture-perfect not to make the cover.

The following year, the test kitchen created a special "gift box" cake for the 1996 issue of *Southern Living Home for the Holidays:* a triple layer white-on-white cake wrapped in buttercream frosting with miniature gingerbread men dancing merrily around the sides. A sparkling red Fruit by the Foot bow tied the whole thing together. At the request of then-Editor-in-Chief John Floyd the cake made a festive leap to our December cover, leaving *Home for the Holidays* cakeless (some stellar chocolate soufflés and a pink peppermint pie made up for the loss). The Gift Box Cake, like the Lemon-Coconut Cake, was such a huge hit that every year since we've featured a white cake on the December cover.

Around the *Southern Living* editorial offices the December cake is known simply as The Big White Cake. Not so much for its actual size (though one year we stacked up a head-turning six layers of red velvet), but for the months of prep and deliciously indecisive madness that go into choosing the perfect cover cake. Planning for next year's cake starts soon after this year's December issue hits the newsstands and usually winds down with a flurry of wintry photo shoots somewhere between the Fourth of July and Labor Day. (Yes, Virginia, it's always a candy-sweet marshmallow world in the *Southern Living* Test Kitchens). Flour is sifted, sugar is measured, mixers

whirl, and cakes tumble from pans. Forks in hand and a nostalgic Johnny Mathis Christmas CD set to replay, the test kitchen often taste-tests a half-dozen cakes each day.

Once we've baked our way through all the contenders and narrowed down the favorites, we break out the cake pans once again for the annual "Big White Cake Showing," a high-glitz cake pageant with lots of bling (think: edible glitter, luster dust, pearl dragées). At the end of the showing, the cake that scores the highest for taste and presentation makes the cover, while the top alternates take center stage on the inside pages.

As with any bonafide Southern tradition, there are always more stories to tell. Like the summer of 2004, when we were photographing the cover cake in front of a roaring fire during a triple-digit heat wave. The homeowner's neighbors, alarmed by the billowing clouds of smoke pouring from the roof, telephoned the fire department. But our favorite stories come from the countless readers who have baked the cover cakes and sent post-Christmas snapshots and selfies of their new holiday traditions in the making. We'd love to see yours this year! Tag us in your social media photos using hashtag #SLwhitecake

—MARY ALLEN PERRY

RED VELVET CHEESECAKE-VANILLA CAKE WITH CREAM CHEESE FROSTING

CHEESECAKE LAYERS

4 1/2 (8-oz.) pkg. cream cheese, softened

2 1/4 cups granulated sugar

6 large eggs, lightly beaten

1 1/2 cups sour cream

3/4 cup whole buttermilk

4 1/2 Tbsp. unsweetened cocoa

2 (1-oz.) bottles liquid red food coloring

1 Tbsp. vanilla extract

1 1/2 tsp. distilled white vinegar

VANILLA CAKE LAYER

1/2 cup (4 oz.) salted butter, softened

1 cup granulated sugar

1 1/2 cups (about 5 5/8-oz.) bleached cake flour

2 tsp. baking powder

1/4 tsp. table salt

2/3 cup whole milk

1 1/2 tsp. vanilla extract

3 large egg whites
Shortening, for greasing pan

CREAM CHEESE FROSTING

2 (8-oz.) pkg. cream cheese, softened

1/2 cup (4 oz.) salted butter, softened

1 (32-oz.) pkg. powdered sugar

2 tsp. vanilla extract

1. Prepare the Cheesecake Layers: Preheat oven to 325°F. Line bottom and sides of 2 (9-inch) round pans with aluminum foil, allowing 2 to 3 inches to extend over sides; lightly grease foil. Beat cream cheese and granulated sugar with an electric mixer on medium speed just until completely combined, about 1 minute. Add eggs, sour cream, buttermilk, cocoa, red food coloring, vanilla, and vinegar, beating on low speed just until fully combined, about 4 minutes. (Do not overbeat.) Pour batter into prepared pans.

2. Bake at 325°F for 10 minutes; reduce heat to 300°F, and bake until center is slightly jiggly, about 1 hour and 5 minutes. Turn oven off. Let cheesecake layers stand in oven 30 minutes. Remove cheesecake layers from oven; cool in pans on wire racks 1 hour. Cover and chill 8 hours.

3. Prepare the Vanilla Cake Layer: Preheat oven to 325°F. Beat butter with a heavy-duty stand mixer on medium speed until creamy; gradually add granulated sugar, beating until light and fluffy, about 5 minutes.

4. Stir together flour, baking powder, and salt in a small bowl; add to butter mixture alternately with milk, beginning and ending with flour mixture. Beat on low speed just until blended after each addition. Stir in vanilla.

5. Beat egg whites in a clean bowl with an electric mixer fitted with whisk attachment on high speed until stiff peaks form; fold about one-third of egg whites into batter. Gradually fold in remaining egg whites. Pour batter into 1 greased (with shortening) and floured 9-inch round cake pan.

6. Bake at 325°F until a wooden pick inserted in center comes out clean, 33 to 36 minutes. Cool in pan on a wire rack 10 minutes. Remove from pan to wire rack; cool completely, about 30 minutes.

7. Prepare the Cream Cheese Frosting: Beat cream cheese and butter with an electric mixer on medium speed until creamy, about 5 minutes. Gradually add powdered sugar, beating at low speed until blended after each addition; stir in vanilla. Increase speed to medium, and beat until light and fluffy.

8. Assemble Cake: Lift Cheesecake Layers from pans, using foil sides as handles. Place 1 Cheesecake Layer, bottom side up, on a cake plate. Place Vanilla Cake Layer on Cheesecake Layer. (This layer will be slightly taller than the Cheesecake Layers; trim the top of the layer, if desired). Top Vanilla Cake Layer with the remaining Cheesecake Layer, bottom side up. Spread a thin layer of Cream Cheese Frosting over top and sides of cake to seal in crumbs. Chill cake 20 minutes. Spread remaining frosting over top and sides of cake.

MAKES 1 cake (serving size: 1 slice)
ACTIVE 1 hour, 6 min. **TOTAL** 13 hours, 24 min., including 8 hours chilling

· Garnish How-To ·

MAKE THE CHOCOLATE CURLS:
Slightly soften an 8-oz. bar of white chocolate by heating it in the microwave at 50% power for 10 seconds. Shave the chocolate into large curls using a vegetable peeler. Pile the curls on top of the frosted cake.

COCONUT CAKE WITH RUM FILLING AND COCONUT ERMINE FROSTING

CAKE LAYERS

1 1/2 cups sweetened shredded coconut
1 1/2 cups heavy cream
2 cups granulated sugar
1 1/2 cups (12 oz.) unsalted butter, softened
3 large egg yolks
2 tsp. vanilla extract
4 cups (about 17 oz.) unbleached cake flour
2 tsp. baking powder
1 tsp. baking soda
1/2 tsp. kosher salt
4 large egg whites
  Shortening, for greasing pans

FILLING

1 1/2 cups half-and-half
3/4 cup packed dark brown sugar
6 Tbsp. cornstarch
3 large egg yolks
1/4 cup (2 oz.) unsalted butter
2 Tbsp. dark rum

FROSTING

1 cup granulated sugar
1 cup whole milk
1/2 cup (about 2 1/8 oz.) all-purpose flour
1/2 tsp. kosher salt
2 cups (16 oz.) unsalted butter, softened
1 Tbsp. coconut extract
2 tsp. vanilla extract

1. Prepare the Cake Layers: Pulse shredded coconut in a food processor until finely chopped, about 20 times. Transfer to a small bowl. Heat heavy cream in a small saucepan over medium just until warm and beginning to release steam, about 5 minutes. Pour warmed cream over coconut, and cool completely, about 30 minutes.

2. Preheat oven to 350°F. Beat granulated sugar and butter with an electric mixer on medium speed until light and fluffy, about 2 minutes. Add egg yolks, 1 at a time, and beat until blended after each addition. Add vanilla, and beat just until smooth. Whisk together flour, baking powder, baking soda, and salt in a medium

bowl. Add flour mixture, in batches, alternately with cream mixture, beginning and ending with flour mixture. Beat on low speed just until blended after each addition.

3. Beat egg whites in a clean bowl with an electric mixer fitted with whisk attachment on high speed until stiff peaks form. Stir about one-third of egg whites into batter; fold in remaining egg whites. Pour batter into 4 greased (with shortening) and floured 8-inch round cake pans.

4. Bake in preheated oven until a wooden pick inserted in center comes out clean, 25 to 30 minutes. Cool in pans on wire racks 20 minutes; remove from pans to wire racks, and cool completely, about 30 minutes.

5. Prepare the Filling: Stir together half-and-half, brown sugar, cornstarch, and egg yolks in a small saucepan. Cook over medium-high, whisking constantly, just until mixture thickens and comes to a boil, 10 to 12 minutes. Immediately remove from heat, and whisk in butter and rum until smooth. Transfer to a glass bowl, and place plastic wrap directly on warm custard (to keep a film from forming). Cool completely, about

30 minutes. Chill until ready to use.

6. Prepare the Frosting: Whisk together granulated sugar, milk, flour, and salt in a medium saucepan. Cook over medium, whisking constantly, until mixture thickens, about 10 minutes. Immediately pour mixture into a medium-size metal bowl, and cool completely, about 30 minutes, stirring occasionally.

7. Beat butter with an electric mixer on medium speed until smooth and creamy. Slowly add cooled custard to butter mixture, 1/4 cup at a time, and beat until smooth after each addition. Add coconut extract and vanilla, and beat until smooth. Spoon 1 cup of the Frosting into a zip-top plastic freezer bag with 1 corner snipped or a pastry bag.

8. Assemble Cake: Place 1 Cake Layer on a cake plate, and pipe a 1/2-inch-thick ring of Frosting around the outer edge of the layer. Spread about 2/3 cup of the Filling over the layer. Repeat with second and third Cake Layers. Place the final layer on top, and frost sides and top with remaining Frosting.

MAKES 1 cake (serving size: 1 slice)
ACTIVE 1 hour, 22 min. **TOTAL** 3 hours, 51 min.

• Garnish How-To •

MAKE THE TREE COOKIES: Preheat oven to 350°F. Roll out 1 (18-oz.) pkg. refrigerated sugar cookie dough to 1/8-inch-thickness. Use 1 3/4-inch and 2 3/4-inch tree-shaped cookie cutters to create about 18 small cookies. Use 2 3/4-inch, 4-inch, and 5 1/2-inch tree-shaped cookie cutters to make about 5 large cookies. Bake the cookies at 350°F for 7 to 9 minutes. Let the cookies cool completely on a wire rack.

DECORATE THE TREE COOKIES: To make Royal Icing, beat 16 oz. powdered sugar, 2 tsp. meringue powder, and 5 to 6 Tbsp. warm water with an electric mixer on high speed 5 minutes or until glossy. Pipe the icing onto the cooled cookies. Top with white coarse sanding sugar and white Disco Dust.

EMBELLISH THE CAKE: Drag a 1-inch-wide spatula up and down the sides of the frosted cake to create ridges. Arrange the large tree cookies on the top of the cake. Press the small tree cookies into the sides of the cake. Top the cake with 1/2 cup shredded sweetened coconut flakes for "snow."

WHITE CHOCOLATE POINSETTIA CAKE

CAKE LAYERS

- 1 (4-oz.) white chocolate baking bar, chopped
- 1 cup boiling water
- 1 3/4 cups granulated sugar
- 1 1/4 cups (10 oz.) salted butter, softened
- 7 large egg whites, at room temperature, lightly beaten
- 3 1/2 cups (about 13 1/8 oz.) bleached cake flour
- 4 tsp. baking powder
- 1/4 tsp. table salt
- 2 tsp. vanilla bean paste
  Shortening, for greasing pans

WHITE CHOCOLATE MOUSSE FILLING

- 1 cup white chocolate morsels
- 1 1/4 cups heavy cream, divided
- 1 Tbsp. crème de cacao

FROSTING

- 1 (4-oz.) white chocolate baking bar, chopped
- 1/3 cup heavy cream
- 1 cup (8 oz.) salted butter, softened
- 1 (32-oz.) pkg. powdered sugar
- 1/4 cup heavy cream
- 1/8 tsp. table salt
- 2 tsp. vanilla extract

1. Prepare the Cake: Place white chocolate in a small bowl. Pour boiling water over chocolate, and let stand 1 minute. Stir mixture until chocolate is melted and smooth. Cool completely, about 20 minutes.

2. Preheat oven to 350°F. Beat granulated sugar and butter with a heavy-duty stand mixer on medium speed until light and fluffy, about 5 minutes. Gradually add egg whites, one-third at a time, beating well after each addition.

3. Sift together cake flour, baking powder, and salt; add to butter mixture alternately with white chocolate mixture, beginning and ending with flour mixture. Beat on low speed just until blended after each addition. Stir in vanilla bean paste. Pour batter into 3 greased (with shortening) and floured 9-inch round cake pans.

4. Bake in preheated oven until a wooden pick inserted in center comes out clean, 22 to 25 minutes. Cool in pans on wire racks 10 minutes; remove from pans to wire racks, and cool completely, about 30 minutes.

5. Prepare the Mousse Filling: Microwave white chocolate morsels and 1/4 cup of the heavy cream in a small microwave-safe glass bowl on MEDIUM (50% power) until melted and smooth, 1 1/2 to 2 minutes, stirring every 30 seconds. Stir in crème de cacao. Cool 5 minutes.

6. Beat remaining 1 cup cream with an electric mixer on medium speed until soft peaks form; fold cream into white chocolate mixture. Chill while preparing frosting.

7. Prepare the Frosting: Microwave chopped chocolate and 1/3 cup heavy cream in a microwave-safe bowl on MEDIUM (50% power) until melted and smooth, 1 to 1 1/2 minutes, stirring every 30 seconds. (Do not overheat.) Cool completely, about 20 minutes.

8. Beat butter with an electric mixer on medium speed until creamy; gradually add powdered sugar beating on low speed until blended after each addition. Add 1/4 cup heavy cream, 1 tablespoon at a time, beating on low speed until blended after each addition. Add salt and white chocolate mixture, and beat on low speed until combined; increase speed to high, and beat until light and fluffy. Stir in vanilla.

9. Assemble the Cake: Place 1 Cake Layer on a serving plate. Pipe a 1/2-inch-thick ring of Frosting around edge of Cake Layer. Spread half of White Chocolate Mousse Filling inside Frosting border; top with 1 Cake Layer. Pipe a 1/2-inch-thick ring of Frosting around edge of Cake Layer. Spread remaining White Chocolate Mousse Filling inside Frosting border. Place remaining Cake Layer on top, and spread top and sides of cake with remaining Frosting.

MAKES 1 cake (serving size: 1 slice)
ACTIVE 52 min. **TOTAL** 2 hours, 37 min.

• Garnish How-To •

MAKE THE POINSETTIA COOKIES: Preheat the oven to 350°F. Roll out 1 (18-oz.) pkg. refrigerated sugar cookie dough to 1/8-inch-thickness. Cut the dough into 12 petals using a 3-inch leaf cookie cutter. Cut 3 small petals from dough using a 2-inch leaf cutter and the center of the poinsettia using a 1 1/2-inch flower cutter. Bake the cookies at 350°F for 7 to 9 minutes.

DECORATE THE COOKIES: To make Royal Icing, beat 16 oz. powdered sugar, 2 tsp. meringue powder, and 5 to 6 Tbsp. warm water with an electric mixer at high speed 5 minutes. Pipe the icing onto the cooled cookies. Top the center poinsettia cookie with gold dragées, if desired. (Remove before eating.) Let the cookies dry. Use a paintbrush to paint the cookies with edible ivory luster dust and gold luster dust.

FROST THE CAKE: Make another batch of Frosting. Spoon it into a zip-top plastic bag, and snip 1 corner of the bag. Pipe a column of 4 (1-inch) dots of frosting down the side of the frosted cake. (The dots should touch.) Place a 1-inch-wide spatula on the center of the first dot, and drag the frosting outward, creating a petal-like shape. Repeat with the remaining 3 dots, wiping the spatula clean. Pipe a second column of dots on top of the swiped edges, and drag the frosting outward. Repeat, covering the cake, ending with 1 column of dots.

PEPPERMINT CAKE WITH SEVEN-MINUTE FROSTING

CAKE LAYERS

2   cups granulated sugar
1 1/4 cups (10 oz.) unsalted butter, softened
4   large eggs
2   Tbsp. vanilla extract
4   cups (about 17 oz.) unbleached cake flour
1   Tbsp. baking powder
1/2 tsp. baking soda
1/2 tsp. kosher salt
1   cup whole milk
    Shortening, for greasing pans

PEPPERMINT BUTTERCREAM

3   cups (about 12 oz.) powdered sugar
1   cup (8 oz.) unsalted butter, softened
1/2 cup finely crushed hard peppermint candies (about 20 candies)
1   tsp. vanilla extract
1/2 tsp. kosher salt
1   to 2 tsp. whole milk
2   to 3 drops of liquid red food coloring

SEVEN-MINUTE FROSTING

12   large egg whites

3   cups granulated sugar
3   Tbsp. corn syrup
1   tsp. kosher salt
1/2 tsp. peppermint extract

1. Prepare the Cake Layers: Preheat oven to 350°F. Beat granulated sugar and butter with an electric mixer on medium speed until light and fluffy, about 2 minutes. Add eggs, 1 at a time, and beat just until combined after each addition. Add vanilla, and beat just until combined. Whisk together flour, baking powder, baking soda, and salt in a medium bowl. Add flour mixture, in batches, alternately with milk, beginning and ending with flour mixture. Beat on low speed just until blended after each addition. Pour batter into 2 greased (with shortening) and floured 9-inch round cake pans.
2. Bake in preheated oven until a wooden pick inserted in center comes out clean, 28 to 30 minutes. Cool in pans on wire racks 20 minutes; remove from pans to wire racks, and cool completely, about 30 minutes.
3. Prepare the Peppermint Buttercream: Beat powdered sugar and butter with electric mixer on medium speed until smooth, about 2 minutes. Add crushed peppermints, vanilla, and salt; beat until blended. Beat in 1

teaspoon of the milk. Beat in up to 1 more teaspoon of milk, 1/4 teaspoon at a time, until desired consistency is reached. Beat in food coloring, 1 drop at a time, until desired color is reached.
4. Prepare the Seven-Minute Frosting: Pour water to a depth of 2 inches into bottom of a saucepan or double boiler; bring to a simmer over medium. Stir together egg whites, granulated sugar, corn syrup, and salt in a heatproof bowl or top of double boiler. Place bowl over simmering water, and whisk constantly until sugar dissolves and mixture is hot, about 7 minutes. Remove from heat, and beat with an electric mixer on medium-high until stiff peaks form and mixture is completely cooled, about 10 minutes. Beat in peppermint extract.
5. Assemble Cake: Place 1 Cake Layer on a cake plate. Spread Peppermint Buttercream in an even layer, about 1/2-inch thick, to within 1/2 inch of cake edge. Top with remaining Cake Layer.
6. Spread cooled Seven-Minute Frosting over top and sides of cake.

MAKES 1 cake (serving size: 1 slice)
ACTIVE 1 hour, 20 min. **TOTAL** 2 hours, 40 min.

· Garnish How-To ·

PREPARE THE CANDY: Roughly crush 1 cup hard peppermint candies into small pieces. Crush an additional 1/4 cup candies into fine pieces and set aside. Add 1 tsp. white Disco Dust (white edible glitter) to 1 cup crushed candy, and stir to combine.

DECORATE THE CAKE: Spoon the remaining Seven-Minute Frosting into a zip-top plastic bag. Snip 1 corner of the bag to make a 1/2-inch-wide hole. Pipe swirls of frosting on the top of the cake. Lightly press the Disco Dust-coated crushed candy into the sides of the frosted cake until the sides of the cake are coated. Sprinkle the piped swirls with the finely crushed candy and an additional 1/2 tsp. Disco Dust.

A Carolina Christmas

THE PAST AND PRESENT INTERTWINE DELICIOUSLY ON NORTH CAROLINA CHEF
VIVIAN HOWARD'S HOLIDAY TABLE

FROM THE VINTAGE TREE TOPPER to the special dinner blessing the whole family knows by heart, Christmas is about tradition—unless you're Vivian Howard. At her two Kinston, North Carolina, restaurants, Chef & the Farmer and Boiler Room, and on her award-winning PBS show "A Chef's Life," Howard has made a name for herself by putting her own stamp on the classic dishes of her native eastern North Carolina. And the holidays are no different.

Throughout her childhood in Deep Run, a tiny farming community near Kinston, Christmas morning meant a hearty breakfast cooked by her mother, Scarlett: grilled sausage on biscuits with muscadine preserves and mustard, a baked egg casserole, creamy grits, and pecan pie, a carryover from Christmas Eve dinner. "It's the least exciting of all the pies my mom made, so we would save it for breakfast," Howard explains.

Now Howard is the one cooking her family's Christmas meal (winning a James Beard Award will do that for you). It's still breakfast—but with a few unexpected twists. She shares several of these recipes in her new cookbook, *Deep Run Roots,* including baked eggs with crispy ham chips and tangy stewed tomatoes, and grits and greens topped with a simple but delicious brown butter-hot sauce vinaigrette.

These updated family favorites have gone over well with her crowd. She's kept the pecan pie and the sausage biscuits to satisfy the traditionalists, but she can't help making the biscuits from scratch rather than from a can, the way her mother did. "Now that I do the cooking, I make a lot in advance so I can throw it in the oven and

Home for the Holidays
Vivian Howard in her modern farm-house kitchen in Deep Run, NC.

spend more time with everyone that morning," Howard says.

The Christmas meal may be breakfast, but the holiday fun doesn't start there. Howard's five-year-old twins, Theo and Flo, ensure that she and her husband, artist Ben Knight, are up very early to exchange gifts around the tree. Then it's time to load up the presents and head out for the traveling gift exchange at "Howardville," as the family calls it. First, they head next door to Howard's parents' house. Next stop is Howard's sister's house up the road, then across the street to her childhood home, where out-of-town family stays. When everyone's ready to eat, the festivities wind their way back to Howard's modern farmhouse, a symbol of her ability to merge the past with the present.

Having a tight-knit family is something Howard appreciates all year long but especially at Christmastime. "I love that we're able to hop from house to house," she says. "I hope my kids understand how lucky they are to live somewhere where they have their whole family around them. I hope they feel the warmth of their family and how special it is." It's one tradition she has no desire to change.

GRITS AND GREENS WITH BROWN BUTTER HOT SAUCE

You can substitute any hearty winter green you like but don't skip the hot and tangy vinaigrette—it makes the dish.

GRITS AND GREENS

- 3 1/4 cups whole milk
- 1 cup uncooked stone-ground grits
- 2 Tbsp. salted butter, divided
- 2 1/2 tsp. table salt, divided
- 1 lb. fresh turnip greens
- 2 Tbsp. olive oil
- 4 garlic cloves, minced
- 1/4 tsp. crushed red pepper
- 4 oz. Parmigiano-Reggiano cheese, grated (about 1 cup)
- 1 cup chicken stock
- 1 tsp. black pepper

BROWN BUTTER HOT SAUCE

- 4 Tbsp. salted butter
- 2 Tbsp. fresh lemon juice (from 1 lemon)
- 1 Tbsp. Tabasco hot sauce
- 1/4 tsp. table salt

Grits and Greens with Brown Butter Hot Sauce

1. Prepare the Grits and Greens: Stir together milk and grits in a double boiler. Using a small wire-mesh strainer, skim any hulls that float to the top of the milk. (This ensures there will be no hard bits in your creamy finished product.) Cook over medium-high, whisking often to ensure grits don't stick to sides and bottom of pan, until milk is completely absorbed and grits are thickened and tender, 25 to 40 minutes. Stir in 1 tablespoon of the butter and 1 1/2 teaspoons of the salt. Remove from heat.
2. Preheat oven to 400°F. Cut and discard tough ends from turnip greens, and slice stems and leaves into 1 1/2-inch pieces. Heat oil and remaining 1 tablespoon butter in a 12-inch cast-iron skillet until butter melts. Add garlic, and cook, stirring occasionally, just until garlic starts to sizzle. (Be careful garlic does not start to turn brown and burn.) Add greens, crushed red pepper, and remaining 1 teaspoon salt. Using tongs, toss greens until they are just wilted. Add greens mixture and any accumulated liquids to grits in double boiler. Add cheese, stock, and black pepper; stir to combine.
3. Spoon grits mixture into the same skillet (do not wipe skillet clean). Bake in preheated oven, uncovered, until set, about 30 minutes.
4. Prepare the Hot Sauce: Melt butter in an 8-inch skillet over medium until it starts to foam and turn slightly brown. Stir butter to distribute evenly on bottom of skillet, and cook, undisturbed, until butter browns and smells nutty. Stir in lemon juice, Tabasco, and salt. Cook, undisturbed, until bubbly, about 15 seconds. Spoon hot vinaigrette over baked grits.

SERVES 4 (serving size: about 1 cup)
ACTIVE 16 min. **TOTAL** 1 hour, 21 min.

AMBROSIA BREAKFAST

"Ambrosia is the cranberry sauce of the Christmas table," Howard says. "We always have a ton of citrus at Christmas because the high schools sell boxes of oranges around this time."

PEANUT CRUMBLE

- 1 1/4 cups salted roasted peanuts, roughly chopped

- 1 cup uncooked regular rolled oats
- 1/2 cup unsweetened shredded coconut
- 1 large egg white
- 1/4 cup granulated sugar
- 1/4 cup unrefined coconut oil, melted
- 1 tsp. Madras curry powder
- 1 tsp. ground coriander
- 1/2 tsp. cayenne pepper
- 1/2 tsp. table salt

YOGURT AND FRUIT

- 1 qt. plain Greek yogurt
- 3 Tbsp. cream of coconut (such as Coco López)
- 2 Tbsp. orange zest (from 1 orange)
- 2 oranges
- 1 tangerine
- 1 grapefruit
- 1/2 cup pomegranate arils

1. Prepare the Peanut Crumble: Preheat oven to 300°F. Stir together peanuts, oats, and shredded coconut in a large bowl. Whisk egg white in a separate bowl until frothy. Add sugar, coconut oil, curry powder, coriander, cayenne, and salt to egg white; whisk until combined. Pour egg white

Ambrosia Breakfast: Citrus and Pomegranate with Coconut Yogurt and Peanut Crumble

mixture over peanut mixture; stir well to combine. Spread in a thin layer on a large rimmed baking sheet lined with parchment paper. Bake in preheated oven until golden brown, fragrant, and caramelized on bottom, about 50 minutes. Let cool completely; crumble into pieces. (This is by no means just for breakfast. It's a go-to snack and is delicious sprinkled on salads.)

2. Prepare the Yogurt and Fruit: Stir together the yogurt, cream of coconut, and zest in a bowl; set aside. Cut a 1/4-inch-thick slice from each end of oranges, tangerine, and grapefruit using a serrated paring knife. Place fruit, cut side down, on a cutting board. Peel fruit; cut away bitter white pith. Slice each fruit between membranes, and gently remove whole segments, holding fruit over a bowl to collect juices. Discard membranes and seeds. Stir up to 1/2 cup citrus juice into yogurt mixture until mixture reaches desired consistency.

3. Divide yogurt mixture evenly among 6 bowls, and top evenly with citrus segments, peanut crumble, and pomegranate arils.

SERVES 6 (serving size: 2/3 cup yogurt, 1/2 cup crumble, 1/3 cup fruit) **ACTIVE** 18 min. **TOTAL** 1 hour, 8 min.

PECAN-CHEWY PIE

CRUST AND STREUSEL

- 1 1/4 cups (about 5 3/8 oz.) all-purpose flour
- 1 cup granulated sugar
- 5 Tbsp. cold butter, divided
- 2 cups very finely chopped pecans
- 1 Tbsp. cold water
- 1 large egg, beaten

CHEWY PECAN FILLING

- 1 cup white chocolate morsels
- 1/2 cup (4 oz.) salted butter
- 1/2 cup dark brown sugar
- 4 large egg yolks, at room temperature
- 1 cup heavy cream, at room temperature
- 1 1/2 cups roughly chopped toasted pecans
- 2/3 cup (about 2 7/8 oz.) all-purpose flour
- 1 tsp. table salt

ADDITIONAL INGREDIENT

Ice cream

1. Prepare the Crust and Streusel: Preheat oven to 350°F. Stir together flour and granulated sugar in a medium bowl. Using a fork or pastry cutter, cut 4 tablespoons of the butter into flour mixture until it resembles small pebbles. Stir in pecans, water, and egg until mixture is damp. Grease 2 (9-inch) pie pans with remaining 1 tablespoon butter. Divide pecan mixture into thirds. Place 1/3 mixture into each prepared pie pan, pressing to cover bottom and sides of pans. Set aside remaining 1/3 mixture. Bake crusts on middle rack of oven until the edges are lightly browned, about 10 minutes. Cool 10 minutes.

2. Prepare the Filling: Melt white chocolate morsels and butter in a double boiler over low. (It's OK if mixture separates.) Whisk together brown sugar and egg yolks in a medium bowl until thoroughly combined. Pour white chocolate mixture into brown sugar mixture; whisk to combine. Whisk in heavy cream. Stir together pecans, flour, and salt in a small bowl. Fold pecan mixture into white chocolate mixture just until incorporated.

3. Reduce oven temperature to 325°F. Divide filling mixture evenly between

2 piecrusts. Sprinkle remaining 1/3 cup streusel mixture evenly over pies. Bake until golden brown and set, about 35 minutes. Serve warm or at room temperature with ice cream. Pies will keep 3 days covered with plastic wrap.

MAKES 2 (9-inch) pies **ACTIVE** 35 min. **TOTAL** 1 hour, 10 min.

STEWED TOMATO SHIRRED EGGS WITH HAM CHIPS

STEWED TOMATOES

- 2 Tbsp. salted butter
- 2 cups finely chopped yellow onion (from 1 large onion)
- 1 tsp. table salt
- 8 cups diced fresh tomatoes, with their juices (about 3 1/2 lb. tomatoes)
- 1/4 cup packed fresh basil leaves, chopped
- 2 Tbsp. light brown sugar
- 1 Tbsp. red wine vinegar
- 4 garlic cloves, sliced or minced
- 1/4 tsp. crushed red pepper
- 1/2 cup soft, fresh breadcrumbs

ADDITIONAL INGREDIENTS

- 8 thin country ham or prosciutto slices (about 4 oz.)
- 6 large eggs
- 1/2 tsp. table salt
- 1/2 tsp. black pepper
  Fresh basil, flat-leaf parsley, or chervil leaves
  Crusty bread (optional)

1. Prepare the Stewed Tomatoes: Melt butter in a 3- to 6-quart heavy saucepan or Dutch oven over medium. Add onions and salt; cook, stirring occasionally, until slightly caramelized, about 10 minutes. Stir in tomatoes, chopped basil, brown sugar, vinegar, garlic, and crushed red pepper. Cover and increase heat to medium-high; bring to a boil. Reduce heat to medium-low, and simmer 30 minutes. Uncover and cook 10 minutes. Stir in breadcrumbs, and cook until tomato mixture is slightly thickened, about 5 minutes. Proceed with recipe as directed, or chill overnight in an airtight container. (Stewed Tomatoes are best the next day.) If chilling overnight, bring to a

Sausage-Stuffed Honey Buns

simmer before proceeding with recipe.

2. Preheat oven to 350°F. Place ham slices in a single layer on a parchment paper-lined baking sheet; top with another piece of parchment paper. Place a second baking sheet on top of parchment to weigh it down. Bake on middle rack in preheated oven until ham is crisp and brown, 12 to 15 minutes. Cool to room temperature. (Ham will continue to crisp as it cools.) Remove and discard parchment; store ham chips in an airtight container up to 2 days.

3. Spoon simmering Stewed Tomatoes into a greased large shallow baking dish or ovenproof 12-inch skillet. Using the back of a spoon, press 6 evenly spaced indentations in Stewed Tomatoes. Crack eggs, and slide 1 egg into each indentation. Sprinkle eggs evenly with salt and black pepper. Bake at 350°F on middle rack until whites are a little jiggly and yolks are barely set, 12 to 15 minutes.

4. Divide eggs and Stewed Tomatoes evenly among 4 bowls. Top evenly with herbs. Stand ham chips upright in bowls. Serve with crusty bread, if desired.

Note: You can substitute canned tomatoes in lieu of fresh.

SERVES 4 (serving size: 1 ½ cups tomato mixture, 1 ½ eggs, 2 prosciutto slices) **ACTIVE** 41 min. **TOTAL** 1 hour, 36 min.

SAUSAGE-STUFFED HONEY BUNS

HONEY GLAZE

- ³/₄ cup (6 oz.) salted butter
- 1 cup honey
- ¹/₃ cup corn syrup
- 2 Tbsp. granulated sugar
- 2 Tbsp. orange zest plus ¹/₂ cup fresh juice (from 1 orange)
- 2 thyme sprigs

SAUSAGE FILLING

- 1 lb. ground pork sausage (such as Jimmy Dean)
- ¹/₂ cup (4 oz.) butter, at room temperature
- ¹/₂ cup honey
- ¹/₄ cup dark brown sugar

BUN DOUGH

- 1 ¹/₄ cups whole milk
- ¹/₄ cup warm water
- 1 (¹/₄-oz.) envelope active dry yeast (2 ¹/₄ tsp.)
- 1 ¹/₂ tsp. table salt
- 5 cups (about 21 ¹/₄ oz.) all-purpose flour, divided
- ²/₃ cup, plus 1 Tbsp. granulated sugar, divided
- ¹/₂ cup shortening
- 2 large eggs

1. Prepare the Honey Glaze: Melt butter in a 2- to 3-quart saucepan over medium. Stir in honey, corn syrup, granulated sugar, orange zest, orange juice, and thyme. Increase heat to medium-high, and bring to a boil; cook 1 minute. Remove from heat, and set aside. (Glaze may be refrigerated in an airtight container up to 1 week.)

2. Prepare the Sausage Filling: Cook sausage in a 12-inch cast-iron skillet over medium, stirring to crumble, until browned and done. Remove from heat; drain well. Beat butter, honey, and brown sugar with a heavy-duty electric stand mixer fitted with the paddle attachment on medium speed until incorporated. Add sausage, and beat until incorporated. Set aside. (Filling may be refrigerated in an airtight container up to 3 days. Bring to room temperature before proceeding with recipe.)

3. Prepare the Bun Dough: Heat milk in a 3-quart saucepan over medium until bubbles begin to form around the edge of pan. Remove from heat. Combine warm water and yeast in a

1-cup measuring cup. Let stand 10 minutes. Add yeast mixture, salt, 2 cups of the flour, and 1 tablespoon of the granulated sugar to warm milk; stir until relatively smooth. Place mixture in a warm place (85°F) until bubbly, 10 to 15 minutes.

4. Meanwhile, beat shortening with a heavy-duty electric mixer fitted with the paddle attachment on medium-high speed until fluffy. Add remaining ²/₃ cup granulated sugar; beat until combined. Add eggs, 1 at a time, beating just until blended after each addition. With mixer on low, gradually add bubbly yeast mixture to shortening mixture until fully incorporated. Add remaining 3 cups flour, in 4 batches, beating just until blended after each addition. Replace the paddle attachment with the dough hook; beat dough on medium speed until smooth, 10 to 12 minutes.

5. Turn dough out onto a floured work surface; knead until very smooth, about 2 minutes. Transfer dough to a lightly oiled bowl; cover with plastic wrap. Let stand in a warm place (85°F) until dough doubles in size, about 1 hour.

6. Place 2 ¹/₂ cups of the Honey Glaze in a 12-inch cast-iron skillet. Place dough on a lightly floured surface; punch dough down, and divide in half. Roll 1 dough half out into a 10- x 8-inch rectangle. Spread half of the Sausage Filling over dough rectangle, leaving a 1-inch border. Starting from 1 long side, roll dough up to enclose filling. Place dough cylinder seam side down; cut off and discard 2 short ends to create smooth ends. Cut cylinder crosswise into 4 to 5 (1 ¹/₂-inch-thick) rounds. Starting in center of skillet and working outward, place rounds, cut side down, on Honey Glaze in skillet. Repeat process. Place skillet in a warm place (85°F); let stand until dough rounds have plumped up and press against each other, 20 to 30 minutes.

7. Preheat oven to 375°F. Bake honey buns on middle oven rack until golden brown on top, 55 minutes to 1 hour. (If buns are getting too brown, cover with aluminum foil after baking 30 minutes.)

8. Carefully invert honey buns onto a serving platter. Serve warm or at room temperature, drizzled with remaining Honey Glaze.

SERVES 10 (serving size: 1 honey bun) **ACTIVE** 1 hour, 8 min. **TOTAL** 3 hours, 3 min.

THE SOUTHERN LIVING

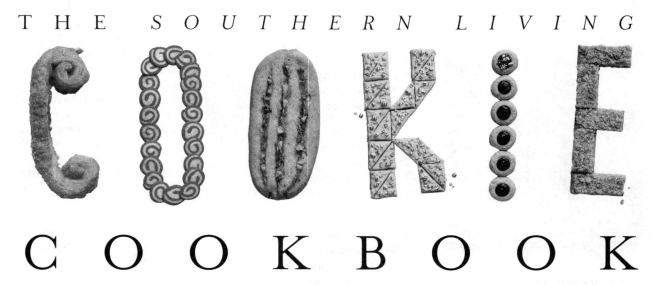

COOKBOOK

BREAK OUT THE COOKIE TINS! WE'VE GOT 30 DELIGHTFULLY DELICIOUS CHRISTMAS COOKIES TO SHARE WITH FRIENDS AND FAMILY—AND SANTA, OF COURSE. TAKE YOUR PICK FROM SLICE-AND-BAKE, CUTOUTS, SANDWICH COOKIES, AND MORE

THEY SAY THE WAY TO A MAN'S HEART is through his stomach, and Saint Nick is no exception to the rule … he just happens to have a sweet tooth. But it's not a slice of coconut cake or buttermilk pie we leave out in his honor; when Christmas Eve rolls around, only a cookie will do. And what better gift for the elf who has it all? Cookies are small but mighty, encompassing a range of flavors and traditions as diverse as the South.

Whether thick and chewy or thin and crisp, Christmas cookies are something Southerners do particularly well. Maybe it's our appreciation for White Lily flour or our steadfast refusal to skimp on fresh butter; maybe it's because we keep a bag of fat pecans at the ready or that we've got the best sorghum and molasses in the world. Then again, maybe it's the wild blackberries and scuppernongs we turn into jam or that we count cookie cutters and rolling pins among our most precious family heirlooms.

In my family, Christmas cookies were a herald of the season, appearing in my Kentucky home as soon as we'd recovered from Thanksgiving. I can remember being small enough to sit on the kitchen counter, dunking spoonfuls of sticky dough into a dish of cane sugar, then graduating to jammy thumbprint cookies, frosted gingerbread men, and ever more elaborate creations from year to year.

The recipes my brother and I tackled invariably came from *Southern Living* and the infinite back issues Momma kept in wicker baskets by her reading chair. She made no effort to protect them from our messy hands, and today they're a batter-stained, cinnamon-scented, chocolate-splattered testament to holidays spent together in the kitchen.

Which is why I'm so excited to find myself within these very pages to introduce this year's Christmas cookie feature—a collection of memories in the making. With six categories of treats, from laid-back bars to frosted cutouts with a decidedly artistic flair, these recipes offer something for every baker.

—Stella Parks

~BAR~

WHITE CHOCOLATE-PEPPERMINT BLONDIES

We gave the classic blondie a Christmas makeover with peppermints and minty icing.

BLONDIES
- 1 cup (8 oz.) salted butter, softened, plus more for greasing pan
- 1 cup granulated sugar
- 2 large eggs
- 2 tsp. vanilla extract
- 1/2 tsp. table salt
- 2 1/4 cups (about 9 5/8 oz.) all-purpose flour
- 1/2 cup white chocolate morsels
- 1 cup coarsely crushed peppermint candies (about 40 candies), divided

ICING
- 2 cups (about 8 oz.) powdered sugar
- 1/4 cup salted butter, softened
- 1 tsp. vanilla extract
- 1/4 tsp. peppermint extract
- 2 to 3 Tbsp. heavy cream

1. Preheat oven to 350°F. Grease a 13- x 9-inch baking pan with butter. Line pan with parchment paper, allowing parchment to extend over sides of pan. Grease paper.

2. Prepare the Blondies: Combine butter and granulated sugar in a large bowl. Beat with an electric mixer on medium speed until well combined, about 3 minutes. Add eggs, 1 at a time, beating until combined after each addition. Beat in vanilla and salt. Add flour; beat on low speed just until combined, 1 to 2 minutes. Stir in white chocolate morsels and 1/2 cup of the crushed peppermints, reserving remaining crushed peppermints to sprinkle on top.

3. Spread batter in prepared pan; smooth top with a spatula. Bake in preheated oven until a wooden pick inserted in center comes out clean, 20 to 22 minutes. Cool completely in pan. Lift blondies from pan using parchment paper as handles. Remove and discard paper; trim browned edges.

4. Prepare the Icing: Combine powdered sugar, butter, vanilla, and peppermint extract in a medium bowl; beat on medium speed until smooth. Beat in 2 tablespoons of the cream. Add up to 1 additional tablespoon cream, if necessary, until Icing reaches a spreadable consistency. Spread Icing over top of Blondies. Sprinkle with reserved crushed peppermints. Cut into 3-inch squares; cut squares into triangles.

MAKES about 4 1/2 dozen (serving size: 1 triangle)
ACTIVE 20 min. **TOTAL** 1 hour, 40 min.

NO-BAKE FUDGY TOFFEE BARS

These rich and gooey bars will be your new favorite no-bake cookie this holiday season and beyond.

- Salted butter for greasing pan
- 1 1/2 cups heavy cream
- 3 Tbsp. powdered sugar
- 3 (4-oz.) semisweet chocolate baking bars, finely chopped
- 1 tsp. vanilla extract
- 2 (11-oz.) pkg. caramels
- 1/3 cup evaporated milk
- 17 graham cracker sheets
- 2 (1.4-oz.) chocolate-covered toffee candy bars (such as Heath), coarsely chopped

1. Line a 9-inch square baking pan with parchment paper, allowing parchment to extend over sides of pan. Grease paper with butter.

White Chocolate-Peppermint Blondies

2. Combine heavy cream and powdered sugar in a small saucepan. Bring to a simmer over medium-low, stirring occasionally. (Do not bring to a boil.) Place chopped chocolate in a medium bowl. Pour cream mixture over chocolate; let stand 1 minute. Gently stir mixture until chocolate melts and mixture is smooth. Stir in vanilla.

3. Combine caramels and evaporated milk in a medium saucepan over medium-low. Cook, stirring often, until caramels melt and mixture is smooth, 9 to 10 minutes. Remove from heat; let stand 10 minutes.

4. Place 1 layer of graham cracker sheets in bottom of prepared pan, breaking crackers to fit as needed. Pour one-third of the caramel mixture over crackers. Using an offset spatula, smooth caramel to edges of pan. Pour one-third chocolate mixture over caramel; smooth chocolate to edges of pan. Repeat layers 2 times with remaining graham cracker sheets, caramel mixture, and chocolate mixture, ending with chocolate. Sprinkle chopped toffee candy bars over top. Chill, uncovered, 4 hours or overnight.

5. Lift toffee bar mixture from pan using parchment as handles. Trim edges if necessary. Cut into 16 pieces. Serve chilled.

SERVES 16 (serving size: 1 piece)
ACTIVE 30 min. **TOTAL** 4 hours, 30 min., including 4 hours chilling

LEMON CRUMBLE BARS

Lemon bars are always a crowd-pleaser, and they'll be even more popular when topped with a sweet oat crumble.

COOKIE BASE
- 1 1/4 cups (about 5 3/8 oz.) all-purpose flour
- 1/2 cup (about 2 oz.) powdered sugar
- 1/4 tsp. table salt
- 10 Tbsp. (5 oz.) cold salted butter, cut into 1/2-inch pieces, plus more for greasing pan

FILLING
- 1 cup granulated sugar
- 2/3 cup fresh lemon juice (from about 4 lemons)

1/4 cup cornstarch
1/4 tsp. table salt
2 large eggs
2 large egg yolks
1 Tbsp. salted butter

TOPPING

1/2 cup (about 2 1/8 oz.) all-purpose flour
3 Tbsp. powdered sugar
2 tsp. lemon zest
1/8 tsp. table salt
3/8 cup (3 oz.) salted butter
1/2 cup uncooked regular rolled oats

1. Prepare the Cookie Base: Preheat oven to 350°F. Grease an 8-inch square baking pan with butter. Line pan with parchment paper, allowing paper to extend past edges of pan. Grease parchment. Pulse flour, powdered sugar, and salt in a food processor until combined, about 3 times. Add butter; pulse until mixture resembles coarse sand, 6 to 7 times. Press flour mixture into prepared pan. Bake in preheated oven 15 minutes.
2. Prepare the Filling: Combine granulated sugar, lemon juice, cornstarch, and salt in a medium saucepan; bring to a simmer over medium-high. (Do not bring to a boil.) Lightly beat eggs and yolks in a medium bowl. Add 1/2 cup of the hot sugar mixture to eggs, whisking constantly. Gradually add egg mixture to remaining sugar mixture in saucepan; whisking constantly. Cook, whisking constantly, until thick and bubbly, about 2 minutes. Remove from heat. Stir in butter until melted and combined. Spread hot filling evenly over prepared cookie base.
3. Prepare the Topping: Pulse flour, powdered sugar, lemon zest, and salt in a food processor until combined, 5 to 6 times. Add butter, pulse until mixture forms pea-sized pieces, 4 to 5 times. Add oats; pulse until combined, 2 to 3 times. Using your hands, press mixture together into small clumps. Sprinkle clumps evenly over filling, pressing lightly to adhere. Bake at 350°F until top is lightly browned, 35 to 40 minutes.

4. Cool completely in pan. Lift Lemon Crumble from pan using parchment as handles. Trim edges, if necessary, and cut into 16 bars.

SERVES 16 (serving size: 1 bar) **ACTIVE** 25 min. **TOTAL** 1 hour

CRANBERRY SHORTBREAD BARS

Freeze the shortbread dough, then grate it in a food processor for the lightest, most tender crust.

1 1/2 cups fresh or frozen cranberries
1/4 cup water
1 cup granulated sugar, divided
3/4 cup (6 oz.) salted butter, softened, plus more for greasing pan
1/4 tsp. table salt
2 large egg yolks
1 tsp. vanilla extract
1 3/4 cups (about 7 1/2 oz.) all-purpose flour

1. Bring cranberries, water, and 1/4 cup of the sugar to a boil in a small saucepan over medium-high. Cook, stirring and smashing berries occasionally, until mixture thickens, 10 to 12 minutes. Remove from heat, and cool completely.
2. Beat butter, salt, and remaining 3/4 cup sugar in a large bowl with an electric mixer on medium speed until light and fluffy, 3 to 5 minutes. Add egg yolks and vanilla; beat on low speed until combined, 1 to 2 minutes. Add flour to butter mixture; beat on low speed just until combined.
3. Turn dough out onto a lightly floured work surface; knead until dough comes together, 3 to 4 times. Shape dough into a 14-inch-long log. Cover with plastic wrap, and freeze at least 1 hour or overnight.
4. Preheat oven to 350°F. Line a 9-inch square baking pan with parchment paper, allowing paper to extend past edges of pan. Grease parchment.
5. Remove plastic wrap from dough; cut dough log in half crosswise, and cut each piece in half lengthwise. Feed dough log quarters through the food chute of a food processor fitted with a shredding blade. Lightly press half of

grated dough into the bottom of prepared pan. Spread cranberry mixture evenly over dough, leaving a 1/2-inch border. Top with remaining half of grated dough, pressing lightly to seal edges.
6. Bake in preheated oven until firm and golden brown, 33 to 35 minutes. Cool completely in pan. Lift cranberry shortbread from pan using parchment as handles. Cut into rectangles; then cut into triangles.

SERVES 24 (serving size: 1 bar)
ACTIVE 20 min. **TOTAL** 2 hours, 5 min.

~CUTOUT~

SPICY MOLASSES GINGERBREAD PEOPLE

We gave the traditional gingerbread cookies a kick with warm spices, orange and lemon zests, and the deep flavor of molasses. The icing is made with meringue powder, which can be found at craft or baking supply stores.

COOKIES

1/4 cup dark molasses
1 large egg
1 large egg yolk
3 1/2 cups (about 14 7/8 oz.) all-purpose flour
1 cup packed light brown sugar
1/2 cup granulated sugar
1 Tbsp. ground ginger
1 Tbsp. lemon zest
2 tsp. orange zest
2 tsp. ground cinnamon
1 tsp. ground cloves
1/2 tsp. table salt
1/2 tsp. baking soda
1 cup (8 oz.) cold salted butter, cut into 1/2-inch pieces

ICING

1 1/2 cups (about 6 oz.) powdered sugar
1 Tbsp. meringue powder
4 to 6 tsp. water

1. Prepare the Cookies: Whisk together molasses, egg, and egg yolk in a small bowl.
2. Process flour, brown sugar, granulated sugar, ginger, lemon zest,

Almond Stars and Chocolate Cutout Cookies

orange zest, cinnamon, cloves, salt, and baking soda in a food processor until well combined, about 1 minute. Add butter; pulse until mixture resembles coarse sand, 5 to 6 times. Add molasses mixture; pulse until mixture begins to clump, 5 to 6 times.
3. Turn mixture out onto a lightly floured work surface, and knead until mixture comes together, 5 to 6 times. Divide dough in half; shape each half into a 4-inch disk. Wrap each disk in plastic wrap, and chill 1 hour or up to 2 days.
4. Preheat oven to 350°F. Unwrap 1 dough disk, and roll to 1/4-inch thickness on a lightly floured surface. Cut with a 5- x 3-inch cookie cutter, rerolling scraps once. Place 1 inch apart on parchment paper-lined baking sheets.
5. Bake in preheated oven until set, 11 to 12 minutes, switching pans top rack to bottom rack halfway through baking. Cool on pans 2 minutes; remove cookies to wire racks, and cool completely, about 30 minutes. Repeat with remaining dough disk.
6. Prepare the Icing: Beat powdered sugar, meringue powder, and 4 teaspoons of the water on medium speed in a medium bowl until well combined, 4 to 5 minutes. Add up to 2 teaspoons water, 1/4 teaspoon at a time, and beat until desired consistency is reached. Spread icing on cookies, and decorate as desired.

MAKES about 2 1/2 dozen cookies (serving size: 1 cookie) **ACTIVE** 30 min. **TOTAL** 2 hours, 10 min.

SOFT SUGAR COOKIE TREES

These tender cookies are even better when topped with cream cheese frosting. The dough can be made up to 2 days ahead and will be easier to roll out when it is very cold.

COOKIES

- 1 cup (8 oz.) salted butter, softened
- 1 1/2 cups (about 6 oz.) powdered sugar
- 1 large egg
- 1 large egg yolk
- 2 tsp. vanilla extract
- 2 1/2 cups (about 9 3/8 oz.) cake flour
- 1/4 tsp. baking powder
- 1/4 tsp. table salt

ICING

- 1 (4-oz.) pkg. cream cheese, softened
- 1/4 cup salted butter, softened
- 2 1/2 cups (about 10 oz.) powdered sugar
- 1/2 tsp. vanilla extract
- 1/4 tsp. table salt

ADDITIONAL INGREDIENT

Green sparkling sugar

1. Prepare the Cookies: Beat butter with an electric mixer on medium-low speed until creamy. Add powdered sugar, egg, egg yolk, and vanilla; beat on medium speed until light and fluffy, about 5 minutes.
2. Whisk together flour, baking powder, and salt in a bowl. Add flour mixture to butter mixture; beat on low speed until combined, about 2 minutes. (Dough will be very soft and sticky.)
3. Transfer half of dough onto plastic wrap, and wrap tightly, shaping into a 4-inch disk. Repeat process with remaining half of dough. Chill 2 to 12 hours.
4. Preheat oven to 350°F. Unwrap 1 dough disk, and roll to 1/4-inch thickness on a lightly floured surface. Cut with a 5- x 3 1/2-inch tree-shaped cutter, rerolling scraps once. Place cookies, 2 inches apart, on parchment paper-lined baking sheets.
5. Bake in preheated oven until set, 8 to 9 minutes, switching pans top rack to bottom rack halfway through baking. (Cookies should not brown.) Cool on pans 2 minutes. Remove cookies to wire racks, and cool completely, about 30 minutes. Repeat process with remaining dough disk.
6. Prepare the Icing: Beat cream cheese and butter on medium speed until well combined and smooth, about 2 minutes. Add powdered sugar, vanilla, and salt; beat on medium-low speed until smooth, about 3 minutes. Add sour cream, and beat until incorporated.
7. Spread icing over cookies, and sprinkle with sparkling sugar.

MAKES about 1 1/2 dozen cookies (serving size: 1 cookie) **ACTIVE** 30 min. **TOTAL** 3 hours.

CHOCOLATE CUTOUT COOKIES

Cutout cookies don't have to be vanilla! Try a dark chocolate version this year. Be sure to dust your cutting board with cocoa powder.

COOKIES

- 3/4 cup (6 oz.) salted butter
- 1/2 (4-oz.) 60% cacao bittersweet chocolate baking bar, finely chopped
- 2 (1-oz.) unsweetened chocolate baking squares, finely chopped
- 1 cup granulated sugar
- 1 cup packed light brown sugar
- 2 large eggs
- 1 tsp. vanilla extract
- 1 1/2 cups (about 6 3/8 oz.) all-purpose flour
- 1 tsp. baking soda
- 1/2 tsp. table salt
- 1 cup unsweetened cocoa, divided

ICING

- 1 1/2 cups (about 6 oz.) powdered sugar
- 1 Tbsp. meringue powder
- 4 to 5 tsp. water
  Red liquid food coloring
  Green liquid food coloring

ADDITIONAL INGREDIENTS

Red sparkling sugar
Green sparkling sugar

1. Prepare the Cookies: Combine butter, bittersweet chocolate, and unsweetened chocolate in a microwave-safe bowl, and microwave on HIGH until chocolate melts and mixture is smooth, about 1 minute, stirring every 15 seconds.

2. Beat chocolate mixture, granulated sugar, and brown sugar with an electric mixer on medium speed until well combined, about 3 minutes. Add eggs, 1 at a time, beating well after each addition. Add vanilla, and beat until incorporated.

3. Whisk together flour, baking soda, salt, and 3/4 cup of the cocoa in a bowl. Add flour mixture to chocolate mixture; beat on low speed until well combined, about 2 minutes. (Dough will be very soft.) Transfer half of dough onto plastic wrap, and wrap tightly, shaping into a disk. Repeat process with remaining half of dough. Chill dough 2 hours.

4. Preheat oven to 325°F. Let 1 dough disk stand at room temperature 10 minutes. Sprinkle work surface with 2 tablespoons of the cocoa. Unwrap dough disk, and roll to 1/4-inch thickness on cocoa. Cut with a 2 1/2-inch round cutter, rerolling scraps once. Place cookies 2 inches apart on parchment paper-lined baking sheets.

5. Bake in preheated oven until just set, about 8 minutes, switching pans top rack to bottom rack halfway through baking. Cool on pans 5 minutes; remove cookies to wire racks, and cool completely, about 30 minutes. Repeat process with remaining dough disk and 2 tablespoons cocoa.

6. Prepare the Icing: Beat powdered sugar, meringue powder, and 4 teaspoons of the water on medium speed until well combined, 3 to 4 minutes. Add up to 1 teaspoon more water, 1/4 teaspoon at a time, and beat until desired consistency is reached. Divide icing between 2 bowls. Stir in food coloring, 1 drop at a time, until icing reaches desired shades of green and red. Place icing into piping bags and pipe trees onto tops of cookies. Sprinkle with sparkling sugar.

MAKES 40 cookies (serving size: 1 cookie) **ACTIVE** 30 min. **TOTAL** 3 hours

SPARKLING SNOWFLAKE SUGAR COOKIES

Adults will love these elegant blue and white cookies made with a touch of brandy and topped with sparkling sugar.

COOKIES

- 3 cups (about 12 3/4 oz.) all-purpose flour
- 1 cup granulated sugar
- 1/2 tsp. table salt
- 1 cup (8 oz.) cold salted butter, cut into 1/2-inch pieces
- 2 large egg yolks
- 2 Tbsp. brandy or whole milk

ICING

- 2 cups (about 8 oz.) powdered sugar
- 4 tsp. meringue powder
- 2 to 3 Tbsp. water
- Blue liquid food coloring
- Blue sparkling sugar
- White sparkling sugar

1. Prepare the Cookies: Pulse flour, granulated sugar, and salt in a food processor until combined, 3 to 4 times. Add butter, and pulse until mixture resembles coarse sand, 5 to 6 times. Add egg yolks and brandy; process until clumps begin to form, 30 seconds to 1 minute. Turn mixture out onto a lightly floured work surface; knead until dough comes together, 3 to 4 times. Divide dough in half; shape each half into a 6-inch disk. Wrap each disk with plastic wrap, and chill 1 hour.

2. Preheat oven to 350°F. Let 1 dough disk stand at room temperature 10 minutes. Unwrap dough disk, and roll to 1/4-inch thickness on a lightly floured surface. Cut with a 3 1/2-inch snowflake-shaped cutter, rerolling scraps once. Place cookies 2 inches apart on parchment paper-lined baking sheets.

3. Bake in preheated oven until set and beginning to brown on edges, 9 to 10 minutes, switching pans top rack to bottom rack halfway through baking. Cool on pans 2 minutes; remove cookies to wire racks, and cool completely, about 20 minutes. Repeat process with remaining dough disk.

4. Prepare the Icing: Beat powdered sugar, meringue powder, and 2 tablespoons of the water on medium speed in a medium bowl until well combined, 3 to 4 minutes. Add up to 1 tablespoon water, 1/4 teaspoon at a time, until desired consistency is reached. Add food coloring, 1 drop at a time, and beat until frosting is desired color. Spread icing on cookies, and sprinkle with sparkling sugars.

MAKES about 3 1/2 dozen cookies (serving size: 1 cookie) **ACTIVE** 30 min. **TOTAL** 2 hours, 10 min.

ALMOND STARS

These flavorful cookies are made with almond flour (look for it in the gluten-free section of your supermarket) and almond paste (found in the baking aisle). Boxed or canned almond paste is softer and easier to work with.

COOKIES

- 1 cup (about 3 1/2 oz.) almond flour
- 1 1/2 cups (12 oz.) salted butter, softened
- 1/2 cup almond paste, crumbled
- 2 tsp. vanilla extract
- 2 cups (about 8 oz.) powdered sugar
- 2 1/4 cups (about 9 5/8 oz.) all-purpose flour
- 1/2 tsp. table salt

ICING

- 2 cups (about 8 oz.) powdered sugar
- 4 tsp. meringue powder
- 6 to 7 tsp. water

ADDITIONAL INGREDIENT

- 1 cup sliced almonds, toasted

1. Prepare the Cookies: Preheat oven to 350°F. Spread almond flour in an even layer on a parchment paper-lined baking sheet. Bake in preheated oven until lightly toasted, about 10 minutes.

2. Beat butter, almond paste, and vanilla with an electric mixer on medium-low speed until well combined and smooth, about 4 minutes. Add powdered sugar; beat on low speed until well combined, about 2 minutes.

3. Whisk together all-purpose flour, toasted almond flour, and salt in a bowl. Add flour mixture to butter mixture; beat on low speed until just combined. Turn dough out onto a work surface; knead until dough comes together, 4 to 5 times. Divide dough in half. Shape each half into a 6-inch disk, and wrap each disk in plastic wrap. Chill 1 hour.

4. Preheat oven to 350°F. Let 1 dough disk stand at room temperature 10 minutes. Unwrap dough disk, and roll to ¼-inch thickness on a lightly floured surface. Cut with a 3 ½-inch star-shaped cookie cutter, rerolling scraps once. Place cookies 2 inches apart on parchment paper-lined baking sheets.

5. Bake in preheated oven until edges are golden brown, 9 to 10 minutes, switching pans top rack to bottom rack halfway through baking. Cool on pans 2 minutes. Remove cookies to wire racks, and cool completely, about 20 minutes. Repeat process with remaining dough disk.

6. Prepare the Icing: Beat powdered sugar, meringue powder, and 6 teaspoons of the water on medium speed until well combined, 3 to 4 minutes. Add up to 1 teaspoon water, ¼ teaspoon at a time, and beat until desired consistency is reached. Spread icing over cookies, and top with toasted almonds.

MAKES about 2 dozen cookies (serving size: 1 cookie) **ACTIVE** 30 min. **TOTAL** 2 hours, 10 min.

~DROP~

TRIPLE MINT COOKIES

Mint lovers will fall head over heels for these rich, brownie-like cookies filled with chopped mint candies and topped with minty icing.

- 1 cup 60% cacao bittersweet chocolate morsels
- ½ cup (4 oz.) unsalted butter
- 1 cup granulated sugar
- 2 large eggs
- 1 tsp. vanilla extract
- ½ tsp. mint extract, divided
- 2 cups (about 8 ½ oz.) all-purpose flour
- ½ cup unsweetened cocoa
- ¾ tsp. baking powder
- ¾ tsp. kosher salt

Pecan Tea Cakes

- 1 cup chopped thin crème de menthe chocolate mints (such as Andes)
- 2 cups (about 8 oz.) powdered sugar
- 3 to 4 Tbsp. whole milk
- 5 to 6 drops green food coloring

1. Preheat oven to 375°F with oven racks in the top third and bottom third of oven. Combine chocolate morsels and butter in a large microwave-safe bowl, and microwave on MEDIUM (50% power) until melted and smooth, about 2 minutes, stirring every 30 seconds. Whisk in sugar, eggs, vanilla, and ¼ teaspoon of the mint extract until smooth. Whisk together flour, cocoa, baking powder, and salt in a medium bowl. Stir flour mixture into chocolate mixture; fold in chopped mints. Drop cookies by 2 tablespoonfuls inches apart onto 2 parchment paper-lined baking sheets.

2. Bake in preheated oven until cookies are just set on top, about 10 minutes, switching pans top rack to bottom rack halfway through baking. Remove pans to wire racks, and immediately flatten domed cookie tops with the bottom of a heatproof dry measuring cup. Cool cookies on pans 5 minutes; transfer cookies to wire racks, and cool completely, about 30 minutes.

3. Whisk together powdered sugar, 3 tablespoons of the milk, and remaining ¼ teaspoon mint extract in a small bowl. Stir in up to 1 more tablespoon of milk, 1 teaspoon at a time, until desired consistency is reached. Transfer 2 tablespoons of the icing to a separate small bowl, and stir in desired amount of food coloring.

4. Spoon remaining white icing into a zip-top plastic freezer bag with 1

corner snipped or a piping bag. Pipe circles of white icing over cooled cookies. Drop 4 to 5 drops of green icing onto white icing circles, and swirl with a wooden pick to create a marbled effect. Let stand at room temperature until set, about 1 hour.

MAKES about 2 ½ dozen **ACTIVE** 30 min. **TOTAL** 1 hour, 55 min.

PECAN TEA CAKES

- 1 cup toasted pecans, chopped
- ¼ cup whole milk
- ½ cup (4 oz.) unsalted butter, softened
- ¾ cup, plus 1 Tbsp. granulated sugar, divided
- 1 large egg
- 1 tsp. vanilla extract
- 2 cups (about 8 oz.) self-rising flour
- 48 to 50 pecan halves (about 1 ¼ cups)
- 1 large egg white, lightly beaten

1. Place chopped toasted pecans and milk in a small bowl, and let stand at room temperature until milk is mostly absorbed, about 30 minutes.

2. Preheat oven to 375°F with oven racks in the top third and bottom third of oven. Beat butter and ¾ cup of the sugar with an electric mixer on medium speed until light and fluffy, about 2 minutes. Add egg and vanilla, and beat on low speed just until combined. Add flour and chopped toasted pecans alternately to butter mixture, beginning and ending with flour. Beat on low speed just until incorporated after each addition. Drop by tablespoonfuls about 2 inches apart on parchment paper-lined baking sheets. Press 1 pecan half into top of each cookie. Brush pecans lightly with egg white, and sprinkle evenly with remaining 1 tablespoon sugar.

3. Bake in preheated oven until cookies are just set, about 10 minutes, switching pans top rack to bottom rack halfway through baking. Cool on pans on wire rack 5 minutes; transfer cookies to wire rack, and cool completely, about 30 minutes.

MAKES about 4 dozen **ACTIVE** 1 hour **TOTAL** 1 hour, 30 min.

SPICED MOLASSES DROPS

You've never had spice cookies like these. A secret ingredient—black pepper—adds a hint of heat.

- 1/2 cup (4 oz.) unsalted butter, softened
- 3/4 cup packed light brown sugar
- 1/4 cup light molasses
- 1 tsp. vanilla extract
- 1 large egg
- 2 cups (about 8 1/2 oz.) all-purpose flour
- 1 1/2 tsp. baking powder
- 1/2 tsp. baking soda
- 1/4 tsp. kosher salt
- 1/4 tsp. ground cinnamon
- 1/4 tsp. ground ginger
- 1/4 tsp. black pepper
- 1/2 cup sanding sugar or sparkling sugar

1. Preheat oven to 375°F with oven racks in top third and bottom third of oven. Beat butter and brown sugar with an electric mixer on medium speed until light and fluffy, about 2 minutes. Add molasses and vanilla, and beat on low speed just until combined. Add egg, and beat on medium speed until mixture thickens slightly, about 30 seconds. Whisk together flour, baking powder, baking soda, salt, cinnamon, ginger, and pepper in a medium bowl. Gradually add to butter mixture, and beat on low speed just until combined after each addition.
2. Place sanding sugar in a shallow dish or bowl, and drop dough by heaping tablespoonfuls into sugar, rolling to coat. Place half of coated dough balls about 2 inches apart on parchment paper-lined baking sheets.
3. Bake in preheated oven until cookies are just set, 8 to 9 minutes, switching pans top third to bottom rack halfway through baking. Cool on pans 5 minutes; remove cookies to wire racks, and cool completely, about 30 minutes. Repeat with remaining dough.

MAKES about 4 dozen **ACTIVE** 30 min. **TOTAL** 1 hour, 13 min.

RASPBERRY JAM THUMBPRINTS

You can make the dough for all three thumbprint cookies a day in advance; store in the refrigerator.

- 1 cup (8 oz.) unsalted butter, softened
- 3/4 cup (about 3 oz.) powdered sugar
- 1/4 cup packed light brown sugar
- 1 large egg yolk
- 1 tsp. vanilla extract
- 3 cups (about 12 3/4 oz.) all-purpose flour
- 1/2 tsp. kosher salt
- 1/2 tsp. baking powder
- 1/3 cup seedless raspberry jam
- 4 oz. white chocolate baking bar, chopped
- 1/4 cup heavy cream

1. Preheat oven to 375°F with oven racks in the top third and bottom third of oven. Beat butter and both sugars with an electric mixer on medium speed until smooth, about 1 minute. Add egg yolk and vanilla, and beat on low speed just until incorporated. Whisk together flour, salt, and baking powder in a small bowl, and gradually add to butter mixture, beating on low speed just until incorporated after each addition.
2. Drop dough by tablespoonfuls 1 inch apart onto parchment paper-lined baking sheets. Press thumb or end of a wooden spoon into each ball, forming an indentation.
3. Bake in preheated oven until cookies are set and beginning to brown, about 12 minutes, switching pans top rack to bottom rack halfway through baking. Cool on pans on wire racks 5 minutes; remove cookies to wire racks, and cool completely, about 30 minutes.
4. Fill each indentation with about 1/2 teaspoon jam, and let stand at room temperature 15 minutes.
5. Combine white chocolate and cream in a small heatproof bowl. Bring a small saucepan filled with 1 inch of water to a simmer over medium, and place bowl with chocolate mixture over simmering water. Cook, stirring often, until chocolate is melted and smooth, about 2 minutes. Cool 10 minutes. Spoon chocolate mixture into a zip-top plastic freezer bag with 1 corner snipped or a piping bag, and pipe mixture over cookies.

MAKES about 4 dozen **ACTIVE** 40 min. **TOTAL** 1 hour, 30 min.

COCONUT THUMBPRINTS WITH DULCE DE LECHE

Don't forget to top these cookies with a pinch of flaky salt—it balances the luscious caramel filling and sweet toasted coconut.

- 1 cup sweetened shredded coconut
- 1 cup (8 oz.) unsalted butter, softened
- 3/4 cup (about 3 oz.) powdered sugar
- 1/4 cup packed light brown sugar
- 1 large egg yolk
- 1 tsp. vanilla extract
- 3 cups (about 12 3/4 oz.) all-purpose flour
- 1/2 tsp. kosher salt
- 1/2 tsp. baking powder
- 1/2 cup jarred or canned dulce de leche
- 2 tsp. flaked sea salt

1. Preheat oven to 375°F with oven racks in the top third and bottom third of oven. Pulse coconut in a food processor until finely chopped, about 10 times. Transfer to a shallow dish or bowl.
2. Beat butter and both sugars with an electric mixer on medium speed until smooth, about 1 minute. Add egg yolk and vanilla, and beat on low speed just until incorporated. Whisk together flour, kosher salt, and baking powder in a small bowl, and add to butter mixture, beating on low speed just until incorporated.
3. Drop dough by tablespoonfuls into chopped coconut, and roll lightly to coat. Place cookies 1 inch apart on parchment paper-lined baking sheets. Press thumb or end of a wooden spoon into each ball, forming an indentation.
4. Bake in preheated oven until cookies are set and coconut is browned, about 11 minutes, switching pans top rack to bottom rack halfway

through baking. Transfer baking sheets to wire racks, and immediately reshape indentations by pressing again with your thumb. Cool cookies completely, about 30 minutes.

5. Fill each indentation with about ¹/₂ teaspoon of the dulce de leche. Sprinkle cookies evenly with sea salt.

MAKES about 4 dozen **ACTIVE** 30 min. **TOTAL** 1 hour

CHOCOLATE GANACHE THUMBPRINTS WITH CRUSHED PEPPERMINTS

This chocolate ganache is impossibly rich and incredibly easy to make in the microwave.

- 1 cup (8 oz.) unsalted butter, softened
- ³/₄ cup (about 3 oz.) powdered sugar
- ¹/₄ cup packed light brown sugar
- 1 large egg yolk
- 1 tsp. vanilla extract
- 3 cups (about 12 ³/₄ oz.) all-purpose flour
- ¹/₂ tsp. kosher salt
- ¹/₂ tsp. baking powder
- ³/₄ cup semisweet chocolate morsels
- 3 Tbsp. heavy cream
- ¹/₄ cup crushed hard peppermint candies (about 12 candies)

1. Preheat oven to 375°F with oven racks in the top third and bottom third of oven. Beat butter and both sugars with an electric mixer on medium speed until smooth, about 1 minute. Add egg yolk and vanilla, and beat on low speed just until incorporated. Whisk together flour, salt, and baking powder in a small bowl, and gradually add to butter mixture, beating on low speed just until incorporated after each addition.

2. Drop dough by tablespoonfuls 1 inch apart onto parchment paper-lined baking sheets. Press thumb or end of a wooden spoon into each ball, forming an indentation.

3. Bake in preheated oven until cookies are set and beginning to brown, about 12 minutes, switching pans top rack to bottom rack halfway through baking. Cool on pans on wire racks 5 minutes; remove cookies to wire racks, and cool completely, about 30 minutes.

4. Combine chocolate morsels and cream in a microwave-safe bowl, and microwave on MEDIUM (50% power) until melted and smooth, about 1 ¹/₂ minutes, stirring every 30 seconds. Cool 5 minutes. Fill each indentation with about ¹/₂ teaspoon of the ganache. Sprinkle cookies evenly with crushed peppermints, and let stand 15 minutes before serving.

MAKES about 4 dozen **ACTIVE** 40 min. **TOTAL** 1 hour, 30 min.

~SANDWICH~

RED VELVET CRACKLE SANDWICH COOKIES

All the flavors of red velvet cake in a cute little package! A small trigger-handled ice cream scoop makes the work of getting uniform cookies a breeze.

- 3 oz. semisweet baking chocolate, chopped
- ¹/₄ cup unsalted butter
- 1 cup granulated sugar
- 2 large eggs
- 1 Tbsp. red liquid food coloring
- 2 cups (about 8 ¹/₂ oz.) all-purpose flour
- 2 Tbsp. unsweetened cocoa
- 1 tsp. baking powder
- ¹/₂ tsp. baking soda
- ¹/₂ tsp. kosher salt
- 2 cups (about 8 oz.) powdered sugar, divided
- 4 oz. cream cheese, softened

1. Preheat oven to 375°F with oven racks in the top third and bottom third of oven. Melt chocolate and butter in a large microwave-safe glass bowl on MEDIUM (50% power) until melted and smooth, about 1 ¹/₂ minutes, stirring every 30 seconds. Whisk in granulated sugar, eggs, and food coloring until smooth.

2. Whisk together flour, cocoa, baking powder, baking soda, and salt, and add to butter mixture, stirring gently just to combine.

Lemony Sandwich Cookies and Eggnog Whoopie Pies

3. Place 1 cup of the powdered sugar in a small bowl. Drop dough by tablespoonfuls into powdered sugar, rolling to coat, and place 1 inch apart on parchment-lined baking sheets. Using the heal of your hand, gently flatten domed tops of dough. Bake in preheated oven until cookies are almost set and outsides are crackled, 10 to 11 minutes. Transfer pans to wire racks, and cool cookies completely, about 30 minutes.

4. Beat cream cheese and remaining 1 cup powdered sugar with an electric mixer on medium speed until smooth. Spread 1 ¹/₂ teaspoons cream cheese filling onto flat side of half of the cookies. Cover with remaining half of cookies, flat side down, and gently press.

MAKES 21 sandwich cookies **ACTIVE** 30 min. **TOTAL** 40 min.

PEANUT BUTTER-AND-JELLY LINZER COOKIES

- 1 cup (8 oz.) unsalted butter, softened
- ¹/₂ cup granulated sugar
- ¹/₂ cup packed light brown sugar
- ¹/₂ cup creamy peanut butter
- 1 large egg yolk
- 1 tsp. vanilla extract
- 3 cups (about 12 ³/₄ oz.) all-purpose flour
- ¹/₂ tsp. kosher salt
- ¹/₂ tsp. baking powder
- ¹/₂ cup (about 2 oz.) powdered sugar
- ¹/₂ cup strawberry jam

1. Preheat oven to 375°F with oven racks in the top third and bottom third of oven. Beat butter, granulated sugar, brown sugar, and peanut butter with an electric mixer on medium speed until smooth, about 1 minute. Add egg yolk and vanilla, and beat on low speed just until incorporated. Whisk together flour, salt, and baking powder, and gradually add to butter mixture, beating on low speed just until incorporated.

2. Place dough on a well-floured surface, and roll to 1/4-inch thickness. Cut dough with a 2 1/2-inch round cutter. Gently reroll scraps once, and repeat process with round cutter. Place half of the dough rounds on parchment paper-lined baking sheets. Using a 1-inch star-shaped cutter, cut out and remove dough star shapes from the center of the remaining half of dough rounds. (Reserve and bake dough star cutouts for later, if desired.) Transfer dough rounds with star cutouts removed to lined baking sheets.

3. Bake cookies in preheated oven until cookies are set and beginning to brown, 12 to 13 minutes, switching pans top rack to bottom rack halfway through baking. Transfer pans to wire racks, and cool cookies completely, about 30 minutes.

4. Sift powdered sugar over cookies with star cutouts. Spread 1 1/2 teaspoons jam on 1 side of remaining cookies. Place a star cutout cookie, powdered sugar side up, over each jam covered cookie, and gently press.

MAKES 18 cookies **ACTIVE** 40 min. **TOTAL** 1 hour, 30 min.

SPICED STARS WITH COOKIE BUTTER

Sweet, creamy cookie butter (also called speculoos spread) tastes even better when sandwiched between two ultra-thin spice cookies. Don't roll the dough more than twice; it will make the cookies a bit tough.

- 1/2 **cup (8 oz.) unsalted butter, softened**
- 1/2 **cup packed light brown sugar**
- 1/4 **cup powdered sugar**
- 1 **large egg**
- 1 **tsp. vanilla extract**
- 2 **cups (about 8 1/2 oz.) all-purpose flour**
- 1 **tsp. baking powder**
- 1/2 **tsp. baking soda**
- 1/4 **tsp. kosher salt**
- 1/4 **tsp. ground cinnamon**
- 1/4 **tsp. ground nutmeg**
- 1/2 **cup cookie butter spread (such as Biscoff)**

1. Preheat oven to 375°F with oven racks in the top third and bottom third of oven. Beat butter and sugars with an electric mixer on medium speed until light and fluffy, about 2 minutes. Add egg and vanilla and beat on low speed just until combined and mixture thickens slightly, about 1 minute. Whisk together flour, baking powder, baking soda, salt, cinnamon, and nutmeg, and add to butter mixture, beating on low speed until combined.

2. Place dough on a well-floured surface, and roll to 1/8-inch thickness. Cut dough using a 2-inch star-shaped cutter. Gently reroll scraps once, and repeat process. Place star dough cookies about 2 inches apart on parchment paper-lined baking sheets. Bake in preheated oven until just set, about 8 minutes, switching pans top rack to bottom rack halfway through baking. Transfer to wire racks, and cool cookies on pans 5 minutes. Remove cookies from pans to wire racks, and cool completely, about 30 minutes.

3. Spread 1 teaspoon cookie spread onto flat side of half of star cookies. Cover with remaining half of star cookies, flat side down, and gently press.

MAKES 27 star cookies **ACTIVE** 40 min. **TOTAL** 1 hour, 30 min.

LEMONY SANDWICH COOKIES

These soft cookies have loads of lemon flavor and beautifully crackled tops.

- 1 **cup granulated sugar**
- 3/4 **cup (6 oz.) unsalted butter, at room temperature, divided**
- 1 **large egg**
- 1 **large egg yolk**
- 1 **tsp. vanilla extract**
- 1/8 **tsp. yellow food coloring gel**
- 2 **Tbsp. lemon zest, plus 1 tsp. fresh juice (from 1 lemon), divided**
- 2 **cups (about 8 oz.) self-rising flour**
- 1/2 **cup sanding or sparkling sugar**
- 1 **cup (about 4 oz.) powdered sugar**
- 4 **tsp. whole milk**

1. Preheat oven to 375°F with oven racks in the top third and bottom third of oven. Beat granulated sugar and 1/2 cup of the butter with an electric mixer on medium speed until light and fluffy. Add egg, egg yolk, vanilla, food coloring gel, and 1 tablespoon of the lemon zest, and beat on low speed until just combined. Add flour to butter mixture, beating on low speed just until flour is incorporated. Place sanding sugar in a shallow dish. Drop dough by tablespoonfuls into sugar, rolling to coat, and place 2 inches apart on parchment paper-lined baking sheets.

2. Bake in preheated oven until cookies are just set, about 8 minutes, switching pans top rack to bottom rack halfway through baking. Transfer to wire racks, and cool cookies on pans 5 minutes. Remove cookies from pans to wire racks, and cool completely, about 30 minutes.

3. Beat powdered sugar, milk, lemon juice, and remaining 1/4 cup butter and 1 tablespoon lemon zest on medium speed until light and fluffy. Pipe 2 teaspoons lemon filling onto flat side of half of the cookies. Cover with remaining half of cookies, flat side down, and gently press.

MAKES about 20 sandwich cookies **ACTIVE** 40 min. **TOTAL** 1 hour, 30 min.

EGGNOG WHOOPIE PIES

The rich, creamy filling can be made ahead up to 3 days then piped onto fresh, cooled cookies. The bourbon makes these cookies truly over-the-top, but you can omit the booze to make them kid-friendly.

- 1/2 **cup (4 oz.) unsalted butter, softened**
- 1 **cup granulated sugar**
- 1/2 **cup packed light brown sugar**
- 2 **large eggs**
- 2 **tsp. vanilla extract, divided**
- 2 1/2 **cups (about 10 5/8 oz.) all-purpose flour**
- 1 **tsp. baking powder**
- 1/4 **tsp. baking soda**
- 1/4 **tsp. ground cinnamon**
- 1 **tsp. kosher salt, divided**
- 1/3 **cup whole milk**
- 4 **oz. cream cheese, softened**
- 2 **Tbsp. bourbon**
- 1/4 **tsp. ground nutmeg**
- 1 1/3 **cups (about 5 1/3 oz.) powdered sugar, divided**
- 1/2 **cup heavy cream**

1. Preheat oven to 375°F with oven racks in the top third and bottom third of oven. Beat butter, granulated sugar, and brown sugar with an electric mixer on medium speed until smooth, about 1 minute. Add eggs, one at a time, beating on low speed just until incorporated. Add 1 teaspoon of the vanilla, and beat just until combined. Whisk together flour, baking powder, baking soda, cinnamon, and 3/4 teaspoon of the salt, and add to butter mixture alternately with milk, beginning and ending with flour mixture and beating on low speed just until each is incorporated.

2. Using a 1-inch cookie scoop, drop dough about 3 inches apart onto parchment paper-lined baking sheets. Bake in preheated oven until cookies are just set and beginning to brown, 9 to 11 minutes, switching pans top rack to bottom rack halfway through baking. Transfer to wire racks, and cool cookies on pans 5 minutes. Remove cookies from pans to wire racks, and cool completely, about 30 minutes.

3. Beat cream cheese on medium speed until fluffy, about 2 minutes, scraping down sides of the bowl as needed. Add bourbon, nutmeg, 1 cup of the powdered sugar, and remaining 1 teaspoon vanilla and 1/4 teaspoon salt; beat until smooth. Beat heavy cream in a small bowl until stiff peaks form; fold into cream cheese mixture. Pipe 1 tablespoon cream cheese filling onto flat side of half of the cookies. Cover with remaining half of cookies, flat side down, and gently press. Sift with remaining 1/3 cup powdered sugar.

MAKES about 22 cookie "pies"
ACTIVE 45 min. **TOTAL** 1 hour, 15 min.

~SHAPED~

SPARKLING ORNAMENT COOKIES

These richly colored cookies are perfect for little hands—the more sprinkles, the better!

- 1 1/2 **cups (12 oz.) salted butter, softened**
- 3/4 **cup granulated sugar**
- 1/2 **tsp. vanilla extract**
- 1/8 **tsp. almond extract**
- 3 3/4 **cups (about 16 oz.) all-purpose flour**
- **Food coloring gel in blue, red, green, and yellow**
- **White sparkling sugar or sanding sugar**
- **Assorted sprinkles, sugar pearls, silver dragées**

Chocolate-Bourbon-Fudge Balls and Sparkling Ornament Cookies

1. Beat butter and sugar with a heavy-duty stand mixer on medium speed until creamy; add vanilla and almond extract, and beat until incorporated. Gradually add flour, and beat on low speed until incorporated after each addition.

2. Divide dough into 4 equal portions, and place each portion in a small bowl. Add desired amount of food coloring gel to each bowl, and stir with a fork until food coloring is incorporated. Cover bowls, and chill 1 hour.

3. Preheat oven to 250°F. Shape 1 dough portion into about 12 (1 1/2-inch) balls, and roll in sparkling sugar or sanding sugar. Press sprinkles, sugar pearls, or silver dragées into dough balls. Place decorated balls about 2 inches apart on parchment paper-lined baking sheets. Repeat with remaining dough portions.

4. Bake in preheated oven until lightly browned on bottom, 25 to 30 minutes, switching pans top rack to bottom rack halfway through baking. Cool on pans 5 minutes. Remove cookies to wire racks, and cool completely, about 30 minutes.

MAKES about 4 dozen (serving size: 1 cookie)
ACTIVE 30 min. **TOTAL** 2 hours, 30 min.

WALNUT CRESCENTS

These delicate cookies are soft and tender on the inside, with delectable nutty flavor from browned butter and toasted walnuts.

- 1/2 **cup (4 oz.) salted butter, softened**
- 1/3 **cup granulated sugar**
- 1 **tsp. vanilla extract**
- 1 **cup (about 4 1/4 oz.) all-purpose flour**
- 1 **cup finely chopped toasted walnuts (about 4 1/2 oz.)**
- 1 **cup (about 4 oz.) powdered sugar, plus more for dusting**

1. Preheat oven to 400°F. Beat butter with a heavy-duty stand mixer on medium speed until creamy. Add sugar and vanilla, and beat until well incorporated; add flour, and beat until blended. Stir in walnuts.

2. Shape into 16 (1-inch) balls, and roll each ball into a 3-inch rope. Place ropes 2 inches apart on parchment paper-lined baking sheets, and curve into crescents.

3. Bake in preheated oven until golden brown, 9 to 10 minutes, switching pans top rack to bottom rack halfway through baking. Cool on pans 1 minute. Roll warm cookies in powdered sugar, and cool completely, about 30 minutes. Dust with additional powdered sugar, if desired.

MAKES 16 cookies (serving size: 1 cookie) **ACTIVE** 20 min. **TOTAL** 1 hour

KEY LIME TASSIES

Not only are these mini tarts irresistibly good, they are truly make-ahead: The tart shells can be made and frozen up to a month in advance and the Key lime curd can be made up to 5 days ahead and stored, covered, in the refrigerator.

CURD
- 2 cups granulated sugar
- 1/2 cup (4 oz.) salted butter, softened
- 4 large eggs, at room temperature
- 1 cup bottled Key lime juice (such as Nellie & Joe's Famous Key West Lime Juice), at room temperature

CREAM CHEESE PASTRY
- 1 (8-oz.) pkg. cream cheese, softened
- 1 cup (8 oz.) salted butter, softened
- 1/4 cup granulated sugar
- 3 1/2 cups (about 14 7/8 oz.) all-purpose flour

ADDITIONAL INGREDIENTS
- Powdered sugar
- Lime zest (optional)

1. Prepare the Curd: Beat 2 cups granulated sugar and 1/2 cup butter with an electric mixer on medium speed until blended. Add eggs, 1 at a time, beating just until blended after each addition. Gradually add Key lime juice to butter mixture, beating at low speed just until blended after each addition. (Mixture may separate at this stage, but will emulsify as it is heated and whisked.)

2. Transfer mixture to a heavy 4-quart saucepan. Cook over medium-low,

whisking constantly, until mixture thickens and just begins to bubble, 14 to 16 minutes. Remove from heat, and cool 30 minutes. Place heavy-duty plastic wrap directly on surface of warm curd (to prevent a film from forming), and chill until firm, about 4 hours. Refrigerate in an airtight container up to 2 weeks.

3. Prepare the Cream Cheese Pastry: Beat cream cheese, 1 cup butter, and 1/4 cup granulated sugar with a heavy-duty electric stand mixer on medium speed until creamy. Gradually add flour to butter mixture, beating at low speed just until blended after each addition. Shape dough into 60 (1-inch) balls, and place on a baking sheet; cover and chill 1 hour.

4. Preheat oven to 400°F. Place 1 chilled dough ball into each cup of lightly greased miniature muffin pans; press dough into bottoms and up sides of cups, forming shells.

5. Bake in preheated oven until lightly browned, 10 to 12 minutes. Remove shells from pans to wire racks, and cool completely, about 20 minutes.

6. Spoon about 1 1/2 teaspoons of the Curd into each pastry shell. Cover filled shells, and chill until ready to serve. Just before serving, sprinkle filled shells with powdered sugar and, if desired, garnish with lime zest.

Note: You will have leftover curd. It is great to use on warm biscuits or scones, as a topping for pound cake, or a dip for fresh fruit.

MAKES 60 cookies (serving size: 1 cookie) **ACTIVE** 45 min. **TOTAL** 4 hours, 45 min.

CARAMEL-STUFFED GINGER COOKIES

These spice cookies have an ooey-gooey caramel center and are best served warm, either straight from the oven or reheated in the microwave.

- 1 1/2 cups packed dark brown sugar
- 1/2 cup (4 oz.) plus 2 Tbsp. salted butter, softened
- 2 large eggs
- 1 tsp. vanilla extract

- 3 cups (about 12 3/4 oz.) all-purpose flour
- 1/4 cup chopped crystallized ginger
- 2 tsp. baking powder
- 1 tsp. table salt
- 16 caramel candies, cut in half
- 1/2 cup Demerara sugar

1. Beat brown sugar, butter, eggs, and vanilla with a heavy-duty stand mixer on medium speed until mixture is blended and smooth.

2. Process flour, ginger, baking powder, and salt in a food processor until ginger is very finely chopped and mixture is well blended, 1 to 2 minutes. Gradually add flour mixture to sugar mixture, and beat on low speed just until blended after each addition. Shape dough into a disk, and wrap in plastic wrap. Chill 4 to 24 hours.

3. Preheat oven to 350°F. Shape dough into about 32 (1 1/2-inch) balls. Flatten each dough ball in the palm of your hand, and place 1 caramel half in center of dough. Wrap dough around caramel, and reshape into a ball by rolling in hand, completely covering caramel. Place dough balls 2 inches apart on parchment paper-lined baking sheets. Sprinkle each cookie lightly with Demerara sugar. (Chill assembled balls until ready to bake.)

4. Bake in preheated oven until flattened and lightly browned on the bottom, 11 to 12 minutes, switching pans top rack to bottom rack halfway through baking. Cool on pans 8 minutes. Serve warm.

MAKES about 32 cookies (serving size: 1 cookie) **ACTIVE** 30 min. **TOTAL** 5 hours, 45 min.

CHOCOLATE-BOURBON-FUDGE BALLS

These delightfully tipsy (and no bake!) treats will be a hit at all your holiday parties. You can make the mixture up to 2 days in advance and the actual balls can be stored in the refrigerator up to 5 days in an airtight container.

- 2 (4-oz.) bittersweet chocolate baking bars, chopped
- 1 (4-oz.) semisweet chocolate baking bar, chopped
- 1 1/2 Tbsp. salted butter, cubed

9 Tbsp. heavy cream
1/4 cup bourbon
2 tsp. vanilla extract
1 (5.3-oz.) pkg. pure butter shortbread cookies (such as Walkers), finely crushed
1/2 tsp. fine sea salt
2 cups finely chopped toasted pecans

1. Combine bittersweet chocolate, semisweet chocolate, and butter in a large glass bowl. Cook cream and bourbon in a small saucepan over medium until mixture is hot but not boiling, 3 to 4 minutes. (Bubbles will form around the edge.) Pour mixture over chocolate. Let stand 1 minute.
2. Stir chocolate mixture until melted and smooth. (If mixture doesn't melt completely, microwave on HIGH 30 seconds to 1 minute, stirring after 30 seconds.) Stir in vanilla. Stir in crushed cookies. Cover and chill 3 hours or until firm. (Mixture can be prepared and chilled up to 2 days ahead.)
3. Shape mixture into about 40 (1-inch) balls. Sprinkle each ball with a very small amount of sea salt, and coat balls in chopped pecans. Place on wax paper-lined baking sheets, and chill 1 hour. Refrigerate in an airtight container up to 5 days.

MAKES about 40 cookies (serving size: 1 cookie)
ACTIVE 25 min. **TOTAL** 4 hours, 25 min.

~SLICE & BAKE~

PEACHY PISTACHIO ICEBOX COOKIES

With its fun stripes and unusually tasty flavor combination of peach preserves and salted pistachios, this cookie will stand out in any cookie tin.

1/2 cup (4 oz.) salted butter, softened
1 cup granulated sugar
1 large egg
1 tsp. vanilla extract
1 3/4 cups (about 7 1/2 oz.) all-purpose flour
1 tsp. baking powder
1/4 tsp. table salt

Peppermint Pinwheels

1/2 cup peach preserves
1/2 cup finely chopped roasted salted pistachios

1. Cut parchment paper into 8 (12- x 6-inch) rectangles. Beat butter with a heavy-duty stand mixer on medium speed until creamy, about 2 minutes; add sugar, and beat until light and fluffy, about 3 minutes. Add egg and vanilla, and beat until combined.
2. Stir together flour, baking powder, and salt in a small bowl. Gradually add flour mixture to butter mixture, beating on low speed just until blended.
3. Transfer dough to work surface, and divide into 4 equal portions. Place 1 dough portion between 2 parchment rectangles. Roll out dough to a 9- x 3 1/2- inch rectangle about 1/4-inch thick. Repeat with remaining dough portions and prepared parchment paper rectangles. Place dough rectangles (still between parchment paper) on a baking sheet, and freeze 30 minutes.
4. Pulse peach preserves in a food processor just until large pieces are broken apart, 2 to 3 times.
5. Remove dough from freezer. Remove top pieces of parchment from dough rectangles. Spread about 2 1/2 tablespoons of the preserves over 1 dough rectangle. Sprinkle with about 8 teaspoons of the finely chopped pistachios. Top with 1 dough rectangle. Repeat layers with remaining preserves, pistachios, and dough rectangles, leaving the top rectangle uncoated. Trim dough stack to an 8 1/2- x 3 1/4-inch brick. Wrap dough in plastic wrap, and freeze 1 hour.
6. Preheat oven to 350°F. Remove dough from freezer, and slice into 1/4-inch-thick rectangles; place on parchment paper-lined baking sheets.

7. Bake in preheated oven until lightly browned around edges, 13 to 15 minutes. Cool on baking sheets 5 minutes. Transfer to wire racks, and cool completely, about 20 minutes.

MAKES 2 dozen (serving size: 2 cookies)
ACTIVE 30 min. **TOTAL** 2 hours, 30 min.

ORANGE PALMIERS

You'd never guess these impressive-looking cookies are made with just four ingredients. Demerara sugar is a coarse brown sugar; look for it in the baking aisle at the supermarket.

3/4 cup Demerara sugar
1 tsp. ground cinnamon
1 (17.3-oz.) pkg. frozen puff pastry sheets, thawed
2/3 cup orange marmalade, divided

1. Combine sugar and cinnamon in a small bowl. Sprinkle 1/4 cup sugar mixture over a 12-inch square on a work surface. Unfold 1 pastry sheet on top of sugar, and roll sheet into a 12- x 9-inch rectangle. Spread 1/3 cup marmalade over dough, leaving a 1/2-inch border around edges. Starting with 1 long side, roll up pastry, jelly-roll fashion, to center of pastry sheet. Roll opposite side to center. (The shape will resemble a scroll.) Wrap in plastic wrap, and freeze 20 minutes. Repeat procedure with 1/4 cup of the sugar mixture and remaining pastry sheet and 1/3 cup marmalade.
2. Preheat oven to 375°F. Remove 1 pastry roll from freezer, and cut into 1/2-inch-thick slices; place 2 inches apart on a parchment paper-lined baking sheet. Sprinkle each slice with a small amount of the remaining sugar mixture.
3. Bake in preheated oven until light golden brown on the bottom, 14 to 16 minutes. Remove from oven, and carefully turn each cookie over. Return to oven, and bake until crisp and golden brown, 8 to 10 more minutes. Transfer cookies to a wire rack, and cool completely, about 30 minutes. Repeat procedure with remaining pastry roll.

MAKES about 3 1/2 dozen (serving size: 2 cookies)
ACTIVE 20 min. **TOTAL** 1 hour, 25 min.

CHEWY AMBROSIA BISCOTTI

1 1/2 cups (about 6 3/8 oz.) all-purpose flour
3/4 tsp. baking powder
1/4 tsp. table salt
1/4 tsp. baking soda
3/4 cup granulated sugar
2 large eggs
1 tsp. vanilla extract
1 cup sweetened shredded coconut
1/2 cup chopped maraschino cherries, drained and patted dry
1 Tbsp. orange zest

1. Preheat oven to 300°F. Stir together flour, baking powder, salt, and baking soda in a small bowl. Beat sugar, eggs, and vanilla with an electric mixer on medium speed until thick and pale, about 2 minutes. Stir in flour mixture, coconut, cherries, and orange zest. (Dough will be very sticky.)
2. Turn dough out onto a heavily floured surface; knead lightly 8 or 9 times. Shape dough into a 15- x 3-inch loaf, and place on a parchment paper-lined baking sheet; pat to 3/4-inch thickness.
3. Bake in preheated oven until loaf is golden brown, about 40 minutes. Cool on pan on a wire rack 5 minutes. Cut loaf diagonally into 22 (1/2-inch-thick) slices. Place slices in a single layer on same parchment paper-lined baking sheet, and bake 20 minutes, turning slices over halfway through baking. Remove from baking sheet; cool completely on wire rack, about 20 minutes.

MAKES 22 pieces (serving size: 2 pieces) **ACTIVE** 25 min. **TOTAL** 2 hours

PEPPERMINT PINWHEELS

Kids will love baking—and eating—these swirly, not-too-minty cookies. Feel free to swap out the red food coloring for green, if you prefer.

1 cup (8 oz.) salted butter, softened
1 1/2 cups granulated sugar
1 large egg
1 tsp. peppermint extract
1 tsp. vanilla extract
2 1/2 cups (about 10 5/8 oz.) all-purpose flour
1 1/2 tsp. baking powder
1/4 tsp. table salt
Red food coloring paste or gel

1. Beat butter with a heavy-duty stand mixer on medium speed until creamy, about 2 minutes; gradually add sugar, beating well. Add egg, peppermint extract, and vanilla, beating until combined.
2. Stir together flour, baking powder, and salt in a small bowl. Gradually add to butter mixture, beating on low speed just until blended.
3. Divide dough in half; add desired amount of red food coloring to 1 portion, and knead until color is distributed. Shape dough halves into disks; wrap in plastic wrap, and chill until firm, about 1 hour.
4. Divide each half of dough into 2 equal portions. Roll out each portion on floured wax paper into an 8-inch square, trimming edges if necessary.
5. Invert 1 white dough square onto 1 red dough square; peel wax paper from white dough. Tightly roll up dough, jelly-roll fashion, peeling wax paper from red dough as you roll. Repeat with remaining dough squares. Wrap rolls in plastic wrap, and chill 2 hours. (Dough can be tightly wrapped and frozen for up to 1 month.)
6. Preheat oven to 350°F. Remove dough from refrigerator, and cut into 1/4-inch-thick slices; place slices 2 inches apart on parchment paper-lined baking sheets. (Keep unbaked dough chilled while baking cookies.)
7. Bake, in batches, in preheated oven until bottoms are lightly browned, 10 to 12 minutes. Remove cookies from pans to wire racks, and cool completely, about 20 minutes.

MAKES about 5 dozen (serving size: 1 cookie) **ACTIVE** 30 min. **TOTAL** 4 hours

DARK CHOCOLATE SABLÉS

These French sugar cookies have a slightly crumbly texture ("sablé" means "sand") and loads of chocolate flavor. The recipe makes a lot of cookies—ideal for gifts or a cookie exchange.

1 cup (8 oz.) salted butter, softened
1 cup (about 4 oz.) powdered sugar
1 tsp. vanilla extract
2 cups (about 8 1/2 oz.) all-purpose flour
1/3 cup unsweetened cocoa
1/2 tsp. kosher salt
2 1/2 (4-oz.) 60% cacao bittersweet chocolate baking bars
Sea salt or chopped toasted pecans (optional)

1. Beat butter and sugar with an electric mixer on medium speed until creamy; add vanilla, and beat until combined. Stir together flour, cocoa, and salt. Gradually add flour mixture to butter mixture, beating at low speed until combined after each addition. Finely chop 1 of the bittersweet chocolate baking bars; stir into cookie dough until well incorporated.
2. Divide dough in half; shape each into an 8-inch-long log. Wrap each log tightly in plastic wrap, and freeze until firm, about 30 minutes. (Dough may be frozen up to 1 month.)
3. Preheat oven to 350°F. Cut dough into 1/4-inch-thick slices, and place 2 inches apart on parchment paper-lined baking sheets. (Keep dough logs refrigerated while cookies bake.)
4. Bake in preheated oven until bottoms are lightly browned, 11 to 13 minutes. Cool on pans 5 minutes; remove cookies to wire racks, and cool completely, about 20 minutes.
5. Chop remaining 1 1/2 bittersweet chocolate baking bars, and place in a small microwave-safe bowl. Microwave on HIGH until chocolate is melted and smooth, 1 to 1 1/2 minutes, stirring every 30 seconds.
6. Dip half of top side of each cookie in melted chocolate. Sprinkle lightly with sea salt or chopped toasted pecans, if desired. Place cookies on a parchment paper-lined baking sheet, and chill just until chocolate sets, about 15 minutes. Layer cookies between wax paper, and store in an airtight container at room temperature up to 5 days.

MAKES about 4 1/2 dozen **ACTIVE** 20 min. **TOTAL** 1 hour, 40 min.

Oyster Casserole

ON TABLES THROUGHOUT THE COASTAL SOUTH, IT WOULDN'T BE CHRISTMAS WITHOUT
THIS RICH AND CREAMY DISH. WE CAME UP WITH THE ULTIMATE RECIPE USING PLUMP,
BRINY OYSTERS, BUTTERY BREADCRUMBS, AND A VELVETY SAUCE

3. Using a fine wire-mesh strainer, strain oyster mixture; discard liquid. Add oyster mixture to cheese sauce; stir until fully incorporated. Stir in salt, pepper, and nutmeg. Spread mixture in a lightly greased (with cooking spray) 11- x 7-inch baking dish. Melt remaining 2 tablespoons of butter; toss breadcrumbs with melted butter. Sprinkle breadcrumbs over oyster mixture.
4. Broil on middle rack of oven until breadcrumbs are deep golden brown and mixture is bubbly, 4 to 5 minutes.

SERVES 4 (serving size: ³/₄ cup)
ACTIVE 20 min. **TOTAL** 30 min.

Shuck Like a Pro

Let your fishmonger do the dirty work, or grab an oyster knife and dig in. Here's how:

1 Place the oyster, curved-side down, on a clean kitchen towel. The hinge (where the two shells meet) should be facing out. Carefully wiggle an oyster knife into the hinge until you feel the seal between the two shells pop.

2 Use the tip of your knife to cut along the perimeter, severing the muscle that connects the top shell to the oyster. Remove and discard the top shell, being careful not to spill the liquid inside.

3 Wipe your knife clean, then slide it under the oyster to sever the muscle that connects it to the bottom shell. Remove any stray bits of shell or debris.

OYSTER CASSEROLE

- 5 Tbsp. salted butter, divided
- ¼ cup chopped yellow onion
- ¼ cup chopped green bell pepper
- ¼ cup chopped celery
- 2 scallions, thinly sliced (about ¹/₂ cup)
- 1 tsp. minced garlic
- 2 (16-oz.) containers fresh oysters, drained well
- 4 oz. fresh mushrooms, sliced (about 1 ¹/₂ cups)
- 2 Tbsp. all-purpose flour
- ¹/₂ cup heavy cream
- 1 oz. Parmesan cheese, grated (about ¹/₄ cup)
- ³/₄ tsp. kosher salt
- ¹/₄ tsp. black pepper
- ¹/₄ tsp. ground nutmeg

- 1 cup coarse fresh breadcrumbs (from ¹/₄ baguette)

1. Preheat broiler. Melt 2 tablespoons of the butter in a large skillet over medium-high. Add onion, bell pepper, celery, scallions, and garlic. Cook, stirring often, until vegetables soften, 5 to 7 minutes. Stir in oysters and mushrooms. Bring to a simmer, and cook, stirring often, 5 minutes. Remove from heat.
2. Melt 1 tablespoon of the butter in a small saucepan over medium. Whisk in flour, and cook, whisking constantly, until smooth, 30 seconds to 1 minute. Whisk in cream, and cook, whisking constantly, until very thick and just beginning to bubble. Whisk in Parmesan, and cook, whisking constantly, until cheese is melted. Remove from heat.

cooking ◆SL◆ school

TIPS, TRICKS, AND TECHNIQUES FROM THE SOUTHERN LIVING TEST KITCHEN

PANTRY PRIMER

BAKING ESSENTIALS BREAKDOWN

VANILLA, COCOA POWDER, AND BUTTER ARE IN HEAVY ROTATION THIS TIME OF YEAR. MAKE SURE YOU'RE USING THE RIGHT KIND FOR ALL YOUR HOLIDAY BAKING PROJECTS.

VANILLA

❶ REAL VANILLA EXTRACT: Use this expensive extract in recipes that don't require high heat, which can degrade the delicate flavor.

IMITATION VANILLA EXTRACT: For recipes that have strong flavors like chocolate or spice, it's perfectly fine to use imitation vanilla. Made from vanillin, a vanilla by-product, imitation vanilla has a stronger scent than the real stuff.

❷ VANILLA BEANS: Use vanilla beans for their rich, concentrated flavor and beautiful black seeds. One vanilla bean is roughly equal to three teaspoons of extract.

❸ VANILLA BEAN PASTE: This syrupy liquid gives you strong vanilla flavor and seeds without having to scrape any pods. If a recipe calls for one vanilla bean pod, use one tablespoon of paste. If the recipe calls for extract, use the same amount.

COCOA

❹ DUTCH PROCESS COCOA POWDER: Dutch process cocoa offers richer chocolate flavor with less bitterness. You can't always use it in place of natural cocoa. Because Dutch cocoa isn't acidic, it won't react with baking soda alone, so make sure your recipe also calls for baking powder.

❺ NATURAL COCOA: Natural cocoa hasn't been treated and is, as a result, more acidic. It has a lighter, almost reddish color and sharper chocolate flavor. Most recipes call for natural cocoa.

BUTTER

❻ Unsalted butter allows you to control the amount of salt and, since salt is a preservative, it may also be sweeter and more fresh than its salted counterpart. If a recipe calls for unsalted butter but you have only salted, simply omit half of the salt in the recipe.

COOKIE SHEET SHOWDOWN

THREE SECRETS TO BAKING BETTER BATCHES

1 What's the difference between a baking sheet and a cookie sheet, anyway? Baking sheets have higher edges to keep liquid from rolling out of the pan.

2 Choose aluminum. A basic aluminum cookie sheet is affordable and conducts heat evenly. A rimless baking sheet makes it easier to transfer cookies to cooling racks.

3 Keep it cool. When you're baking several batches of cookies at once, it's tempting to put raw cookie dough on a hot cookie sheet. Keep your cookies from spreading by letting the sheets cool down in between batches or by running tepid water over the sheets to bring the temperature down.

PAM LOLLEY

SL Test Kitchen Professional

"Don't reroll cookie dough scraps more than twice. The dough will get overworked and turn out tough."

Southern Living

50 YEARS

OUR BEST CAKE & PIE COVERS

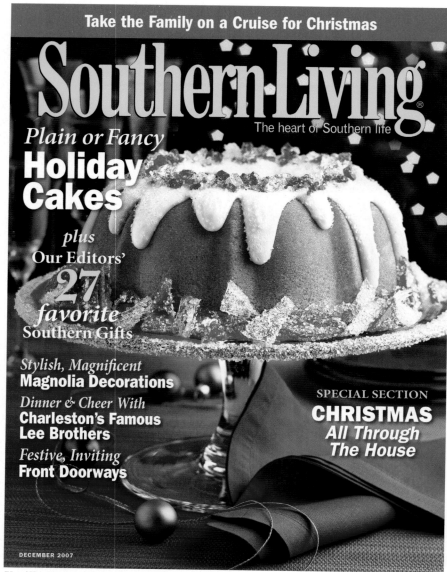

Vanilla Butter Cake, page 330

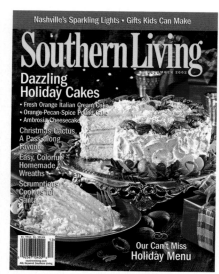

Fresh Orange Italian Cream Cake, page 327

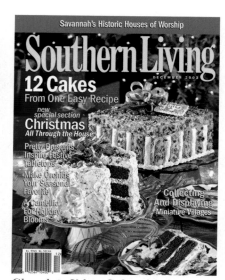

Chocolate Velvet Cake with Cream Cheese-Butter Pecan Frosting, page 328

Holiday Lane Cake, page 326

Banana Pudding Pie, page 329

Lemon-Coconut Cake, page 328

Caramel-Filled Butter Pecan Cake,
page 323

Cranberry Streusel Pie and
Apple-Pear Pull-Up Pie, page 326

Cherry-Berry Pie, page 325

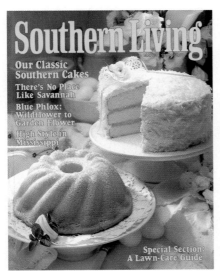

Sour Cream Pound Cake and
Coconut-Pineapple Cake, page 324

Spicy Blueberry Pie, page 325

Coconut Cream Pie, page 325;
Red, White, and Blueberry Pie,
page 326

Apple Tart with Cheese Pastry, page 323

Strawberry Shortcake, page 322

Orange-Pecan Pie, page 322

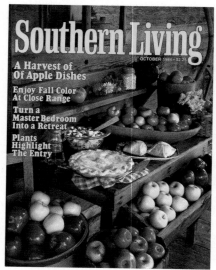

Apple Cider Pie, page 322

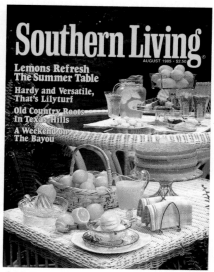

Old-Fashioned Lemon Layer Cake, page 322

Butternut Squash Pie, page 323

Fresh Strawberry Meringue Cake,
page 336

Brown Sugar-Bourbon Bundt and
Black Bottom Pumpkin Pie, page 337

Mrs. Billett's White Cake, page 338

Caramel Apple Blondie Pie,
page 338

Red Velvet-White Chocolate Cheesecake, page 339

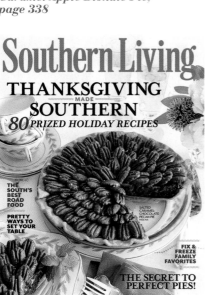

Salted Caramel-Chocolate Pecan
Pie, page 339

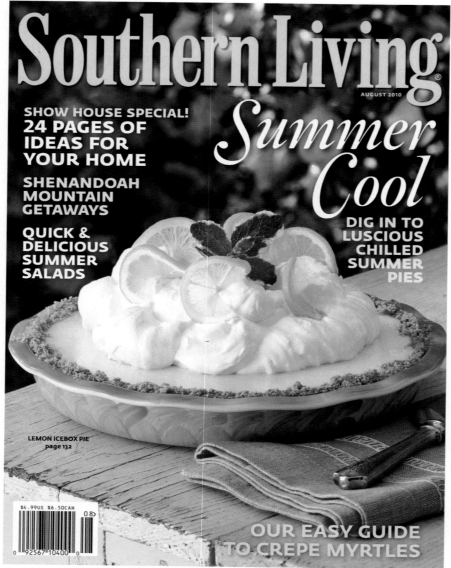

Zesty Lemon Pie, page 334

Sweet Potato Pie with Marshmallow Meringue, page 334

Elegant Citrus Tart, page 335

Strawberry Swirl Cream Cheese Pound Cake, page 335

Brown Sugar-Cinnamon Peach Pie, page 335

Lemon Meringue Ice-Cream Pie, page 336

Heavenly Angel Food Cake, page 330

Double Apple Pie with Cornmeal Crust, page 331

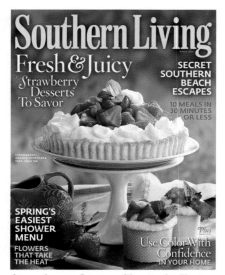

Strawberry-Orange Shortcake Tart, page 333

Pumpkin Pie Spectacular, page 332

Chocolate-Citrus Cake with Candied Oranges, page 333

Basic Vanilla Cake Batter—Our Easiest Layer Cake Ever, page 332

Lemon-Lime Pound Cake, page 340

Strawberry-Lemonade Layer Cake, page 341

Honey-Balsamic-Blueberry Pie, page 341

Apple Stack Cake, page 342

Pumpkin Tart with Whipped Cream and Almond Toffee, page 342

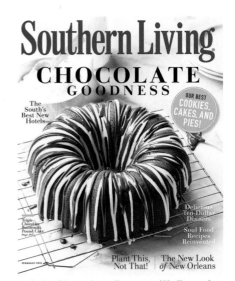

Triple-Chocolate Buttermilk Pound Cake, page 343

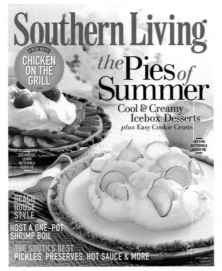

Key Lime-Buttermilk Icebox Pie, page 343; Strawberry-Lemon-Buttermilk Icebox Pie, page 344

Caramel Apple Cake, page 344

Spice Cake with Cranberry Filling, page 345

Southern Living
50 Years
1966-2016

OUR BEST CAKE & PIE COVERS

FOR 50 YEARS COOKS HAVE TURNED to the pages of *Southern Living* with confidence for the Test Kitchen-perfected recipes that they know they can trust to deliver delicious results every time. Since the very start, mile-high layer cakes with billowy frosting and over-the-top flourishes along with swoon-worthy deep-dish pies of every persuasion have been reader favorites. From old-fashioned classics such as *Holiday Lane Cake* and *Coconut Cream Pie* to new spins on Southern standards such as *Red Velvet-White Chocolate Cheesecake* and *Strawberry-Lemonade Layer Cake*, we bring you 50 decadent recipes for cakes and pies that have graced covers of the magazine over the years. This tasty homage to all things sweet is our delicious bonus to you, our dedicated readers. We invite you to continue on the journey with us as we embark on the next 50 years. So raise a fork (or two) and dig in! We thank you for making *Southern Living* the South's most iconic lifestyle brand.

STRAWBERRY SHORTCAKE
May 1981

- 1 quart strawberries, sliced
- 1/4 to 1/2 cup sugar
- 4 ounces (1/2 cup) butter, softened
- 2 cups (9 ounces) all-purpose flour
- 1/4 cup sugar
- 1 tablespoon plus 1 teaspoon baking powder
- 1/4 teaspoon table salt
  Dash of ground nutmeg
- 1/2 cup milk
- 2 large eggs, separated
- 1/4 cup sugar
- 1 cup whipping cream
- 1/4 cup (.8 ounce) sifted powdered sugar
  Whole strawberries

1. Combine the sliced strawberries and 1/4 to 1/2 cup sugar; stir gently, and chill 1 to 2 hours.
2. Preheat the oven to 450°F. Grease 2 (9-inch) cake pans with 1/2 tablespoon of the butter each.
3. Combine the flour, 1/4 cup sugar, baking powder, salt, and nutmeg in a large mixing bowl; cut in remaining butter with a pastry blender until mixture is crumbly.
4. Combine the milk and egg yolks; beat well. Add to the flour mixture; stir with a fork until a soft dough forms. Pat the dough out evenly into prepared pans. (Dough will be sticky; moisten fingers with egg whites as necessary.)
5. Beat the egg whites until stiff but not dry. Brush the surface of dough with beaten egg whites; sprinkle evenly with 1/4 cup sugar. Bake at 450°F for 10 to 12 minutes or until layers are golden brown. Cool on wire racks. (Layers will be thin.)
6. Beat the whipping cream until foamy; gradually add powdered sugar, beating until soft peaks form.
7. Place 1 of the cake layers on a serving plate. Spoon on half of the whipped cream, and arrange half of the sliced strawberries on top. Repeat procedure with the remaining cake, whipped cream, and strawberries, reserving small amount whipped cream. Top the cake with remaining whipped cream and whole berries.

SERVES 8 to 10 **ACTIVE** 30 minutes
TOTAL 1 hour, 40 minutes

ORANGE-PECAN PIE
October 1983

- 3 large eggs, beaten
- 1/2 cup sugar
- 1 cup dark corn syrup
- 1 tablespoon orange zest
- 1/3 cup orange juice
- 1 tablespoon all-purpose flour
- 1/4 teaspoon table salt
- 1 cup chopped pecans
- 1 unbaked 9-inch pastry shell
- 3/4 cup pecan halves

Preheat the oven to 350°F. Combine the first 7 ingredients; beat at medium speed with an electric mixer until blended. Stir in the chopped pecans. Pour the mixture into pastry shell. Arrange the pecan halves over top. Bake at 350°F for 55 to 60 minutes.

SERVES 6 to 8 **ACTIVE** 15 minutes
TOTAL 1 hour, 10 minutes

APPLE CIDER PIE
October 1984

PASTRY FOR DOUBLE-CRUST 9-INCH PIE

- 2 cups (9 ounces) all-purpose flour
- 1/2 teaspoon table salt
- 3/4 cup shortening
- 5 to 6 tablespoons cold water

FILLING

- 1 cup apple cider
- 2/3 cup sugar
- 6 1/2 cups peeled, sliced Stayman, Winesap, or other cooking apples
- 2 tablespoons cornstarch
- 1 tablespoon water
- 1/2 teaspoon ground cinnamon
- 1 tablespoon butter

1. Make the pastry: Preheat the oven to 375°F. Combine the flour and salt in a medium bowl; cut in shortening with a pastry blender until mixture is crumbly. Sprinkle with the cold water, 1 tablespoon at a time, over surface of mixture in bowl; stir with a fork until dry ingredients are moistened. Shape dough into a ball; chill.
2. Roll half of pastry to 1/8-inch thickness on a lightly floured surface; line a 9-inch pie plate with pastry. Roll remaining half of pastry to 1/8-inch thickness into an 11-inch circle.
3. Make the filling: Combine the cider and sugar in a large saucepan; bring to a boil. Add the apples; cook, uncovered, 8 minutes or until apples are tender. Drain, reserving syrup. Add enough water to syrup to measure 1 1/3 cups liquid; return syrup mixture and apples to saucepan. Combine the cornstarch and 1 tablespoon water, stirring well; add to apple mixture. Stir in the cinnamon; cook, stirring constantly, until thickened. Stir in the butter. Spoon the mixture into pastry-lined pie plate. Cover with remaining top crust. Trim the edges of pastry; seal and flute edges. Cut slits in top of crust for steam to escape.
4. Bake at 375°F for 45 to 50 minutes (cover edges with foil to prevent overbrowning, if necessary). Serve warm or cool.

SERVES 6 to 8 **ACTIVE** 30 minutes
TOTAL 1 hour, 15 minutes

OLD-FASHIONED LEMON LAYER CAKE
August 1985

CAKE

  Shortening
- 8 1/2 ounces (1 cup plus 1 tablespoon) butter, softened
- 2 1/4 cups sugar
- 6 large eggs, separated
- 3 1/4 cups (14.6 ounces) all-purpose flour
- 1 tablespoon baking powder
- 1/8 teaspoon table salt
- 1 cup plus 2 tablespoons milk
- 3/4 teaspoon lemon zest
- 1 3/4 teaspoons lemon juice

LEMON FILLING

- 2 1/4 cups sugar
- 1/4 cup plus 1 1/2 tablespoons (1.1 ounces) all-purpose flour
- 2 tablespoons lemon zest

½ cup lemon juice
1 large egg, beaten
2 tablespoons butter
Garnishes: lemon zest, lemon twist

1. Make the cake: Preheat the oven to 350°F. Lightly grease (with shortening) and flour 3 (9-inch) round cake pans. Beat the butter at medium speed with a mixer until creamy; gradually add sugar, beating well until blended. Add the egg yolks, 1 at a time, beating well after each addition.

2. Combine the flour, baking powder, and salt; add to butter mixture alternately with milk, beginning and ending with flour mixture. Mix well after each addition. Stir in lemon zest and juice. Beat the egg whites at medium speed until stiff peaks form; fold into batter.

3. Pour the batter into prepared pans. Bake at 350°F for 25 to 30 minutes or until a wooden pick inserted in center comes out clean. Cool in pans 10 minutes. Remove the layers; cool completely.

4. Make the filling: Combine the sugar, flour, lemon zest, lemon juice, and beaten egg in a heavy saucepan; cook over medium, stirring constantly, until smooth and thickened. Remove from heat. Add the butter; stir until melted. Cool.

5. Split each layer in half horizontally. Spread the filling between layers and on top.

SERVES 8 to 10 **ACTIVE** 20 minutes
TOTAL 1 hour, 20 minutes

BUTTERNUT SQUASH PIE
October 1987

PIE

1 (2-pound) butternut squash
¾ cup sugar
1 teaspoon ground cinnamon
½ teaspoon ground allspice
½ teaspoon ground nutmeg
¼ teaspoon ground cloves
¼ teaspoon table salt
1 (12-ounce) can evaporated milk
2 large eggs, beaten

PASTRY

1½ cups (6.75 ounces) all-purpose flour
½ teaspoon table salt
½ cup shortening
4 to 5 tablespoons milk

1. Make the pie: Preheat the oven to 350°F. Slice the squash in half lengthwise, and remove seeds. Place cut side down in a shallow baking pan; add water to a depth of ¾ inch. Bake, uncovered, at 350°F for 45 minutes or until tender. Drain and cool. Peel squash; mash pulp thoroughly. Set aside 1¼ cups mashed squash; store remainder in refrigerator for other uses. Increase oven temperature to 400°F.

2. Make the pastry: Combine the flour and salt; cut in shortening with a pastry blender until mixture is crumbly. Sprinkle the milk, 1 tablespoon at a time, over surface of mixture in bowl; stir with a fork until dry ingredients are moistened. Shape dough into a ball, and place on a lightly floured surface; roll dough into a circle 2 inches larger than inverted 9-inch pie plate. Place in pie plate, and trim edges. Fold edges under; flute.

3. Combine the pulp, sugar, spices, and salt; stir well. Gradually stir in the milk and eggs. Pour into the pastry shell; bake at 400°F for 10 minutes. Reduce heat to 350°F, and bake 40 more minutes or until set. Cool.

SERVES 6 to 8 **ACTIVE** 30 minutes
TOTAL 2 hours, 5 minutes

APPLE TART WITH CHEESE PASTRY
October 1988

1½ cups (13.5 ounces) all-purpose flour
½ teaspoon table salt
½ cup shortening
1 cup (4 ounces) shredded Cheddar cheese
4 to 5 tablespoons ice-cold water
½ cup powdered nondairy coffee creamer
½ cup firmly packed brown sugar
½ cup granulated sugar

⅓ cup (1.5 ounces) all-purpose flour
¼ teaspoon table salt
1 teaspoon ground cinnamon
½ teaspoon ground nutmeg
2 ounces (¼ cup) butter
6 cups (½-inch-thick) apple slices
2 tablespoons lemon juice

1. Preheat the oven to 450°F. Combine 1½ cups flour and ½ teaspoon salt; cut in shortening with a pastry blender until mixture is crumbly. Stir in the cheese. Sprinkle the ice water, 1 tablespoon at a time, over surface of mixture in bowl, and stir with a fork until dry ingredients are moistened. Shape into a ball. Roll dough to ⅛-inch thickness on a floured surface. Place in a 12-inch tart pan with removable bottom.

2. Combine the coffee creamer and next 6 ingredients; sprinkle half of the mixture evenly over pastry. Cut the butter into remaining mixture.

3. Arrange the apple slices in a circle in pastry shell, overlapping slices. Sprinkle with the lemon juice and remaining sugar mixture. Bake at 450°F for 30 minutes or until apples are tender. Remove from tart pan to serve.

SERVES 8 to 10 **ACTIVE** 40 minutes
TOTAL 1 hour, 10 minutes

CARAMEL-FILLED BUTTER PECAN CAKE
December 1988

CAKE

Shortening
Parchment paper
1 cup shortening
2 cups sugar
4 large eggs
3 cups (11.3 ounces) sifted cake flour
2½ teaspoons baking powder
½ teaspoon table salt
1 cup milk
1 teaspoon almond extract
1 teaspoon vanilla extract

CARAMEL FILLING

- 3 cups sugar
- 3/4 cup milk
- 1 large egg, beaten
  Pinch of table salt
- 4 ounces (1/2 cup) butter, cut up

BUTTERCREAM FROSTING

- 3 ounces (1/3 cup) butter, softened
- 3 cups (9.75 ounces) sifted powdered sugar
- 2 to 3 tablespoons half-and-half
- 1/2 teaspoon vanilla extract
- 1 cup chopped pecans
  Pecan halves

1. Make the cake: Preheat the oven to 375°F. Grease (with shortening) 3 (9-inch) round cake pans, and line with parchment paper; grease paper. Beat 1 cup shortening in a large mixing bowl at medium speed with an electric mixer until fluffy; gradually add sugar, beating well. Add the eggs, 1 at a time, beating well after each addition.

2. Combine the cake flour, baking powder, and salt; add to shortening mixture alternately with milk, beginning and ending with flour mixture, beating until blended after each addition. Stir in the flavorings.

3. Pour batter into prepared pans; bake at 375°F for 22 to 25 minutes or until a wooden pick inserted in center comes out clean. Cool in pans 10 minutes; remove from pans, and cool completely on wire racks.

4. Make the filling: Sprinkle 1/2 cup of the sugar in a large heavy saucepan. Place over medium, and cook, stirring constantly, until sugar melts and syrup is light golden brown. Combine remaining 2 1/2 cups sugar, milk, egg, and salt, stirring well; stir in butter. Stir butter mixture into hot caramelized sugar. (The mixture will tend to lump, becoming smooth with further cooking.) Cook over medium, stirring frequently, until a candy thermometer registers 230°F (15 to 20 minutes). Cool 5 minutes. Beat with a wooden spoon to almost spreading consistency. Spread Caramel Filling between layers and on top of cake.

5. Make the frosting: Beat the butter at medium speed with an electric mixer until creamy; gradually add powdered sugar alternately with half-and-half, beating until light and fluffy. Stir in the vanilla. Spread the Buttercream Frosting on sides of cake. Press chopped pecans into frosting on sides of cake. Top with pecan halves.

SERVES 8 to 10 ACTIVE 30 minutes
TOTAL 2 hours, 15 minutes, including filling and frosting

SOUR CREAM POUND CAKE

March 1989

  Shortening
- 6 ounces (3/4 cup) butter, softened
- 2 1/4 cups sugar
- 4 large eggs
- 2 1/4 cups (11.25 ounces) all-purpose flour
- 1/8 teaspoon baking soda
- 3/4 cup sour cream
- 1 teaspoon vanilla extract
- 1/4 teaspoon almond extract
- 1/4 teaspoon lemon extract
  Powdered sugar (optional)
  Lemon slices (optional)
  Lemon zest (optional)
  Fresh mint sprigs (optional)

1. Preheat the oven to 325°F. Grease (with shortening) and flour a 10-inch Bundt pan. Beat butter at medium speed with an electric mixer until creamy; gradually add sugar, beating 5 to 7 minutes. Add eggs, 1 at a time, beating just until yellow disappears.

2. Combine the flour and soda; add to butter mixture alternately with sour cream, beginning and ending with flour mixture. Beat at low speed just until blended after each addition. Stir in the flavorings.

3. Pour the batter into prepared pan. Bake at 325°F for 1 hour and 5 minutes or until a wooden pick inserted in center comes out clean. Cool in pan on a wire rack 10 to 15 minutes; remove from pan to wire rack, and cool completely on wire rack. If desired, sprinkle with powdered sugar, and top with lemon slices, lemon zest, and mint sprigs.

Note: Cake may be baked in a greased and floured 2 1/2-quart Turk's-head or Kugelhopf mold for 1 1/2 hours or until a wooden pick inserted in center comes out clean.

SERVES 10 to 12 ACTIVE 20 minutes
TOTAL 1 hour, 35 minutes

COCONUT-PINEAPPLE CAKE

March 1989

CAKE

  Shortening
- 8 ounces (1 cup) butter, softened
- 2 cups sugar
- 4 large eggs
- 3 cups (11.3 ounces) sifted cake flour
- 1 tablespoon baking powder
- 1/4 teaspoon table salt
- 1 cup milk
- 1 teaspoon vanilla extract
- 1 teaspoon almond extract

PINEAPPLE FILLING

- 1 cup sugar
- 3 tablespoons all-purpose flour
- 2 large eggs, beaten
- 1 (8-ounce) can crushed pineapple, undrained
- 2 tablespoons lemon juice
- 1/2 ounce (1 tablespoon) butter
- 1 teaspoon vanilla extract

SEVEN-MINUTE FROSTING

- 1 1/2 cups sugar
- 1/4 cup plus 1 tablespoon cold water
- 2 large egg whites
- 1 tablespoon light corn syrup
  Dash of table salt
- 1 teaspoon vanilla extract
- 2 cups grated coconut

1. Make the cake: Preheat the oven to 350°F. Grease (with shortening) and flour 3 (9-inch) round cake pans. Beat the butter in a large bowl at medium speed with an electric mixer until creamy; gradually add sugar, beating well. Add the eggs, 1 at a time, beating well after each addition.

2. Combine the flour, baking powder, and salt; add to butter mixture alternately with milk, beginning and ending with flour mixture, beating at low speed after each addition until blended. Stir in the flavorings.

3. Pour the batter into prepared pans. Bake at 350°F for 25 to 30 minutes or until a wooden pick inserted in center comes out clean. Cool in pans on wire racks 10 minutes; remove from pans, and cool completely on wire racks.

4. Make the filling: Combine the sugar and flour in a small saucepan; add eggs and next 4 ingredients. Cook over medium, stirring constantly, until thickened (about 2 minutes). Cool.

5. Make the frosting: Combine first 5 ingredients in top of a large double boiler. Beat at low speed with a handheld mixer 30 seconds or just until blended. Place over boiling water; beat constantly at high speed 7 minutes or until stiff peaks form. Remove from heat. Add the vanilla; beat 2 minutes or until frosting is thick enough to spread.

6. Spread 1 layer with half of the Pineapple Filling; sprinkle 1/3 cup of the coconut over filling. Repeat procedure with the second layer, filling, and coconut. Place the third layer on top, and spread Seven-Minute Frosting on top and sides of cake; sprinkle with remaining coconut.

Note: To prepare coconut: Carefully pierce eyes of coconut with screwdriver or ice pick; drain liquid. Place coconut in pan. Heat at 350°F for 15 to 30 minutes or until cracks appear. Remove from oven; cool. Tap with hammer to open. Remove dark skin with vegetable peeler.

SERVES 8 to 10 **ACTIVE** 1 hour, 10 minutes **TOTAL** 2 hours, 10 minutes, including filling and frosting

CHERRY-BERRY PIE
December 1992

- 1 (10-ounce) package frozen red raspberries, thawed
- 1 (16-ounce) can pitted red cherries, undrained
- 1 cup sugar
- 1/4 cup (1 ounce) cornstarch
- 2 ounces (1/4 cup) butter
- 1/4 teaspoon almond extract
- 1/4 teaspoon red liquid food coloring

- 1 (14.1-ounce) package refrigerated piecrusts
- 1 teaspoon all-purpose flour
  Garnishes: fresh raspberries, powdered sugar

1. Preheat the oven to 375°F. Drain the raspberries and cherries, reserving 1 cup combined juices; set fruit aside. Combine the sugar and cornstarch in a medium saucepan; gradually stir in juices. Cook over medium, stirring constantly, until mixture begins to boil. Cook 1 minute, stirring constantly. Remove from heat; stir in the butter, almond extract, and food coloring. Gently fold in reserved fruit; cool slightly.

2. Unfold 1 of the piecrusts, and press out fold lines; sprinkle with flour, spreading over surface. Place, floured side down, in a 9-inch pie plate; fold edges under, and flute. Spoon in the filling. Roll remaining piecrust to press out fold lines. Cut 5 leaves with a 3 1/4-inch leaf-shaped cutter, and mark veins using a pastry wheel or knife. Cut remaining pastry into 1/2-inch strips, and arrange in a lattice design over filling. Top with the pastry leaves. Bake at 375°F for 45 minutes. Cool on a wire rack.

SERVES 6 to 8 **ACTIVE** 30 minutes **TOTAL** 1 hour, 15 minutes

SPICY BLUEBERRY PIE
June 1996

- 3/4 cup granulated sugar
- 1/4 cup firmly packed brown sugar
- 1/2 cup (2.25 ounces) all-purpose flour
- 1/2 teaspoon ground cinnamon
- 1/4 teaspoon ground allspice
- 5 cups fresh blueberries
- 1 tablespoon lemon juice
- 1 tablespoon butter, melted
- 1 (14.1-ounce) package refrigerated piecrusts
- 1 tablespoon milk
- 1 teaspoon granulated sugar

1. Preheat the oven to 400°F. Combine the first 8 ingredients, tossing gently.
2. Fit 1 of the piecrusts into a 9-inch pie plate according to package directions.

Spoon the blueberry mixture into pastry shell.

3. Roll the remaining piecrust to 1/8-inch thickness; cut into 6 (2 1/2-inch-wide) strips. Arrange the strips in a lattice design over filling; fold edges under, and crimp. Brush pastry with the milk; sprinkle with 1 teaspoon sugar.

4. Bake at 400°F for 40 to 45 minutes or until golden, shielding edges with strips of aluminum foil during last 20 minutes of baking to prevent excessive browning.

SERVES 6 to 8 **ACTIVE** 15 minutes **TOTAL** 55 minutes

COCONUT CREAM PIE
June 1998

- 1/2 cup sugar
- 1/4 cup (1 ounce) cornstarch
- 2 cups half-and-half
- 4 large egg yolks
- 1 1/2 ounces (3 tablespoons) butter
- 1 cup sweetened flaked coconut
- 2 teaspoons vanilla extract
- 1 baked 9-inch pastry shell
- 1 cup whipping cream
- 1/4 cup sugar
  Garnish: toasted coconut chips

1. Combine 1/2 cup sugar and cornstarch in a heavy saucepan; gradually whisk in half-and-half and egg yolks. Bring to a boil over medium, whisking constantly; boil 1 minute. Remove the mixture from heat.

2. Stir in the butter, 1 cup flaked coconut, and 1 teaspoon of the vanilla. Cover tightly with plastic wrap, and cool to room temperature. Spoon the custard mixture into baked pastry shell, and chill 30 minutes or until set.

3. Beat whipping cream at high speed with an electric mixer until foamy; gradually add 1/4 cup sugar and remaining 1 teaspoon vanilla, beating until soft peaks form. Spread or pipe whipped cream over pie.

SERVES 6 to 8 **ACTIVE** 15 minutes **TOTAL** 1 hour

RED, WHITE, AND BLUEBERRY PIE

June 1998

- ½ cup sugar
- ⅓ cup (1.5 ounces) all-purpose flour
- 1½ cups half-and-half
- 2 large eggs
- 1 teaspoon vanilla extract
- 1 baked 9-inch pastry shell
- 1½ cups fresh blueberries
- ⅔ cup sugar
- 2 tablespoons cornstarch
- 2 tablespoons strawberry gelatin
- ⅔ cup water
- 3 pints fresh strawberries
  Garnish: fresh mint sprigs

1. Combine ½ cup sugar and flour in a heavy saucepan; gradually whisk in half-and-half and eggs. Bring to a boil over medium, whisking constantly; boil 1 minute or until thickened. Add the vanilla, and cool.

2. Spoon custard mixture into baked pastry shell. Arrange blueberries over custard mixture.

3. Combine ⅔ cup sugar, cornstarch, and gelatin in a saucepan; gradually stir in ⅔ cup water. Bring to a boil, stirring constantly; boil 1 minute. Pour half of the mixture over blueberries. Chill 30 minutes or until set.

4. Arrange strawberries over blueberries; drizzle with remaining gelatin mixture. Chill until set.

SERVES 6 to 8 **ACTIVE** 50 minutes **TOTAL** 50 minutes

CRANBERRY STREUSEL PIE

November 1998

- ½ (14.1-ounce) package refrigerated piecrusts
- 2 cups fresh or frozen cranberries
- ¼ cup granulated sugar
- ¼ cup firmly packed light brown sugar
- ½ cup chopped walnuts
- ½ teaspoon ground cinnamon
- 1 large egg

- 2 ounces (¼ cup) butter, melted
- ⅓ cup granulated sugar
- 3 tablespoons all-purpose flour

1. Preheat the oven to 400°F. Fit the piecrust into a 9-inch pie plate according to package directions; fold edges under, and crimp.

2. Stir together the cranberries and next 4 ingredients, and spoon into piecrust.

3. Whisk together the egg and next 3 ingredients, and pour over cranberry mixture. Bake at 400°F for 20 minutes. Reduce oven temperature to 350°F, and bake 30 minutes.

SERVES 6 to 8 **ACTIVE** 10 minutes **TOTAL** 1 hour

APPLE-PEAR PULL-UP PIE

November 1998

- Parchment paper
- Shortening
- 6 large Granny Smith apples, peeled and quartered*
- 6 large Bartlett pears, peeled and quartered**
- 2 cups sugar
- 1 tablespoon lemon juice
- 4 ounces (½ cup) butter
- 1 (14.1-ounce) package refrigerated piecrusts
- 1 large egg
- 1 tablespoon water
- 5 tablespoons sugar
- 1 cup whipping cream
- 2 tablespoons orange liqueur (optional)

1. Preheat the oven to 425°F. Line a baking sheet with parchment paper, and grease (with shortening) parchment paper. Lightly grease (with shortening) the sides of a 9-inch springform pan. Toss together the apples, pears, sugar, and lemon juice in a large bowl.

2. Melt the butter in a large skillet over medium-high; add apple mixture, and cook, stirring often, 15 to 20 minutes or until tender. Remove the apple mixture with a slotted spoon, reserving juices in skillet. Cook the

juices over medium-high, stirring occasionally, 10 to 15 minutes or until slightly thickened and caramel colored. Remove caramel sauce from heat.

3. Unfold piecrusts, and stack on a lightly floured surface. Roll into a 15-inch circle. Place on prepared baking sheet. Arrange apples and pears, cut sides down, in center of pastry, leaving a 3-inch border around edges. Lift pastry edges, and pull over fruit, leaving a 4- to 6-inch circle of fruit showing in center; press folds gently to secure. Stir together egg and 1 tablespoon water; brush over pastry. Sprinkle with 2 tablespoons of the sugar.

4. Place the prepared pan with clasp open around pie; close clasp. Bake on lowest oven rack at 425°F for 30 to 35 minutes or until golden brown. Run a knife around edges of pie to loosen. Cool on baking sheet on a wire rack 10 minutes. Remove pan sides.

5. Heat the caramel sauce over medium. Beat the whipping cream at medium speed with an electric mixer until foamy; gradually add remaining 3 tablespoons sugar and, if desired, liqueur, beating until soft peaks form. Serve sauce and whipped cream with pie.

Note: Do not substitute wax paper or aluminum foil in this recipe. Parchment paper is packaged similarly to wax paper.

*Gala or Rome apples may be substituted for Granny Smith.
**Bosc or Anjou pears may be substituted for Bartlett.

SERVES 6 to 8 **ACTIVE** 40 minutes **TOTAL** 2 hours

HOLIDAY LANE CAKE

December 1999

HOLLY LEAVES

- 1 (12-ounce) package green candy melts
- ⅓ cup light corn syrup
  Powdered sugar

CANDY BOW

- 1 (12-ounce) package red candy melts
- 1/3 cup light corn syrup
  Powdered sugar

CAKE

  Shortening
- 1 (18.25-ounce) package white cake mix
- 3 large eggs
- 1 1/4 cups buttermilk
- 1/4 cup vegetable oil

NUTTY FRUIT FILLING

- 4 ounces (1/2 cup) butter
- 8 large egg yolks
- 1 cup sugar
- 1 cup toasted chopped pecans
- 1 cup chopped sweetened dried cranberries or dried cherries
- 1 cup sweetened flaked coconut
- 1/2 cup diced red or green candied cherries
- 1/3 cup orange juice
- 1 (7.2-ounce) package fluffy white frosting mix
- 1/2 cup boiling water

ADDITIONAL INGREDIENTS

  Assorted red candies
  Fruit-shaped candies (optional)
  White sugar crystals

1. Make the leaves: Microwave the candy melts in a glass bowl at MEDIUM (50% power), stirring once, 1 minute or until melted. Stir in the corn syrup. Place in a zip-top plastic bag; seal and let stand 8 hours.

2. Knead 2 to 3 minutes or until soft (about 12 times). Turn out onto a surface dusted with powdered sugar. Roll to 1/16-inch thickness. Cut with 1- and 2-inch holly leaf-shaped cutters. Score leaves with a knife. Place on wax paper and over sides of an inverted cake pan for a curved shape. Let stand 3 to 4 hours. Store in an airtight container up to 3 days, if desired.

3. Make the bow: Microwave the candy melts in a glass bowl at MEDIUM (50% power), stirring once, 1 minute or until melted. Stir in the corn syrup. Place in a zip-top plastic bag; seal and let stand 8 hours.

4. Knead 2 to 3 minutes or until soft (about 12 times). Turn out onto a surface dusted with powdered sugar. Roll to 1/16-inch thickness.

5. Cut into 6 (12- x 1/2-inch) strips and 1 (1/2-inch) square using a fluted pastry cutter. Place ends of 2 strips together to form loops. Shape each loop into a heart. Place tops of hearts together to form half of bow. Place ends of 2 strips together to form 2 more loops, and place each on top of bow half. Wrap 1/2-inch square around center of bow. Place the bow on side of an inverted cake pan. Place ends of remaining 2 strips under center of bow. Shape strips into streamers; place them on sides of cake pan. Let dry at least 30 minutes. Store in an airtight container up to 3 days.

6. Make the cake: Preheat the oven to 350°F. Grease (with shortening) and flour 3 (8-inch) round or square cake pans. Combine the cake mix and next 3 ingredients in a bowl. Beat at medium speed with an electric mixer 2 minutes. Pour into prepared pans.

7. Bake at 350°F for 15 to 20 minutes or until a wooden pick inserted in center comes out clean. Cool in pans on wire racks 10 minutes. Remove from pans, and cool completely on wire racks.

8. Make the filling: Melt the butter in a heavy saucepan over low. Whisk in egg yolks and sugar; cook, whisking constantly, 11 minutes or until mixture thickens. Stir in the pecans and next 4 ingredients. Cool. Spread the Nutty Fruit Filling between layers.

9. Beat the frosting mix and 1/2 cup boiling water at low speed with an electric mixer 30 seconds. Scrape down sides of bowl; beat at high speed 5 to 7 minutes or until stiff peaks form. Spread the frosting on top and sides of cake. Arrange the Holly Leaves around top of cake to resemble a wreath. Arrange the candies for berries, and place the Candy Bow on wreath. Place the fruit candies between leaves, if desired. Sprinkle the cake with sugar crystals.

Note: We used M&M's and Skittles for red candies. Swiss Petite Fruit may be added to wreath.

SERVES 8 to 10 **ACTIVE** 1 hour, 25 minutes
TOTAL 10 hours, 25 minutes

FRESH ORANGE ITALIAN CREAM CAKE
December 2002

CAKE

  Shortening
- 4 ounces (1/2 cup) butter, softened
- 1/2 cup shortening
- 2 cups sugar
- 5 large eggs, separated
- 1 tablespoon vanilla extract
- 2 cups (9 ounces) all-purpose flour
- 1 teaspoon baking soda
- 1 cup buttermilk
- 1 cup sweetened flaked coconut

FRESH ORANGE CURD

- 1 cup sugar
- 1/4 cup (1 ounce) cornstarch
- 2 cups fresh orange juice (about 4 pounds navel oranges)
- 3 large eggs, lightly beaten
- 2 ounces (1/4 cup) butter
- 1 tablespoon orange zest

PECAN-CREAM CHEESE FROSTING

- 1 (8-ounce) package cream cheese, softened
- 4 ounces (1/2 cup) butter
- 1 tablespoon vanilla extract
- 1 (16-ounce) package powdered sugar
- 1 cup toasted chopped pecans
- 1/2 cup sweetened flaked coconut, lightly toasted (optional)

GLAZED PECAN HALVES (OPTIONAL)

  Parchment paper
  Vegetable cooking spray
- 2 cups pecan halves
- 1/3 cup light corn syrup

1. Make the cake: Preheat the oven to 350°F. Grease (with shortening) and flour 3 (9-inch) round cake pans. Beat the butter and shortening at medium speed with an electric mixer until fluffy; gradually add sugar, beating well. Add the egg yolks, 1 at a time, beating until blended after each addition. Add the vanilla; beat until blended.

2. Combine the flour and soda; add to sugar mixture alternately with buttermilk, beginning and ending with flour mixture. Beat at low speed until blended after each addition. Stir in 1 cup flaked coconut.

3. Beat the egg whites at high speed until stiff peaks form; fold into batter. Pour the batter into prepared pans.

4. Bake at 350°F for 25 minutes or until a wooden pick inserted in center comes out clean. Cool in pans on wire racks 10 minutes; remove from pans, and cool completely on racks.

5. Make the curd: Combine the sugar and cornstarch in a 3-quart saucepan; gradually whisk in the orange juice. Whisk in lightly beaten eggs. Bring to a boil (5 to 6 minutes) over medium, whisking constantly. Cook, whisking constantly, 1 to 2 minutes or until mixture reaches a pudding-like thickness. Remove from heat, and whisk in the butter and orange zest. Cover, placing plastic wrap directly on curd, and chill 8 hours. Spread 3/4 cup chilled curd between layers; spread remaining curd on top of cake. (The curd layer on top will be very thick.) If desired, loosely cover cake, and chill 8 hours. (Chilling the cake with the curd between the layers helps keep the layers in place and makes it much easier to spread the frosting.)

6. Make the frosting: Beat the first 3 ingredients at medium speed with an electric mixer until creamy. Gradually add the powdered sugar, beating at low speed until blended. Beat at high speed until smooth; stir in the pecans and coconut, if desired. Spread 3 cups frosting on sides of cake, reserving remaining frosting for another use. Sprinkle 1/2 cup toasted coconut over top of cake, if desired.

7. Make the pecan halves: Preheat the oven to 350°F. Line a 15- x 10-inch jelly-roll pan with parchment paper or aluminum foil; coat with cooking spray. Combine pecan halves and corn syrup, stirring to coat pecans. Arrange pecan halves in an even layer in prepared pan. Bake at 350°F for 12 minutes; stir using a rubber spatula. Bake at 350°F for 8 more minutes. Remove from oven, and stir; arrange in an even layer on wax paper, and cool completely. Arrange Glazed Pecan Halves around top edge of cake, if desired. Store the cake in refrigerator until ready to serve.

SERVES 12 to 16 **ACTIVE** 45 minutes
TOTAL 16 hours, 20 minutes, including chilling time

CHOCOLATE VELVET CAKE WITH CREAM CHEESE-BUTTER PECAN FROSTING
December 2003

CAKE
Shortening
1 1/2 cups semisweet chocolate morsels
4 ounces (1/2 cup) butter, softened
1 (16-ounce) package light brown sugar
3 large eggs
2 cups (9 ounces) all-purpose flour
1 teaspoon baking soda
1/2 teaspoon table salt
1 (8-ounce) container sour cream
1 cup hot water
2 teaspoons vanilla extract
CREAM CHEESE-BUTTER PECAN FROSTING
2 cups chopped pecans
2 ounces (1/4 cup) butter, melted
2 (8-ounce) packages cream cheese, softened
4 ounces (1/2 cup) butter, softened
2 (16-ounce) packages powdered sugar
2 teaspoons vanilla extract
  Garnishes: sugared silk ivy leaves, raspberry candies, toffee peanut candies, cracked partially shelled pecans

1. Make the cake: Preheat the oven to 350°F. Grease (with shortening) and flour 3 (8-inch) round cake pans. Microwave the semisweet chocolate morsels in a microwave-safe bowl at HIGH 1 1/2 minutes to 2 minutes or until melted and smooth, stirring at 30-second intervals.

2. Beat 1/2 cup butter and brown sugar at medium speed with an electric mixer, beating about 5 minutes or until well blended. Add the eggs, 1 at a time, beating just until blended after each addition. Add the melted chocolate, beating just until blended.

3. Sift together the flour, baking soda, and salt. Gradually add to the chocolate mixture alternately with sour cream, beginning and ending with flour mixture. Beat at low speed just until blended after each addition. Gradually add 1 cup hot water in a slow, steady stream, beating at low speed just until blended. Stir in the vanilla.

4. Spoon the cake batter evenly into prepared pans. Bake at 350°F for 25 to 30 minutes or until a wooden pick inserted in center comes out clean. Cool in pans on a wire rack 10 minutes; remove from pans, and cool completely on wire rack.

5. Make the frosting: Stir together the chopped pecans and 1/4 cup melted butter. Spread in an even layer in a 13- x 9-inch baking pan. Bake at 350°F for 15 minutes or until pecans are toasted. Remove from oven, and cool.

6. Meanwhile, beat the cream cheese and 1/2 cup butter at medium speed with an electric mixer until creamy. Gradually add the powdered sugar, beating until light and fluffy. Stir in the pecans and vanilla. Spread Cream Cheese-Butter Pecan Frosting between layers and on top and sides of cake.

Note: To sugar the silk ivy leaves, brush leaves lightly with corn syrup, and sprinkle with granulated sugar.

SERVES 12 **ACTIVE** 25 minutes
TOTAL 1 hour, 25 minutes

LEMON-COCONUT CAKE
December 2006

CAKE
Shortening
8 ounces (1 cup) butter, softened
2 cups sugar
4 large eggs, separated
3 cups (13.5 ounces) all-purpose flour
1 tablespoon baking powder
1 cup milk
1 teaspoon vanilla extract

LEMON FILLING

- 1 cup sugar
- ¼ cup (1 ounce) cornstarch
- 1 cup boiling water
- 4 large egg yolks, lightly beaten
- 2 teaspoons lemon zest
- ⅓ cup fresh lemon juice
- 2 tablespoons butter

CREAM CHEESE FROSTING

- 4 ounces (½ cup) butter, softened
- 1 (8-ounce) package cream cheese, softened
- 1 (16-ounce) package powdered sugar
- 1 teaspoon vanilla extract
- 2 cups sweetened flaked coconut

  Garnishes: fresh rosemary sprigs, gumdrops

1. Make the cake: Preheat the oven to 350°F. Grease (with shortening) and flour 3 (9-inch) round cake pans. Beat the butter at medium speed with an electric mixer until fluffy; gradually add sugar, beating well. Add the egg yolks, 1 at a time, beating until blended after each addition.

2. Combine the flour and baking powder; add to butter mixture alternately with milk, beginning and ending with flour mixture. Beat at low speed until blended after each addition. Stir in the vanilla.

3. Beat the egg whites at high speed with electric mixer until stiff peaks form; fold one-third of the egg whites into batter. Gently fold in remaining beaten egg whites just until blended. Spoon the batter into prepared pans.

4. Bake at 350°F for 18 to 20 minutes or until a wooden pick inserted in center comes out clean. Cool in pans on wire racks 10 minutes; remove from pans, and cool completely on wire racks.

5. Make the filling: Combine the sugar and cornstarch in a medium saucepan; whisk in 1 cup boiling water. Cook over medium, whisking constantly, until sugar and cornstarch dissolve (about 2 minutes). Gradually whisk about one-fourth of hot sugar mixture into egg yolks; add yolk mixture to remaining hot sugar

mixture in pan, whisking constantly. Whisk in lemon zest and juice.

6. Cook, whisking constantly, until mixture is thickened (about 2 to 3 minutes). Remove from heat. Whisk in the butter; cool completely, stirring occasionally. Spread Lemon Filling between layers.

7. Make the frosting: Beat the butter and cream cheese at medium speed with an electric mixer until creamy. Gradually add the powdered sugar, beating at low speed until blended; stir in vanilla. Spread the Cream Cheese Frosting on top and sides of cake. Sprinkle top and sides with coconut.

SERVES 12 **ACTIVE** 25 minutes **TOTAL** 1 hour

BANANA PUDDING PIE

February 2007

CRUST

- 1 (12-ounce) box vanilla wafers
- 4 ounces (½ cup) butter, melted
- 2 large bananas, sliced

VANILLA CREAM FILLING

- ¾ cup sugar
- ⅓ cup (1.5 ounces) all-purpose flour
- 2 large eggs
- 4 large egg yolks
- 2 cups milk
- 2 teaspoons vanilla extract
- 4 large egg whites
- ½ cup sugar

1. Make the crust: Preheat the oven to 350°F. Set aside 30 vanilla wafers; pulse remaining vanilla wafers in a food processor 8 to 10 times or until coarsely crushed. (Yield should be about 2½ cups.) Stir together the crushed vanilla wafers and butter until blended. Firmly press on bottom, up sides, and onto lip of a 9-inch pie plate.

2. Bake at 350°F for 10 to 12 minutes or until lightly browned. Remove to a wire rack, and cool 30 minutes or until completely cool.

3. Arrange the banana slices evenly over bottom of crust.

4. Make the filling: Whisk together the sugar and next 4 ingredients in a heavy saucepan. Cook over medium-low, whisking constantly, 8 to 10 minutes or until it reaches the thickness of chilled pudding. (Mixture will just begin to bubble and will be thick enough to hold soft peaks when whisk is lifted.) Remove from heat, and stir in vanilla. Spread half of the hot filling over bananas; top with 20 vanilla wafers. Spread remaining hot filling over vanilla wafers. (Filling will be about ¼ inch higher than top edge of crust.)

5. Beat the egg whites at high speed with an electric mixer until foamy. Add the sugar, 1 tablespoon at a time, beating until stiff peaks form and sugar dissolves. Spread the meringue evenly over hot filling, sealing the edges.

6. Bake at 350°F for 10 to 12 minutes or until golden brown. Remove from oven, and cool 1 hour on a wire rack or until completely cool. Coarsely crush remaining 10 vanilla wafers, and sprinkle evenly over top of pie. Chill 4 hours.

Note: We tested with Nabisco Nilla Wafers.

SERVES 8 **ACTIVE** 20 minutes
TOTAL 5 hours, 10 minutes, including chilling time

VANILLA BUTTER CAKE

December 2007

CAKE

Shortening

8 ounces (1 cup) butter, softened

2 1/2 cups sugar

5 large eggs

3 cups (13.5 ounces) all-purpose flour

1 teaspoon baking powder

1/4 teaspoon table salt

3/4 cup half-and-half

1 tablespoon vanilla extract

FLUFFY WINTRY-WHITE ICING (OPTIONAL)

2 cups (8 ounces) powdered sugar

3 to 4 tablespoons milk

1 teaspoon vanilla extract

1 teaspoon meringue powder

SPARKLING PEPPERMINT CANDY (OPTIONAL)

Vegetable oil

2 cups granulated sugar

3/4 cup light corn syrup

1/2 cup water

1 teaspoon peppermint flavoring

1/2 teaspoon red food coloring paste

Clear sparkling sugar

1. Make the cake: Preheat the oven to 325°F. Grease (with shortening) and flour a 12-cup Bundt pan. Beat the butter at medium speed with an electric mixer until creamy. Gradually add the sugar, beating at medium speed until light and fluffy. Add the eggs, 1 at a time, beating just until blended after each addition.

2. Sift together the flour, baking powder, and salt. Add to the butter mixture alternately with half-and-half, beginning and ending with flour mixture. Beat at low speed just until blended after each addition. Stir in the vanilla. Pour into prepared pan.

3. Bake at 325°F for 1 hour to 1 hour and 10 minutes or until a long wooden pick inserted in center of cake comes out clean. Cool in pan on a wire rack 15 minutes. Remove from pan to wire rack; cool 30 minutes or until completely cool.

4. If desired, make the icing: Combine powdered sugar and next 3 ingredients. Beat at medium speed with an electric mixer until light and fluffy.

5. If desired, make the candy: Generously oil the bottom and sides of a 15- x 10-inch jelly-roll pan. Stir together the granulated sugar, 1/2 cup of the corn syrup, and 1/2 cup water in an oiled 3 1/2-quart heavy sauce-pan over medium until a candy thermometer registers 300°F to 310°F (hard crack stage, about 15 to 20 minutes).

6. Remove from heat, and carefully stir in peppermint flavoring and food coloring until well blended; quickly pour mixture onto prepared pan. Cool 45 minutes or until completely cool. Carefully break into pieces.

7. Carefully brush or dip edges (some edges will be jagged and sharp) of candy pieces with remaining 1/4 cup corn syrup, allowing excess syrup to drip off. Spoon icing over cake, decorate with candy, and sprinkle with clear sparkling sugar, if desired.

Note: For Clear Sparkling Peppermint Candy, omit the red food coloring. Proceed with recipe as directed.

SERVES 12 **ACTIVE** 30 minutes **TOTAL** 2 hours, 30 minutes

HEAVENLY ANGEL FOOD CAKE

April 2008

CAKE

2 1/2 cups sugar

1 1/2 cups (6.8 ounces) all-purpose flour

1/4 teaspoon table salt

2 1/2 cups egg whites

1 teaspoon cream of tartar

1 teaspoon vanilla extract

1 teaspoon fresh lemon juice

LEMON-CREAM CHEESE FROSTING

1 1/2 (8-ounce) packages cream cheese, softened

2 ounces (1/4 cup) butter, softened

1/4 cup fresh lemon juice

1 (16-ounce) package powdered sugar

2 teaspoons lemon zest

GARNISHES (OPTIONAL)

Gumdrop Rose Petals
Gumdrops
Granulated sugar
Fresh mint leaves

1. Make the cake: Preheat the oven to 375°F. Line the bottom and sides of a 13- x 9-inch pan with aluminum foil, allowing 2 to 3 inches to extend over sides of pan. (Do not grease pan or foil.) Sift together the first 3 ingredients.

2. Beat the egg whites and cream of tartar at high speed with a heavy-duty electric stand mixer until stiff peaks form. Gradually fold in the sugar mixture, 1/3 cup at a time, folding just until blended after each addition. Fold in the vanilla and lemon juice. Spoon the batter into prepared pan. (Pan will be very full. The batter will reach almost to the top of the pan.)

3. Bake at 375°F on an oven rack one-third up from bottom of oven 30 to 35 minutes or until a wooden pick inserted in center of cake comes out clean. Invert cake onto a lightly greased wire rack; cool, with pan over cake, 1 hour or until completely cool. Remove pan; peel foil off cake. Transfer cake to a serving platter.

4. Make the frosting: Beat the cream cheese and butter at medium speed with an electric mixer until creamy; add lemon juice, beating just until blended. Gradually add the powdered sugar, beating at low speed until blended; stir in lemon zest. Spread Lemon-Cream Cheese Frosting evenly over top of cake.

5. If desired, make the rose petals: Using your thumbs and forefingers, flatten 1 small gumdrop to 1/8-inch thickness, lengthening and widening to form a petal shape. Dredge lightly in granulated sugar to prevent sticking as you work. Repeat procedure for desired number of petals. Place petals on a wire rack, and let stand uncovered for 24 hours. Holding each petal between your thumbs and forefingers, use your thumb to press the lower center portion of the petal inward, cupping the petal. Gently curl the top outer edges of the petal backward.

6. Use a single brightly colored gumdrop to shape the petals, or knead 2 colors together—such as red and white to make pink. Add more white to soften the color and create a paler pink, or add a pinch of yellow to highlight a portion of the petal. Experiment with different color combinations to see which you like best. For the prettiest petals, don't overblend the colors or be too exact with the shaping.

7. Dampen fingertips to prevent sticking when kneading gumdrops together. (A folded paper towel moistened with water works great—it's like a stamp pad for your fingertips.) It's easier to work with just 3 or 4 gumdrops at a time when blending new colors. After kneading several together, dredge lightly in sugar, and divide the mixture into small gumdrop-size portions for shaping individual petals and flowers.

8. Decorate cake with gumdrop petals and mint, if desired.

SERVES 15 **ACTIVE** 20 minutes
TOTAL 1 hour, 50 minutes, plus 1 day for garnishes

DOUBLE APPLE PIE WITH CORNMEAL CRUST

September 2008

PIE

2 1/4   **pounds Granny Smith apples (about 5 apples)**
2 1/4   **pounds Braeburn apples (about 5 apples)**
1/4   **cup (1.1 ounces) all-purpose flour**
2   **tablespoons apple jelly**
1   **tablespoon fresh lemon juice**
1/2   **teaspoon ground cinnamon**
1/4   **teaspoon table salt**
1/4   **teaspoon ground nutmeg**
1/3   **cup sugar**
CORNMEAL CRUST DOUGH
2 1/3   **cups (10.5 ounces) all-purpose flour**
1/4   **cup (1.1 ounces) plain yellow cornmeal**
2   **tablespoons sugar**
3/4   **teaspoon table salt**

6   **ounces (3/4 cup) cold butter, cut into 1/2-inch pieces**
1/4   **cup chilled shortening, cut into 1/2-inch pieces**
8   **to 10 tablespoons chilled apple cider**
  Wax paper
3   **tablespoons sugar**
1   **tablespoon butter, cut into pieces**
1   **teaspoon sugar**
BRANDY-CARAMEL SAUCE
1   **cup whipping cream**
1 1/2   **cups firmly packed brown sugar**
2   **tablespoons to 2 ounces (1/4 cup) butter**
2   **tablespoons brandy***
1   **teaspoon vanilla extract**

1. Make the pie: Peel and core the apples; cut into 1/2-inch-thick wedges. Place the apples in a large bowl. Stir in the flour and next 6 ingredients. Let stand 30 minutes, gently stirring occasionally.

2. Make the dough: Stir together the flour and next 3 ingredients in a large bowl. Cut the butter and shortening into flour mixture with a pastry blender until mixture is crumbly. Mound mixture on 1 side of bowl.

3. Drizzle 1 tablespoon apple cider along edge of mixture in bowl. Using a fork, gently toss a small amount of flour mixture into cider just until dry ingredients are moistened; move mixture to other side of bowl. Repeat procedure with remaining cider and flour mixture.

4. Gently gather dough into 2 flat disks. Wrap in plastic wrap, and chill 1 to 24 hours. Place 1 Cornmeal Crust Dough disk on a lightly floured piece of wax paper; sprinkle dough lightly with flour. Top with another sheet of wax paper. Roll dough to about 1/8-inch thickness (about 11 inches wide).

5. Preheat the oven to 425°F. Remove and discard top sheet of wax paper. Starting at 1 edge of dough, wrap dough around rolling pin, separating dough from bottom sheet of wax paper as you roll. Discard bottom sheet of wax paper. Place rolling pin over a 9-inch glass pie plate, and unroll dough over pie plate. Gently press dough into pie plate

6. Stir apple mixture; reserve 1 tablespoon juices. Spoon apples into crust, packing tightly and mounding in center. Pour remaining juices in bowl over apples. Sprinkle the apples with 3 tablespoons sugar; dot with butter.

7. Roll remaining Cornmeal Crust Dough disk as directed in Step 4, rolling dough to about 1/8-inch thickness (13 inches wide). Remove and discard wax paper, and place dough over filling; fold edges under, sealing to bottom crust, and crimp. Brush top of pie, excluding fluted edges, lightly with reserved 1 tablespoon juices from apples; sprinkle with 1 teaspoon sugar. Place pie on a jelly-roll pan. Cut 4 to 5 slits in top of pie for steam to escape.

8. Bake at 425°F on lower oven rack 15 minutes. Reduce oven temperature to 350°F; transfer pie to middle oven rack, and bake at 350°F for 35 minutes. Cover loosely with aluminum foil to prevent excessive browning, and bake at 350° for 30 more minutes or until juices are thick and bubbly, crust is golden brown, and apples are tender when pierced with a long wooden pick through slits in crust. Remove to a wire rack. Cool 1 1/2 to 2 hours before serving.

9. Make the sauce: Bring the whipping cream to a light boil in a large saucepan over medium, stirring occasionally. Add the sugar, and cook, stirring occasionally, 4 to 5 minutes or until sugar is dissolved and mixture is smooth. Remove from heat, and stir in butter, brandy, and vanilla. Cool 10 minutes. Serve pie with Brandy-Caramel Sauce.

*Apple cider may be substituted.

Note: To make the sauce ahead, prepare recipe as directed. Store in an airtight container in refrigerator up to 1 week. To reheat, let the sauce stand at room temperature 30 minutes. Place the mixture in a microwave-safe bowl, and microwave at HIGH 1 minute, stirring after 30 seconds.

SERVES 8 **ACTIVE** 30 minutes
TOTAL 3 hours, 50 minutes

BASIC VANILLA CAKE BATTER – OUR EASIEST LAYER CAKE EVER

March 2009

BASIC VANILLA CAKE BATTER

- 2 cups sugar
- 8 ounces (1 cup) butter, softened
- 3 large eggs
- 1 teaspoon vanilla extract
- 1/4 teaspoon almond extract
- 3 cups (11.3 ounces) cake flour
- 1 1/2 teaspoons baking powder
- 1/4 teaspoon table salt
- 1 cup buttermilk

1. Beat the sugar and butter at medium speed with a heavy-duty electric stand mixer until creamy and fluffy (about 5 minutes). Add the eggs, 1 at a time, beating until blended after each addition. Beat in the vanilla and almond extracts.

2. Whisk together the flour, baking powder, and salt in a bowl; add to sugar mixture alternately with buttermilk, beginning and ending with flour mixture. Beat at medium-low speed just until blended after each addition. (Batter will be thick.) Use immediately.

MAKES 6 cups **ACTIVE** 20 minutes
TOTAL 20 minutes

Ultimate Vanilla Cake Batter: Substitute 2 teaspoons vanilla bean paste for vanilla extract. Proceed with recipe as directed.

BASIC LAYER CAKE

Shortening
Basic Vanilla Cake Batter or Ultimate Vanilla Cake Batter
Vanilla Buttercream Frosting
Garnishes as desired

Preheat the oven to 350°F. Grease (with shortening) and flour 2 (8-inch) round (2-inch-deep) cake pans, spreading to edges. Bake at 350°F for 34 to 38 minutes or until a wooden pick inserted in center comes out clean. Cool in pans on a wire rack 10 minutes. Remove from the pans to wire rack, and cool completely (about 1 hour). Spread Vanilla Buttercream Frosting on top and sides of cake.

SERVES 10 to 12 **ACTIVE** 10 minutes
TOTAL 1 hour, 54 minutes

VANILLA BUTTERCREAM FROSTING

- 4 ounces (1/2 cup) butter, softened
- 1 teaspoon vanilla extract
- 1/8 teaspoon table salt
- 1 (16-ounce) package powdered sugar
- 3 to 5 tablespoons milk

1. Beat the first 3 ingredients at medium speed with an electric mixer until creamy.

2. Gradually add the powdered sugar alternately with 3 tablespoons milk, 1 tablespoon at a time, beating at low speed until blended and smooth after each addition. Beat in up to 2 tablespoons additional milk for desired consistency.

Ultimate Vanilla Buttercream Frosting: Substitute 2 teaspoons vanilla bean paste for vanilla extract. Proceed with recipe as directed.

MAKES about 2 3/4 cups **ACTIVE** 10 minutes
TOTAL 10 minutes

PUMPKIN PIE SPECTACULAR

November 2009

PIE

- 1/2 (14.1-ounce) package refrigerated piecrusts
- 2 cups crushed gingersnaps (about 40 gingersnaps)
- 1 cup pecans, finely chopped
- 1/2 cup (2 ounces) powdered sugar
- 2 ounces (1/4 cup) butter, melted
- 1 (15-ounce) can pumpkin
- 1 (14-ounce) can sweetened condensed milk
- 2 large eggs, beaten
- 1/2 cup sour cream
- 1 teaspoon ground cinnamon
- 1/2 teaspoon vanilla extract
- 1/4 teaspoon ground ginger

PECAN STREUSEL

- 1/4 cup (1.1 ounces) all-purpose flour
- 1/4 cup firmly packed dark brown sugar
- 2 tablespoons butter, melted
- 3/4 cup pecans, coarsely chopped
- 7 thin ginger cookies, halved

GINGER-SPICE TOPPING (OPTIONAL)

- 1 (8-ounce) container frozen whipped topping, thawed
- 1/4 teaspoon ground cinnamon, plus more for dusting
- 1/4 teaspoon ground ginger

1. Make the pie: Preheat the oven to 350°F. Fit the piecrust into a 9-inch deep-dish pie plate according to package directions; fold edges under, and crimp.

2. Stir together the crushed gingersnaps and next 3 ingredients. Press the mixture on bottom and 1/2 inch up sides of piecrust.

3. Bake at 350°F for 10 minutes. Cool on a wire rack (about 30 minutes).

4. Stir together the pumpkin and next 6 ingredients until well blended. Pour into prepared crust. Place pie on an aluminum foil-lined baking sheet. Bake at 350°F for 30 minutes.

5. Meanwhile, make the streusel: Stir together the flour, brown sugar, melted butter, and chopped pecans. Sprinkle the Pecan Streusel around edge of crust. Bake at 350°F for 40 to 45 more minutes or until set, shielding edges with aluminum foil during last 25 to 30 minutes of baking, if necessary. Insert ginger cookies around edge of crust. Cool completely on a wire rack (about 1 hour).

6. If desired, make the topping: Stir together the thawed whipped topping, cinnamon, and ginger. Dollop the pie with Ginger-Spice Topping; dust with cinnamon.

Note: We tested with Anna's Ginger Thins.

SERVES 8 **ACTIVE** 20 minutes
TOTAL 3 hours, 10 minutes

CHOCOLATE-CITRUS CAKE WITH CANDIED ORANGES

December 2009

WHIPPED GANACHE FILLING

- 1 (12-ounce) package semi-sweet chocolate morsels
- 1 1/2 cups whipping cream
- 1 tablespoon orange liqueur

CAKE

- Shortening
- Parchment paper
- 2 (4-ounce) bittersweet chocolate baking bars, chopped
- 4 ounces (1/2 cup) butter, softened
- 1 2/3 cups granulated sugar
- 1/3 cup firmly packed light brown sugar
- 3 large eggs
- 2 cups (9 ounces) all-purpose flour
- 1 teaspoon baking soda
- 1/2 teaspoon table salt
- 1 (8-ounce) container sour cream
- 1 teaspoon vanilla extract
- 1 cup hot brewed coffee

CANDIED ORANGES

- 4 cups water
- 2 large navel oranges, thinly sliced
- Parchment paper
- 2 cups granulated sugar
- 2 cups water
- 1/2 vanilla bean, split

SEVEN-MINUTE FROSTING

- 2 large egg whites
- 1 1/4 cups granulated sugar
- 1 tablespoon corn syrup
- 1 teaspoon orange liqueur
- 1/4 cup water
- Garnishes: fresh citrus leaves, cranberries

1. Make the ganache filling: Microwave the chocolate morsels and whipping cream in a 3-quart microwave-safe glass bowl at HIGH 2 1/2 minutes or until melted and smooth, stirring at 30-second intervals. Whisk in the liqueur until smooth. Cover and chill 2 hours or until mixture is thickened. Beat the ganache at medium speed with an electric mixer 20 to 30 seconds or until soft peaks form and ganache lightens in color. (Do not overmix.)

2. Make the cake: Preheat oven to 350°F. Grease (with shortening) and flour 2 (9-inch) round cake pans. Line the bottoms of pans with parchment paper. Lightly grease (with shortening) parchment paper.

3. Microwave the chocolate in a microwave-safe bowl at HIGH 1 1/2 minutes or until melted and smooth, stirring at 30-second intervals.

4. Beat the butter and sugars at medium speed with a heavy-duty electric stand mixer until well blended (about 3 minutes). Add the eggs, 1 at a time, beating just until blended after each addition. Add the melted chocolate, beating just until blended.

5. Sift together the flour, baking soda, and salt. Gradually add to chocolate mixture alternately with sour cream, beginning and ending with flour mixture. Beat at low speed just until blended after each addition. (Mixture will be thick.)

6. Stir the vanilla into hot coffee. Gradually add the coffee mixture to batter in a slow, steady stream, beating at low speed just until blended. Pour the batter into prepared pans.

7. Bake at 350°F for 38 to 42 minutes or until a wooden pick inserted in center comes out clean. Cool in pans on a wire rack 10 minutes. Remove from pans to wire rack, and cool completely (about 1 hour).

8. Spread the Whipped Ganache Filling between layers, spreading to edges of cake and leveling with an offset spatula. Gently press the top cake layer down, pressing out a small amount of ganache filling from between layers, and spread filling around sides of cake, filling in any gaps between layers.

9. Make the candied oranges: Bring 4 cups water to a boil in a 3- to 3 1/2-quart saucepan over medium-high. Add the oranges. Return to a boil; cook 5 minutes. Transfer oranges to a parchment paper-lined jelly-roll pan, using a slotted spoon; discard water.

10. Combine the sugar and 2 cups water in saucepan. Scrape the seeds from vanilla bean into water; add vanilla bean to water. Bring to a boil over medium-high, stirring occasionally, until sugar is dissolved. Add the orange slices. Return to a boil; cover, reduce heat to medium, and simmer 10 minutes. Uncover and cook, stirring occasionally, 35 to 45 minutes or until rinds are softened and translucent. Remove the oranges, using tongs; arrange on parchment paper-lined jelly-roll pan, folding oranges as desired. Blot with paper towels. Pour the syrup through a fine wire-mesh strainer into a bowl, reserving syrup and vanilla bean for another use. Discard solids. Let oranges stand 15 minutes.

11. Make the frosting: Pour water to a depth of 1 1/2 inches into a 2- to 2 1/2-quart saucepan; bring to a boil over medium-high. Reduce heat to medium, and simmer. Combine the egg whites, sugar, corn syrup, orange liqueur, and 1/4 cup water in a 2 1/2-quart glass bowl; beat at high speed with an electric mixer until blended. Place the bowl over simmering water, and beat at high speed 5 to 7 minutes or until soft peaks form; remove from heat. Beat to spreading consistency (about 2 to 3 minutes). Spread the Seven-Minute Frosting over top and sides of cake. Swirl frosting using back of a spoon, if desired. Top with the Candied Oranges.

SERVES 16 **ACTIVE** 1 hour
TOTAL 6 hours, 40 minutes, including candied oranges

STRAWBERRY-ORANGE SHORTCAKE TART

April 2010

- Shortening
- 1 3/4 cups (7.9 ounces) all-purpose flour
- 1/4 cup (1.1 ounces) plain yellow cornmeal
- 2 tablespoons sugar
- 3/4 teaspoon baking powder
- 1/2 teaspoon table salt
- 3 ounces (6 tablespoons) cold butter, cut into pieces
- 1 large egg, lightly beaten

2/3 cup buttermilk
1 tablespoon orange marmalade
1 (16-ounce) container fresh strawberries, cut in half
1/2 cup orange marmalade
2 cups heavy cream
2 tablespoons sugar
Garnishes: fresh mint sprigs, sweetened whipped cream

1. Preheat the oven to 425°F. Lightly grease (with shortening) a 9-inch tart pan. Place the flour and next 5 ingredients (in order of ingredient list) in a food processor. Process 20 seconds or until mixture resembles coarse sand. Transfer to a large bowl.
2. Whisk together the egg and buttermilk; add to flour mixture, stirring just until dry ingredients are moistened and a dough forms. Turn the dough out onto a lightly floured surface, and knead 3 or 4 times. Press dough on bottom and up sides of prepared pan.
3. Bake at 425°F for 20 to 22 minutes or until golden and firm to touch.
4. Microwave 1 tablespoon marmalade at HIGH 10 seconds; brush over crust. Cool 45 minutes.
5. Stir together strawberries and 1/2 cup marmalade.
6. Beat heavy cream with 2 tablespoons sugar at medium speed with an electric mixer until soft peaks form. Spoon onto cornmeal crust; top with strawberry mixture.

SERVES 8 **ACTIVE** 20 minutes
TOTAL 1 hour, 5 minutes

ZESTY LEMON PIE
August 2010

1 cup graham cracker crumbs
3 tablespoons powdered sugar
1 1/2 ounces (3 tablespoons) butter, melted
6 large egg yolks
2 (14-ounce) cans sweetened condensed milk
1 cup fresh lemon juice
1 cup whipping cream
2 tablespoons powdered sugar
Garnishes: lemon slices, fresh mint leaves

1. Preheat the oven to 350°F. Stir

together the first 2 ingredients; add butter, stirring until blended. Press mixture on the bottom and up sides of a 9-inch deep-dish pie plate. Bake at 350°F for 10 minutes. Cool completely on a wire rack (about 30 minutes).
2. Whisk together the egg yolks, sweetened condensed milk, and lemon juice. Pour into prepared crust.
3. Bake at 350°F for 15 minutes. Cool completely on a wire rack (about 1 hour). Cover and chill 4 hours.
4. Beat the whipping cream at high speed with an electric mixer until foamy; gradually add powdered sugar, beating until soft peaks form; dollop over chilled pie.

SERVES 8 **ACTIVE** 20 minutes
TOTAL 5 hours, 30 minutes

SWEET POTATO PIE WITH MARSHMALLOW MERINGUE
November 2010

CRUST
1/2 (14.1-ounce) package refrigerated piecrusts
Parchment paper
1 large egg yolk, lightly beaten
1 tablespoon whipping cream
FILLING
2 ounces (1/4 cup) butter, melted
1 cup sugar
1/4 teaspoon table salt
3 large eggs
3 cups lightly packed, mashed, cooked sweet potatoes (about 2 1/2 pounds sweet potatoes)
1 cup half-and-half
1 tablespoon lemon zest
3 tablespoons lemon juice
1/4 teaspoon ground nutmeg
MARSHMALLOW MERINGUE
3 large egg whites
1/2 teaspoon vanilla extract
1/8 teaspoon table salt
1/4 cup sugar
1 (7-ounce) jar marshmallow crème

1. Make the crust: Preheat the oven to 425°F. Roll the piecrust into a 13-inch

circle on a lightly floured surface. Fit into a 9-inch pie plate; fold edges under, and crimp. Prick bottom and sides with a fork. Line piecrust with parchment paper; fill with pie weights or dried beans. Bake at 425°F for 9 minutes. Remove weights and parchment paper.
2. Whisk together the egg yolk and cream; brush bottom and sides of crust with yolk mixture. Bake at 425°F for 6 to 8 more minutes or until crust is golden. Transfer to a wire rack, and cool. Reduce oven temperature to 350°F.
3. Make the filling: Stir together the melted butter, 1 cup sugar, and next 2 ingredients in a large bowl until mixture is well blended. Add the sweet potatoes and next 4 ingredients; stir until mixture is well blended. Pour the sweet potato mixture into prepared piecrust. (Pie will be very full.)
4. Bake at 350°F for 50 to 55 minutes or until a knife inserted in center comes out clean, shielding with aluminum foil to prevent excessive browning. Transfer the pie to wire rack, and cool completely (about 1 hour).
5. Make the meringue: Preheat the oven to 400°F. Beat the egg whites and next 2 ingredients at high speed with a heavy-duty electric stand mixer until foamy. Gradually add sugar, 1 tablespoon at a time, beating until stiff peaks form.
6. Beat one-fourth of marshmallow crème into egg white mixture; repeat 3 times with remaining marshmallow crème, beating until smooth (about 1 minute). Spread over pie.
7. Bake at 400°F for 6 to 7 minutes or until meringue is lightly browned.

Note: Pie can be made up to a day ahead. Prepare recipe as directed through Step 4; cover and chill up to 24 hours. Proceed as directed in Steps 5 through 7.

SERVES 8 to 10 **ACTIVE** 25 minutes
TOTAL 2 hours, 30 minutes

ELEGANT CITRUS TART

January 2011

TART

1/3 cup sweetened flaked coconut

2 cups (9 ounces) all-purpose flour

2/3 cup (2.7 ounces) powdered sugar

6 ounces (3/4 cup) cold butter, cut into pieces

1/4 teaspoon coconut extract

3 tablespoons water

BUTTERY ORANGE CURD

2/3 cup sugar

2 1/2 tablespoons cornstarch

1 1/3 cups orange juice

1 large egg, lightly beaten

1 1/2 ounces (3 tablespoons) butter

2 teaspoons orange zest
Pinch of table salt

9 assorted citrus fruits, peeled and sectioned

1. Make the tart: Preheat the oven to 350°F. Bake the coconut in a single layer in a shallow pan 4 to 5 minutes or until toasted and fragrant, stirring halfway through; cool completely (about 15 minutes).

2. Pulse the coconut, flour, and powdered sugar in a food processor 3 or 4 times or until combined. Add the butter and coconut extract, and pulse 5 or 6 times or until crumbly. With processor running, gradually add 3 tablespoons water, and process until dough forms a ball and leaves sides of bowl.

3. Roll dough into a 12 1/2- x 8-inch rectangle (about 1/4 inch thick) on a lightly floured surface; press on bottom and up sides of a 12- x 9-inch tart pan with removable bottom. Trim excess dough, and discard.

4. Bake at 350°F for 30 minutes. Cool completely on a wire rack (about 40 minutes).

5. Make the curd: Combine the sugar and cornstarch in a 3-quart saucepan; gradually whisk in orange juice. Whisk in the egg. Bring to a boil; boil, whisking constantly, 3 to 4 minutes.

6. Remove from heat; whisk in the butter, zest, and salt. Place heavy-duty

plastic wrap directly on curd (to prevent a film from forming), and chill 8 hours. Spread the Buttery Orange Curd over crust. Top with the citrus sections. Store leftovers in refrigerator up to 3 days.

Note: To make a round tart, roll dough into a 10-inch circle (about 1/4 inch thick) on a lightly floured surface; press on bottom and up sides of a 9-inch round tart pan with removable bottom. Trim excess dough, and discard. Bake as directed.

SERVES 8 **ACTIVE** 40 minutes
TOTAL 10 hours, 5 minutes

STRAWBERRY SWIRL CREAM CHEESE POUND CAKE

March 2011

Shortening

12 ounces (1 1/2 cups) butter, softened

3 cups sugar

1 (8-ounce) package cream cheese, softened

6 large eggs

3 cups (13.5 ounces) all-purpose flour

1 teaspoon almond extract

1/2 teaspoon vanilla extract

2/3 cup strawberry glaze

1 (6-inch) wooden skewer

1. Preheat the oven to 350°F. Grease (with shortening) and flour a 10-inch (14-cup) tube pan. Beat the butter at medium speed with a heavy-duty electric stand mixer until creamy. Gradually add the sugar, beating at medium speed until light and fluffy. Add the cream cheese, beating until creamy. Add the eggs, 1 at a time, beating just until yellow disappears.

2. Gradually add the flour to butter mixture. Beat at low speed just until blended after each addition, stopping to scrape bowl as needed. Stir in the almond and vanilla extracts. Pour one-third of the batter into prepared pan (about 2 2/3 cups batter). Dollop 8 rounded teaspoonfuls strawberry glaze over batter, and swirl with a wooden skewer. Repeat procedure

once, and top with remaining third of batter.

3. Bake at 350°F for 1 hour to 1 hour and 10 minutes or until a long wooden pick inserted in center comes out clean. Cool in the pan on a wire rack 10 to 15 minutes; remove from pan to wire rack, and cool completely (about 1 hour).

Note: We tested with Marzetti Glaze for Strawberries.

SERVES 12 **ACTIVE** 25 minutes
TOTAL 2 hours, 35 minutes

BROWN SUGAR-CINNAMON PEACH PIE

July 2011

11 ounces (1 1/3 cups) cold butter

4 1/4 cups (19.1 ounces) all-purpose flour

1 1/2 teaspoons table salt

1/2 to 3/4 cup ice-cold water

8 large fresh, firm, ripe peaches (about 4 pounds)

1/2 cup firmly packed light brown sugar

1/3 cup granulated sugar

1 teaspoon ground cinnamon

1/8 teaspoon table salt

1 1/2 tablespoons butter, cut into pieces

1 large egg, beaten

1 1/2 tablespoons granulated sugar

1. Cut 1 1/3 cups butter into small cubes, and chill 15 minutes. Stir together 4 cups of the flour and 1 1/2 teaspoons salt. Cut the butter into flour mixture with a pastry blender until mixture is crumbly. Gradually stir in 1/2 cup of the ice water with a fork, stirring until dry ingredients are moistened and dough begins to form a ball and leaves sides of bowl, adding more ice water, 1 tablespoon at a time, if necessary. Turn the dough out onto a piece of plastic wrap; press and shape dough into 2 flat disks. Wrap each disk in plastic wrap, and chill 30 minutes to 24 hours.

2. Preheat oven to 425°F. Place 1 dough disk on a lightly floured surface; sprinkle dough lightly with flour. Roll the dough to about 1/4-inch thickness. Starting at 1 edge of dough, wrap dough around a rolling pin. Place the rolling pin over a 9-inch pie plate, and unroll dough over pie plate. Press the dough into pie plate.

3. Roll remaining dough disk to about 1/4-inch thickness on a lightly floured surface.

4. Peel the peaches, and cut into 1/2-inch-thick slices; cut slices in half. Stir together the brown sugar, next 3 ingredients, and remaining 1/4 cup flour in a bowl; add peaches, stirring to coat. Immediately spoon the peach mixture into piecrust in pie plate, and dot with 1 1/2 tablespoons butter. (Do not make mixture ahead or it will become too juicy.)

5. Carefully place remaining piecrust over filling; press edges of crusts together to seal. Cut off the excess crust, and reserve. Crimp the edges of pie. If desired, reroll the excess crust to 1/4-inch thickness. Cut into 3-inch leaves using a knife. Brush the top of pie with beaten egg; top with leaves. Brush the leaves with egg; sprinkle leaves and top of pie with 1 1/2 table-spoons granulated sugar. Cut 4 or 5 slits in top of pie for steam to escape.

6. Freeze the pie 15 minutes. Mean-while, heat a jelly-roll pan in oven 10 minutes. Place the pie on hot jelly-roll pan.

7. Bake at 425°F on lower oven rack 15 minutes. Reduce oven temperature to 375°F; bake 40 minutes. Cover loosely with aluminum foil to prevent excessive browning, and bake at 375°F for 25 more minutes or until juices are thick and bubbly (juices will bubble through top). Transfer to a wire rack; cool 2 hours before serving.

SERVES 8 **ACTIVE** 30 minutes
TOTAL 4 hours, 50 minutes

LEMON MERINGUE ICE-CREAM PIE
August 2011

PIE
2 pints vanilla ice cream
VANILLA WAFER CRUST
2 1/2 cups coarsely crushed vanilla wafers
1/4 cup (1 ounce) powdered sugar
4 ounces (1/2 cup) butter, melted
HOMEMADE LEMON CURD
2 cups sugar
4 ounces (1/2 cup) butter, coarsely chopped
2 tablespoons lemon zest
1 cup fresh lemon juice (about 6 lemons)
4 large eggs, lightly beaten
16 vanilla wafers
MERINGUE TOPPING
2 large egg whites
1 1/4 cups sugar
1 tablespoon light corn syrup
1 teaspoon vanilla extract
1/4 cup water

1. Make the pie: Preheat the oven to 350°F. Let the ice cream stand at room temperature 5 minutes or just until soft enough to spread.

2. Make the crust: Stir together crushed vanilla wafers, powdered sugar, and melted butter; firmly press on bottom, up sides, and onto lip of a lightly greased 9-inch pie plate. Bake at 350°F for 10 to 12 minutes or until golden brown. Remove from oven, and cool completely (about 1 hour).

3. Make the curd: Stir together the sugar and next 3 ingredients in a large heavy saucepan over medium, and cook, stirring constantly, 3 to 4 minutes or until sugar dissolves and butter melts. Whisk about one-fourth of the hot sugar mixture gradually into eggs; add egg mixture to remaining hot sugar mixture, whisking constantly. Cook over medium-low, whisking constantly, 15 minutes or until mixture thickens and coats back of a spoon. Remove from heat; cool completely (about 1 hour), stirring occasionally.

4. Spoon 1 pint ice cream into Vanilla Wafer Crust. Top with 3/4 cup of the lemon curd; repeat with remaining ice cream and lemon curd. Gently swirl ice cream and curd with a knife or small spatula. Insert vanilla wafers around edge of pie. Cover and freeze 8 hours.

5. Make the topping: Pour water to a depth of 1 1/2 inches into a 3 1/2-quart saucepan; bring to a boil over medium-high. Reduce heat to medium, and simmer.

6. Combine the egg whites and next 4 ingredients in a 2 1/2-quart glass bowl; beat mixture at high speed with an electric mixer until blended. Place bowl over simmering water, and beat at high speed 5 to 7 minutes or until soft peaks form; remove from heat. Beat to spreading consistency (about 2 to 3 minutes). Immediately spread the Meringue Topping over pie. If desired, brown the meringue using a kitchen torch, holding torch 1 to 2 inches from pie and moving torch back and forth. (If you do not have a torch, preheat the broiler with oven rack 8 inches from heat; broil 30 to 45 seconds or until golden.) Serve immediately, or cover loosely with plastic wrap, and freeze 4 hours or up to 1 week.

Note: Plan ahead when making this recipe to allow time for the crust and curd to cool. The recipe for the lemon curd makes two cups. Reserve remaining amount in an airtight container in the refrigerator up to 2 weeks and enjoy it as a topping on pound cake or angel food cake.

SERVES 8 **ACTIVE** 15 minutes
TOTAL 11 hours, 25 minutes

FRESH STRAWBERRY MERINGUE CAKE
April 2012

Parchment paper
Masking tape
2 tablespoons cornstarch
1/8 teaspoon table salt
1 cup toasted chopped pecans
2 cups sugar
7 large egg whites, at room temperature
1/2 teaspoon cream of tartar
2 (8-ounce) containers mascarpone cheese

2 teaspoons vanilla extract
3 cups whipping cream
4 1/2 cups sliced fresh strawberries
Halved fresh strawberries

1. Preheat the oven to 250°F. Cover 2 large baking sheets with parchment paper. Draw 2 (8-inch) circles on each piece of paper. Turn paper over; secure with masking tape.
2. Process cornstarch, salt, toasted pecans, and 1/2 cup of the sugar in a food processor 40 to 45 seconds or until pecans are finely ground.
3. Beat the egg whites and cream of tartar at high speed with an electric mixer until foamy. Gradually add 1 cup of the sugar, 1 tablespoon at a time, beating at medium-high speed until glossy, stiff peaks form and sugar dissolves (2 to 4 minutes; do not overbeat). Add half of the pecan mixture to egg white mixture, gently folding just until blended. Repeat procedure with remaining pecan mixture.
4. Gently spoon egg white mixture onto circles drawn on parchment paper (about 1 1/2 cups mixture per circle), spreading to cover each circle completely.
5. Bake at 250°F for 1 hour, turning baking sheets after 30 minutes. Turn oven off; let meringues stand in closed oven with light on 2 to 2 1/2 hours or until surface is dry and meringues can be lifted from paper without sticking to fingers.
6. Just before assembling cake, stir together mascarpone cheese and vanilla in a large bowl just until blended.
7. Beat whipping cream at low speed until foamy; increase speed to medium-high, and gradually add remaining 1/2 cup sugar, beating until stiff peaks form. (Do not overbeat or cream will be grainy.) Gently fold whipped cream into mascarpone mixture.
8. Carefully remove 1 meringue from parchment paper; place on a serving plate. Spread one-fourth of the mascarpone mixture (about 2 cups) over meringue; top with 1 1/2 cups of the sliced strawberries. Repeat layers

2 times; top with remaining meringue, mascarpone mixture, and halved strawberries. Serve immediately, or chill up to 2 hours. Cut with a sharp, thin-bladed knife.

SERVES 10 to 12 **ACTIVE** 1 hour
TOTAL 4 hours, 10 minutes

BROWN SUGAR-BOURBON BUNDT
November 2012

Shortening
8 ounces (1 cup) butter, softened
1/2 cup shortening
1 (16-ounce) package light brown sugar
5 large eggs
1 (5-ounce) can evaporated milk
1/2 cup bourbon
3 cups (13.5 ounces) all-purpose flour
1/2 teaspoon baking powder
1/2 teaspoon table salt
1 tablespoon vanilla bean paste
2 tablespoons powdered sugar
Garnishes: candied oranges, magnolia leaves

1. Preheat the oven to 325°F. Grease (with shortening) and flour a 10-inch (12-cup) Bundt pan. Beat the butter and shortening at medium speed with a heavy-duty electric stand mixer until creamy. Gradually add the brown sugar, beating at medium speed until light and fluffy. Add the eggs, 1 at a time, beating just until yellow disappears.
2. Stir together the evaporated milk and bourbon in a bowl. Stir together the flour, baking powder, and salt in another bowl. Add the flour mixture to butter mixture alternately with milk mixture, beginning and ending with flour mixture. Beat at low speed just until blended after each addition. Stir in the vanilla bean paste. Pour batter into prepared pan.
3. Bake at 325°F for 1 hour and 5 minutes to 1 hour and 10 minutes or until a long wooden pick inserted in center comes out clean. Cool in pan on a wire rack 10 to 15 minutes;

remove from pan to wire rack. Cool completely (about 1 hour). Dust top lightly with powdered sugar.

SERVES 12 **ACTIVE** 20 minutes
TOTAL 2 hours, 35 minutes

BLACK BOTTOM PUMPKIN PIE
November 2012

Shortening
1 cup cinnamon graham cracker crumbs
1 cup crushed gingersnaps
4 ounces (1/2 cup) butter, melted
1/2 cup toasted chopped pecans
1 cup semisweet chocolate morsels
2 cups whipping cream
2 (1.4-ounce) chocolate-covered toffee candy bars, finely chopped
3/4 cup sugar
1/3 cup (1.5 ounces) all-purpose flour
2 large eggs
4 large egg yolks
2 cups milk
1 cup canned pumpkin
1 tablespoon vanilla bean paste*
1/2 cup maple syrup
Garnish: semisweet chocolate shavings

1. Preheat the oven to 350°F. Lightly grease (with shortening) a 10-inch pie plate. Stir together the graham cracker crumbs, next 2 ingredients, and toasted pecans until blended. Press the crumb mixture on bottom, up sides, and onto lip of prepared pie plate.
2. Bake at 350°F for 10 to 12 minutes or until lightly browned. Transfer to a wire rack, and cool completely (about 30 minutes).
3. Microwave 1 cup semisweet chocolate morsels and 1/2 cup of the whipping cream in a small microwave-safe bowl at HIGH 1 minute or until melted, stirring at 30-second intervals. Spoon the chocolate mixture over bottom of pie crust; sprinkle candy bars over chocolate mixture. Cover and chill 1 hour or until chocolate mixture is set.

4. Meanwhile, whisk together the sugar and flour in a heavy 3-quart saucepan; add eggs, egg yolks, and milk, and whisk until blended. Cook over medium, whisking constantly, 8 to 10 minutes or until a pudding-like thickness. (Mixture will just begin to bubble and will hold soft peaks when whisk is lifted.) Remove from heat, and whisk in pumpkin and vanilla bean paste. Transfer to a bowl. Place heavy-duty plastic wrap directly on the warm filling (to prevent a film from forming); chill 30 minutes. Spoon the pumpkin mixture over chocolate; cover and chill 8 to 24 hours or until filling is firm.

5. Beat remaining 1 1/2 cups cream at high speed with an electric mixer until foamy; gradually add syrup, beating until soft peaks form. Spread or pipe over pie.

*Vanilla extract may be substituted.

SERVES 6 to 8 **ACTIVE** 30 minutes
TOTAL 10 hours, 20 minutes

MRS. BILLETT'S WHITE CAKE
December 2012

CAKE
Shortening
Parchment paper
1 cup milk
1 1/2 teaspoons vanilla extract
8 ounces (1 cup) butter, softened
2 cups sugar
3 cups (13.5 ounces) cake flour
1 tablespoon baking powder
5 large egg whites
VANILLA BUTTERCREAM FROSTING
8 ounces (1 cup) butter, softened
1/4 teaspoon table salt
1 (32-ounce) package powdered sugar
6 to 7 tablespoons milk
1 tablespoon vanilla extract
Garnish: Fondant Snowflakes

1. Make the cake: Preheat the oven to 350°F. Grease (with shortening) 3 (8-inch) round cake pans; line

bottoms with parchment paper, and grease (with shortening) and flour paper.
2. Stir together the milk and vanilla.
3. Beat 1 cup butter at medium speed with a heavy-duty electric stand mixer until creamy; gradually add sugar, beating until light and fluffy. Sift together the flour and baking powder; add to butter mixture alternately with milk mixture, beginning and ending with flour mixture. Beat at low speed just until blended after each addition.
4. Beat the egg whites at medium speed until stiff peaks form; gently fold into batter. Pour the batter into prepared pans.
5. Bake at 350°F for 20 to 23 minutes or until a wooden pick inserted in center comes out clean. Cool in the pans on wire racks 10 minutes. Remove from the pans to wire racks; discard parchment paper. Cool completely (about 40 minutes).
6. Make the frosting: Beat 1 cup butter and salt at medium speed with an electric mixer 1 to 2 minutes or until creamy; gradually add powdered sugar alternately with 6 tablespoons milk, beating at low speed until blended and smooth after each addition. Stir in the vanilla. If desired, beat in remaining 1 tablespoon milk, 1 teaspoon at a time, for desired consistency. Spread the Vanilla Buttercream Frosting between layers (about 1 cup per layer) and on top and sides of cake.

SERVES 10 to 12 **ACTIVE** 40 minutes
TOTAL 2 hours

Fondant Snowflakes (OPTIONAL)

1 (24-ounce) package white rolled fondant
Powdered sugar
Vodka
White edible glitter
Pearl sparkling dust (such as Wilton Shimmer Dust)

1. If desired, make the snowflakes: Roll half of package of fondant to 1/4-inch thickness on a flat surface lightly dusted with powdered sugar. Cut fondant with small and large snow-

flake cutters. Transfer to baking sheets; let stand at room temperature 12 hours.
2. Lightly brush dry snowflakes with the vodka, and sprinkle with the glitter and sparkling dust. Arrange on cake as desired, using frosting to adhere. Press white no. 5 dragées around bottom edge of cake, if desired.

CARAMEL APPLE BLONDIE PIE
September 2013

PIE
6 large Granny Smith apples (about 3 pounds)
2 tablespoons all-purpose flour
2 cups firmly packed light brown sugar
8 ounces (1 cup) butter
1 1/2 cups (6.9 ounces) all-purpose flour
1 1/2 teaspoons baking powder
1/2 teaspoon table salt
3 large eggs, lightly beaten
3 tablespoons bourbon
3/4 cup coarsely chopped toasted pecans
1/2 (14.1-ounce) package refrigerated piecrusts
APPLE CIDER CARAMEL SAUCE
1 cup apple cider
1 cup firmly packed light brown sugar
4 ounces (1/2 cup) butter
1/4 cup whipping cream

1. Make the pie: Peel the apples, and cut into 1/4-inch-thick wedges. Toss with 2 tablespoons flour and 1/2 cup of the brown sugar in a large bowl. Melt 1/4 cup of the butter in a large skillet over medium-high; add apple mixture, and sauté 15 minutes or until apples are tender and liquid is thickened. Remove from heat; cool completely (about 30 minutes).
2. Meanwhile, preheat the oven to 350°F. Melt remaining 3/4 cup butter. Stir together 1 1/2 cups flour and next 2 ingredients in a large bowl. Add the eggs, bourbon, 3/4 cup melted butter, and remaining 1 1/2 cups brown sugar, stirring until blended. Stir in the pecans.
3. Fit the piecrust into a 10-inch cast-iron

skillet, gently pressing piecrust all the way up the sides of skillet. Spoon two-thirds of apple mixture over bottom of piecrust, spreading and gently pressing apple slices into an even layer using the back of a spoon. Spoon the batter over apple mixture; top with remaining apple mixture.

4. Place the pie on lower oven rack, and bake at 350°F for 1 hour and 10 minutes to 1 hour and 20 minutes or until a wooden pick inserted in center comes out with a few moist crumbs. Remove from oven; cool pie completely on a wire rack.

5. Make the sauce: Cook the cider in a 3-quart saucepan over medium, stirring often, 10 minutes or until reduced to ¼ cup. Stir in 1 cup firmly packed light brown sugar and next 2 ingredients. Bring to a boil over medium-high, stirring constantly; boil, stirring constantly, 2 minutes. Remove from heat, and cool completely. Refrigerate up to 1 week. To reheat, microwave at HIGH 10 to 15 seconds or just until warm; stir until smooth. Drizzle the cooled pie with ⅓ cup Apple Cider Caramel Sauce. Serve with remaining sauce.

SERVES 8 to 10 **ACTIVE** 40 minutes
TOTAL 4 hours, 30 minutes

SALTED CARAMEL-CHOCOLATE PECAN PIE
November 2013

CHOCOLATE FILLING

- 1 ½ cups sugar
- 6 ounces (¾ cup) butter, melted
- ⅓ cup (1.5 ounces) all-purpose flour
- ⅓ cup (1.07 ounces) 100% cacao unsweetened cocoa
- 1 tablespoon light corn syrup
- 1 teaspoon vanilla extract
- 3 large eggs
- 1 cup toasted chopped pecans
- 1 (9-inch) unbaked deep-dish piecrust shell

SALTED CARAMEL TOPPING

- ¾ cup sugar
- 1 tablespoon fresh lemon juice

- ¼ cup water
- ⅓ cup heavy cream
- 2 ounces (¼ cup) butter
- ¼ teaspoon table salt
- 2 cups toasted pecan halves
- ½ teaspoon sea salt

1. Make the filling: Preheat the oven to 350°F. Stir together first 6 ingredients in a large bowl. Add the eggs, stirring until well blended. Fold in the chopped pecans. Pour mixture into the pie shell.

2. Bake at 350°F for 35 minutes. (Filling will be loose but will set as it cools.) Remove from oven to a wire rack.

3. Make the topping: Bring ¾ cup sugar, 1 tablespoon lemon juice, and ¼ cup water to a boil in a medium saucepan over high. (Do not stir.) Boil, swirling occasionally after sugar begins to change color, 8 minutes or until dark amber. (Do not walk away from the pan, as the sugar could burn quickly once it begins to change color.) Remove from heat; add cream and ¼ cup butter. Stir constantly until bubbling stops and butter is incorporated (about 1 minute). Stir in the table salt.

4. Arrange the pecan halves on pie. Top with the warm caramel. Cool 15 minutes; sprinkle with sea salt.

Note: We tested with Hershey's 100% Cacao Special Dark Cocoa and Maldon Sea Salt Flakes.

SERVES 8 **ACTIVE** 25 minutes
TOTAL 1 hour, 20 minutes

RED VELVET-WHITE CHOCOLATE CHEESECAKE
December 2013

CHEESECAKE LAYERS

- 2 (8-inch) round disposable aluminum foil cake pans
  Shortening
- 1 (12-ounce) package white chocolate morsels
- 5 (8-ounce) packages cream cheese, softened
- 1 cup granulated sugar
- 2 large eggs
- 1 tablespoon vanilla extract

RED VELVET LAYERS
Shortening
- 3 (8-inch) round disposable aluminum foil cake pans
- 8 ounces (1 cup) butter, softened
- 2 ½ cups granulated sugar
- 6 large eggs
- 3 cups (13.5 ounces) all-purpose flour
- 3 tablespoons unsweetened cocoa
- ¼ teaspoon baking soda
- 1 (8-ounce) container sour cream
- 2 teaspoons vanilla extract
- 2 (1-ounce) bottles red liquid food coloring

WHITE CHOCOLATE FROSTING
- 2 (4-ounce) white chocolate baking bars, chopped
- ½ cup boiling water
- 8 ounces (1 cup) butter, softened
- 1 (32-ounce) package powdered sugar, sifted
- ⅛ teaspoon table salt

GARNISHES
White Candy Leaves: Nontoxic leaves, such as bay leaves

About 2 ounces vanilla candy coating

Parchment paper

Store-bought coconut candies

1. Make the Cheesecake Layers: Preheat the oven to 300°F. Line the bottom and sides of 2 disposable cake pans with aluminum foil, allowing 2 to 3 inches to extend over sides; lightly grease (with shortening) foil.

2. Microwave the white chocolate morsels in a microwave-safe bowl according to package directions; cool 10 minutes.

3. Beat the cream cheese and melted chocolate at medium speed with an electric mixer until creamy; gradually add 1 cup sugar, beating well. Add the 2 eggs, 1 at a time, beating just until yellow disappears after each addition. Stir in 1 tablespoon vanilla. Pour into the prepared pans.

4. Bake at 300°F for 30 to 35 minutes or until almost set. Turn oven off. Let the cheesecakes stand in oven, with door closed, 30 minutes. Remove from oven to wire racks; cool completely (about 1 1/2 hours). Cover and chill 8 hours, or freeze 24 hours to 2 days.

5. Make the Red Velvet Layers: Preheat the oven to 350°F. Grease (with shortening) and flour 3 (8-inch) disposable cake pans. Beat 1 cup butter at medium speed with a heavy-duty electric stand mixer until creamy. Gradually add the 2 1/2 cups sugar, beating until light and fluffy. Add the 6 eggs, 1 at a time, beating just until blended after each addition.

6. Stir together the flour and next 2 ingredients; add to butter mixture alternately with sour cream, beginning and ending with flour mixture. Beat at low speed just until blended after each addition. Stir in the 2 teaspoons vanilla; stir in food coloring. Spoon the batter into prepared pans.

7. Bake at 350°F for 20 to 24 minutes or until a wooden pick inserted in center comes out clean. Cool in pans on wire racks 10 minutes. Remove from pans to wire racks; cool completely (about 1 hour).

8. Make the frosting: Whisk together the chocolate and 1/2 cup boiling water until chocolate melts. Cool 20 minutes; chill 30 minutes.

9. Beat 1 cup butter and chilled chocolate mixture at low speed until blended. Beat at medium speed 1 minute. Increase speed to high; beat 2 to 3 minutes or until fluffy. Gradually add the powdered sugar and salt, beating at low speed until blended. Increase speed to high; beat 1 to 2 minutes or until smooth and fluffy.

10. Assemble the cake: Place 1 layer Red Velvet on a serving platter. Top with 1 layer Cheesecake. Repeat with remaining layers of Red Velvet and Cheesecake, alternating and ending with Red Velvet on top. Spread top and sides of cake with White Chocolate Frosting. Store in refrigerator.

11. Make the White Candy Leaves: Select nontoxic leaves, such as bay leaves. Thoroughly wash the leaves, and pat dry. Melt the vanilla candy coating in a saucepan over low heat until melted (about 3 minutes). Stir until smooth. Cool slightly. Working on parchment paper, spoon a 1/8-inch-thick layer of candy coating over backs of leaves, spreading to edges.

12. Transfer the leaves gently, by their stems, to a clean sheet of parchment paper, resting them candy-coating sides up; let stand until candy coating is firm (about 10 minutes). Gently grasp each leaf at stem end, and carefully peel the leaf away from the candy coating. Store candy leaves in a cold, dry place, such as an airtight container in the freezer, up to 1 week.

13. Handle leaves gently when garnishing or they'll break or melt. Arrange candy leaves around the base of the cake and store-bought coconut candies (such as Confetteria Raffaello Almond Coconut Treats) in the center of the cake. Accent the top of the cake with additional candy leaves. For candy pearls, simply roll any remaining candy coating into balls, and let stand until dry.

SERVES 10 to 12 **ACTIVE** 45 minutes
TOTAL 13 hours, 45 minutes

LEMON-LIME POUND CAKE

February 2014

CAKE

Shortening
12 ounces (1 1/2 cups) butter, softened
3 cups sugar
5 large eggs
2 tablespoons lemon zest
1 teaspoon vanilla extract
1 teaspoon lemon extract
3 cups (13.5 ounces) all-purpose flour
1 cup lemon-lime soft drink (such as 7UP)

LEMON-LIME GLAZE

2 cups (8 ounces) powdered sugar
2 teaspoons lemon zest
1 1/2 tablespoons fresh lemon juice
1 tablespoon fresh lime juice
1 tablespoon fresh lemon juice (optional)

CANDIED LEMONS (OPTIONAL)

2 medium lemons
4 cups water
2 cups granulated sugar
Garnish: lime zest twists

1. Make the cake: Preheat the oven to 350°F. Grease (with shortening) and flour a 10-inch Bundt pan. Beat the butter at medium speed with a heavy-duty electric stand mixer until creamy. Gradually add 3 cups sugar; beat at medium speed 3 to 5 minutes or until light and fluffy. Add the eggs, 1 at a time, beating just until blended after each addition. Stir in 2 tablespoons lemon zest and extracts.

2. Add the flour to butter mixture alternately with lemon-lime soft drink, beginning and ending with flour. Beat at low speed just until blended after each addition. Pour the batter into prepared pan.

3. Bake at 350°F for 1 hour and 5 minutes to 1 hour and 15 minutes or until a long wooden pick inserted in center comes out clean, shielding with aluminum foil after 45 to 50 minutes to prevent excessive browning. Cool in pan on a wire rack 10 minutes; remove cake from pan to wire rack.

4. Make the glaze: Whisk together the powdered sugar, lemon zest, 1 1/2 tablespoons fresh lemon juice, and lime juice in a bowl until blended and smooth. (For a thinner glaze, stir in an additional 1 tablespoon fresh lemon juice, 1 teaspoon at a time, if desired.) Spoon the glaze over warm or room temperature cake.

5. If desired, make the lemons: Cut lemons into 1/8-inch-thick slices; discard seeds. Stir together 4 cups water and sugar in a large heavy saucepan. Bring to a light boil, stirring just until sugar dissolves. Add the lemon slices; reduce heat to medium-low. Gently simmer 45 minutes or until rinds are very soft and lemons are translucent, turning lemons every 15 minutes. Remove with a slotted spoon, and place in a single layer on a wire rack. Cool completely. Top cake with the Candied Lemons.

SERVES 12 **ACTIVE** 20 minutes
TOTAL 1 hour, 35 minutes, not including glaze and candied lemons

STRAWBERRY-LEMONADE LAYER CAKE

April 2014

CAKE

Shortening
8 ounces (1 cup) butter, softened
2 cups sugar
4 large eggs, separated
3 cups (13.5 ounces) cake flour
1 tablespoon baking powder
1/8 teaspoon table salt
1 cup milk
1 tablespoon lemon zest
1 tablespoon fresh lemon juice

STRAWBERRY-LEMONADE JAM

2 1/2 cups coarsely chopped fresh strawberries
3/4 cup sugar
1/4 cup fresh lemon juice
3 tablespoons cornstarch

STRAWBERRY FROSTING

1 (8-ounce) package cream cheese, softened
2/3 cup sugar
2/3 cup chopped fresh strawberries
1 drop of pink food coloring gel (optional)
1 1/2 cups heavy cream
3 tablespoons fresh lemon juice

1. Make the cake: Preheat the oven to 350°F. Grease (with shortening) and flour 4 (9-inch) round cake pans. Beat the butter at medium speed with an electric mixer until creamy; gradually add 2 cups sugar, beating until light and fluffy. Add the egg yolks, 1 at a time, beating until blended after each addition.

2. Stir together the flour and next 2 ingredients; add to butter mixture alternately with milk, beginning and ending with flour mixture. Beat at low speed just until blended. Stir in zest and 1 tablespoon juice.

3. Beat the egg whites in a large bowl at high speed until stiff peaks form. Gently stir one-third of the egg whites into batter; fold in remaining egg whites. Spoon the batter into prepared pans.

4. Bake at 350°F for 16 to 20 minutes or until a wooden pick inserted in center comes out clean. Cool in pans on wire racks 10 minutes; remove from pans to wire racks, and cool completely.

5. Make the jam: Process 2 1/2 cups strawberries in a blender until smooth; press through a wire-mesh strainer into a 3-quart saucepan, using back of a spoon to squeeze out juice; discard pulp. Stir in 3/4 cup sugar.

6. Whisk together 1/4 cup lemon juice and cornstarch; gradually whisk into strawberry mixture. Bring the mixture to a boil over medium, and cook, whisking constantly, 1 minute. Remove from heat. Place plastic wrap directly on warm jam; chill 2 hours or until cold. Refrigerate in an airtight container up to 1 week.

7. Make the frosting: Beat the cream cheese and 1/3 cup of the sugar with an electric mixer until smooth; add 2/3 cup strawberries and food coloring (if desired); beat until blended.

8. Beat the cream and 3 tablespoons juice at medium speed until foamy; increase speed to medium-high, and slowly add remaining 1/3 cup sugar, beating until stiff peaks form. Fold half of the cream mixture into cheese mixture; fold in remaining cream mixture.

9. Place 1 cake layer on a serving platter, and spread with about 1/2 cup Strawberry-Lemonade Jam, leaving a 1/2-inch border around edges. Spoon 1 cup Strawberry Frosting into a zip-top plastic freezer bag. Snip 1 corner of bag to make a small hole. Pipe a ring of frosting around cake layer just inside the top edge. Top with second and third cake layers, repeating procedure with filling and frosting between each layer. Top with last cake layer, and spread remaining Strawberry Frosting on top and sides of cake.

SERVES 12 **ACTIVE** 45 minutes
TOTAL 4 hours, 30 minutes, including jam and frosting

HONEY-BALSAMIC-BLUEBERRY PIE

June 2014

CRUST

3 cups (13.5 ounces) all-purpose flour
6 ounces (3/4 cup) cold butter, sliced
6 tablespoons cold shortening, sliced
1 teaspoon kosher salt
4 to 6 tablespoons ice-cold water

FILLING

7 cups fresh blueberries
1/4 cup (1 ounce) cornstarch
2 tablespoons balsamic vinegar
1/2 cup sugar
1/3 cup honey
1 teaspoon vanilla extract
1/4 teaspoon kosher salt
1/4 teaspoon ground cinnamon
1/8 teaspoon finely ground black pepper
Butter
2 tablespoons butter, cut into 1/4-inch cubes
1 large egg
1 tablespoon water

1. Make the crust: Process first 4 ingredients in a food processor until mixture is crumbly. With processor running, gradually add 4 tablespoons ice-cold water, 1 tablespoon at a time, and process until dough forms a ball and pulls away from sides of bowl, adding up to 2 tablespoons more water, 1 tablespoon at a time, if necessary. Divide dough in half, and flatten each half into a disk. Wrap each disk in plastic wrap, and chill 2 hours to 2 days.

2. Make the filling: Place 1 cup of the blueberries in a large bowl; crush blueberries with a wooden spoon. Stir the cornstarch and vinegar into crushed berries until cornstarch dissolves. Stir the sugar, next 5 ingredients, and remaining 6 cups blueberries into crushed berry mixture.

3. Grease (with butter) a 9-inch deep-dish pie plate. Unwrap 1 dough disk, and place on a lightly floured surface. Sprinkle with the flour. Roll the dough to 1/8-inch thickness. Fit dough into prepared pie plate. Repeat rolling procedure with remaining dough disk; cut dough into 12 to 14 (1/2-inch-wide) strips. (You will have dough leftover.)

4. Pour the blueberry mixture into piecrust, and dot with butter cubes. Arrange the piecrust strips in a lattice design over filling. Trim the excess dough.

5. Reroll remaining dough, and cut into 6 (9- x 1/2-inch) strips. Twist together 2 strips at a time. Whisk together the egg and 1 tablespoon water. Brush a small amount of egg mixture around edge of pie. Arrange the twisted strips around edge of pie, pressing lightly to adhere. Brush the entire pie with remaining egg mixture. Freeze 20 minutes or until dough is firm.

6. Preheat the oven to 425°F. Bake the pie on an aluminum foil-lined baking sheet 20 minutes. Reduce oven temperature to 375°F, and bake at 375°F for 20 minutes. Cover pie with aluminum foil to prevent excessive browning, and bake at 375°F for 25 to 30 more minutes (65 to 70 minutes total) or until crust is golden and filling bubbles in center. Remove from baking sheet to a wire rack; cool 1 hour before serving.

SERVES 8 **ACTIVE** 40 minutes
TOTAL 5 hours, 5 minutes

APPLE STACK CAKE
September 2014

FILLING
- 3 **pounds tart apples (such as Granny Smith), peeled and cut into 1/2-inch wedges (about 6 apples)**
- 3 **pounds crisp apples (such as Braeburn or Honeycrisp), peeled and chopped (about 6 apples)**
- 1 **cup firmly packed light brown sugar**
- 1/2 **lemon, sliced**

CAKE
- **Vegetable cooking spray**
- 6 **(8-inch) round disposable aluminum foil cake pans**
- **Parchment paper**
- 8 **ounces (1 cup) butter, softened**
- 2 **cups granulated sugar**
- 5 **large eggs, separated**
- 1 1/2 **teaspoons apple pie spice**

- 3 **cups (13.5 ounces) all-purpose flour**
- 1 **cup buttermilk**
- 1 **teaspoon baking soda**
- 1 **cup chopped toasted pecans**
- 1 **cup apple butter**

GLAZE
- 1 **cup granulated sugar**
- 1/2 **cup apple cider**
- 4 **ounces (1/2 cup) butter**
- 1 **tablespoon light corn syrup**
- 1 **teaspoon vanilla extract**

1. Make the filling: Bring the first 4 ingredients to a light boil in a Dutch oven over medium-high. Reduce heat to medium-low, and simmer, stirring often, 25 to 30 minutes or until apples are tender and juices thicken. Discard lemon slices. Cool completely (about 2 hours). Cover and chill until ready to use.

2. Make the cake: Lightly grease (with cooking spray) disposable cake pans; line bottoms of pans with parchment paper, and lightly grease parchment paper.

3. Preheat the oven to 350°F. Beat 1 cup butter at medium speed with a heavy-duty electric stand mixer until creamy. Gradually add the sugar, beating until light and fluffy. Add the egg yolks, 1 at a time, beating just until blended after each addition.

4. Stir together the apple pie spice and 2 3/4 cups of the flour in a medium bowl; stir together buttermilk and baking soda in a small bowl. Add the flour mixture to butter mixture alternately with buttermilk mixture, beginning and ending with flour mixture. Beat at low speed just until blended after each addition.

5. Stir together the pecans and remaining 1/4 cup flour. Fold the pecan mixture and apple butter into batter.

6. Beat the egg whites at high speed with an electric mixer until stiff peaks form. Stir about one-third of the egg whites into batter; fold in remaining egg whites.

7. Divide the cake batter among prepared pans, spreading with an offset spatula.

8. Bake at 350°F for 7 minutes; rotate pans from top rack to bottom rack. Bake at 350°F for 7 to 9 more minutes

or until a wooden pick inserted in center comes out clean.

9. Meanwhile, make the glaze: Bring 1 cup sugar, apple cider, 1/2 cup butter, and corn syrup to a boil in a small heavy saucepan over medium-high, stirring constantly. Reduce heat to medium, and cook, stirring constantly, 4 minutes. Remove from heat, and stir in vanilla.

10. Remove the cake layers from oven, and brush each with 2 to 3 tablespoons of the warm glaze. (Reserve remaining glaze.) Cool the cake layers in pans on wire racks 10 minutes. Remove from pans to wire racks; discard parchment paper. Cool completely (about 30 minutes).

11. Assemble the cake: Place 1 layer, glaze-side up, on serving platter. Top with 1 1/2 cups filling. Repeat with remaining layers and filling. Top the last layer with any remaining filling, and drizzle cake with desired amount of reserved glaze.

Note: If necessary, microwave glaze in a microwave-safe bowl at HIGH 10 to 20 seconds before drizzling over cake.

SERVES 12 to 14 **ACTIVE** 1 hour
TOTAL 4 hours, 15 minutes

PUMPKIN TART WITH WHIPPED CREAM AND ALMOND TOFFEE
November 2014

TART
- 1/2 **(14.1-ounce) package refrigerated piecrusts**
- 3/4 **cup granulated sugar**
- 1 1/2 **tablespoons all-purpose flour**
- 2 **teaspoons pumpkin pie spice**
- 1/4 **teaspoon ground cloves**
- 3 **cups canned pumpkin**
- 1/2 **cup blackstrap molasses**
- 3 **ounces (6 tablespoons) butter, melted**
- 4 **large eggs**
- 1 **(12-ounce) can evaporated milk**

ALMOND TOFFEE
- 1/2 **cup firmly packed light brown sugar**
- 2 **ounces (1/4 cup) butter**

1 cup slivered almonds
Vegetable cooking spray
Parchment paper
WHIPPED CREAM
2 1/2 cups heavy cream
1/4 teaspoon pumpkin pie spice
1/2 cup (2 ounces) plus 2 tablespoons powdered sugar

1. Make the tart: Preheat the oven to 350°F. Fit the piecrust into a 9-inch deep-dish tart or quiche pan with removable bottom; press into fluted edges. Whisk together the granulated sugar and next 3 ingredients in a large bowl. Whisk together pumpkin and next 2 ingredients in a separate bowl. Whisk pumpkin mixture into sugar mixture. Add the eggs, 1 at a time, whisking until blended after each addition. Whisk in the evaporated milk, and pour into crust.

2. Bake at 350°F for 1 hour and 30 minutes or until a knife inserted in center comes out clean. Cool completely on a wire rack. Cover and chill 8 to 24 hours.

3. Make the toffee: Cook the brown sugar and butter in a small skillet over medium, stirring constantly, until bubbly. Add the almonds, and cook, stirring constantly, 2 minutes or until golden. Pour the mixture onto lightly greased (with cooking spray) parchment paper; cool completely. Break into pieces.

4. Make the whipped cream: Beat the cream and 1/4 teaspoon pumpkin pie spice at medium-high speed with an electric mixer until foamy; gradually add powdered sugar, beating until soft peaks form. Top the tart with whipped cream; sprinkle with toffee.

SERVES 8 to 10 **ACTIVE** 45 minutes
TOTAL 13 hours

TRIPLE-CHOCOLATE BUTTERMILK POUND CAKE
February 2015

CAKE
Shortening
2 cups (9 ounces) all-purpose flour
3/4 cup (2.44 ounces) unsweetened cocoa

1/2 teaspoon baking powder
1 teaspoon table salt
12 ounces (1 1/2 cups) butter, softened
3 cups granulated sugar
5 large eggs, at room temperature
1 1/4 cups buttermilk
2 teaspoons instant espresso
2 teaspoons vanilla extract
1 cup 60% cacao bittersweet chocolate morsels
CHOCOLATE GLAZE
3/4 cup semisweet chocolate morsels
3 ounces (3 tablespoons) butter
1 tablespoon light corn syrup
1/2 teaspoon vanilla extract
BUTTERMILK GLAZE
1 cup (4 ounces) powdered sugar
1 to 2 tablespoons buttermilk
1/4 teaspoon vanilla extract

1. Make the cake: Preheat the oven to 325°F. Grease (with shortening) and flour a 12-cup Bundt pan. Whisk together the flour and next 3 ingredients in a medium bowl. Beat 1 1/2 cups butter in a medium bowl at medium-high speed with an electric mixer until smooth. Gradually add granulated sugar, beating until light and fluffy. Add the eggs, 1 at a time, beating just until yellow disappears. Combine 1 1/4 cups buttermilk and next 2 ingredients. Add the flour mixture to egg mixture alternately with buttermilk mixture, beginning and ending with flour mixture. Beat at low speed after each addition. Fold in the bittersweet chocolate morsels. Pour the batter into prepared pan. Sharply tap pan on counter to remove air bubbles.

2. Bake at 325°F for 1 hour and 15 minutes to 1 hour and 25 minutes or until a wooden pick inserted in center comes out clean. Cool in pan on a wire rack 20 minutes. Remove from pan; cool completely on rack.

3. Make the Chocolate Glaze: Combine the semisweet morsels, 3 tablespoons butter, and 1 tablespoon corn syrup in a microwave-safe glass bowl. Microwave at MEDIUM (50% power) 1 to 1 1/2 minutes or until morsels begin to melt, stirring after 1 minute. Stir until smooth. Stir in 1/2 teaspoon vanilla.

4. Make the Buttermilk Glaze: Whisk together the powdered sugar, 1 tablespoon of the buttermilk, and 1/4 teaspoon vanilla in a small bowl until smooth. Add up to 1 tablespoon buttermilk, if desired. Drizzle warm glazes over cooled cake.

SERVES 10 to 12 **ACTIVE** 45 minutes
TOTAL 4 hours, 25 minutes

Mini Triple-Chocolate Buttermilk Pound Cakes: Prepare recipe as directed through Step 1, pouring batter into 2 lightly greased (with vegetable cooking spray) 12-cup Bundt brownie pans, filling each about three-fourths full. Bake at 325°F for 26 to 30 minutes. Cool in pans on wire racks 10 minutes; remove from pans, and cool completely. Proceed with recipe as directed in Steps 3 and 4.

MAKES 2 dozen **ACTIVE** 45 minutes
TOTAL 1 hour, 25 minutes

KEY LIME-BUTTER-MILK ICEBOX PIE WITH BAKED BUTTERY CRACKER CRUST
June 2015

BUTTERY CRACKER CRUST
1 1/2 cups crushed round buttery crackers
1/4 cup sugar
3 ounces (6 tablespoons) butter, melted
Vegetable cooking spray
PIE
1 (14-ounce) can sweetened condensed milk
1 tablespoon loosely packed lime zest
1/2 cup Key lime juice
3 large egg yolks
1/4 cup buttermilk
Vegetable cooking spray
SWEETENED WHIPPED CREAM
2 cups heavy cream
1 teaspoon vanilla extract
1/4 cup (1 ounce) powdered sugar

1. Make the crust: Preheat the oven to 325°F. Process crushed crackers and sugar in a food processor until finely crushed and well combined. Add the melted butter, and process until thoroughly combined. Press on bottom, up sides, and onto lip of a lightly greased (with cooking spray) 9-inch regular pie plate or 9-inch deep-dish pie plate. Bake the crust at 325°F 8 to 10 minutes or until lightly browned.

2. Meanwhile, make the pie: Whisk together sweetened condensed milk and next 2 ingredients in a bowl.

3. Beat the egg yolks with a handheld mixer in a medium bowl at high speed 4 to 5 minutes or until yolks become pale and ribbons form on surface of mixture when beater is lifted. Gradually whisk in the sweetened condensed milk mixture, and whisk until thoroughly combined; whisk in buttermilk. Pour the mixture into prepared crust.

4. Bake at 325°F for 20 to 25 minutes or until set around edges. (Pie will be slightly jiggly.) Cool on a wire rack 1 hour. Cover the pie with lightly greased (with cooking spray) plastic wrap, and freeze 4 to 6 hours.

5. Make the sweetened cream: Beat the cream and vanilla at medium-high speed with an electric mixer until foamy; gradually add powdered sugar, beating until soft peaks form. Top the pie with Sweetened Whipped Cream.

SERVES 8 **ACTIVE** 20 minutes
TOTAL 6 hours, 20 minutes

STRAWBERRY-LEMON-BUTTER-MILK ICEBOX PIE WITH BAKED GINGERSNAP CRUST

June 2015

GINGERSNAP CRUST

1 1/2 cups crushed gingersnaps
1/4 cup sugar
1 teaspoon kosher salt
3 ounces (6 tablespoons) butter, melted
Vegetable cooking spray

PIE

1 (14-ounce) can sweetened condensed milk
1 tablespoon loosely packed lemon zest
1/2 cup fresh lemon juice
1/2 cup strawberry jam
3 large egg yolks
1/4 cup buttermilk
Vegetable cooking spray
3 tablespoons strawberry jam
16 ounces sliced strawberries

1. Make the crust: Preheat the oven to 325°F. Process the crushed cookies, sugar, and salt in a food processor until finely crushed and well combined. Add the melted butter, and process until thoroughly combined. Press on bottom, up sides, and onto lip of a lightly greased (with cooking spray) 9-inch regular pie plate or 9-inch deep-dish pie plate. Bake the crust at 325°F for 8 to 10 minutes or until lightly browned.

2. Meanwhile, make the pie: Whisk together the sweetened condensed milk and next 3 ingredients in a bowl.

3. Beat the egg yolks with a handheld mixer in a medium bowl at high speed 4 to 5 minutes or until yolks become pale and ribbons form on surface of mixture when beater is lifted. Gradually whisk in the sweetened condensed milk mixture, and whisk until thoroughly combined; whisk in buttermilk. Pour the mixture into prepared crust.

4. Bake at 325°F for 20 to 25 minutes or until set around edges. (Pie will be slightly jiggly.) Cool on a wire rack 1 hour. Cover the pie with lightly greased (with cooking spray) plastic wrap, and freeze 4 to 6 hours.

5. Microwave 3 tablespoons strawberry jam in a medium-size microwave-safe bowl at HIGH 20 seconds. Stir the sliced strawberries into jam. Top the pie with strawberry mixture just before serving.

SERVES 8 **ACTIVE** 25 minutes
TOTAL 6 hours, 25 minutes

CARAMEL APPLE CAKE

September 2015

CAKE

Shortening
1 1/3 cups firmly packed light brown sugar
6 ounces (3/4 cup) butter, softened
3 large eggs
1 teaspoon vanilla extract
2 cups (9 ounces) all-purpose flour
1 teaspoon baking powder
1 teaspoon table salt
1 teaspoon ground cinnamon
1/2 teaspoon baking soda
3/4 cup buttermilk

APPLES

2 pounds McIntosh apples (about 6 apples, 6 to 7 ounces each)
1/2 cup firmly packed light brown sugar
1 teaspoon cornstarch
1/4 teaspoon ground cinnamon
Pinch of table salt
2 tablespoons butter

APPLE BRANDY-CARAMEL SAUCE

1/2 cup firmly packed light brown sugar
2 ounces (1/4 cup) butter
1/4 cup heavy cream
Pinch of table salt
1 tablespoon apple brandy
1 tablespoon powdered sugar

1. Make the cake: Preheat the oven to 350°F. Grease (with shortening) and flour a 9-inch round cake pan. Beat the brown sugar and butter at medium speed with a heavy-duty electric stand mixer until light and fluffy. Add the eggs, 1 at a time, beating just until blended after each addition; stir in vanilla.

2. Whisk together the flour and next 4 ingredients in a medium bowl. Add the flour mixture to sugar mixture alternately with buttermilk, beginning and ending with flour mixture. Beat just until blended after each addition. Spread the batter into prepared pan.

3. Bake at 350°F for 50 minutes or until a wooden pick inserted in center comes out clean, shielding with aluminum foil after 35 to 40 minutes to prevent excessive browning, if necessary. Cool in the pan on a wire rack 10 minutes. Remove from the pan, and cool completely (about 1 hour).

4. Meanwhile, make the apples. Cut the apples into 1/2-inch-thick wedges. Toss together the apples, 1/2 cup brown sugar, and next 3 ingredients. Melt 2 tablespoons butter in a large skillet over medium-high; add apple mixture, and sauté 5 to 6 minutes or until crisp-tender and golden. Cool completely (about 30 minutes).

5. Make the sauce: Bring the brown sugar, 1/4 cup butter, cream, and salt to a boil in a small saucepan over medium, stirring constantly. Boil, stirring constantly, 1 minute. Remove from heat, and stir in apple brandy. Whisk in the powdered sugar; cool 15 minutes before serving.

6. Arrange sautéed apples over cooled cake, and drizzle with desired amount of warm Apple Brandy-Caramel Sauce; serve with remaining sauce.

SERVES 8 to 10 **ACTIVE** 20 minutes **TOTAL** 2 hours, 20 minutes

SPICE CAKE WITH CRANBERRY FILLING
December 2015

CRANBERRY FILLING
- 2 cups fresh or frozen whole cranberries
- 1 cup granulated sugar
- 3 tablespoons fresh orange juice
- 2 tablespoons cornstarch
- 1 tablespoon cold water
- 1/2 cup chopped fresh or frozen whole cranberries
- 2 tablespoons butter

CAKE
- Shortening
- 4 (8 1/2-inch) round disposable aluminum foil cake pans
- 8 ounces (1 cup) butter, softened
- 2 cups granulated sugar
- 4 large eggs
- 3 cups (13.5 ounces) all-purpose flour
- 2 teaspoons baking powder
- 1 teaspoon ground cinnamon

- 1/2 teaspoon table salt
- 1/2 teaspoon baking soda
- 1/2 teaspoon ground ginger
- 1/4 teaspoon ground nutmeg
- 1 1/2 cups buttermilk
- 2 teaspoons vanilla extract

APPLE CIDER FROSTING
- 1 cup apple cider
- 8 ounces (1 cup) butter, softened
- 1/4 teaspoon table salt
- 1 (32-ounce) package powdered sugar
- 2 teaspoons vanilla extract
- 4 to 5 tablespoons whole milk
- Garnish: decorated sugar cones

1. Make the filling: Stir together the first 3 ingredients in a small saucepan. Whisk together the cornstarch and cold water in a small bowl until smooth. Stir the cornstarch mixture into cranberry mixture, and cook over medium-low, stirring often, 4 to 5 minutes or until cranberry skins begin to split and mixture comes to a boil. Cook, stirring constantly, 1 more minute or until thickened and translucent. Stir in the chopped cranberries and 2 tablespoons butter, and cook, stirring constantly, 1 minute or until butter is melted. Remove from heat, and cool completely (about 30 minutes). Cover and chill 8 to 24 hours.

2. Make the cake: Preheat the oven to 350°F. Grease (with shortening) and flour 4 (8 1/2-inch) round disposable aluminum foil cake pans. Beat 1 cup butter at medium speed with a heavy-duty electric stand mixer until creamy. Gradually add the 2 cups granulated sugar, beating until light and fluffy. Add the eggs, 1 at a time, beating just until blended after each addition.

3. Whisk together the flour and next 6 ingredients until well blended. Add the flour mixture to butter mixture alternately with buttermilk, beginning and ending with flour mixture. Beat at low speed just until blended after each addition. Stir in 2 teaspoons vanilla. Pour the batter into prepared pans.

4. Bake at 350°F for 18 to 20 minutes or until a wooden pick inserted in center comes out clean. Cool in the pans on wire racks 10 minutes; remove from pans. Cool completely on wire racks (about 1 hour).

5. Meanwhile, make the frosting: Cook cider in a small saucepan over medium, stirring often, 10 to 15 minutes or until reduced to 1/4 cup. Cool completely (about 20 minutes).

6. Beat the 1 cup butter and 1/4 teaspoon salt at medium speed with a heavy-duty electric stand mixer until creamy. Gradually add the powdered sugar alternately with reduced apple cider, 2 teaspoons vanilla, and 4 tablespoons of the milk, beating well after each addition. If needed, add up to 1 tablespoon milk, 1 teaspoon at a time, and beat to desired consistency.

7. Place 1 cake layer on a cake plate or platter. Spoon 1 cup Apple Cider Frosting into a zip-top plastic freezer bag. Snip 1 corner of bag to make a small hole. Pipe a ring of frosting around cake layer just inside the top edge. Spread cake layer with about 2/3 cup chilled Cranberry Filling, spreading to edge of piped frosting. Repeat with 2 more layers. Top with remaining cake layer. Spread remaining frosting over top and sides of cake.

Note: If using the sugar cones garnish, double the frosting recipe.

SERVES 10 to 12 **ACTIVE** 1 hour, 15 minutes **TOTAL** 11 hours, 15 minutes, not including sugar cone garnish

Decorated Sugar Cones

- 6 to 10 sugar cones
- Silver dragées

1. Make the cones: Let 6 to 10 sugar cones stand at room temperature, uncovered, 24 hours.

2. Cut bottom from several cones to make trees of varying heights.

3. Prepare an extra batch of Apple Cider Frosting. Using 1 cup at a time, place the frosting in a zip-top plastic freezer bag. Snip 1 corner of bag to make a 1/4-inch hole. Pipe small dots of frosting onto each cone, starting at bottom and lifting up to create a snowy branch effect. Cover cones completely with frosting.

4. Carefully press the silver dragées into wet frosting. Let cones dry 24 hours. Place around edge and on top of cake.

Appendices

handy substitutions

ingredient	substitution
baking products	
Baking powder, 1 teaspoon	· ½ teaspoon cream of tartar plus ¼ teaspoon baking soda
Chocolate	
semisweet, 1 ounce	· 1 ounce unsweetened chocolate plus 1 tablespoon sugar
unsweetened, 1 ounce or square	· 3 tablespoons cocoa plus 1 tablespoon fat
chips, semisweet, 6-ounce package, melted	· 2 ounces unsweetened chocolate, 2 tablespoons shortening plus ½ cup sugar
Cocoa, ¼ cup	· 1 ounce unsweetened chocolate (decrease fat in recipe by ½ tablespoon)
Corn syrup, light, 1 cup	· 1 cup sugar plus ¼ cup water
	· 1 cup honey
Cornstarch, 1 tablespoon	· 2 tablespoons all-purpose flour or granular tapioca
Flour	
all-purpose, 1 tablespoon	· 1½ teaspoons cornstarch, potato starch, or rice starch
	· 1 tablespoon rice flour or corn flour
	· 1½ tablespoons whole-wheat flour
all-purpose, 1 cup sifted	· 1 cup plus 2 tablespoons sifted cake flour
cake, 1 cup sifted	· 1 cup minus 2 tablespoons all-purpose flour
self-rising, 1 cup	· 1 cup all-purpose flour, 1 teaspoon baking powder plus ½ teaspoon salt
Shortening	
melted, 1 cup	· 1 cup cooking oil (don't use cooking oil unless recipe calls for melted shortening)
solid, 1 cup (used in baking)	· 1⅛ cups butter (decrease salt called for in recipe by ½ teaspoon)
Sugar	
brown, 1 cup firmly packed	· 1 cup granulated white sugar
powdered, 1 cup	· 1 cup sugar plus 1 tablespoon cornstarch (processed in food processor)
granulated white, 1 teaspoon	· ⅛ teaspoon noncaloric sweetener solution or follow manufacturer's directions
granulated white, 1 cup	· 1 cup corn syrup (decrease liquid called for in recipe by ¼ cup)
	· 1 cup honey (decrease liquid called for in recipe by ¼ cup)
Tapioca, granular, 1 tablespoon	· 1½ teaspoons cornstarch or 1 tablespoon all-purpose flour
dairy products	
Butter, 1 cup	· ⅞ to 1 cup shortening or lard plus ½ teaspoon salt
	· 1 cup margarine (2 sticks; do not substitute whipped or low-fat margarine)
Cream	
heavy (30% to 40% fat), 1 cup	· ¾ cup milk plus ⅓ cup butter (for cooking and baking; will not whip)
light (15% to 20% fat), 1 cup	· ¾ cup milk plus 3 tablespoons butter or margarine (for cooking and baking)
	· 1 cup evaporated milk, undiluted
half-and-half, 1 cup	· ⅞ cup milk plus ½ tablespoon butter or margarine (for cooking and baking)
	· 1 cup evaporated milk, undiluted
whipped, 1 cup	· 1 cup frozen whipped topping, thawed
Egg	
1 large	· ¼ cup egg substitute
2 large	· 3 small eggs or ½ cup egg substitute
	· 1 large egg plus 2 egg whites
1 egg white (2 tablespoons)	· 2 tablespoons egg substitute
Milk	
buttermilk, 1 cup	· 1 tablespoon vinegar or lemon juice plus whole milk to make 1 cup (let stand 10 minutes)
	· 1 cup plain yogurt
	· 1 cup whole milk plus 1¾ teaspoons cream of tartar
fat-free, 1 cup	· 4 to 5 tablespoons nonfat dry milk powder plus enough water to make 1 cup
	· ½ cup evaporated skim milk plus ½ cup water
whole, 1 cup	· 4 to 5 tablespoons nonfat dry milk powder plus enough water to make 1 cup
	· ½ cup evaporated milk plus ½ cup water

handy substitutions

ingredient	substitution
Milk (continued)	
sweetened condensed, 1 (14-ounce) can (about 1¼ cups)	· Heat the following ingredients until sugar and butter dissolve: ⅓ cup plus 2 tablespoons evaporated milk, 1 cup sugar, 3 tablespoons butter. · Add 1 cup plus 2 tablespoons nonfat dry milk powder to ½ cup warm water. Mix well. Add ¾ cup sugar, and stir until smooth.
Sour cream, 1 cup	· 1 cup plain yogurt plus 3 tablespoons melted butter or 1 tablespoon cornstarch · 1 tablespoon lemon juice plus evaporated milk to equal 1 cup
Yogurt, 1 cup (plain)	· 1 cup buttermilk

miscellaneous

ingredient	substitution
Broth, beef or chicken canned broth, 1 cup	· 1 bouillon cube or 1 teaspoon bouillon granules dissolved in 1 cup boiling water
Garlic	
1 small clove	· ⅛ teaspoon garlic powder or minced dried garlic
garlic salt, 1 teaspoon	· ⅛ teaspoon garlic powder plus ⅞ teaspoon salt
Gelatin, flavored, 3-ounce package	· 1 tablespoon unflavored gelatin plus 2 cups fruit juice
Herbs, fresh, chopped, 1 tablespoon	· 1 teaspoon dried herbs or ¼ teaspoon ground herbs
Honey, 1 cup	· 1¼ cups sugar plus ¼ cup water
Mustard, dried, 1 teaspoon	· 1 tablespoon prepared mustard
Tomatoes, fresh, chopped, 2 cups	· 1 (16-ounce) can (may need to drain)
Tomato sauce, 2 cups	· ¾ cup tomato paste plus 1 cup water

alcohol substitutions

alcohol	substitution
Amaretto, 2 tablespoons	· ¼ to ½ teaspoon almond extract*
Bourbon or sherry, 2 tablespoons	· 1 to 2 teaspoons vanilla extract*
Brandy, fruit-flavored liqueur, port wine, rum, or sweet sherry, ¼ cup or more	· Equal amount of unsweetened orange or apple juice plus 1 teaspoon vanilla extract or corresponding flavor
Brandy or rum, 2 tablespoons	· ½ to 1 teaspoon brandy or rum extract*
Grand Marnier or other orange liqueur, 2 tablespoons	· 2 tablespoons unsweetened orange juice concentrate or 2 tablespoons orange juice and ½ teaspoon orange extract
Kahlúa or other coffee or chocolate liqueur, 2 tablespoons	· ½ to 1 teaspoon chocolate extract plus ½ to 1 teaspoon instant coffee dissolved in 2 tablespoons water
Marsala, ¼ cup	· ¼ cup white grape juice or ¼ cup dry white wine plus 1 teaspoon brandy
Wine	
red, ¼ cup or more	· Equal measure of red grape juice or cranberry juice
white, ¼ cup or more	· Equal measure of white grape juice or nonalcoholic white wine

Add water, white grape juice, or apple juice to get the specified amount of liquid (when the liquid amount is crucial).

equivalent measures

3 teaspoons	= 1 tablespoon	2 tablespoons (liquid)	= 1 ounce	⅛ cup	= 2 tablespoons
4 tablespoons	= ¼ cup	1 cup	= 8 fluid ounces	⅓ cup	= 5 tablespoons plus 1 teaspoon
5⅓ tablespoons	= ⅓ cup	2 cups	= 1 pint (16 fluid ounces)		
8 tablespoons	= ½ cup			⅔ cup	= 10 tablespoons plus 2 teaspoons
16 tablespoons	= 1 cup	4 cups	= 1 quart		
		4 quarts	= 1 gallon	¾ cup	= 12 tablespoons

baking at high altitudes

Liquids boil at lower temperatures (below 212°F), and moisture evaporates more quickly at high altitudes. Both of these factors significantly impact the quality of baked goods. Also, leavening gases (air, carbon dioxide, water vapor) expand faster. If you live at 3,000 feet or below, first try a recipe as is. Sometimes few, if any, changes are needed. But the higher you go, the more you'll have to adjust your ingredients and cooking times.

A Few Overall Tips

- Use shiny new baking pans. This seems to help mixtures rise, especially cake batters.
- Use butter, flour, and parchment paper to prep your baking pans for nonstick cooking. At high altitudes, baked goods tend to stick more to pans.
- Be exact in your measurements (once you've figured out what they should be). This is always important in baking, but especially so when you're up so high. Tiny variations in ingredients make a bigger difference at high altitudes than at sea level.
- Boost flavor. Seasonings and extracts tend to be more muted at higher altitudes, so increase them slightly.
- Have patience. You may have to bake your favorite sea-level recipe a few times, making slight adjustments each time, until it's worked out to suit your particular altitude.

ingredient/temperature adjustments

CHANGE	AT 3,000 FEET	AT 5,000 FEET	AT 7,000 FEET
Baking powder or baking soda	• Reduce each tsp. called for by up to ⅛ tsp.	• Reduce each tsp. called for by ⅛ to ¼ tsp.	• Reduce each tsp. called for by ¼ to ½ tsp.
Sugar	• Reduce each cup called for by up to 1 Tbsp.	• Reduce each cup called for by up to 2 Tbsp.	• Reduce each cup called for by 2 to 3 Tbsp.
Liquid	• Increase each cup called for by up to 2 Tbsp.	• Increase each cup called for by up to 2 to 4 Tbsp.	• Increase each cup called for by up to 3 to 4 Tbsp.
Oven temperature	• Increase 3° to 5°	• Increase 15°	• Increase 21° to 25°

METRIC EQUIVALENTS

The recipes that appear in this cookbook use the standard United States method for measuring liquid and dry or solid ingredients (teaspoons, tablespoons, and cups). The information on this chart is provided to help cooks outside the U.S. successfully use these recipes. All equivalents are approximate.

METRIC EQUIVALENTS FOR DIFFERENT TYPES OF INGREDIENTS

A standard cup measure of a dry or solid ingredient will vary in weight depending on the type of ingredient. A standard cup of liquid is the same volume for any type of liquid. Use the following chart when converting standard cup measures to grams (weight) or milliliters (volume).

Standard Cup	Fine Powder (ex. flour)	Grain (ex. rice)	Granular (ex. sugar)	Liquid Solids (ex. butter)	Liquid (ex. milk)
1	140 g	150 g	190 g	200 g	240 ml
¾	105 g	113 g	143 g	150 g	180 ml
⅔	93 g	100 g	125 g	133 g	160 ml
½	70 g	75 g	95 g	100 g	120 ml
⅓	47 g	50 g	63 g	67 g	80 ml
¼	35 g	38 g	48 g	50 g	60 ml
⅛	18 g	19 g	24 g	25 g	30 ml

USEFUL EQUIVALENTS FOR DRY INGREDIENTS BY WEIGHT

(To convert ounces to grams, multiply the number of ounces by 30.)

1 oz	=	1/16 lb	=	30 g
4 oz	=	¼ lb	=	120 g
8 oz	=	½ lb	=	240 g
12 oz	=	¾ lb	=	360 g
16 oz	=	1 lb	=	480 g

USEFUL EQUIVALENTS FOR LENGTH

(To convert inches to centimeters, multiply the number of inches by 2.5.)

1 in				=	2.5 cm		
6 in	=	½ ft		=	15 cm		
12 in	=	1 ft		=	30 cm		
36 in	=	3 ft	=	1 yd	=	90 cm	
40 in				=	100 cm	=	1 m

USEFUL EQUIVALENTS FOR LIQUID INGREDIENTS BY VOLUME

¼ tsp						=	1 ml	
½ tsp						=	2 ml	
1 tsp						=	5 ml	
3 tsp	=	1 Tbsp			=	½ fl oz	=	15 ml
		2 Tbsp	=	⅛ cup	=	1 fl oz	=	30 ml
		4 Tbsp	=	¼ cup	=	2 fl oz	=	60 ml
		5⅓ Tbsp	=	⅓ cup	=	3 fl oz	=	80 ml
		8 Tbsp	=	½ cup	=	4 fl oz	=	120 ml
		10⅔ Tbsp	=	⅔ cup	=	5 fl oz	=	160 ml
		12 Tbsp	=	¾ cup	=	6 fl oz	=	180 ml
		16 Tbsp	=	1 cup	=	8 fl oz	=	240 ml
	1 pt		=	2 cups	=	16 fl oz	=	480 ml
	1 qt		=	4 cups	=	32 fl oz	=	960 ml
						33 fl oz	=	1000 ml = 1 l

USEFUL EQUIVALENTS FOR COOKING/OVEN TEMPERATURES

	Fahrenheit	Celsius	Gas Mark
Freeze Water	32° F	0° C	
Room Temperature	68° F	20° C	
Boil Water	212° F	100° C	
Bake	325° F	160° C	3
	350° F	180° C	4
	375° F	190° C	5
	400° F	200° C	6
	425° F	220° C	7
	450° F	230° C	8
Broil			Grill

Month-by-Month Index

This index alphabetically lists every food article and accompanying recipes by month.

General Recipe Index

This index alphabetically lists every recipe by exact title.

©2016 Time Inc. Books

Published by Oxmoor House, an imprint of Time Inc. Books
225 Liberty Street, New York, NY 10281

Senior Editor: Katherine Cobbs
Project Editor: Lacie Pinyan
Designer: Carol Damsky
Junior Designer: AnnaMaria Jacob
Photographers: Iain Bagwell, Jennifer Causey, Greg DuPree, Alison Miksch,
   Hector Sanchez
Prop Stylist: Kay Clarke
Food Stylists: Victoria E. Cox, Margaret Monroe Dickey, Blakeslee Giles,
   Rishon Hanners, Ana Kelly, Kellie Kelley, Catherine Crowell Steele,
   Chelsea Zimmer
Recipe Developers and Testers: Robin Bashinsky, Jiselle Basile, Mark Driskill,
   Paige Grandjean, Emily Hall, Adam Hickman, Julia Levy, Pam Lolley,
   Robby Melvin, Karen Rankin, Deb Wise
Senior Production Manager: Greg A. Amason
Assistant Production Director: Sue Chodakiewicz
Copy Editor: Donna Baldone
Proofreader: Rebecca Brennan
Indexer: Mary Ann Laurens
Fellows: Audrey Davis, Helena Joseph, Hailey Middlebrook, Kyle Grace Mills

ISBN-13: 978-0-8487-4536-3
ISSN: 0272-2003

First Edition 2016

Printed in the United States of America

10 9 8 7 6 5 4 3 2 1

Time Inc. Books products may be purchased for business or promotional use.
For information on bulk purchases, please contact Christi Crowley in the
Special Sales Department at (845) 895-9858.

We welcome your comments and suggestions about Time Inc. Books.
Please write to us at:
Time Inc. Books
Attention: Book Editors
P.O. Box 62310
Tampa, Florida 33662-2310

Cover: Peppermint Cake with Seven-Minute Frosting, page 301
Page 1: Ambrosia Pudding Pie, page 284;
German Chocolate-Pecan Pie, page 280

Favorite Recipes Journal

Jot down your family's and your favorite recipes for quick and handy reference. And don't forget to include the dishes that drew rave reviews when company came for dinner.

Recipe	Source/Page	Remarks

Recipe	Source/Page	Remarks